THE SEARCH FOR MEANING

AND

THE MYSTERY OF CONSCIOUSNESS

—◊—

A Psychologist's Journey
Through Gurdjieff and Jung

by Stephen Aronson

THE KARNAK
PRESS

THE SEARCH FOR MEANING
AND
THE MYSTERY OF CONSCIOUSNESS

A Psychologist's Journey Through Gurdjieff and Jung

Second Edition: September 2023
ISBN: 978-1-957278-00-1
Printed in the United States of America

THE KARNAK PRESS
Austin, Texas

This book is dedicated to my daughter, Courtney, and all those like her, who search for the Kingdom East of the Sun and West of the Moon

THE SEARCH FOR MEANING
AND
THE MYSTERY OF CONSCIOUSNESS

—⁓—

A Psychologist's Journey
Through Gurdjieff and Jung

There are more things in heaven and earth, Horatio, than are dreamt of in your philosophy.

~William Shakespeare

Contents

Foreword

S tephen Aronson begins his account of a search for meaning by auspiciously referencing the famous Golden Tablet of Hermes Trismegistus. He describes his experience in encountering this text forty years earlier as "electrifying, bringing tears to his eyes." One line of the quotation he provides reads, "I am the child of Earth and starry Heaven."

Such a moment, a moment of an intense aliveness of one's essential self, an experience of being outside any conditioning, is an experience that Aronson studies from a number of different points of view. It can be termed "the witness state." Since such an experience lies outside our conditioning, we have been taught to brush it aside, to ignore it, or suppress it, whereas it has the potential to lead us to who and what we really are. A central aim of this book is to awaken in the reader an interest in making contact with this essential self that could then lead to an ongoing exploration, a quest.

Beginning the book in this way makes clear right from the start that experience will be central to Aronson's exposition of his "Journey through Gurdjieff and Jung." Of course, ideas and concepts from Gurdjieff, Jung, and elsewhere are presented, but without using a specialized vocabulary. The reader is continually brought back to actual experiences of those ideas and concepts. For example, in the Chapter *Control and Influence* the reader is led through some of the author's experiences in such a way as to suggest how the reader might conduct his or her own experiments.

Aronson expounds on the centrality of experience: *"Ideas are one thing. The actual experience behind an idea is a totally different level akin to a new dimension. To know is not the same as to understand. To make an idea real, and not just a theory, we need to go beyond the hearing or reading of it to try to find a way to make it our own through some aspect of our individual experience."* One must verify for oneself the truth of anything one has read. Such verification must be connected to feeling and make use of the physical body's capacity to sense what is real.

Although experience is central there are also numerous chapters of carefully reasoned exposition such as the chapter *Consciousness*. written in the form of a letter to Aronson's daughter Courtney. Another example is the chapter *Religion, Secular and Spiritual.*

Through describing many experiences as well as drawing on his professional training, Aronson provides helpful guidance on the use of the word "Imagination" and how it must be distinguished from fantasy. For example, the creative imagination of the architect making plans is definitely not fantasy but is instead a natural human capacity. Experiencing a clear vision of a staircase to heaven has the potential of being equally "real," depending on the state of the experiencer.

In Aronson's down-to-earth practical approach to learning, I am reminded of the book *A Master in Life*, by Tcheslaw Tchekhovitch (Dolmen Meadow Editions, 2006), which is really a book of teaching stories of experiences with Gurdjieff. And like Tchekhovitch, who wrote about his precognitive dreams (in the French edition of his book), Aronson is not afraid to address the forbidden but important topic of paranormal experiences. His experience and investigation is taken up in some detail in the final chapters *The Breadcrumb Trail* and *What is Real?*

Aronson's book is a delight. What impressed me most was my perception of an author who is able to convey what cannot be conveyed in words, the unnamable. The first paragraph of the book's preface is an example of this craft:

> *"At an early age, I almost "touched" ... I can't really say what ... something ... totally surprising and intense. At the time it felt like what, today, I could call The Source. I was at the edge of my teens when I was surprised and overwhelmed by a feeling of being very, very close to It. ... so, so close... just a little bit further ... I could feel its proximity growing stronger and stronger... almost there.. and then I suddenly "fell" back into my body on the bed where I had been lying?"* *

Jack Cain, Canadian Hypnotherapist

---

* Reprinted from a *Parabola* book review.

Acknowledgements

I would like to publicly acknowledge a number of people, past and present, whose contributions to my life journey made this book possible. Their influence has been inspirational as well as practical.

Dr. Keith Buzzell, Author, Country Doctor, Spiritual Mentor, Friend and Shimon Malin, Emeritus Professor of Physics, both of whom modeled the reality of the Fourth Way practice and principles.

Jungian analysts Rev. Michael Dwinell and Eleanor Mattern, whose creativity and skill first showed me the door to my inner world.

Federico Balsa, my wonderful editor whose humor, belief in the aims of this project and perseverance kept me on task.

Jack Cain, who wrote the preface, which was also published as a review of this book in the Fall Edition of Parabola, 2023

Robin Bloor, my publisher, a man of serious intent, prodigious intellect, and a vision for the future.

Richard Webb, architect, and intellectual companion whose contributions to my thinking process and assistance with the diagrams in this book, were truly collaborative.

Joan Dow, publicist, and creative designer whose guidance on issues of style and appearance have been invaluable.

Paula Schmidt for her advice in helping increase the clarity of my writing.

Courtney Sparks, my daughter and librarian, for her help with research and as an inspiration for my search to discover an approach to sharing these complex ideas in a practical format.

Ocke De Boer, my friend and colleague, who shared with me his experience of communication with my wife, Susan, after her death.

Dr. Scott Roby, my longtime friend, and the man who long ago handed me a strange book which led directly to my captivation by Gurdjieff's astounding ideas and methods.

Carl Gustav Jung, who first opened for me the doorway to the hidden world behind our ordinary consciousness and showed me the wisdom of dreams and symbols.

And George Ivanovich Gurdjieff, the man whose lifetime of effort in support of future generations he would never meet, has irrevocably led to a transformation that changed the course of my understanding and experience of Life and the mystery of myself.

Preface

At an early age, I almost "touched" ... I can't really say what ... something ... totally surprising and intense. At the time it felt like what, today, I could call *The Source*. I was at the edge of my teens when I was surprised and overwhelmed by a feeling of being very, very close to *It* ... so, so close... just a little bit further... I could feel its proximity growing stronger and stronger... almost there.... and then I suddenly "fell" back into my body on the bed where I had been lying.

I had been experimenting with visualizing. I had begun the process by imaging myself floating above the bed and looking down on my body. Slowly I moved the position of my perspective higher until I was looking down at the roof of our house over the bedroom where my body lay. The distance gradually increased until I could "see" the house in the center of the surrounding neighborhood. I continued to move further upwards. Gradually, the island, on which I lived and the surrounding water came into view.

This continued until I was above the continent when I "saw" the whole Earth, then moved outward through the solar system, planet by planet. I "left" the solar system and moved out and up above the galaxy. More and more galaxies appeared in my peripheral vision from behind me and then receded into the distance with the Earth with the continued movement of my viewpoint.

To my surprise, as this expansion continued, I felt a growing sense and overwhelming feeling of being close to *The Answer*. The answer to what question? I couldn't say then or now, other than it felt like The Answer to the meaning of life and existence. The tension and longing mounted. The response to my unspoken question began to feel palpable ... nearly within reach ... I thought I began to see something ... a brilliant illumination just up ahead ... the sense of "others" and the beginning of a feeling of "pressure" as if I were approaching a *Something* ... and then ... without warning, I was once again lying on my bed. The transition was instantaneous. It took me by surprise. Only the memory of the feeling remained. I tried to return to this experience a few times, but these efforts always remained an intellectual visualization without the profound emotional component.

Background

The personal culture of my childhood in the 1950s was scientific, not religious. Reason, alone, was the modeled vehicle for searching the mysteries of Nature and the Universe. The focus was on how things worked, but not what they meant, not their purpose in existing, an inherent limitation of science. Religion, which does focus on meaning, was viewed as quaint, primitive or accepted at face value, without critically evaluating the explanations it offered for these questions. It offered explanations as to theological purpose, but not for how apparently miraculous phenomena could occur in violation of the laws of Nature.

At that time, the energy of *mystery* in the dominant culture, to the extent I was aware of it, had shifted away from the Divine, or subjects with traditional religious overtones, to the quests of both "official" and what established science calls "fringe-pseudo-science" (i.e., parapsychology and UFO's). I was interested in both types of sciences. As a growing boy, I flowed with the scientific currents because I could follow the taste of mystery, which I did not sense in the religious expressions around me. Looking back, it is my impression that for me, science fiction took the place of religion, as I suspect it did with many others. So, it was the path of science I initially followed without surrendering my search for a deeper reality. I loved the exploration of how the Universe worked, but my primary interest remained on what it all meant.

I loved science for its remarkable creativity. How could some people be so smart, so inventive, so intuitive, as to actually be uncovering how life and the universe actually seem to work? I so appreciated the aim of science to unfold the mysterious mechanics of existence. Even more, I loved the fact that no matter how deeply into nature it looked, no matter what amazing things it found with its astoundingly intelligent instruments, the question of meaning remained an enigma. Each reconfirmation of the continuing unknown beyond each new advance of science pointed, for me, to the question of another deeper reality ... the mystery that I longed to understand. It was as if, as science probed further and further, when it came to the meaning of its discoveries, it always reached the same abyss. I loved standing at the edge of the chasm and looking into the darkness ... and feel its pull on me.

On the practical side of life, I earned a Bachelor-of-Science, followed by a Master's-Degree and Ph.D. in clinical psychology. Psychology offered the possibility of approaching the mystery of consciousness, which science, at that time, was unwilling and unable to address. Understanding that I could not help anyone unless I knew how to help myself, I spent a total of twenty years, intermittently, from my early twenties through my mid-fifties, as a patient in different approaches to psychotherapy, the last twelve in Jungian analysis.

Jung and Gurdjieff

Just as the impact of Carl Jung's vision into the "collective unconscious" was unveiling for me a confirmation of that hidden reality for which I had so long been seeking verification, I met the teaching of G. I. Gurdjieff. These two methodologies, primarily the latter, transformed and gave practical direction to my search for verification of another reality behind and actually determining what we call ordinary life.

Specifically, Gurdjieff made two assertions at the outset of his writings that immediately appealed to me. The first was that nothing be accepted, regardless of the source, unless it could be personally confirmed to one's own satisfaction through direct experience. The second was that he sought to unite the "wisdom of the East with the knowledge of the West" as a prerequisite to the search for the meaning of life, existence and consciousness. I felt this was a precise formulation of the need to reconcile the rational, logical intellect with our feeling-intuition and the wisdom of our body as a foundation for actual experiences which could subjectively illuminate the search for meaning.

As both a psychotherapist and a long-time member of various groups studying Gurdjieff's system of "inner transformation," I have been able to talk and listen to many, many people. I noticed years ago that when I said something that was obvious to me, sometimes others were "amazed." They had never "looked at it that way." I was puzzled because, from my perspective, what I had said was obvious ... to me. How could they not see it? Of course, I now recognize that others see perspectives that I do not. That is the point of sharing. But then it left me with a question ... or, more practically, a problem. I did not know what I knew that others did not know. So how was I to know when to offer something or stay silent? I didn't want to insult people or have them think I was pontificating (which I sometimes may have been) by stating the obvious. Yet all testimonies are generated from a particular perspective and I saw that I did occasionally have a perspective some people found valuable.

The Role of Mystery

Humans are both very similar and very different from each other. The type of person drawn to mystery as the center of their life interest is different from other types that feel called by other trumpets. Personality tests suggest that such people are a very small portion of the population. Each and every one of us has a role to play in our families, our workplaces, our communities, and ultimately in the drama of Life Itself. So too does the mystic, the seeker after, and recipient of, mystery.

I have found a way to make this journey that represents both my type and my idiosyncratic nature. I am not recommending to anyone that they should or could follow anyone else's path. In fact, one aspect of my search, as I indicated above, has been to not believe, not accept on face value, anything I hear or read. I may adopt it provisionally as a working hypothesis, whether from science or religion ... or politics, but, until I can confirm it, through my own experience, to my own satisfaction, it is only hearsay, speculation, other peoples' opinion.

Due to my training as a scientist, I know that an "accepted" theory is only the most satisfactory of the current contending explanations. New discoveries are always being made, previous theories discarded, and new theories invented to try to understand them. Even religious doctrine changes over time, as do the interpretations of what a religion's founder meant and intended. One can give the benefit of the doubt without extending one's belief that something is the ultimate Truth.

Discovery and Sharing

What I discover for myself, from myself, inside myself, may then be of real help to me because, whether "right" or "wrong" in the larger scheme of things, the discovery has been made through my own efforts. Something in me has "grown" by these efforts. This new something is now part of my inner world, something to explore ... and something that can be used for exploring.

What is discovered can be shared with others who have a similar interest, perhaps through music or painting or poetry, but only in a very limited way by ordinary words. Typically, the actual experience that led to the discovery can only be imperfectly shared because it was an *experience*. In rare instances, a gifted individual can, through art, poetry, dance, and especially music, convey an experience directly, transmitting emotional information through resonance into another person and re-creating a specific feeling in them

For the most part, what can be shared are descriptions or representations of the experience … but not the actual experiencing of it … and the verbal formulation of the meaning derived from the experience for the experiencer. But this dialogue can still be invaluable if it can be approached with an attitude of interest rather than mechanical critique, with an openness to take in new ideas and test them for oneself, with a comfort of exploring for the love of exploring rather than to search for specific answers that can be nailed down once and for all. If one has this attitude, then what follows may be of interest … and perhaps even of help.

Self-Exploration

There is a selfish aspect to this writing effort. I discover that writing calls for memory to surface from my subconscious and respond to that call through offering up associational links, image by image, event by event, slowly revealing the storyline of what I call my Life. If I want to understand my life, I must understand the subjective entity inside my body that, through its choices, its conditioned patterns, its neuroses, and its higher potentials, has shaped, to a large extent, the life in which I find myself. If I have a purpose in life, what else could that be other than to share my experiences in this search for mystery? And through what lens could I share it but from the perspective of my training as a psychologist and student of the "Perennial Wisdom"?

I have been blessed in my search through the stories and reflections told by those who have made this journey before me, both those in literature and history, as well as those living beings who have been my guides and mentors in this life. As they shared with me, because I asked, I offer these personal reflections for those who may be interested. What follows is a description, a map of my journey, told in story and essay, to be shared with any reader who has had similar experiences and feels the value of the pursuit of mystery as a pathway to deeper understanding.

My Aim

In this collection of essays and reflections, I have three aims. The first is to re-explore certain memories associated with the taste of mystery in my inner life through the two lenses supplied by Carl Jung and George Ivanovich Gurdjieff.

The second is to write in a way that I hope will evoke in you, dear Reader, a wish to engage in your own inner exploration as you read and reflect along with me. I hope that you may establish personal confirmation of the phenomena I am trying to illuminate.

The third is to share the essence of these two methods of psychological transformation, as I have come to understand them, in a practical way, through my own words and experiences, rather than repeating the language and examples used by these two teachers in their own writings. In doing so, I hope to demonstrate a way these two systems can become vehicles to explore your own psychological dimension such that a deeper quality of life may open for you.

If my reflections resonate with you, dear Reader, then perhaps you might be inspired to make your own investigation of the path offered by this sharing. What I can offer are representations of how their example and guidance have transformed the view, for one person, of the nature of reality and the deepest mystery of conscious awareness appearing to arise out of inert matter.

PART ONE

Essays and Explorations

The Golden Tablet

Nearly forty years ago, I came across a fragment of reputedly ancient writing. As I read it, I was electrified. Something in me resonated, vibrating like a bell. Tears came to my eyes. I felt these words. Their wish was not unknown to me. Whatever they meant was affecting something that had always been inside of me but long asleep. I felt that these were also my words, my longings. But … what did they mean? I did not know. But I knew that they were mine. They were intended for me. I read that they were inscribed on the "Golden Tablet of Hermes Trismegistus."

"To its Guardians, cry thus:
I am the child of Earth and starry Heaven;
But my race is heavenly; and this you know yourselves.
I am parched with thirst and I perish;
but give me quickly that draught of ice-cold memory!"

Around this time, an image appeared in my mind … a naked man, his feet like tree roots holding him to the Earth. His hands are clenched in frustration and longing as he gazes up at the night sky and he cries towards the heavens. I drew a number of versions of this image over a period of several months. Gradually, the man changed slightly. His lower legs emerged from the earth and he stood on his own two feet with the ability now to move if he wished to. His body was more at ease. The longing was there, but the intense frustration had abated. Looking at this transformation of the original image, the words from the Golden Tablet appeared in my mind. Was this what the figure had been crying heavenward?

The feeling stimulated in me by this image was the same quality of emotion I had experienced on first reading the ancient, evocative, mysterious words of Hermes. Even after all these years, I still feel that strange but familiar taste on encountering them.

Of interest to me is that only now, in writing about this experience nearly four decades later, have I taken the time to investigate the source of this quote which has riveted me all these years. Being able to absorb what I will share below may have necessitated my waiting all this time, so that I might now be able to understand what I have discovered about both the Golden Tablet and about myself since encountering this invitation from humanity's distant past to visit, now, what it was trying to convey to me from Its time back then.

The object known as the Golden Tablet was uncovered at an ancient Greek site in the 1830s in Southern Italy. The inscription is archaic Greek and estimated to date from 300-200 BC. The tablet claims to be a message from Hermes Trismegistus, Hermes the "thrice-greatest," presumed to have been an ancient philosopher and teacher whose actual biography has now long been lost to legend. In ancient Egypt, his teaching became blended with the god Toth and the two were seen as the same personification. In ancient Greek legend he is blended with the prophet Orpheus, whose followers established a mystery cult that initiated its adherents into an understanding of life after death. It is presumed that the Golden Tablet came from one of the many shrines in the ancient world dedicated to this belief. Other gold-leaf tablets have been found in graves from 400 BC, which give instructions to the dead about passage into the afterlife.

What is this about? Why do these words, engraved on a gold tablet over 2,500 years ago, resonate so deeply within me? What have I to do with that distant time and age? Somehow. I am connected with this message, these people, this yearning to remember.

Time

When I was in my early twenties and in graduate studies, long, long before discovering these instructions from an ancient mystery school, I became very interested in, and increasingly uncomfortable with, the constant flow of Time. My life seemed to be flowing by without my being able to really savor it, hold on to it, remember it. I realized that I could not hold on to a moment, stretch it, save it, because it was immediately followed by another moment and then another and then another. How long was a moment?

Try this for yourself, dear Reader. Right now, whether you pause your reading or continue … and try to catch the moment you are in right now. Can you hold it still? What happens the moment after you try? Is that now a different moment? Are the two connected? How long can you stretch your awareness of the moment before you realize you have forgotten to try?

What is the "Present"? The Present, the moment I became aware of it, seemed to immediately evaporate into the Past, to be replaced by an endless lineup of Future Moments waiting for their turn to become the Present Instant before sliding by into the expanding Past. I still recall feeling a moment of terror, those many years ago, at this realization. My life was being stolen, eaten, by this constant current of rushing moments, each tearing from my grasp the instant I had just been trying to hold onto, and replacing it with another, which was then ripped away and sent rushing into the ever-expanding past, to add to the dark ocean of all the other barely digested moments of my life.

Changing Perspective

Today, on writing this almost six decades later, I see this from a different viewpoint. From the angle of my original frightened perspective, the moment was so infinitesimally brief as to nearly take no time at all. And, as the sense of my existing seemed confined to a given moment in time, if I could not hold on to that moment, I could not hold on to myself either. Somehow, I was constantly disappearing because the moment I existed in barely had time to breathe before being replaced by the next moment.

Yet, from a different viewpoint, because the moment seems to take no time at all, the moment must, in some way, be outside of time … and … that suggests … that the Moment is time-less. If the Present Moment is timeless, then Time cannot be carrying it away. That suggests that the Moment is not in motion. Something else must be in continuous movement. Perhaps it is my attention that cannot hold still and remain for a while in the Present Moment. Maybe the impression of the flow of time has to do with the unsteadiness of my attention.

The Past and Future have shape—a form, content and duration—as they stretch out in time. The Present seems to have no duration, no length or width. In another strange way, although the Present was always disappearing into the Past, it was simultaneously always present. It is always the Present Moment. What other moment in time could it possibly be, other than this one right now? The Present was always here and could never be anywhere else. This must mean that I am always in the Present. Perhaps if I stopped trying to hold onto it, my attention wouldn't constantly be pulled out of the Present and lose its hold on the Moment. If the Present Moment is timeless ... and I only exist in the Present Moment ... does that mean that in some way ... I am also timeless ... outside of Time?

During that period, I was also under the impression that I had very little memory of my past. When I looked back, I would find a few disconnected vignettes scattered over the years, but there was no continuous record, just fragments. What was wrong such that I could not remember so much of what I had lived through? Hadn't I been there for those events? If so, where were the memories? If not, who had been occupying my body as it moved through its life year after year? I recall feeling a sense of injustice. This was not fair! It was *my* life! Why couldn't I hold onto my life? Why did I have the sense it was being stolen from me, moment by moment? What was the point of a life if it was continually in a state of being lost to memory?

Memory Aids and the Sense of Time

Initially, I decided to write down my impressions of events so I had a record I could revisit to prove to myself that I had actually existed before the present moment. "See? There! Those are my words so there is proof I existed before this moment even if I don't remember writing it." As these writings accumulated, I would visit them to remind myself of what had happened in prior moments. When I look now at this writing by a very young man, I see that it was primarily intellectual. I did not yet understand how to utilize or learn from my feelings, much less write about them. The efforts that did contain subtle feelings were attempts at descriptive poetry, trying to paint a word picture of the situation that was evoking the feeling.

Then, I discovered photography. As years passed, I looked at the accumulating collection of images and realized two things. I recognized that I had an ability to capture on film perspectives that most of those around me did not see. I would notice a small part of a large scene, isolate it with a telephoto lens and extract from the larger whole, an angle of reality not immediately noticeable in the overwhelming big picture. On a number of occasions, I saw something that I knew would have a certain appearance at a certain time of day, under certain lighting conditions at a certain time of year. I would wait. And, when a season, day and time that matched my vision arrived, I would find that location and capture the image and feeling that I had "seen" in my mind's eye. I had looked into the future, and now that that particular future had arrived, I could memorialize it for futures yet to come.

After a number of years, I realized that when my eye was functioning as a camera, time evaporated. I would become "lost" in the scouting of the terrain, the setting up of the photo, the playing with light. I recognized that at those times, hours could go by without any sense of the flow of time. In this particular mental-emotional state, time was no longer the thief of memory, but rather it seemed to expand and leave in my mental library a beautiful, long moment, enhanced by a quality of depth, not the shallow slivers of time that ordinary life imposed on me. Something was different inside me at those instances that appeared to influence my relationship with Time. Perhaps in that state, I had momentarily accessed a new dimension. I realized that this activity put me into a type of emotional state. The creative feeling opened depth to the moments that, without it, now felt flat.

When my children were born, I began photographing them … and their mother … and my friends. I recognized that a change had occurred in me. For years, I was drawn to recording nature, large vistas, tiny flowers, the beautiful play of light through windows, shadows and reflections… but my early collection was relatively devoid of people. Now, something had shifted in me, and I became interested in candid portraits and recording moments of ordinary life, but from interesting angles.

I recognized that when looking at a photograph I had taken, the image brought to mind a cascade of impressions associated with that moment, conversations, events leading up to it and afterwards, the feeling of the relationship with people or landscape. When viewing a photograph I have taken, I can often recall the time, place, feelings, and even what I was thinking about at the time of the picture. Each photo had a mnemonic quality which unlocked associated reminiscences that were not available to me with the written word alone.

I also, belatedly, recognized that each picture was a recording of what I was experiencing in my mind at that time. The memory itself was a type of photograph of what was happening in my psychological world when I recorded the outside world events through the camera lens. The resulting image allowed me to share a tiny portion of my inner world with others, let them look through my eyes and mind for that frozen moment in time captured in the picture, a sharing of the idiosyncratic quality of my mind with the minds around me. It also allowed me to see into my own mind at the moment it recorded the image. I was beginning to learn about myself by looking at what had caught my attention in the past.

After many years and thousands of pictures, I recognized, with a shock, that I had been living much of my life through my camera lens. I had found a way to preserve moments for future recall, but I still had not been fully present in those moments because I was so busy recording. I was not fully experiencing it. At that point, I dramatically reduced the use of the camera as a memory assistant and began to learn how to imprint the moment on my memory, not only in my mind but in my feelings and in my body.

Imprinting the Moment: The Witnessing State

My primary source for unlocking this capacity was the teaching and methods of mystic-philosopher G. I. Gurdjieff. Appropriately, the core of his teaching refers to the importance of a state of awareness he calls "Self-Remembering." The key to beginning this system of self-study is learning how to intentionally divide attention so that part of it is focused on the world outside myself, landscape, people, relationships, events while, simultaneously, the other part is intentionally focused inside myself on the sensations of my body, my fluctuating feelings and emotional reactions and the thoughts, assumptions, attitudes and images flowing through my mind. When these three functions, thinking, feeling and sensing, come into focus at the same moment, there also appears a qualitatively different, palpable, experience of myself as the point in the middle, the *Witness* of the experience and relationship between these two worlds of outer and inner. This state of expanded attention alters my subjective experience of time and relationship with memory.

After some practice, I began to notice something else. With the accumulating impressions of how my personality interacts with outside events, sometimes in response to them, sometimes instigating them according to how outside events are framed through the lens of my attitude or mood of the moment, I increasingly saw, in myself, inconsistencies between the newly emerging impressions of myself and my prevailing self-image. I was not always, or certainly not entirely, the person I imagined myself to be ... wanted to believe myself to be... hoped I was ... or the image I tried to convey to the people around me.

In addition, repeated moments of experiencing myself, as the *Observer* between two worlds, the outside and my psychological interior, raised profound questions about whether I might be much more than my body and personality. The taste of being a relatively objective witness of this interplay between personality/ego and outer life helped me recognize that the Observer was not, Itself, the personality reactions that were being observed.

Over time, when in this Witnessing-State, I realized that I did not so easily believe in my thoughts, attitudes and reactions to real or perceived slights. I began to study my negative reactions to find their roots in my past. I saw that much which upset me was a reflection of reactions conditioned into my nervous system from past events. I noticed my reactivity often decreased with increased understanding. Something new seemed to be developing in me ... a new perspective, a new understanding of what I had believed I was. As I now looked at the world around me, I also began to see, with a different insight, why humanity was as it was and what could, and could not, be done about it.

Studying Inner States: Ego

Early on, at the beginning of this inner self-study, I made a decision to try to reduce my self-centered qualities and work towards developing more humility. After two years of this effort, I recall walking in the woods reviewing my attempts at this change. As I did so, my assessment was that I had been successful. The thought appeared in my mind that I was, now, the most humble person I knew. An instant later, I burst out laughing at myself ... or that part of myself that was so subtly egoistic it believed it could become the most humble man in the world ... itself, a most egoistic aim. I recall thinking, after my laughter stopped, "Well, that was a waste of two years. I guess it doesn't work that way. I need a different approach". Of course, I probably had to spend two years on this fruitless endeavor to realize, and accept, that I could not get rid of my egoism by acting humble on the outside and suppressing its opposite on the inside ... and even trying to hide it from myself.

Just a couple of years ago, I was having a conversation with an individual whose respect and assistance I wished to gain. I was raising a concern about a situation in which I myself occupied an essential role, but I also wanted to avoid the perception of any self-interest in bringing this to his attention. My interest in doing so, I told myself, was purely altruistic ... at least from one level. But, as I spoke, I heard within the vibration of my voice a recognition that even this genuine altruism, if recognized, would make me look good ... which I actually wished for ...

even though I wasn't trying to engineer it.

At that moment, an image appeared in my mind of my egoism, my self-serving-wish-for-self-promotion, winding like a snake, around every manifestation I emitted. I could not separate it from any other motive. There suddenly seemed to be no pure motives. It was as if this self-oriented part might be an aspect of every motive, from altruism to narcissism.

If that is so ... then ... Ego must also be in this part of me that is now noticing the egoism in another part of me. I am aware of It. I am also aware of myself being aware of It. I feel pleased and interested that I can see It. I am pleased ... with myself ... pleased for myself ... for my pleasure ... hmmm ... there is the taste of Ego again ... but now I sense it in the part of me that is trying to study egoism in another part of me.

If it is with me always ... in every thought or feeling or manifestation ... then ... it is a part of me ... it is me! It is an aspect of my awareness of myself as a conscious entity ... although perhaps limited in its view and understanding of the larger Whole to which It belongs. I have been like a dog chasing its tail. ... only to catch myself. I've been seeing a movement in my peripheral vision and chasing it ... chasing it ... until I realized ... it is a part of me. I've been chasing myself. How did I become divided so that I did not recognize myself in this other part? To become Whole, we must merge. We? A moment ago, I just realized that It was Me. Did I forget that just a moment later? It is all Me. The merging comes with the recognition.

Expanding Awareness of "Self"

I am now much more aware of an expanded version of what I call Myself. There is now much more to be aware of. It feels like coming home. When I am functioning only in a state of egoism, the assumption that life should center around me, a state where my attention continually gravitates towards my comfort level to the exclusion of most other concerns, the characteristic attitude, understanding and feeling is reflected as "I am God." When consciousness is in the Witnessing-Observer, the recognition, understanding and knowing is that God and I are one. God is in me ... and I am in God ... but only the merged "I" remembers and can experience the connection.

Ego, when seen as a snake, as in the Garden of Eden metaphor, represents one-half of the caduceus. The egoistic striving: "I," "I," "I,"

16

"Me," "Me," "Me," must represent the survival instinct built into all life. In my psychological world, it is a constant drumbeat representing a drive to solidify a sense of myself, of who and what I am. The built-in conscious striving to understand this mystery also insists on its survival as the guiding principle in my inner world, just as the urge to physically survive permeates my body.

Is Ego an evolutional or involutional movement? If Ego is in all aspects of all my manifestations, then it is in both the movement up and the movement down, the movement in and the movement out. Perhaps Ego is a manifestation of the quality of existence we call "Movement" manifesting in my psychological world.

Perhaps, DNA is the location where the movement downward into material existence meets the movement back upwards towards the possibility of reuniting an awareness of the nature of their entwinement. Where else would the blueprint for each living organism, with all its nearly infinite number of built-in, self-regulating functions, originate? The DNA molecule carries the plan already intact and programmed for each specialized type of being. Something is deposited in non-organic, non-living substances so that they come alive and reproduce themselves endlessly until their environment stops supporting them.

Without striving towards the discovery of who or what I actually am, the striving towards uncovering this mystery is lost. The striving is a homing instinct.

I wish, I need, to remember who I Am. I wish for you, dear Reader, to remember who you actually are ... if that interests you. The drive to understand who I am is what drives me forward. It is a force, like a river carrying me, a gravitational field that is pulling me. I just need to stay in contact with it.

The word *"ego"* in ancient Greek and Latin means the sense of the reality of "I," myself, the mysterious Awareness of my existence. In contemporary thought, Ego is often conflated with "personality" and a preoccupation with self over the needs of others. However, in the original sense of the word, it refers to the miracle that I can be aware of myself as the focal mystery of my existence. There are higher levels, higher qualities and understandings of this phenomenon that I call "myself" that can lead to compassion and altruism.

At the other end of the scale, the term "egoism" more accurately refers to the contemporary limited and self-oriented aspect. "I" and "egoism", may at times seem like two, if the term "Ego," in the sense of selfishness, is only applied to socially unacceptable urges, thoughts or behaviors. But with recognition that both the "acceptable" and the "unacceptable" are two different sides of myself, I can experience both as parts of a larger Whole, a One.

Ego could be thought of as an aspect of the Life Force, a creative quality that even creates its sense of itself from the bits and pieces of experience gathered in relationship with others, for without the mirror of others' responses to me, how would I form an assessment of who I believed I was?

Becoming aware that I, myself, am an aspect of this Force, wakens me in the joining of myself with what I have been seeking ... my larger, more whole Self. Joining with It in recognition opens me to experiencing an expansion of myself as I am united with what had become my lost other, my soul mate. Ironically, we never were actually separated by anything other than lack of awareness and limited perspective.

Somehow my Wholistic experience of myself was at some time split into fragments. Each part carried consciousness and capacity to learn to sense itself within its own subjective sphere ... which each part assumed was the Whole of itself.

Shock of Self-Recognition and Dilation of Time

On occasion, when the psychological wall which separated the awareness of each of these parts from each other collapses, they are left staring at each other in surprise. When they recognize each other in relationship, when consciousness becomes more Whole, there is remembrance of always having been in one part or the other of myself. I remember now being in each fragment, always thinking that where I was in myself in a given moment was the only part of myself. Now the memories stored in each part become merged. Time has expanded because memory has expanded and there is so much more now to recall.

There is now much more Life to reacquaint myself with, gathered in one expanded awareness. This quality moment seems much deeper .... almost timeless. It burns into memory. It is never forgotten ... always there ... somewhere in that enormous library of all the recorded moments of my life.

There appeared an instance when I realized that there are always happenings, and the body always responding, but there is not always something present looking at, experiencing, what is happening. It is that "something" that seems to carry the memories. When it is present, memory is made. When it is absent, nothing, no one, was there to witness, as Witness, to catch, contain and store the moment as a new memory to be added to the library.

When the Witness is present, when the I-AM State is present, the memory is deeply recorded and becomes a part of me. I grow as it adds itself to me. I feed on the memories, the impressions, the vibrations of the events. I eat them. They become part of me. I grow in understanding ... perhaps eventually also in compassion ... for others as well as myself. I need quality vibrations, coherent vibrations, not discordant and non-coherent. But I need vibrations ... my nervous system is fueled by vibrations from both outside and inside. These vibrations, whether sensual, emotional, conceptual, whether positive, negative or neutral, stimulate the electricity which powers my life. But each of these cat-egories has a different potential energy, a different "taste" or "feeling" to them.

If the "positive" level, the highest quality of experiential vibration, the prime beef of my psychological-spiritual diet, is low, then I have to make up the difference in my energy needs by eating more of the negative vibrations, many of which are far more intense, although of a lower quality. It is still food for my nervous system and mind, just much less nutritious ... so more and more are needed to make up the deficit of the high-quality positive coherent vibrations. As the positive increase, fewer of the negative are required. But the fact is that something is feeding ... and it will continuously feed regardless of the food available. The Will to eat is the Will to live. If I were able to bring ... if I could actually Be ... more receptive in outlook, understanding and manifestation, then this higher quality of vibrational food nourishes something in me of a higher quality than that which feeds on negativity.

Digesting My Self

But ... I am both feeding myself and eating myself at the same time. I am like the snake devouring its tail. I am eating myself, digesting my ex-periences and understandings, my reactions and my thoughts, by trying to experience them more objectively. Eating and feeding. Taking in and giving out. Involving and evolving. The breath of Life. In and Out. In and Out. Until In and Out blend and become the same place ... the still place at the center ... the home of the united Ego-I with Its understanding that

It is both, an infinitesimal part of the Whole of Wholes, and simultaneously, in its infinitesimal smallness, it is still aware of itself as an individual part of the Whole, but not as a separate fragment ... then it merges Its sense of identity with the Whole, yet without losing simultaneous awareness of Itself as an infinitesimal atom within the Whole. In this Awareness of Its true nature and place, time is irrelevant because this relationship is outside of Time.

State of Presence and the Expansion of Time

Time is what is at the Moment. If I am Present at that Moment to Witness myself experiencing it, then that moment is memorialized and entered into the story of my life. It is experienced when I am awake enough to actually be aware of myself living in it, thus transferring it to the memory library in the process. Depending on how often the Witness is present to record a moment, I may have a full, rich library or a poor and relatively empty one filled only with rooms of long lines of empty shelving, back in the shadows, waiting to hold memories that will never be uploaded to the library because I was not present to record them.

Conscious experiencing is what captures the moment. It is like an enzyme, digesting the impressions that moment is making on me in order to facilitate its incorporation into memory. If in that instance, the experience is *consciously* being recorded in all three centers of functioning, intellect, emotion and sensation, then the moment can be recorded in multiple modalities, intellectual, emotional and sensory. This creates much richer, more textured, nuanced Memory than if consciousness is in only one or two of our three functional arenas. This may be why some memories are shallow and pale compared to others which are deep and vibrant ... while other events cannot be recalled.

When I find myself in the I-Am-Observer state, I become aware of being connected with a continuous movement of levels of awareness, fluctuating upwards and downwards, as well as inside and outside, like two continuous and interactive waves.

Upwards towards heightened and broader consciousness of my existence within the body and its three centers, and downwards, away from this intense experience of self-existence, into a tunnel vision in which there is no space for awareness of myself as the one who is having the experience of the moment.

The movement of attention upwards and downwards on the scale of

Self-awareness, together with the vacillating fluctuation of attention towards my subjective interior and the sensory world outside, are two-thirds of my psychological structure. The third aspect is my Self ... as the Witness ... who is aware of Itself as the Witness, and aware of the eternal movement of up and down, in and out ... blending the three aspects of head, heart and body with their experiences in the world into a coherent Whole integrated within the Observer's exponentially expanded field of awareness.

Can we look at Time as synonymous with this Movement, both away from and towards this place of Oneness, this place that is aware of both inner psychological activity and external sensory impressions, where continuous movement in one direction or the other can be felt and observed, both at the same time? Might it be the subjective experiencing of this continuous movement of attention, without being aware of oneself as the Observer, that produces the sense of the flow of time?

When my attention is insufficient for Self-awareness, then its continuous movement in-out, up-down, creates this impression of the flow of time. On the other hand, from within the experience of Oneness, this movement is seen and accepted as part of the flow of existence, as two strands of the larger Whole ... intertwining spirals of flowing energy, the anode and cathode of existence. It is a movement of energy up and down, in and out, a continuous flow ... illustrated in the Yin-Yang symbol. We can liken the Witness to the white spot in the dark half. Simultaneously, the dark spot on the white side is also the Witness. The Witness state allows consciousness to be present and experience the events and content of each stream of energy within the unity of its encompassing awareness.

Today, I realize that the I-Am-the-Observer experience began to appear early in my life, leaving footprints in the form of my earliest memories. The Witness had visited my day-to-day experiences, off and on, as I developed ... waiting ... waiting ... for me to notice It, realize its significance and then understand that It was a higher aspect of myself.

Our Fragmented Psychological Nature

I then came to recognize that ordinary life experiences train us to focus on only some parts of our "selves" but not others, to accept and develop parts of ourselves and to ignore or reject or try to kill off other parts.

For the most part, we are born into a world that is more interested in shaping us to fit into the established pattern than helping us discover who we innately are. Our consciousness must fragment to survive such an insane world, trying to withdraw as much of its attention as it can from the parts being discouraged or depressed by its surrounding environment. It takes its socializing education to heart and suppresses awareness of, or hides, the parts of itself labeled dangerous or bad or unacceptable. But this suppressed part may stay alive, full of feelings, desires and repressed energy. It may erupt into existence from time to time, leaving traces of its visit, in the memories of others, but not always in the memory of the person who is now back in their socially acceptable side and, would not "themselves," have said or done what their other part said or did.

I am recalling now occasions where two very different parts of me came together in this space of shared awareness with the Witness. There was a stunning surprise of looking at an aspect of myself that I was shocked to discover was a part of me ... yet, at the same time, there was a mildly embarrassed feeling that, of course, I had always known about this part, but I often pretended to myself that I didn't know about it. It was a self-deception. For example, "I" had always prided myself on my "honesty" until I had to confront the fact that a fearful part of me was capable and willing to distort the truth in order to avoid embarrassment or rejection. Both were components of the same person who was inherently honest until he felt threatened in certain ways. For some reason, at some point in my early life, I had decided ... or something decided ... I should pretend to myself that I didn't know about this part of me. If I could successfully convince myself that this other aspect was not part of me, then it would be easier to hide that part of me from others.

That Draught of Ice-Cold Memory

When I first encountered the Golden Tablet, I was much less aware of the complexity of what I then called "myself." Years later, in a singular moment of the Witnessing state, I realized that the "Steve" I had known and believed was the real me was in some ways a figment of my own imagination; that my sense of Steve consisted of only parts of myself that

Image 1. Gold Orphic tablet and case found in Southern Italy and now displayed in the British Museum

were easily accessible and acceptable, to my more limited internal awareness and preferred self-image. I actually did not know who or what I was, but I did not yet realize this. When I saw this truth, I burst out laughing. Rather than finding this revelation disturbing, I felt liberated.

This deepening understanding of the complexity of myself is invisible to me when the Observing-Witness state is not present. It is an understanding that all great spiritual traditions have in their esoteric core. Originally, they were offerings of help to the people of those times, presented in the language and metaphors of their particular culture, to assist them in coming to a direct perception and understanding of this mystery of our existence ... not only our physical existence but the existence of our subjective awareness inside the materialized form of life we call our body ... and what may be its potential beyond helping us in our ordinary life.

The great spiritual traditions are concerned not only with how to live life but how to live life so that we are prepared for our death. I realized that whether one accepts the premise that death is a portal through which something leaves the dying body and continues a different life and different type of search at a non-material level ... or, whether one believes nothing survives after the body ... it is possible to live in such a way that one can put the puzzle of oneself together. Re-constructing the fragments of one's awareness into a larger whole increases the chances that one may die in peace with a fuller appreciation of one's life and place in the larger scheme of things. I must re-member. I must re-collect the pieces of myself that have been compartmentalized by my fragmented awareness.

The literature of most cultures has stories of a hero, or heroine, going on long journeys with a specific task to accomplish, but then falling asleep far from home, becoming identified with the outer life in the new location and forgetting what they had been sent there to accomplish. The parable of the Prodigal Son, the Grail Quest and the Scandinavian fairy tale, "East of the Sun and West of the Moon," are three that have deeply touched me. The latter tale ends with the promise that although the journey is long and difficult if one successfully makes it to the kingdom east of the sun and west of the moon, one will find a welcome within. These stories have felt to be a personal message and have riveted my heart since my first hearing them, as did the Golden Tablet. I believe this rich history of myth, tradition and stories are different versions of what we have been exploring together, dear Reader, in this essay

Is the discovery of the Witness the doorway to "the hidden kingdom within"? In learning that my true nature may be very, very different than what I have been conditioned to believe, have I begun to drink from that ice-cold pool of memory?

> "To its Guardians, cry thus:
> I am the child of Earth and starry Heaven;
> But my race is heavenly; and this you know yourselves.
> I am parched with thirst and I perish;
> but give me quickly that draught of ice-cold memory!"

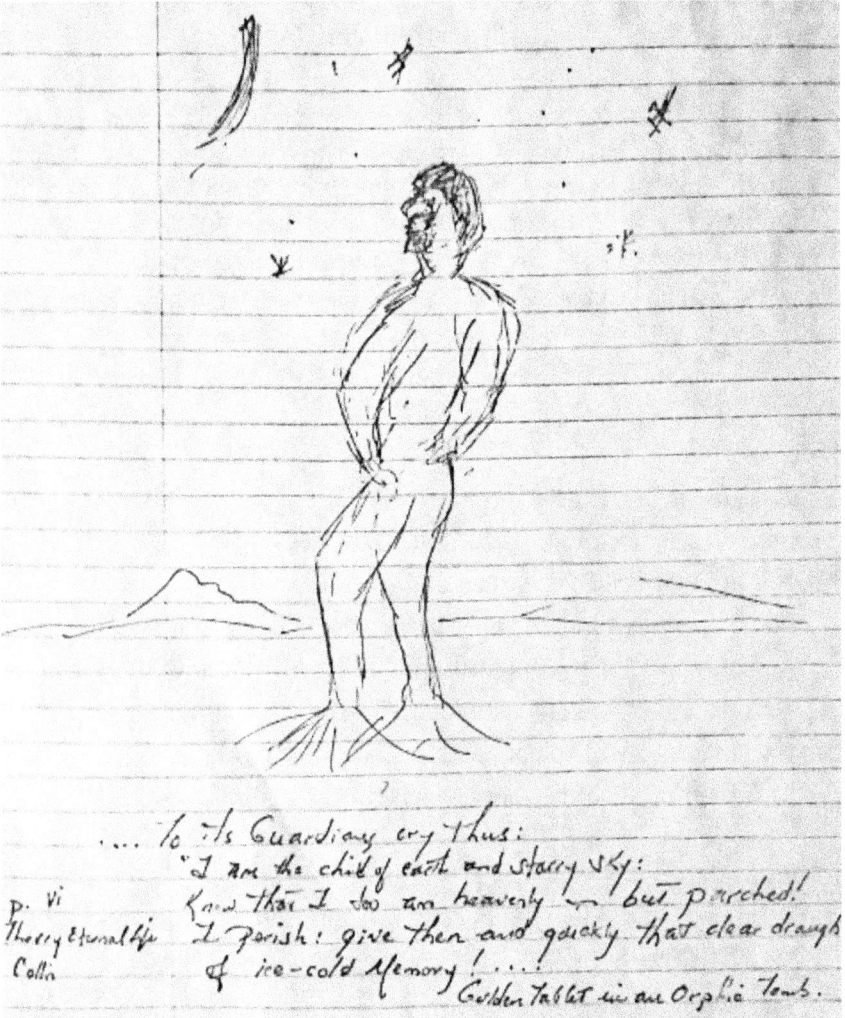

Image 2. Sketch of an image that appeared in my mind's eye joined with the Orphic message.

Translation Note

As with all ancient writings, translation differs with the style and understanding of the translator. Below, in an extended version of what I had originally encountered, are clear instructions to avoid drinking from the lake of "Forgetfulness" (Lethe) but to demand, in a specific formulation, to be allowed to drink from the pool of "Memory" (Mnemosyne).

"You will find in the halls of Hades a spring on the left and standing by it, a glowing white cypress tree;

Do not approach this spring at all.

You will find another, from the lake of Memory, refreshing water flowing forth.

But guardians are nearby.

Say: "I am the child of Earth and starry Heaven;

But my race is heavenly; and this you know yourselves.

I am parched with thirst and I perish; but give me quickly

refreshing water flowing forth from the lake of Memory."

And then they will give you to drink from the divine spring,

And then you will celebrate? [rites? with the other] heroes.

This [is the ? … of Memory, when you are about] to die .."

Now you have died and now you have come into being, O thrice happy one, on this same day.

Tell Persephone* that the Bacchic One himself released you.

---

* Persephone was Queen of the Underworld.

Transmission Through Music

I was in a discussion with my spiritual mentor, Dr. Keith Buzzell, and several colleagues. The conversation concerned an idea from ancient Perennial Wisdom about a way to transmit knowledge across time to people far in the future. The theory was that information could be embedded in architecture, paintings, music, dance, sculpture … mediums that could last a significant period of time and be available in the future when someone, sensitive enough to the type of "vibration" radiating from this intentionally-constructed-medium, would encounter it and receive an impression of the information contained in the medium.

I could confirm for myself that there was something valid in this ancient proposition. I knew that something inside me would occasionally resonate to a medium in a unique and always consistent way that caught my attention. The feeling would be something like, "I *feel* something here. What am I feeling when I look at that … painting … or … hear that piece of music … or … walk through this cathedral? I am drawn to this. Why?"

I had experienced this taste of strange kin-ness on a number of occasions, as with the paintings of William Blake, lines of poetry by Tennyson, the music of the Monks of the Weston Priory, in an ancient underground temple on Malta, at Salisbury Cathedral, with the theories of Carl Jung and intensely with the teachings of G. I. Gurdjieff.

After our discussion had gone on for a while, Keith proposed an experiment. He would play a piece of classical music. We would quietly listen and watch inside ourselves for any impression, image, thought or feeling, that might appear during the music. We were not to look for anything in particular, just keep our inner eye open for whatever came up while listening to the music. Then we would share our impressions.

I did as asked … and listened. After a while, I saw in my mind's eye a vast, empty landscape, devoid of people and towns, stretching to distant mountains deep in shadow. The time of day felt like dusk … visible but darkening. I continued to listen. Then I saw something else. In the sky, high overhead and spanning the whole landscape, was a female figure stretched out across the heavens. She was dressed in gossamer veils, layer upon layer flowing behind her like the wake of a ship. The music continued. I listened. The image persisted. I wondered if I had made up this image but, as I had never seen anything like this before, that did not seem likely. It must have "come to me."

The music stopped and we shared our different impressions. None of the impressions of the others was like mine. When I finally decided to speak, I talked about the desolate landscape but did not mention the floating celestial female. That felt too weird and I still wasn't sure I hadn't created it rather than "received" it. After a while, I asked Keith about the music. I don't recall if I asked for the title or the theme. In either case, he responded, "Mother Russia."

I was stunned. I blurted out the part of the image I had seen but withheld. Keith expressed no surprise. Here was another verification of this ancient art of embedding meaning.

As I am writing this, I searched the internet for images of "Mother Russia" symbolism. I hoped I might find something similar to the image I had seen. There was none. Now I am wondering if I am the only person to have seen "Mother Russia" in this way. If I could paint, I could show you what I still see in my mind when I recall this strange, wonderful memory.

Many years after this experience, I was at the *All and Everything International Humanities Conference* in a small town near Corinth, Greece. This is an annual proceeding held in different locations for people interested in the writings and ideas of G.I. Gurdjieff. I was at this meeting to present a paper. This particular memory begins the morning after a concert of Gurdjieff's music ... his collection of songs and melodies gathered throughout his life and travels in Asia as a young man.

It is strange to me that when I first heard this music, it didn't interest me, but with time I have grown to love and be emotionally moved by it. During the concert, I had an experience similar to that described above with "Mother Russia." The rhythm of this piece of music had always brought to my mind the slow, plodding walking of camels, walking ... walking ... across the desert. The feeling it evoked was one of aching longing and persistent search. No choice but to search and search ... one step in front of the next ... on and on and on ... unceasing effort. The terrain was vast. The sky was vast and glowering. I was very small. I had to continue on. I felt a pull. Something was calling me on, waiting for me to find it.

As I listened to this piece being played, I again felt this soulful-longing feeling. This time there was an image other than trudging camels. My viewpoint was several hundred feet in the sky. The landscape below was dark but for a campfire and a man standing next to it looking up at the night sky. He was feeling this same longing for his love, his soul-mate. He was calling to her. Then, from the space far above me, I heard a female calling back to him. The music was their mutual voice, their shared longing. Whatever "she" represented, she was searching for him, as he was searching for her. I knew this had to do with the creation of a Soul.

In the morning, I was talking with a couple I had met at the conference. We shared our impressions of the evening's concert. I told them about what I had "seen" and felt with this particular piece of music. With excitement, his wife turned to him and asked him to tell me what he had told her at breakfast. He related the same images and feelings as I had just shared with them. We looked at each other with amazement and delight. The idiosyncratic experience of something mysterious is wonderful in itself for me. But, to find someone else who has had the same mysterious experience brings the question of "What is going on here?" to a different level.

Transmission Through Dance

In my early thirties, I was in a bookstore on Harvard Square. There was a book about the Whirling Dervishes. I felt inexorably drawn to the book, to the photograph of the Dervish on the cover, dressed in white, his robe flowing around him, his arms out but hands limp, his head tilted to one side, his eyes closed. I had heard the name Whirling Dervish, and I had seen photographs, but not until this moment did I feel an emotional connection with this label and image. I wanted that book.

For reasons having to do with my maladaptive, conditioned emotional patterning at that time of my life, I resisted what felt like an irrational impulse that I could not logically justify. I left without the book. I thought about that moment for many years. Eventually, I purchased a copy of that book, but I obviously still recall the moment of first recognition in the bookstore over four decades ago. As I sat to write about the below experience, this recollection returned. The two are obviously linked, entangled, in the world out of time we call memory.

As part of the training of attention in the Gurdjieff method, students participate in complex and unusual forms of ancient ritual movements and sacred dances, which he brought with him from half a lifetime of travel in the middle east and Asia. The following reminiscence is from that activity.

I had been involved in a couple of whirling movements before this. Each left me very dizzy and I had to periodically stop to regain my orientation. This time, as I began to whirl, I recalled a suggestion to watch my hand. I kept my attention on it as the speed of the whirling increased. Suddenly I had the strongest impression that I was motionless, and the world was revolving while I watched from the still center. This was not an idea. This was a direct experience. I immediately recognized its relation to other experiences of awakening "behind the scene" or "inside" the moment. The whirling continued and the experience of being at the center of reality while the other world rotated "outside" continued throughout. I was sad when the whirling ended.

I was fortunate to find myself in other whirling Movements from time to time. I never again became dizzy and would periodically touch again, briefly, this original experience. The last time this occurred was a few years ago, when I was in my mid-seventies. I noticed at the end, when the music stopped, I was one of only a few men left standing. I felt as if I could have gone on indefinitely.

Art as Life and Life as Art

When I was an adolescent, there were moments when I looked at drawings that I had made and was surprised at their realism. I also had a talent for writing and photography. In spite of the fact that I occasionally won awards for my work, it was only later in life that I began to feel the value and mystery of these forms of expression. At the time, these experiences never penetrated deeper into me other than as casual facts about some capacities I had, but I never incorporated them into my sense of self or thought much about how they happened ... as I presume is the case with many of us.

But something happened during an intensive Jungian retreat in my late thirties that opened a new perspective and created a burning question that is with me, now, today, even as I try to write about this discovery and its implications. It was a moment when I had a clear impression that there existed a creative process separate from and greater than myself ... and I could come into communion with this mystery.

The retreat was held at my hilltop home in Western Maine. This was a magical location for me. The colonial-era farmhouse dated to 1790 and was one of the first settler structures in what had been the northern New England wilderness. Attached was a magnificent 1820 barn that had been renovated and retrofitted by previous owners. It served as a wonderful retreat center. The view stretched thirty miles to the Presidential Mountain Range in New Hampshire, providing a vision of snow-capped Mount Washington. It was surrounded by thousands of forested acres, with the nearest neighbor a quarter-mile distant.

At the time of this particular Jungian program, I was struggling with myself over the question of whether or not I would publicly acknowledge that I felt drawn to esoteric Christianity even though I was born and raised as a Jew. My emotional strife over this question had been building for a year or more.

At the moment in question, I was alone in a cabin staring at a pile of clay, awaiting an inspiration. As part of the training program, we were to explore allowing "creativity to appear." I stared at the clay. The clay stared back. This silent dialogue between me and the clay continued ... until an image appeared in my mind. It was the image of a wooden cross, twisted, tortured and bent. Nailed at the cross-point in the middle was a Star of David, also distorted in the same way.

My hands, on their own, reached for the clay. I had had no experience with clay since early grade school and did not "know" what to do with it other than twist, pull, pound and try to make a shape that others could recognize. I realized that I was not directing my hands. They were moving on their own. I was startled and began to worry that I should be thinking about how my hands ought to handle the clay so as to recreate the image I had seen in my mind. The moment my attention shifted from watching my hands move on their own to thinking about how my hands should be moving with the clay, they stopped their work. "I don't know what to do next," I thought to myself. Now my hands were slow, awkward and clumsy. I mentally "let go" of my hands and they again began to skillfully handle the clay. I experienced some anxiety at that moment. I felt "out of control." What was directing my hands if I was not? Again, my intellect began to express its concern that it didn't know how this was happening. My hands stopped. Again, I shifted my attention away from thinking and back to my hands. They returned to working with the clay. As I watched them, I realized that what was happening was play… if I would allow it. My hands were playing with the clay, trying different configurations while I watched to see if any accurate form of my image emerged from their explorations.

A few minutes later, there, on the table in front of me, in three dimensions, stood a fairly good replica of the image that had appeared in my mind, a tortured cross with a twisted star nailed at its cross-point. I realized that I had not made this object. I had witnessed it coming into existence … and understood that it had been able to appear because I only watched the process and did not interfere.

This experience momentarily broke the stranglehold my rational mind had on my non-rational mind. Its power shifted the balance to my non-logical mind. I said to myself, "I don't understand what is happening, but I will suspend disbelief and follow this direction. I have no idea where it is taking me, but I will follow."

Suspending Disbelief

I began to pay attention to this phenomenon. I started to play guitar around this time and saw that something resembling music appeared when I kept my attention away from thoughts, particularly thoughts that wanted me to pay attention to feelings of embarrassment, shyness or how silly I might sound to others. Again, I was able to watch my fingers move and listen to my voice sing ... as long as I didn't think about how to do what my body was doing.

Recently I picked up my grandfather's harmonica and, without having had any training, very pleasing music emerged. Again, I saw that if the melody was in my mind, then my mouth, lips and breath would reproduce the music on their own. When my thoughts became involved, "Where is the next note? How is this happening? I don't know how to do this", the music stopped. When I turned my attention to the sensation of my body and away from thoughts, the music resumed. I could only "make" the music by not thinking about it ... which demonstrated that I was not making it. It was making itself through me. When I was able to find an attitudinal posture as "audience" to what was being expressed through my body, the process flowed, and the results were pleasing.

The Mystery of the Creative Process and Artistic Blockage

All those who work with the creative process, whether intellectually like a philosopher, emotionally like an actor, artistically like a painter or physically like an athlete, report similar experiences. But typically, we give ourselves credit for the performance. "Look at what I've done!" As a psychotherapist, I recognized this trap in every artist who came to me seeking help to overcome a "block" and the accompanying anxiety due to the inability to "create." This inability was threatening their sense of themselves.

Often, the initial creative manifestation comes spontaneously and carries a special quality that gains the attention of others. The gift of this "creation" is attributed to the person of the artist and affixed to his or her image as "creator," an image held both by others, and the artist person-ally, who may gladly accept the accolades, perhaps having already appropriated them by self-proclamation. Or ... the artist is actually in awe of what has been brought forth, and not sure how he or she has produced this object of admiration, but now feels compelled to establish credentials as more than a one-time "creator." Under pressure from them-selves and/or from others to continue producing, artists try to create, force and control the process themselves. What results often disappoints.

The cure for artist's block is accepting the fact that I am an instrument in the hands of something I don't understand, which surpasses my comprehension, something far greater, more intelligent and creative than me, myself. To the degree I have been born with the right type of brain and the necessary capacities, which I may have developed through training and practice ... or just discovered were native within me without education ... I can bring into the world creative impulses corresponding to how my individual expression translates my inspiration into some tangible form.

This recognition that I do not have control over manifestations and phenomena that are really important to me ... is unsettling at best. It is definitely an acquired taste. If I feel I must produce manifestations of creativity on a time frame, my own or someone else's, if I am being paid to produce creations pleasing to those who pay me, either with attention, praise, or money, then the process becomes about me. I usurp the role of the mysterious creative impulse and give credit or allow myself to accept the credit given to me by others.

Applying the Creative Principle to Life

This pressure to produce, manifest, to meet the expectations of myself and others, sounds a lot like how I've lived much of my life. How often have I made a decision, not necessarily because I wanted to, but because it was logical, rational, would represent what I was supposed to do? So many times, my heart wanted to move in one direction, but the head said: "No! We need to follow the rules, be responsible. What you are suggesting would upset people and the thought makes me nervous!"

I later realized that what had happened with the experience at the Jungian retreat was that I had "let go". Let go of what? It felt like I had let go of myself, the myself I knew as Steve. I did not know this new part of me. It felt unnerving, alien, powerful. It also felt confident. It knew where it was going. I didn't, but It did. As I followed, it led me to the philosophy and methodology of G. I Gurdjieff, the psychological system that was to alter my relationship with myself and my understanding of what I had known as "reality."

The quality of my life since has changed. I've come to know myself in the manner that I believe Socrates was recommending. As a result, I have discovered a different relationship with life. I've come to see that while I try to paint my wishes on the canvas of the life around me, the life around me is trying to mold me to a shape that fits the energy of the situation. I can feel the push/pull of it at times. I am no longer surprised by or upset by the lack of reality's cooperation with my attempts to arrange life the way I would prefer it to be. I understand that I am not the sole creator of the life around me. I understand it is a result of what I bring to the moment at hand, how that moment has been shaped and energized by all the people and factors that have brought that moment into existence … and … an element of luck, hazard, unpredictable coincidences. Of the three factors, I have influence over only one … myself … and then only to a degree.

Accepting the Unexpected

There is more going on than myself and the canvas, or clay, or the guitar strings, or the keyboard. Intervening is the third element … the Unknown. How do I make peace with the universal constant of chance which makes every outcome uncertain before it takes shape in our reality? Every moment carries the possibility of something unexpected. My intellectual mind gets nervous and starts talking to my non-rational side. "Where is this going?" it argues. "Why is this happening? Could this lead to problems?" it wonders. My non-rational side replies, "Relax. Not knowing makes it more interesting. Why are you afraid of surprises? Just relax let the current carry you. I'll let you know if the feeling of the energy drawing us onward changes. Until then … trust me. Let's see what happens."

Recently, I realized, to my surprise, that I had crossed over into a new phase of my life. For better or worse, I felt I needed to write. The feeling of "rightness" about this call was the same feeling of rightness I experienced at age thirty-eight when I discovered Gurdjieff. It is the same feeling of rightness that has guided my decisions ever since.

I came to realize that life is like the child's game of "Hot and Cold." "You're getting warmer, warmer … no, now colder … ok … warmer again … warmer ... hot. You've found it!" There is a "warmth-cold" meter, an "attraction-repulsion" meter in the center of my chest. When it warms, I know I am on the correct path. When it cools, I know I am not. It is not that I don't think about these choice points, but my rational mind now knows to trust the non-rational when this special feeling is present.

The need to write collided with a very heavy schedule of meetings every week … in all of which I played a central role. These were meetings with people who shared my deepest interests in Gurdjieff's system, people I loved and enjoyed. But I couldn't write without having my solitude continually interrupted for yet another meeting. I was feeling the pressure of this conflict.

Harmonizing Head and Heart

Then I had a dream. In the dream I was with my wife. I was having trouble talking with her and realized that I was having a stroke. I tried to tell her what was happening to me and to call an ambulance. She didn't understand me and did not realize the significance of my inability to communicate. On awakening, I understood immediately that the female figure in the dream did not represent the real-life person sleeping next to me. I realized that this dream was a pictorial representation of the current tension between my genuine feelings for my friends and my role of responsibility with them on the one hand and the yearnings of my essence for the space and solitude that the creative process requires on the other. Something was preventing this yearning part of me from communicating, and its request to be heard was not resonating with the "responsible" part of myself, which wanted to always meet its commitments to others. I could not consistently write and also meet with my colleagues with such frequency. I had to choose.

My intellect and my feelings were having trouble communicating. My feelings were calling to my head, "Wake Up. I am feeling a sense of 'rightness' about this new urging." My logical mind responded, "Yes. I hear you ... but all this group activity is what you have been doing for forty years ... this is your role ... and you love these people and these conversations." My feelings responded "That's true, but I also have a deep feeling that the next stage of my development requires me to write. I need to transfer from my inner understanding to the world outside what I have learned before I die, and for that I need unstructured time to think and read and walk and sit quietly. I can't do that with all these wonderful, enjoyable, but distracting commitments."

Surrender and Acceptance

I have had to "let go" many other times in my life, as have we all, but this time it was different. Previously, I was resisting or grieving involuntary loss. I didn't really choose to let go of something I valued. It was taken from me. The "letting go" was the state of acceptance after a process of grieving. This time I needed to voluntarily let go of activity and time with people that I really enjoyed ... an activity that, up until this moment, had defined my "self" for myself and I had assumed would continue until my death.

An association occurred in response to this experience. I realized that in the end, I would have to either voluntarily let go or have everything taken from me. I could resist and fight or relax and flow. Here was the recognition that I had entered a new chapter in my story without realizing the threshold had been crossed until I was on the other side. I now saw that I could let go of things I still cared for rather than waiting for them to be torn from me.

I realized I had to let go of the version of me, which I had assumed was my completed form (that of a group leader and participant in Gurdjieff's "school" of transformational development). I now had to embrace a new role that I felt I did not deserve, was braggadocio for me to give myself … yet the feeling was right. I "let go" of almost all commitments on my calendar and focused on writing. I did not know who I was writing for. It was a while before I realized I was writing for myself, the Witness to my writing.

Right now, in this moment, as these words appear on the screen in front of me, I am reminded of watching my hands mold the clay. Now I am watching my fingers type the letters which are informing me of how I feel, what I think, what I have come to.

As I am writing this, I notice a new association appearing in my mind with reference to two occurrences in the past six years in which something went wrong in my body and I ended up in a hospital emergency room. I realized how easy it would be to die. I really didn't need to do anything. When my body was ready, it would stop living. I was just along for the ride.

Connected with this memory, I now recall a conversation with my spiritual mentor a year before his passing. I asked him about his remarkable sanguinity about death. He said to me, "I've already died a couple of times and they brought me back. There really is nothing to it. I didn't even know I was dead. I'll just continue to do what I enjoy until one day I'm not here to do so."

Recently, I realized that the center of gravity for my inner life had substantially shifted from accomplishments in the outside world to a wish for being increasingly present to the diminishing moments left to me. As part of this process, I made a deliberate decision to minimize the frequency of my attempting to impose my will on people and events around me. Rather, I am practicing watching and waiting to see what happens. I don't mean to suggest that I don't offer opinions and make suggestions and preferences known. But, if I do share this information, I only add it to the mix and wait to see what emerges. Sometimes it is what I wanted and sometimes not. I accept whichever option appears and work with it.

This produces the same impressions and feelings as the moment I watched my hands mold the clay many decades ago. I have heard the phrase that there is an "art to living" and I've used that phrase myself. But now, I am beginning to understand this phrase more deeply.

Life moves. It flows. Poets and mystics talk about Life as a river. I may have a wish to be carried somewhere, but whether or not that occurs is a combination of my wish, my ability to maneuver in the river and a great deal of luck. Rarely do I end up exactly where I intended. I can fight the current or I can work with it as best I can and wait to see where I am carried.

The "art" is in the attitude. Life is on loan to this body I reside in. I have some choices in most moments, but an infinite range of possible moments is not available to me. As I age, the shape that my life has taken increasingly limits the number of options. How will I play the hand I have been dealt? Sometimes I need to follow reason. Other times I need to follow feelings. Part of the art is distinguishing between the two and knowing which to listen to in a given moment. More importantly, I need to help the longing of my mind to blend with the longing of my heart, so that no choice is necessary.

Nevertheless, the universal constant is chance, hazard, accident, luck. I have no control over this mysterious variable. I must accept its reality, learn to play with it, and accept that resistance is futile. Sometimes fortune favors me. Perhaps, I was intelligent enough to "play the odds" well. Often, good luck eludes, and an unwanted or unexpected situation appears, requiring me to try to be receptive to an impulse that will manifest as a creative response to the new event.

Over the years, I have learned to temper the unnecessary feeling of shock, disappointment or surprise when reality does not conform to my fantasy. I have learned to accept, perhaps even to be open and play with the uncertainty factor.

The Art of Living and Dying

I recently realized that all this practice of "letting go" was preparation for the art of dying. There is a choice, not about inevitable death, but of how I relate to the coming of that end time. One choice is to follow Dylan Thomas and " ... not go gentle into that good night, ... burn and rave at close of day; rage, rage against the dying of the light." But this presumes that death is the end rather than a potential transition to something else. If life is only material, then holding onto life and raging at your dying body is understandable. If existence has meaning, however, then death also has meaning. My experience at that moment may determine what comes next.

Do I want to die in a state of rage and fear or in a state of tranquility, gratefulness and hope?

Do I want to live in a state of rage and fear and frustration or in a state of tranquility, gratefulness and hope?

Practicing the latter will be preparation for the former. The state in which I die will then reflect the state in which I l have lived. In trying to prepare for a graceful death, I am learning how to live more gracefully.

I find, for example, that I am now better able to relax, let people be whoever and whatever they are. We could all relax and do the same for ourselves. What might be the quality of the life remaining to me if I really let go of trying to force life to surrender to my wishes and accept it as it presents itself? Not necessarily accept in the sense of liking it, but in the sense of being realistic. If this is the reality of the moment, how can I best work with it? What choices, if any, are available? If there are none at the moment, and I must just endure, then not wasting energy on what cannot be changed would be a practical attitude to begin with. I always have the choice of enduring with dignity.

What if I could watch myself live my life as I watched my hands mold the clay?

Do I imagine I am the "artist" who can take credit for the form and shape of his life or do I understand that my "artistry" is in how I work with the fact that I am also a channel for the ongoing momentum of events and decisions made by others and circumstances, either contemporary or dating from long before my birth?

Did I "work" life into shape or did life "work" me into a shape that circumstances allowed the possibility for at that time in history?

From one angle, I have applied my skills, native and trained, to draw my intentions on the canvas of life that my birth had painted me onto. From another angle, as the energy of life worked through the structure of my talents and capacities, both in-born and trained, the form of my life took shape.

There has been a creative process at work in my life, in your life also, dear Reader. I, you, we have tried to shape the life around us to conform to the architecture we wish to inhabit. At the same time, the life we are trying to mold has its own shape long pre-existing us. That shape allows for some possibilities and not others, depending on many circumstantial variables. We can only work with what is given and available. We can be creative in what we are able to do, depending again on what actually is possible under the circumstances of the times.

A new question arises now. How have I tried to shape life, people and events into the "picture" I wanted to paint? How do I push, prod, pull at people and events to bring this preferred image into existence? What happens when I meet resistance? Do I tend to always push against it, trying to forcibly move it out of the way? Do I try to accommodate it, work with it, compromise? Do I give up and try a different direction? Or … just give up?

I invite you, dear Reader, to reflect on your life along with me. Can I, can you, remember hopes, plans for what you wanted to be when you grew up? Were there wishes about marriage, family, jobs, finances, travel, rewards and accolades? A useful way to practically explore this question is to make a list of these future projections made so many years ago. Which came into existence and which did not? What happened to create this division? Of those that I "achieved" … how closely did they ultimately resemble the original idea? Do you recognize the disparities in your story, or have you habituated to how things are and rewritten the history of your original aims? To what degree have you been the creator of your life and to what degree have you been carried by events? Are you at all surprised as to where you have ended up in life or is it exactly as you planned?

When I meet with resistance from people and circumstances to my plans and wishes, what do I do? Am I frustrated? Do I continue to push and push to make things turn out as I want? "If at first you don't succeed, try, try again" is practical advice, but is not guaranteed to yield the desired results. … and after a time may become self-defeating. Why do I experience frustration? Do I assume I am the only person with plans who is trying to manipulate people and situations? How about all the people in all the situations I encounter? Every one of them is an "artist" in their own mind, each trying to rearrange the people and events around them ... myself included. To me, they are part of my canvas, clay for me to shape. But, to all of them, I am part of their canvas and clay for them to shape.

Imagine an artist whose brushes, paints, canvas were always moving, changing, often non-compliant with wishes to control them. How does one create under these circumstances? What can one create under these circumstances?

An artist requires a relationship with material, tools and medium. It must be cooperative. A brush and a hand cannot paint a picture by themselves. They require a third component. It is a combination of the artist's intention, skills and attitude that then determines what might come into existence and the degree to which it conforms to the artist's ideal.

It is that way with our lives also. As we experience the ebb and flow of circumstances, the rise and fall of energy, good luck and bad luck, happiness and sadness, success and failure, periods of sickness and health, what attitude do we try to bring to this fluid, fluctuating flow of energy we call our "individual" lives?

When I encountered, so many years ago, that shapeless lump of clay sitting passively in front of me ... and saw, in my mind's eye, the image of the cross and star ... I did not understand then that the experience was the beginning of a tutorial in relating to life and death.

If Existence Has Meaning ...

If I accept that there is purpose behind existence, then, as I am part of existence, so I must have a role in that purpose. If I am part of something much greater than myself ... an infinitely larger extension of myself, then, assuming It and I are holographic in nature, then any part of the Whole will carry a representation of that larger Whole, the outline of which might be seen if the appropriate light is shone through a sliver of the Whole ... such as myself. If I can shine that light ... and who else could? ... I am the only one ... then I shine that light through the focus of my attention. As I peer into the depths of myself, my awareness rides the light-beam of attention. What can I see before I lose control of attention when, distracted by something closer to the surface, it swings away from the deep interior, leaving me with the sorrow of having been so close to something vitally important and then losing it?

I now understand that to play my role with the creative process, my attitude must be one of submission and acceptance.

I must tolerate loss ... loss of control of the process … loss of control over the end product … loss of control of the response it will get from the world … loss over when the Muse will appear again. I am not in total control. Even if my skills are sufficient to produce a quality product, how am I in control? If my skills are so honed that I could say that "I have complete control over my medium," do I know how I move my body so that it is skilled in its gestures... or does its skill manifest automatically?

Creativity appears in my awareness from nowhere and disappears back into nowhere. If I am sensitive to it when it appears, I can allow it to direct my body and my abilities, natural or acquired, to express in a materialized way what it is conveying to me. If I try to control it, the flow is corrupted or lost. I can carry the creative impulse best when I accept my role as instrument, not creator.

Life also appears from nowhere and disappears back into nowhere. "Where was I the moment before my conception?" may be the answer to "where do I go after I die?" We have a taste of this mystery each day when I (consciousness) disappears at night and returns with sunrise. I am not in control of my coming nor of my going.

If I try to force outer life, the process is directed only by my ordinary interests and passions. The true creative impulse will be distorted or absent. If I allow my inner life to follow its innate desires, their expression will be reflected in my interests. They will align and the life that takes shape will be a work of art, a product of the creative energy.

I am not in control of that life energy which seems related to the creative impulse. It comes and goes of its own Will.

When it flows in, I am conceived …

When it flows in, I am born…

When it flows in, I am awakened from sleep …

When it flows in, I wake up to the experience of my own existence.

When it flows out, I lose the experience of my own existence …

When it flows out, I am aware only of impressions around me, but with no awareness of myself …

When it flows out, I become tired and go to sleep …

When it flows out, my body dies.

What will be the artist behind my life? The creative process or the fluctuating whims and worries of my personality? I understand now that those whims and worries are not and can never be the artist. I have learned that by becoming a servant of the creative process, I can allow it to guide me as I paint the form and quality of my life on its canvas.

The Witness to Existence

Just as when I watched my hands molding the clay, I am now trying to observe my body and my personality live their life under the auspices of something much greater than myself. I know I must try not to grasp tight but to keep only a gentle hold so that I won't disturb or fight its flow.

When that process is finished using me, it will withdraw. While I still live, I may become aware of it from time to time. Eventually, it will leave my body and "I" will die. Hopefully, my awareness will leave with it as the passenger of the Creative Process.

I hope I may be gentle at the moment I sense life leaving … and then what happens? Then I become the clay.

Image 3. Contemporary sketch of the image.

Consciousness in Motion

I realize it is morning. I am lying in bed. My body is relaxed, warm, comfortable. I am aware of the feeling of, "I don't want to get up." I don't necessarily hear the words in my head, but I know I don't want to get out of bed. I don't need to tell myself this. I know this directly. My mind is clear. I sense the comfort of my body. I wonder … again without needing to tell myself that I am wondering … "When will I get out of bed? In ten seconds, in one minute, in five minutes?" I know I can make it happen whenever I "choose" to do so, but I am curious. If I lie here in bed and do not initiate a movement, what will happen? I know I will not remain here all day or all morning. If I don't initiate, what will my body do? How will it decide to rise … and how, exactly, does that happen?

I wait and watch. Nothing is changing. I continue to watch with growing interest. I continue to wait … and then, almost surprising me, my body throws a leg out of bed and rises. As it gets up, it carries me with it. It is now walking towards the bathroom for its morning ablutions. I am pretty certain I did not initiate this. Something in me made the decision, but it wasn't the part of me that was watching.

. . . .

I am reading aloud in a group with friends. I hear my voice say the words. I am aware of my tone and emphasis shifting with the content, trying to find a pace and intonation that brings the text to life as I attempt to feel an understanding of the material. Then someone interrupts my reading. I feel the reverberation of his voice inside me. He informs me that I missed a word or skipped a line. I look at the book and realize that he is correct. I am curious. How did that happen?

As I resume reading aloud, I now watch my eye movements. I notice that my eyes are not looking at the word I am pronouncing aloud in that moment. They are scanning ahead several words or sometimes a sentence. In the time it takes for my voice to speak the word, part of my attention has already moved forward to preview what is coming. Clearly, something has recorded, and is processing, individual words for enunciation but is lagging behind my visual scanning. My eyes are in the future of the rendition, while part of my mind is running a fraction of a second behind. I hear my voice finally pronounce the word even as my

46

eyes are roaming ahead.

I have made no decision to do this. It is not a conscious strategy. It is just happening. At the moment, in addition to listening to my voice, to feeling its reverberation in my body, and digesting the content, I now add the intentional watching of my eye movements. Who is actually doing the reading? My voice is reverberating by itself. My eyes have been moving on their own. I am aware that I am making the effort to follow all this simultaneously as I feel for the meaning of the word "content" … but the effort to pay attention seems like the only thing I, myself, am actually doing. The activity of my body and brain seems to be on automatic pilot.

. . . .

I am in conversation with a companion. I notice that my hands and arms have been gesticulating without my initiation. I try an experiment. I hold them still, hands in my lap while I continue to talk. This feels very awkward, unnatural. Then they are moving again, joining in the conversation. I did not initiate this. I lost my attention on them. As soon as they realized they were not being watched, they launched again into their own animated language.

As the conversation continues, I watch my companion. His body is also speaking along with his voice. The motion of his arms and hands, as well as facial expressions, the angle of his body and the modulation of his voice, seem connected to the emotional quality of what he is saying. I wonder if he is aware of his conversational doppelgänger.

How do my arms and hands know how to emphasize and punctuate? I did not intentionally teach them. Social scientists would say that I learned unconsciously from watching others as I grew up. That explanation seems to be a tautology. We learn to gesticulate from others, who learned to gesticulate from others, who learned to gesticulate from others … This begs the question. How does our body know how to speak with … or for us?

As I listen to my voice in conversation, I notice several interesting phenomena. I know the theme of what I want to say, but I have not rehearsed the wording. The words flow nevertheless … including many I did not anticipate. I cannot see what or how the words are being chosen. They seem to flow automatically. Often, I begin in one direction, but the words change course. Often, I am following the theme in my mind while my voice speaks for me. Then I see one, perhaps two or even three divergent associative themes appear in my mind's eye. Which direction to take?

47

Perhaps I pause to think at this point, but sometimes my voice continues on the original theme as I instantly assess the new options, how they tie into the original, where they may lead, how to come back to the starting point if I get "lost."

"Lost." How do I get lost in my own mind? Where do I go? How do I find my way back? If I get lost in my mind, am I my mind or something wandering inside my mind? Is my mind on autopilot also? As I have awoken from thousands of daydreams over the course of a lifetime, this question seems to answer itself.

I notice that, as I am speaking, there are often pictures or thematic outlines forming, on their own, in my mind, ahead of the expression of words. Often, I am assessing them for relevance to the conversation at hand and then deciding which to offer to my voice for verbalizing. Sometimes, when I am talking about a topic that has emotional energy for me, I listen to the words flow out faster than I can think. They often lead in directions I had not anticipated and sometimes verbalize ideas or solutions I did not know I knew until I hear them, along with my listeners, for the first time. Sometimes I hear my voice say something unintended by my mind.

Where do the words come from? As with other motions manifesting from my body, I cannot see the connection between the activity in my mind and the complex modulations of my vocal cords, breath, lips, tongue producing symbolic sounds.

. . . .

I have often been driving while daydreaming, or listening to the radio, or talking with my passenger. I "awaken" suddenly to the fact that I am operating a multi-ton vehicle at sixty miles per hour, maintaining position on a curving road while avoiding collision with other multi-ton vehicles traveling alongside me. I know that you, my Reader, have also experienced this phenomenon.

I am recalling, at this moment of writing, a dark, foggy night in rural Maine. I was halfway home on my hour-long trip, driving a familiar road. I have no recollection of what I was thinking about, but I clearly recall the moment of realizing that I had no idea where I was. What I could make out along the roadside, despite the fog, immediately told me I was no longer on the main road. Where did I turn off? How long ago? How far had I traveled? Where was I?

I thought I could turn around and, if I had made only one wrong turn, I would eventually return to the main road, but if I had made more than one, I might not locate myself for a long time. Or, I could continue until I found a familiar landmark. I chose the latter option. A few minutes later, I intersected with the main road and realized I had unconsciously taken a side loop that I had once driven along in the past.

Who is driving when I am not present to the road?

. . . .

As I round a curve on a country road, I am aware of movement in my peripheral vision. I notice my hands turning the steering wheel as my foot applies pressure to the break. The car modifies its trajectory. Suddenly, a deer enters my direct field of vision, running across the road in front of me. The alteration in the car's angle and speed easily averts a collision. The deer disappears into the forest on the opposite side of the road. My hands readjust the car's position back into alignment with the center line. My foot eases off the break. My heart has not missed a beat. My breath has not sped up. I feel no anxiety. I am totally relaxed. The entire event, as I play it back in my mind, took less than two seconds ... "one thousand one, one thousand two." Yet, during the event, there had been no sense of hurry. Everything had transpired ... v e r y ... s l o w l y.

Time had altered. All the actions my body took were done without my intentional initiation. They just happened as I had watched the event, the car, the deer, my body as if it were a movie.

. . . .

I am walking down a city street. I recall a mental exercise that has been recommended to me.

I put half my attention into the sensation of my body in motion. With most of the remainder, I begin to visualize the alphabet, letter by letter, as my mind says its name. In between each letter, I visualize and say a number, starting from twenty-six and counting backwards to one. When I reach the end, I now visualize and pronounce each letter and the intervening numbers backwards. While mentally working in this way, I try to maintain sensory contact with my body and watch it walking. When I lose this split attention, either on the counting or my body, I start over again. My body continues to walk with confidence and competence, even when much of my attention is occupied in my head. Clearly, my body does not need conscious direction from me in order to know how to move.

. . . .

It is very difficult to pay attention to the body in motion for more than a few seconds. The body's reactions are generally too fast to be thought out step by step. Try catching a ball by thinking about how to do it or think your way downstairs rather than letting the body continually voluntarily fall and catch itself on the step below over and over until the stairway ends.

Clearly, "Thought" is much too slow to control or direct movement.

The learned-academic response to this recognition is that the movement is instinctual or hard-wired due to prolonged practice. This may be correct in terms of brain structure and functions, but it overlooks the mystery of my body being an entity of its own. Sometimes my consciousness and body communicate, but for the most part, it lives its physical life, and I live my psychological life, side-by-side or one-inside-the-other, with only intermittent awareness of each other.

If one is a meditator, an interesting effort to make is to try to maintain awareness and connection with your body when the meditation ends, and you get up and move around again. If the form of meditation you are practicing is focused on strengthening attention, the effort does not end with the meditation. The meditation is practice for strengthening the ability to be attentive in life; standing in a line waiting for my turn, answering the phone, walking from one room to another. The possibilities for this type of practice are limitless … if we can remember in the moment.

One of my favorite Buddhist sayings is, "I have a body, but I am not my body …". This may seem to be a nonsensical statement. Or one may pay lip service to it in theoretical agreement. But to actually verify that this observation is literally true is a totally different experience. The taste of this changes one's sense of reality and one's sense of the very nature of oneself.

Two Realities ... Maybe Three

O ur physical bodies exist in the four-dimensional world of height, width, depth and time. Because we live in material bodies, held fixed on a material planet by gravity, our movements are linear. We walk, drive, ride along the surface of the Earth from one location to another. To us, it seems as if we are traveling along a straight line. After all, we are told that a straight line is the shortest distance between two points. We do not sense that we are actually moving on an arc, our movement following the curved surface of our planet. Nevertheless, we are traveling along a curved line that has, for us, a starting point, a middle and an end at our destination. So, perceptually, we tend only to be concerned with the width and depth of our line of travel unless one is piloting an airplane.

The Horizontal Dimension Perspective

The experience of traveling linearly also gives the impression of a starting point, a middle point and a final destination. The passage of these markers also gives the sense of movement in the direction of my end-point. When we talk about our passage through life, we naturally demarcate events on the line of time. What is behind us we call the *Past*. Where we are now, we call the *Present* and the direction we are headed towards we call the *Future*. These moments *in* time also serve to give the impression of movement along a line. On this line are all my outward movements, experiences, activities ... what I call my life experiences.

Also, connected with this line are what *we thought and felt and sensed at each of those moments remembered* along the line of life. We know that the life events we recall, happened to us. They made an impression on us such that a recording of aspects of the event is embedded in memory. There was something more recorded than just the images, sounds, tastes, feel of the people and scenery around us at the moment the memory was

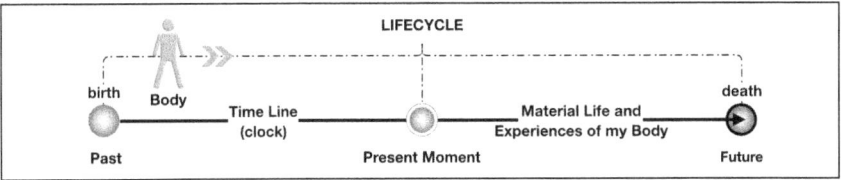

Figure 1. What I call my life experiences.

51

implanted. Also recorded were the thoughts, impressions, feelings, sensations that we experienced in that life situation.

Looking Inside

How was I aware of my thoughts, impressions, feelings, sensations at that moment? My eyes, ears, nose and other senses were looking outward at the life around me, recording, like machines, what they were experiencing. What was recording my thoughts, impressions, feelings, sensations *inside* my mind and body?

If I look at the content of those inner experiences in the context of the outside event, I will see connections between the inner and outer content. I will see that sometimes, what my senses are recording of the world outside, triggers a reaction, positive, neutral or negative, inside. And I will also see that sometimes, the thoughts or feelings or sensations inside color what I am interpreting outside and cause me to react in a way that changes what is happening outside. I will see that my interior psychological world and the outer material world are intimately connected, literally two sides of the same coin. The *interior psychological world lies vertically* to *the horizontal world of the physical body*. My vertical always accompanies my body. Wherever my body goes, my mind goes with it, recording the inner reactions to the outer experience, and influencing my outer manifestations towards the world ... which alters the world's response back to me.

Attitude, Meaning and Memory

Diagram 2 represents the interaction between past attitudes and interpreted meaning of events and what type of future moments will appear based on my past psychological assessments. The upper section of the diagram represents positive psychological attitude and the lower half represents the negative. When my psychological state is positive, the level and quality of experience on the horizontal life-line which accompanies it is experienced and interpreted differently than if the psychological state is in the negative region. Our thoughts about the future are influenced by our attitudes about the past. This often produces a self-fulfilling prophecy. Not only will I be more anxious about the future if I am drawing on negative past memories, but I am likely to bring about, or interpret what actually happens, in light of my expectation.

The vertical axis also demonstrates the relationship between "cre-

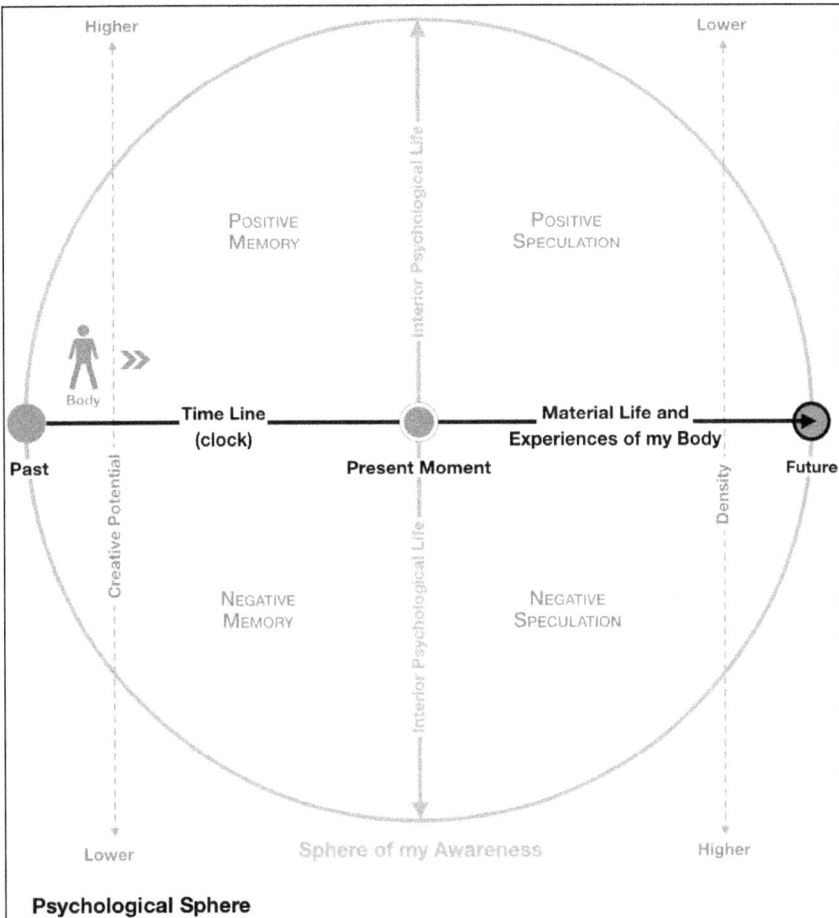

Psychological Sphere
- The body is fixed objectively to the horizontal time line.
- Typically attention is identified with the life of the body on the horizontal timeline, even though our subjective world is experienced in the psychological life on the vertical.
- Attention moves with the present moment horizontally and vertically, which forms our point of view.
- The past is remembered in crystalized events as memories, while the future speculated as potential events.
- Our states are experienced and perceived on the vertical, our subjective world.
- The life of the personality is projected on to the horizontal life of body.
- We experience subjectively on the vertical, yet we project that on the horizontal.

Figure 2. Dimension of Attitude and Meaning.

ativity" and "density". As my attitude and thoughts become heavier, denser in quality, my thinking and feelings become more constricted, less flexible and the possibility for creative, expansive or novel perspectives

53

constrict and my experience of moment sinks downward into negativity. The opposite is true when I "rise above" my conditioned base-line and bring lighter, more flexible, more inquisitive attitude to the moment. When someone suggests that I "lighten up" or "get over it", they are displaying an intuitive sense of these relationships even if they don't actually know how to accomplish this attitude shift.

The "level" of my life experience in the moment is thus a result of my relationship with my interpreted past and speculated future. Thus my experience of "reality" is determined by my location on my interior, vertical dimension.

This perspective immediately shows the criticality of being able to be aware of my inner psychological state simultaneously with being aware of what is happening in the world around me. Typically, my attention switches back and forth, back and forth between the two. Sometimes I am very attentive to my surroundings and at other times, I am oblivious to it, lost in daydream. If attention could be stabilized, I would be able to be aware of, and thus, live in, both worlds at the same time. That would give a more nuanced sense of reality.

In *Figure 2*, we can also see that *memory travels with us*. When we look back in time, where exactly are we looking? Where is memory stored? On the diagram, it is as if we are standing in the present and looking into our vertical world, back into the library of recorded events until we find what we are looking for *in the past*. But we are in the *present*, both when we are looking and when we find it. So, the past and present exist at the same time? I can be with my past, right now, in this present moment.

A Personal Experiment

Try this, dear Reader. Place part of your attention on the sensation of your body and on your breath at the same time you direct the other part of your attention to visit a past memory. Try to hold both worlds in awareness at the same time, both the material world of your body's sensations and your psychological world of memory, with its images and dialogues. This takes effort, which is one reason why our attention tends to continually swing from one to the other without any attempt to hold them together.

The Eternal Present

Any reaction I am experiencing in this moment may have developed many years ago and tends to be triggered by certain events. If I am experiencing it now, there must be something in the current situation similar enough to evoke a resonant echo from my library of conditioned responses. So ... my past is influencing me now, in my present. That means that the past, or the imprint of the past, can *transcend time* and become part of my eternal present ... and unless resolved, it also lies ahead of me, in the "future," waiting to be stimulated again when my body eventually arrives there.

What is the Future? When I look ahead and picture a forthcoming event or a hoped-for or a dreaded possibility, where am I looking? I am in the Present. (See *Figure 3,* on the next page.) If what I see is a future possibility, whether it actually occurs or not when I get to that part of my lifeline, is not the point (i. e. when I am finally standing in that future location I am envisioning now in my *present*). The point is that the dimension of future possibilities exists alongside the present because I can only visit it from my present location.

Somehow, *the present moment is eternal*, encompassing past and future simultaneously. If I maintain my awareness in the present moment, of both inner and outer worlds, including inner world aspects of past and future, positive and negative, then, by implication, I would be experiencing all this from ... *Eternity.* What can this possibly mean?

As our body travels in straight lines, our minds travel in an accompanying but infinitely more complex dimension. In the vertical or interior world, there is an "up" and "down" scale of positive or negative mindset and there is a depth stretching from remembered past to the imagined future. But there is another dimension of *quality* and *meaning* that appears in the vertical. The vertical is a scale of quality from high to low, realistic to illogical, from compassionate to indifferent, from kind to cruel. It is the world where assumptions are made, interpretations created, motives established and plans, and reactions activated by the power of emotion and valuation. It is the realm where we experience what we call our "reality." It is from this subjective, idiosyncratic reality that we manifest out into the horizontal world.

Attention

Just as we have a physical body that can travel the surface of the earth, and with mechanical help, the space above, we must also have a type of *psychological vehicle* that allows us to travel to the heights and depths of

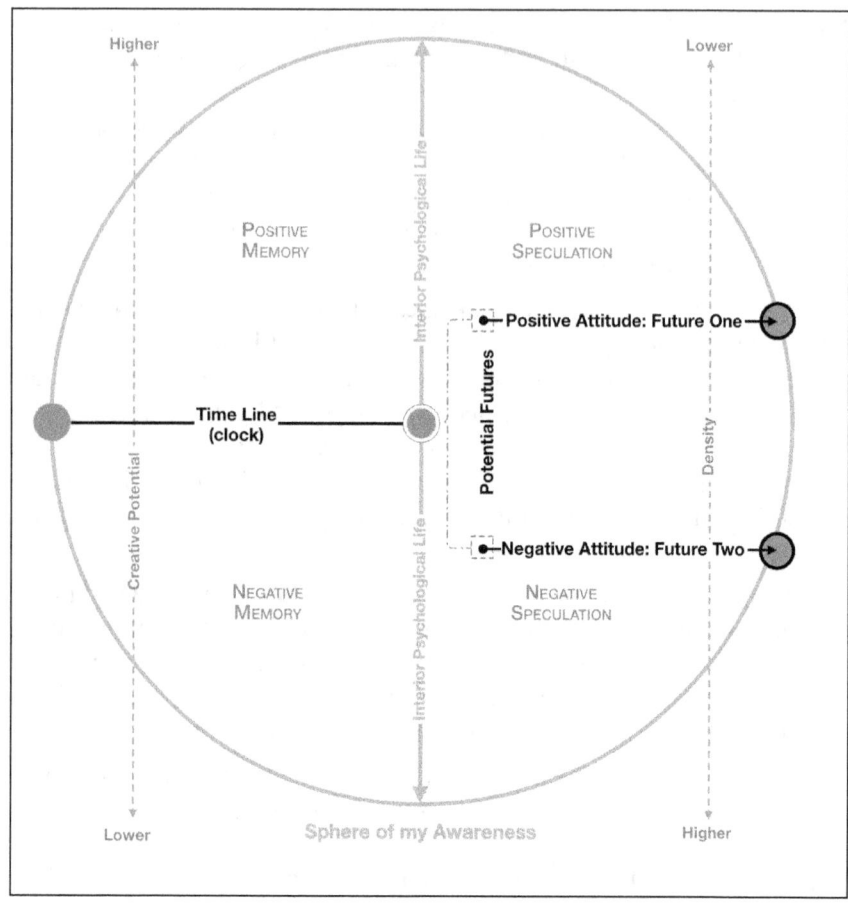

Figure 3. Potential Futures.

human psychology and move freely from past to future and to imaginary worlds that will never exist, …and which also transports us to regions of differing value and levels of meaning!

This *vehicle is attention* … when our inner awareness is directed intentionally for the reason of exploration and understanding of the vertical dimension. But this quality of attention cannot be our ordinary attention. Ordinarily, our attention is either focused outside or inside, alternating between the two but rarely having enough bandwidth to hold both together. To study the interaction between the horizontal and vertical dimensions, we must be able to *look into both realms at the same time.* This experience requires yet another dimension … the *dimension of being aware of being aware* … with a capacity to choose where to direct

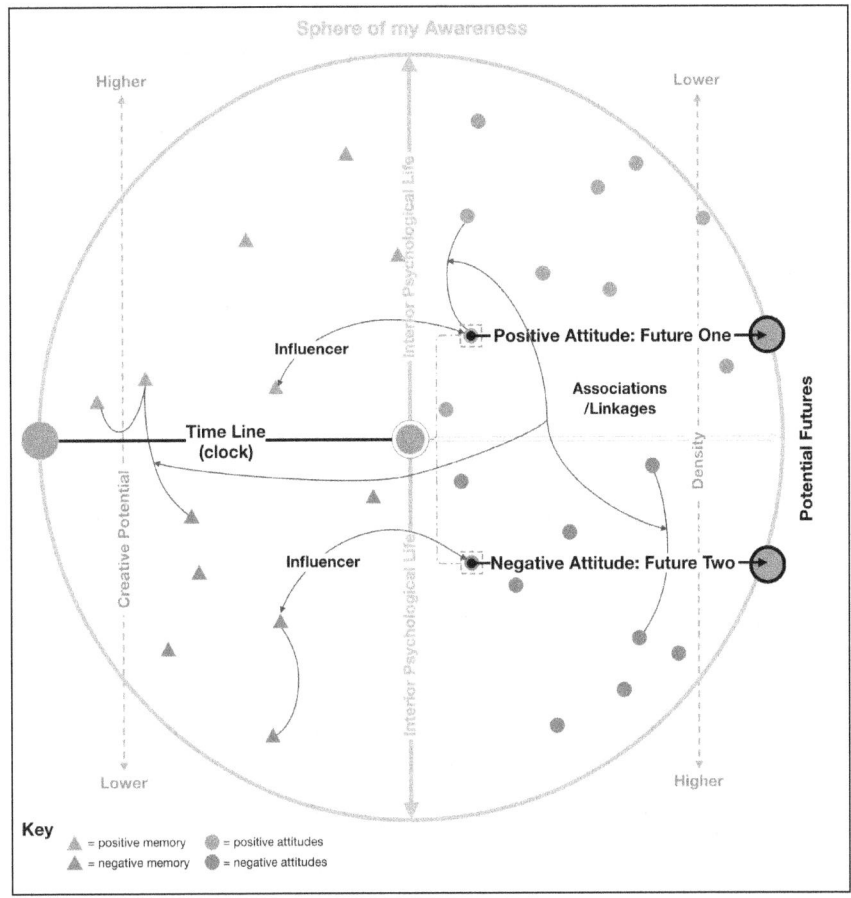

Figure 4. Associations.

attention and for what purpose. It is a dimension that is "higher" than either of the other two and blends both in the field of awareness of the third.

Going in Circles

Going in circles is a phrase often used when there is no sense of "progress" ... even though time is passing along the horizontal line. Where am I searching for this progress? I am looking into the future to see if what I see there is beginning to manifest tangibly in my present. The inability to find a solution to a short-term problem may cause frustration, but the feeling of endlessly cycling, falling into the same responses, being stuck once again in the same issue you hoped you had put behind you, is what leads to the sense of going in circles. In particular, if my wish is to change something in myself, a habit, an irritable response to certain situations that always repeats, or if I wish to learn how to do something differently, or change my attitude towards some things, it often feels that whenever the particular situation comes around again, I find myself at the same place ... in myself ... again and again.

But is this entirely true? It mostly feels as if my life is a straight line, beginning with my birth, a new segment added each year, year after year, like building a road, mile by mile, until I come to the section I am standing on at the moment. When I keep meeting the same problem or unresolved issue over and over again, I start wondering when I will be able to "put it behind me" and presumably never encounter it again.

However, there is another way of visualizing the question. Imagine a circle. Around the circumference lie the days of the year with holidays, birthdays, personally significant repeating events. I am not surprised that I keep running into Christmas or my birthday over and over again each year. Why should I be surprised, for example, that I keep running into the same unresolved issues with family members at each holiday? Viewed this way, time is circular. The "future" of a repeating event lies on the circle at the same location as the past of that event. If I have learned nothing new, if I have tried nothing new, if I am just waiting for *other* people to change, then nothing *inside me* has changed. I have not learned how to "rise above" my conditioned reactions and so, I remain on the same "level" as the original problem. If nothing in the present changes, then it is unlikely that the future will be any different.

If I become *curious* about a repeating pattern rather than *frustrated*, then I can bring an attitude of curiosity to the question. What is the history of this pattern, this response, this behavior? In what situations and with what people does it tend to appear? Who and what seems to trigger it? Perhaps if I can see more deeply into the origins of my reaction, I may learn something that alters my perspective. Eventually, this change in viewpoint will alter the "angle" from which I approach the situation next time. If I am altering my understanding or expectations, then the next time I encounter this repeating pattern, I will not be on the same "level" as I was in prior encounters. My circling around this particular issue has begun to "rise." As I learn more about why my interior world interacts in this way with this situation or this person, my angle of approach continues to alter. Thus, as I "rise above" my initial understanding, the "circle" tilts and becomes a spiral. Each turn around the spiral brings me to a change in my relationship with the issue in question.

Reactions of all living creatures are initiated from their vertical experience. An animal responds when an internal conditioned program reacts to outer circumstances which trigger it. That reaction may be hard-wired by instinct, or it may have been conditioned in a learned stimulus-response pattern. This same principle of mechanically conditioned response patterns holds for humans also ... whenever our outer and inner, our horizontal and vertical worlds, are not *held together in a third world*, the world in which we are aware of both simultaneously. It is in this third world that new perspectives can be discovered, which can change a mind or a heart, and thus bring a new, non-conditioned response into a situation.

Invisibility

In a literal way, we are *invisible*. You can prove this to yourself, dear Reader. Think about the people in your life. Picture them in your mind ... or if someone is present with you while you are reading this, look at them. Take a few moments to try this. Can you hear their thoughts or see their daydreams and know their motives? Perhaps, if the relationship is very close and of long duration, you often make accurate guesses based on past experiences and intuition. But to be certain, you would have to ask, and they would have to honestly answer. In actuality, their vertical psychological world, hidden inside their body, is invisible to you. To bring this home, imagine someone was with you ... or look at the person who may actually be present with you in this moment. Now, think a thought or imagine something that you would *not* want this person to know that you were thinking or imaging. ... Take a few moments for this experiment. ... What happened? Did they read your mind? Is your secret safe? They cannot know what is occurring in your vertical world unless you tell them or display your reaction in some way. And you cannot know for certain where they are in their inner world, either.

All our communication is by muscle movement: voice tone, pitch or volume or facial expression, body posture and timing, whether you touch or not and with what quality ... as well as your words. Without these cues to facilitate guessing on the part of others, there is no way your inner world can be known.

Much of the tragedy of human interactions is due to our poor ability to communicate and read the cues of others ... or realize that others are "reading" us, whether accurately or not, and then acting on their interpretations. Inaccurate interpretations abound, triggering reactions in each other to the *presumed assumptions* we make about what the other means. Worse still is our inability to understand ourselves and why *we react* the way we do to different people and circumstances ... or the rationalizations we may tell ourselves to justify our behavior or attitude.

It is difficult enough that the invisible vertical world of others is hidden from me. It is truly tragic when my own vertical world is hidden from myself. I need to be able to direct attention vertically and horizontally in order to understand why life reacts to me the way it does ... and vice versa.

History

Some may say History is the record of the *activities* of peoples and nations ... in general the story of migrations, subsequent clashes with other people encountered, the rise of strongmen who lead their group in conquest over other groups, attempts at governing the established territories, rebellions, and the rise and fall of these efforts over and over again throughout horizontal time.

History is also the story of discoveries, insights, inspirations, revelations brought to the horizontal from the vertical experiences of thinkers, scientists, philosophers, spiritual seekers. All discoveries, all arts, all the aesthetic aspects of a culture or civilization originate in the vertical psychological dimension and are translated through words or objects or activities into the horizontal plane where they are enacted.

If the interior dimension is dark, fearful, resentful, egoistic, power-seeking, the outer manifestations will lead to conflict and suffering, sometimes for many millions of innocent bystanders. If the interior dimension is filled with light, goodwill and open to inspiration and new ideas, the outer manifestations will lead to beneficial expressions of help, love, creative problem solving ... even inspirational poetry, liturgical music and selfless acts of charity. The *halo* depicted over the head of a Holy Person must represent this high level of light within their inner world.

The manifestations of animals reflect the universal Laws-of-Life inherent inside each living creature. The outer manifestations of humans also reflect the quality of their invisible, vertical world. But humankind has not only been programmed by Nature. Each child is programmed by the quality of the interior worlds of those adults around them in their "formative years" ... the years in which their ways of thinking, feeling, reacting and believing are being *formatted* into their hearts and minds.

This is like a computer program that operates the life behaviors and re-actions until death ... unless something happens to alter the program.

To understand how I have been programmed and to be able to alter aspects of that programming requires that I develop the capacity to see into the interaction between my vertical and horizontal worlds from the third perspective that can see both at the same time ... and also be aware of itself as the repository of both those worlds, lower in both value and potential compared with the one which can hold both in mind and heart together. This expansion in awareness and understanding is trans-formational, a different quality of consciousness, a different capacity for compassion and empathy, a different reality, a different life.

Attitude

Whether aware of the fact or not, we all live simultaneously in two worlds, our attention flitting back and forth between both and often blending them so we cannot tell the difference. My body and most of my attention lives in the material world shown to me by my senses, the world of people and landscapes and interactions between the two. This is the world of concern to my personality, my ego, my self-image. What is typically not noticed is that all our activities in the world outside originate, are initiated from the world inside, from my thoughts, feelings, opinions and conditioned reactions ... the substance of my personality, my ego, my self-image. The world outside is a reflection of processes occurring behind the scenes inside the psychological world of all the people involved. It is this inner psychological activity that produces an interpretation of the meaning of what is happening outside and causes one reaction rather than another.

Experience from the Outside

I am aware of the situation in front of me. I know the person entering the room and about to speak directly to me but did not expect to see them here. I don't know what will be said or why I've been asked here. How do I prepare myself for what is about to happen? Is this to be good news or bad news? I am guessing it must be important, but maybe I am overreacting. Can I assume my imagination about what might possibly be said is correct or am I off target? Should I be defensive or open, relaxed or tense, angry or ...? What type of posture should I take? Should I stand up taller and try to look more impressive or should I relax and look like I have nothing to defend? Should I stand or remain sitting? What should I do if he remains standing? What might that mean? Can I read anything from the expression on his face or the way he is carrying himself? Does he look upset? What is his attitude? I think he looks upset, but I've misread people before.

What should my attitude towards this outside moment be?

Typically, we do not actively engage in the internal conversation outlined above to find an attitude to position ourselves in. Our response is automatic. The original conversation in the mind took place long ago in our subconscious and its conclusions, made then, are now automatically evoked. We may believe our response is instinctive and not within our ability to control. We may recognize its origins in our history but justify it or believe we cannot change it. What we don't see is the attitude, the mental and emotional posture my beliefs put me in whenever they are triggered.

Experience From the Inside

I find that, after many years, I am inexplicably thinking about an old acquaintance. The phone rings and it is my old friend who has called to tell me that I have been on his mind lately and he wanted to reconnect.

. . . .

I recall a dream from last night. All I remember on awakening is a lantern, a split-rail fence and a man, a new acquaintance with whom I seem to have a strong intellectual and spiritual compatibility, standing adjacent to it. I experience an intense rush of ideas in my mind and go to the computer to write them down. The flood of words continues on its own and I find myself taking dictation rather than composing. The words and sentences seem to be writing themselves. I don't know where they are taking me, but I follow like a dutiful servant, allowing my fingers to type the message without seeing where the content is headed. When finished, and I read it, I notice it needs no editing other than typos. Sharing it with a couple of friends, they express amazement at its depth and complexity and say they are deeply moved. I tell them I can take no credit as I was only the stenographer, not the author. When I share this with the man who appeared in the dream, he is amazed and tells me that his personal symbol on the Tarot, the image that he most identifies himself with, is The Hermit ... usually portrayed as a robed and hooded figure holding a lantern.

. . . .

I am in a place I have never been before, in a novel circumstance, with people only recently met. Suddenly, I have the overwhelming feeling that I have been here before, in this situation, with these people. I don't know where this inexplicable impression is coming from. Did I dream it? Was the dream recent or long ago? It feels like both. Could my life be a loop where I come around again and again and "relive" previously lived moments? How is this happening?

. . . .

I am sitting quietly, focusing my attention on my breath in a meditative posture. Suddenly, I experience a surge of "energy." I feel like I am being filled with something that expands inside of me like air in a balloon. I literally feel lifted up. My posture straightens on its own. It takes no effort to maintain my position. It feels like this energy is entering through the top of my head and flowing into my body. It feels like I am being strengthened and held up from the interior by this supporting energy. My mind becomes very still and quiet. My attention is intense. There is a feeling in my chest of warmth and expansion. It is as if my heart opens up and intense feelings of gratitude and intimate relationship bring tears to my eyes. I express thankfulness to the unknown source of this energy.

. . . .

What should my attitude be towards these inner-world events? They do not seem logical. I can't explain them. I can't prove to someone else that they happened ... well, maybe the synchronous phone call from my old friend, if I accept the current scientific explanation of "coincidence," although that label explains nothing, and the statistical odds make no sense. I am the only one who experienced them, so I cannot share the experience with others for confirmation. Do I ignore them? Do I accept them outright as real phenomena unknown to science ... or, at least unexplored as yet ...or explain them away as coincidences without meaning? I know other people talk about similar experiences. Does this mean that this is not personal, in the sense that I am only one of countless people who report these types of events? Do I tell others, or do I keep it private, so I won't be judged? Do I try to delve deeper into these phenomena? Do they have meaning? How could I approach this? Maybe I should just put them out of mind since I can't prove them to my doubting friends and family.

The Inner Filter: Attitude

In aerodynamic terms, a plane's "attitude" is "based on relative positions of the nose and wings on the natural horizon." Rotation about the airplane's vertical axis (yaw) is termed "an attitude relative to the airplane's flight path, but not relative to the natural horizon."

In psychological terms, one's attitude towards a person, a subject, an activity, a point of view, their mental and emotional orientation in the face of the situation is a predisposition that determines the angle of approach to that subject. This will determine "where we land" on certain issues.

If, in my approach, my rotation (attitude) is already tilting toward either yes on one side or no on the other side, what I believe I am dealing with and how I should deal with it are determined by my "tilt," irrespective of the "natural horizon," which could be the guide for an open-minded approach balanced between the gravitational pull towards yes or no, like or dislike, agree or disagree.

How we think about something, how we feel about it, will determine which information concerning it we are attracted to and which information leaves us indifferent or hostile. Attitude will determine what we look for and what we do not look for, what we are willing to look at and what we turn away from. Attitude determines the degree to which we can be aware of the complexity of something, viewpoints, alternative approaches others have that differ from our own... or whether we automatically refuse to look at, consider, or even see, different perspectives that do not reflect our attitude.

If our attitudes are based on notions of logical or illogical, rational or irrational, right or wrong, then there is only one angle of approach. This is a serious limitation on our creativity, flexibility and adaptability. It often leads to disastrous outcomes that could have turned out very differently if other possibilities had been explored. It is in human relationships that the most damage is done, the most possibilities lost. And the primary situation in which this dynamic is played out is during attempts at communication.

Communication

How well do I listen to others? What does "to listen" mean? What role does attention play in my willingness to listen? What is the relationship between my attitude and my willingness to pay attention?

There are two basic attitudes that influence how people communicate:

Do I want to understand this other person's viewpoint, or do I want to be heard and acknowledged?

Is my primary aim to understand the other's position before I consider how, or even if, I wish to respond or to have my orientation to the subject under consideration validated?

Do I wish to explore and deepen the relationship with another person or viewpoint, or do I believe I have all the Truth, all the data, all the background knowledge already, and is acceptance of my opinion above all else my goal?

Do I want to find common ground, or do I wish to "win" the discussion?

Am I interested in learning something new, seeing something from a different angle, or do I want to teach and convert?

If I don't "win" the other to my point of view, have I "lost"?

If we examine the particular quality of communication called dialogue (defined by the dictionary as "an exchange of ideas or opinions on a particular issue, especially a political or religious issue, with a view to reaching an amicable agreement or settlement,"), we will find that the process also begins with an attitude.

In order to choose dialogue, the starting attitudinal position requires a wish to approach an exchange with an emotional/intellectual stance based on genuine interest, with an openness to take in new ideas and test them for oneself, with a comfort of exploring for the love of exploring, rather than mechanical critique and a search for specific answers that can be nailed down once and for all.

If one inhabits this attitude, entirely new options come into existence that were not possible with a less open, less inquisitive posture and a less forgiving and open heart.

Real dialogue can penetrate much deeper than agreement or settlement. Depth dialogue is a method for exploring issues from as many perspectives as possible without a pre-determined or wished-for outcome. A wished-for outcome, and certainly an expected outcome, will prejudice the facts I look for, how I interpret what I find and the meaning I will assign to it. A wished-for outcome is an attitude. It is a filter. Only by stepping outside of a "right or wrong" attitude can I have a better chance for learning and, perhaps, coming closer to a new, deeper, more subtle understanding, not just of particular fact, but of the complexity of life, my fellow humans, and myself.

Types of Attitude

Social scientists talk about four types of attitudes: positive, negative, neutral and hostile. You can explore this inside yourself, dear Reader. Imagine the physical posture that represents each of these four distinct mental/emotional states. See, in your mind's eye, four people standing in front of you, each exhibiting one of these four attitudes. See how they hold their bodies differently, how their facial expression and tone of voice betray their underlying attitude in the moment.

When confronted with something new or unorthodox, something we disapprove of or something we believe is wrong, factually or morally, one of these caricatures is emblematic of the mental/emotional posture we are assuming in our mind and heart ... and perhaps demonstrating through our own body's physical stance. This internal posture of openness, closedness, indifference or hostility, will determine the fate of the encounter because it will determine which of the different possible outcomes will be brought into existence as a result of the attitude carried by one or both parties. It does not matter if my disagreement is with a point of view originating outside myself or whether I "am of two minds" and arguing with myself. The process, and the challenge, are the same.

It is easy to see and feel the impact of the other person's attitude. Unfortunately, we are usually blind to our own, as we tend to experience ourselves as occupying the field of truth. If I am mentally and emotionally in a "yes-no," "right-wrong" attitude, how could there be two different "truths"? If I know I am right, why would I open to another viewpoint?

Increasing my blindness to my own prejudice is the tendency to meld opinion with self-image, the core of my sense of identity. If convinced my opinion is right, that makes me good. If your opinion is thus wrong, that makes you bad. At this concrete level of consciousness, there can be only one good and the others, by definition, must be bad. When attitude merges with ego, changing one's mind feels not only like defeat, but a humiliating diminishment of my image of myself, an attack on my very identity as the more righteous party in the dispute. How can both sides be good and righteous if their viewpoints are different? When my attitude is that my perspective defines my identity, the threat to my sense of existence creates intense resistance. I feel I cannot let go without diminishing or destroying myself.

Do I have to be in a state of doubting myself in order to be open? Can I feel certain that I am correct based on what I have learned and experienced, but also open to the possibility that perhaps there are factors unknown to me that would add a new consideration and maybe a change of mind ... or heart?

An example of this phenomenon is shown in the famous parable of the group of blind men gathered around an elephant. They are touching the animal all over to try to understand what an elephant is. One holds the trunk and says with confidence that the elephant is like a thick snake. One touching an ear says, "No. The elephant is like a giant leaf." "Are you crazy?" asks a third, his arms wrapped around a leg. "The elephant is like a tree trunk."

People rarely take the trouble to examine their own attitude unless it is causing problems in relationships with others or with their life choices. More likely, people project the cause of their difficulty outward, blaming it on other people or circumstances rather than looking at their own contribution. Typically, we will be open to an "attitude change" only when we have run out of formulas to fix a situation. But we don't need to wait until extreme hardship forces an exploration of other perspectives.

Watching for the attitudes behind my assumptions and challenging them will lead to flexibility and enhanced understanding of others and myself. Equally important, it can improve the quality of relationships, reduce conflict and lead to better-informed decisions.

The human brain is designed to seek patterns. We cannot, not, see patterns. Perceived patterns lead to interpretations of the meaning of these apparent patterns. However, the dots can be connected in many different configurations, and correlation does not necessarily mean cause and effect. Nevertheless, if the interpretation is felt to be the truth, it becomes the lens through which I posture my position on the subject. If the meaning changes for me, my orientation toward it changes. Can I be open to allowing a change in meaning to appear in my mind or heart? How could this happen?

To begin the process, I need to discover what my current, prevailing attitude is. Why do I feel this way? What is my history with this type of situation or subject? Am I resistant to the possibility that I may be wrong or limited in my perspective? If so, why? In order to pose these questions to myself, I cannot be in a "black-white" frame of mind. I must be in the part of my mind that wants to expand my understanding, not the part that wants to blindly defend it.

But wait! Are there different parts of my mind? Are there parts that are dogmatically closed and parts that are more flexible, curious and open to learning? If there are different parts, what can notice this fact? Is there a third part that can observe and referee between the other fractions? If I experience a change in mind, a change of heart … what changed? Who experienced the change? Were they a passive or active participant in the change?

Attitude as a State of Consciousness

The term "brainstorming" refers to a process where all possible solutions, perspectives, all the viewpoints that can be imagined are considered before examining each for its strengths and weaknesses. This is an act of creation in which time is temporarily stopped and decision suspended in order to first explore all available data. In this exploration, which can only be utilized with an "open mind," a mind that is receptive to learning, new discoveries are possible which cannot appear in a mind that is closed.

I can discover my hidden attitudes and temporarily suspend their implementation if I will make the effort to impose an intervening step between noticing the activation of an attitude and then allowing it to manifest. This step can only be taken if I am conscious of myself in the situation and aware of the fact that I may, possibly, not be the possessor of Ultimate Truth. Then, I might be curious to know why there is a different viewpoint confronting me. Why has the other party come to a different stance? What has been their experience? How have they come to a different interpretation of the meaning of this situation? If I am in a "right-wrong" mindset … (isn't that an interesting image … a "set mind"?) … then I must be right and the other must be wrong. I must convert them or dismiss them. There is no "I-Thou" attitude that allows the other the same dignity which I feel is owed to me.

To change the "set" of my mind, I cannot afford to be so consumed by my opinion that I forget the times I have, on discovering more information, been wrong, and subsequently, "changed" my mind … or moved to a different part of my mind.

One way to think into the strange idea of having different minds is to recognize the distinction, the actual feel, of a "yes" or a "no," "my way or the highway" attitude and the feel of a "frame of mind" that recognizes the significance of the existence of different viewpoints and is curious about how others experience life, not just myself. The "right-wrong" frame of mind is obviously more narrow, denser and not capable of learning because it assumes it already knows all and has come to the only conclusion possible. The attitude that is interested, and open to learning and change obviously represents a mind-frame that is larger, more flexible, able to grow and evolve. These are two different "states of consciousness," one small and rigid, the other larger and more flexible. This difference can be felt if we pay attention to it. Most of us, for most of our lives, live in the conditioned limiting state of right and wrong.

Attitude is another word for state of consciousness. To *want to listen* …

to *want to learn*, is a more expansive, inclusive state of consciousness than wanting to preach, convert, judge and exile different viewpoints.

This is not to imply that all perspectives are morally, or even factually the same. A quick glance at history, and our contemporary world, demonstrates the cruelty and destruction that can result from ignorant or pathological attitudes. Nevertheless, these situations are rare when compared with the multitude of events in the normal lives of normal people.

In our normal lives, giving the other opinion an open-minded exploration does not mean that our mind will change. Actually, I cannot, will my mind to change or my heart to open. I am not really deciding to change my mind. I may find that my mind has changed as a result of new experiences or a shift in the state of my consciousness. Or I may come to see another point of view yet reaffirm that my original sense of things still makes more sense to me, but at least I have challenged and tested it. However, this can only occur if I have the capacity to stay in a state of indecision ... tolerate not knowing ... keeping possibilities open. Do I have the curiosity and the courage to open myself to other perspectives and see if there is a resulting change in my feeling or thinking? If not, what am I afraid of? What has produced such an attitude of fear that my heart and mind are in a locked and closed attitude? The fear that locks my heart and mind in a closed attitude comes from our outer world, culture, conditioned education, subjective morality, groupthink, demands for conformity.

Freedom from Conditioned Attitude

There is a gate to freedom from the trap of a conditioned mind. There are methods, known for untold thousands of years, for escaping this prison of entrapment in the collective mindset, whether of a civilization, or a family, or a church or politics. They have been called religions, philosophies, traditions, teachings, but all, despite outward differences in shape, share the same essence, providing guidance for an enhanced quality of feeling and thinking, to be able to connect the world inside with the world outside consciously, which then re-sets our emotions on a more even keel.

Much of ancient understanding seems very different in form and metaphor from our world today, and even from each other. Each appeared at different times in human history and took a shape that could speak to people of that era. As time passes, a teaching takes on new forms more digestible by the changing cultures. ... attitudes change with time and vary between cultures. Inevitably and tragically, when the teaching, designed to lift people out of the prison of yes or no, is interpreted by minds still trapped in duality, it is, of course, translated into rules of right or wrong. This is used to justify the rejections and inquisitions that today give religions a deservedly bad name for many who have been hurt and disappointed by their apparent failure to deliver on their promise. Despite this inevitable, nearly lawful deterioration and concretization of the subtlety of the founders' vision, there still exist groups following the essence of the original intent and can be found by those who are willing to search.

Historically the aim of these teachings, in their essence, has been to help consciousness reach a state of elevation such that it could see both sides of a question at the same time. It could see, and feel, the validity on both sides, the logic of each side (given their starting positions) and, the limitations and misunderstandings of each side ... simultaneously. From this location, balanced between the absoluteness of yes or no, right or wrong, not tilted toward judgments of good or evil, one can see a much broader and deeper horizon than is visible from the "either-or" level below. From this higher level, one can experience the feelings of both sides, the wishing, the longing, the hoping, the fear and realize that they are the same on both sides. Yes and no are two sides of one coin. The whole coin suffers while each side believes it is the only side and refuses to recognize the other has a right to exist., But from a higher level of mind, one has the ableness to practice the Golden Rule and follow the precepts of the great spiritual teachers to love our neighbor as ourselves.

At the lower level of consciousness (perhaps we can call this the "lower" mind or the-mind-that-just-reacts-but-doesn't-actually-think), the feeling tone is self-righteousness, anger, rejection, judgment. From the level above, the feeling is empathy and compassion, but also sorrow, because it can be seen from up here that much of the suffering below comes from misunderstanding. It is ultimately unnecessary, but at the same time, it is unavoidable in that world fixated on duality. Friction is a natural outcome when depth of perspective is limited, which in turn places limits on its ability to understand, but nevertheless insists on a forced choice between apparent opposites.

How to Reach this Freedom

How to reach this other, higher perspective? I am trapped in the binary world when I believe it is the only reality, the only way to see and interpret and experience. Then, of course, I give it all my attention. What else would I pay attention to?

If I am willing to provisionally be interested in testing the possibility that there might be more to the question of the moment than "meets the eye," then I could try to listen to the sound of my voice when I talk or try to sense the expression on my face or feel the tension in my posture. What does that information tell me about the position of the stance (the attitude) I am taking intellectually or emotionally at this moment? I can try to practice dividing my attention between watching myself in the situation and what is happening in the situation itself. When I see a strong reaction of preference, positive or negative, agreement or disagreement, there is an attitude underneath. I need to find that attitude, articulate it to myself, and then search through my historical memory for other times, particularly the earliest I can remember. When have I experienced that attitude in the past, in my childhood? How did it form? Was it taught to me? Did I learn to mimic it to fit in and be accepted? Was it true then? Is it true now? Am I willing, just as an experiment, to explore the situation from the perspective of other viewpoints? How would it look from "over there" if I were that person, with their unique history? Might I see it the same as they do … if I were them or shared the kind of life they lived? If I would be willing to set aside who is right and who is wrong and explore with the other what our different experiences have been that led us to our perspective, what might I discover? How might that experience shift my perspective? Might it change my attitude?

As I travel through life, meeting one situation, one opinion after another, I could, attitudinally, be approaching at treetop level, dodging branches and buildings, my view of the terrain limited due to my low altitude and angle at the moment determined by my tilt, left or right. If I were cruising at ten thousand feet and keeping myself balanced between the continual pull from one side or the other, level with the true horizon, the experience would be from another world. Once airborne, what would be my altitude limit? What would "reality" look like from fifty thousand feet, from two hundred miles, from beyond the moon? Between the top of my head and the end of the universe lies only empty space. How high, how deep, could my exploring travel? What form of attitudinal understanding would such a perspective create? Am I interested in finding out?

Religion, Secular and Spiritual

One aspect of human history is the dynamic fluctuation between religious and secular aspects of society. Secularism is defined as "a belief system that rejects religion ... or the belief that religion should not be part of the affairs of the state or part of public education. It denotes attitudes, activities, or other things that have no religious or spiritual basis ... or a clergy not subject to or bound by religious rule; not belonging to or living in a monastic or other order."

The conventional definition of the word "religion" refers to "the belief in and worship of a superhuman controlling power, especially a personal God or gods. It also refers to "a pursuit or interest to which someone ascribes supreme importance (i.e., "consumerism is the new religion") ... "a particular system of faith and worship." The U.S. Supreme Court has interpreted "religion" to mean a sincere and meaningful belief that occupies, in the life of its possessor, a place parallel to the place held by God in the lives of other persons. In this sense, religion does not necessarily have to do with what we call "God." It is what we "worship." Also, Religion can be explained as a set of beliefs concerning the cause, nature, and purpose of the Universe, especially when considered as the creation of a superhuman agency or agencies, usually involving devotional and ritual observances, and often containing a moral code governing the conduct of human affairs.

Religious syncretism is the blending of two or more religious belief systems into a new system or the incorporation into a religious tradition of beliefs from unrelated traditions.

A joining of contemporary science and a spiritual viewpoint would be a new syncretism.

The Object of Worship

What do I ... what do you Reader ... "worship"? Whatever I make of worth to myself is what I worship. Because of the value I give it, it may become my inner "god," my interior North Star. What we worship becomes Lord over us. It Lords over us and we become its servant ... or slave. We best chose well, the Lord we chose to serve.

It seems to me that humans have a built-in need to feel they belong to and perhaps are serving or representing something greater than themselves. Historically, this was understood to apply to a God or Universal Creator or a superhuman agency. These belief systems and practices are what we call "religious." When the world was Pagan, conflict between different belief systems was minimal since Pagans recognized many "gods" behind the manifestations of Nature, so other systems of "gods" could naturally blend into a growing pantheon. The "gods" of other systems were regarded as only different names for the same underlying energies behind manifested phenomena everywhere. This was a magical world where everything was alive with "spirit" and one could communicate and make supplication to the invisible forces behind creation. The veil between the dimensions was gossamer thin. One could experience oneself as part of the Whole. The mystery was imminent.

The appearance, in the minds of men, of the idea of a singular "god," The One God, immediately presented a challenge to the existence of other spiritual systems. If there was only One True God, then the "gods", or "God" of other systems must be in error. If I am a devotee of The One God, then you, my friend, must be wrong in your misbegotten belief in your god. The intermittent warfare between different belief systems has lasted for over twenty-five centuries. Prior to that time, wars were fought for material gains, land, plunder, slaves, women, but not over ideas. The first stage of mankind was a practical, and magical world based in the senses. An ideologically based world would not appear for a long time.

Developmental Sequence

If we look at the history of Humankind and its societies and compare it to the developmental sequence of an individual human, we can find interesting parallels.

Initially, the child's world is composed of sound, touch, taste and meaningless shapes. Over time, the shapes become familiar and associated with certain touches, tastes, sounds. One day these shapes transform into people, food, toys. Everything that moves seems to be alive. It is a magical world in which children have to learn to discern what is real from what is imaginary. "Are there really fairies, daddy? Is there really a Santa Clause? I'm sure there is a monster under my bed." This early stage of a child's developing consciousness is called magical thinking.

I now recall, as I write this, a moment when my son was around three years old. It was a clear autumn afternoon. The ground under us was a carpet of dead leaves recently fallen from the giant maples that stood in front of our 1790 farmhouse near the top of a small mountain in Western Maine. A breeze sent the leaves scuttering around my son's legs. He screamed in terror as the leaves attacked. I immediately picked him up and tried to explain to him that the leaves were not alive and would not hurt him. He was not convinced of this assertion until he was older.

As children, we need to learn how to use our bodies. The world of the child is primarily sensory. Its body is fragile for long years of development, dependent on larger, stronger, more powerful humans to care for and protect it. The child is socialized to control aspects of its emotional world, primarily, so it won't physically act out whatever behaviors its educators consider unwanted or dangerous. This emotional world is ruled by the "god" of right or wrong, yes or no, like or dislike, agree or disagree. It is a binary world where things can't be mixtures but seem that they must be one thing or the other. From ages 6-12, thinking is "concrete," no longer magical but not yet abstract, reflecting the yes or no, good or bad perspective. Not until the teen years do the capacities for abstract thinking, reasoning from known principles to form one's own new ideas and questions, considering many viewpoints to compare ideas and opinions and the ability to be aware of the flow of thought processes, begin. On average, women reach adult conceptual abilities around age eighteen, but some men not until their mid-twenties. Many people do not reach this stage but remain concrete thinkers.

As far as can be determined and intuited, ancient humans were, understandably, inevitably focused on Nature. Survival depended on the study of the patterns of Nature and developing theories for how to influence these patterns to increase chances of survival. How could it have been anything but the primary focus of thought, attention, emotion, worship? Nature is still inconceivably huge, complex and seemingly intelligent for us modern humans. With the recent (in human history) ability to shelter and feed ourselves sufficiently, and the move of the majority of the Earth's population to urban centers, for most people today, Nature is noticed only when it interferes with or facilitates our plans of activity. At those times, its manifestations will have our near-total attention. But, until the past century, everyone was a meteorologist. The famous (in New England) publication, *The Farmer's Almanac*, is a reminder of the farmers' continuing intimacy with Nature, without which we would not have sufficient food to maintain a lifestyle that affords us the luxury of rarely experiencing our self at the mercy of this planetary force we call Nature.

It seems a natural stage of development, even logical, that early man placed the worship of Nature at the core of his psychology and made it his religion. Every Natural manifestation was its own expression of energy, or "spirit," a part of the Whole. Nature was a deep mystery that held the power of life or death. "Mother Nature," "Mother Earth," "Kali," the Mother Goddess, brought both life and death. These were some of the personifications of this force known today as "Nature."

Understanding, and better yet, having a relationship with, or way to influence Nature, was critical. The intuition of these individual manifestations of the Whole became "gods," in the sense of being hidden "energies," or "spirits." Rivers, springs, mountains, wind, sun, moon, animals ... all were manifestations of Nature as Goddess ... as, in fact, they naturally are. Each was a spirit or god that could be related to. Under these circumstances, early men would inevitably begin the Human, many-millennium-long search for our origins and meaning on Earth, with developing a relationship with the different gods, spirits, representative manifestations of the underlying Mystery of existence. (Linguistically, both words, "energy" and "spirit," were used synonymously until the eighteenth century. The word "energy" was adopted by the newly emerging physical sciences to distinguish "science" as exploring something different from non-rational "religion.")

A Related Diversion

The logic of Paganism came home to me one night when I was driving the car along a dark, country road. The light of a full moon was blinking on and off ... on and off ... as it was rhythmically eclipsed by the trees rushing by. My son was in the back seat watching the moonlight. Then he asked, "Dad. Why is the Moon following us?" I looked out my window. The trees were clipping by at a rapid rate ... but the Moon ... the Moon's position held steady with the car. Whether I slowed down or sped up, the Moon would continue to pace us. In that moment, I too saw the Moon following the car! How could it appear anything else to my son who did not yet know about astronomy, physics or the mysteries of perception? My senses also told me that the Moon was intentionally following us. My head had since learned a different perspective that would override the instinctive judgment of my body. Yet, there is our common phrase, "Seeing is believing!" Unfortunately, that is often true even when the belief is in error.

As I watch these words appear on my computer screen, I notice I used the phrases "the trees were rushing" and "clipping" by the car. As I am reliving the event in my memory, I see and feel now what I saw and felt then. Although my intellect knows better, to my eyes the trees are "passing by."

A few years after that, I was walking around our wooded neighborhood on a damp, foggy night. Visibility was very low. I was familiar with the road, so I knew my location. Up ahead was a house light. It illuminated the fog so that its source was not visible behind the diffusion of glowing air, ballooning out into the dark. The lighting created strange shadows. As I walked, something caught my peripheral vision. What I saw was a shadow that looked like a large, wolf-sized dog. I began to watch it cautiously as I continued to walk very slowly. Then, before my eyes, as my perspective of the shifting shadows accompanying my movement started to alter ... it changed shape.! As I had approached it, it changed itself into ... a ... mailbox! "Interesting," I thought. A "shape-shifter." A "werewolf." A "witch." I immediately associated to what I have read about the middle ages. When people back then had experiences like this, how logical of them to attribute it to "spirits." What would you have thought?

Back to Religion as a Developmental Sequence

The appearance of a new idea, that there is ... only One God, represents a view from above duality. Yet when introduced in the magical level of Human consciousness, this higher perspective was only able to raise it to the next level ... the concrete-thinking stage of development. This inability to see that the One God contained everything within It, and thus enveloped all energies, spirits, Natural powers ... the other "gods"... this new stage brought conflict, first between Monotheists and Pagans and later between different Monotheistic movements and even the sects within the same movement. If there is only One God, then who is worshipping the correct God? I can see this stage of development in human reasoning as equivalent to the developmental period of a human child where black and white reasoning begins to appear.

From the Renaissance flowed the Age of Reason. It was as if a critical mass of people had begun to think beyond just senses and emotion. People began to see beyond black and white and employ the scientific method of "observe, test, verify." With this rational, logical approach came a justified suspicion of one-sided passions, feelings, and emotions. These past four hundred years have brought more knowledge about Nature, exponentially with each passing year. Knowing how Nature works has brought a false sense of certainty. Knowing is not understanding.

Gradually over the past several centuries, science first joined and now appears to have surpassed religion as the new dominant, "sincere and meaningful belief that occupies, in the life of its possessor, a place parallel to the place held by God in the lives of other persons." Particularly at the current time in our worldwide society, "Science" is now quoted as was once religious scripture. And, just as with religion, differences among scientists have become politicized ... mostly by non-scientists who pick and choose the research that supports their preferred opinion. Science is now popularly misunderstood as the definitive answer for anything. There is little understanding that science is a method of inquiry, the results of which are always changing with additional discoveries. A "settled science" is a dead science. If the final answer has been found, then science has nothing else to learn. Then that science has become a religion.

The Tension Between "Science" and "Religion"

Over many years I have followed the tension between scientific and religious viewpoints. A modern religious or spiritual viewpoint reasons this way. Science tells us that the Universe appeared from nowhere and is constantly expanding into nowhere. This totally illogical conclusion seems to actually be a fact, even though a paradox. It therefore ... must have ... meaning! ... Which means ... I must also have ... meaning! The Universe is intelligent and was created by something ... for some reason ... so ... to talk about this ... let us call this something ... God ... or ... Endlessness ... or ... The Absolute ... or ... It.

Such a viewpoint may state this position as a *fact*. But how could anyone know if the Universe has meaning or is intelligent or has a creator behind it ... or prove it by the scientific method even if true? This statement is an opinion, a hypothesis, a guess ... unless one has had a direct experience and is convinced themselves. If this viewpoint appeals, one can certainly embrace it.

An experience cannot be argued with. I cannot tell you that you did not have an experience. It is a *fact* that you are telling me that you had an experience. Where we can differ is in the interpreted meaning you have derived from the experience. You see one meaning and I see another. Obviously, we are each having our own experience of your telling me about your original experience.

Materialists also say that the Universe appeared from nowhere and is constantly expanding into nowhere. But, since they came to this conclusion, not intuitively, but from observation through their specialized instruments and mathematics, they conclude that their theory has nothing to do with spirit, God, higher intelligence or anything beyond humans. The Universe just happened and has unfolded mechanically ever since. It has no meaning ... and therefore ... neither do we. This position is stated as a *fact*. But how could anyone know if it is the Ultimate Truth that there is no meaning? That statement cannot be proven by the scientific method. The statement is an opinion, a hypothesis, a guess. If this viewpoint appeals, one can certainly embrace it.

So, materialism or atheism are "sincere and meaningful beliefs that occupy, in the life of their possessor, a place parallel to the place held by God in the lives of other persons." I have wondered why it is important for some atheist groups to insist on banning public expressions of belief by theist groups. Why are atheist groups promoting their viewpoint so vehemently, looking for people to come to their perspective ... actually to convert and become parishioners in the Church-of-No-god? Isn't this what they protest when done by the religious community?

What other beliefs and causes represent "sincere and meaningful beliefs that occupy, in the life of its possessor, a place parallel to the place held by God in the lives of other persons"? Politics is a receptive field for these guiding beliefs. Look at how the names given to ideas become "isms," things in and of themselves: socialism, communism, capitalism, republicanism, federalism, progressivism, conservatism. When searching for something bigger than myself to serve, these philosophies become the *raison d'être* of many lives.

Most problematic is the phenomenon of identifying all of oneself with, or, as a representative of the movement, the cause, the belief. I then become ... I am ... a communist, socialist, capitalist, Catholic, Muslim, Jew, American, Russian, white, black, brown-skinned. If I blend my entire sense of myself with the larger something, then its power flows into me and I feel more than myself. If I identify myself with something that has diminished power, then I also feel myself diminished. When identified in this way, any attack or criticism of my community identity feels like a personal attack on me. Since I am in the good, the other must be in the bad. Confusing theories with provable facts is an indication that one is at the level of binary, concrete thinking.

If a religion is a core set of beliefs that serve as the guiding principles for our lives, then *that* is our inner god, our religion. To be honest, I need to ask myself, what are my core set of beliefs that serve as my guiding principle: money, popularity, safety, being liked, being good at what I do? What group or philosophical labels have become part of my self-definition? When others ask what I do with my life, what I believe ... what adjectives appear as adornments to "my-self." "I am a Liberal. I am a Conservative. I am an American, a Russian. I am a soccer fan. I am a survivor. I am a victim." If you begin with the words "I am ..." what follows?

The Next Stage in Development

The need to experience myself as a part of something much bigger, much more meaningful, appears built into most human beings. Where does one go to find this core interest, principle belief that will become the pole star for my search? The obvious place to look is the world around me and the recommendations of people of the world. The danger is that I then find "religion" disguised as a science or a philosophy, a monetary theory, a political movement. Then my "religion" is at the level of right or wrong. It is a religion of the concrete thinking level.

What would be the guiding principles of the next level of human development? For the individual child, it is the appearance of the capacity to think abstractly, to be able and interested, in holding multiple viewpoints in mind at a time and looking for connections. It is a level that is not interested in deciding right or wrong, but rather trying always to find the bigger picture. Are we at the edge of a new age when increasing numbers of people will develop this capacity? How might that change the world over the next several centuries if the general level of conscious perception rose above the world of opposites?

How might your world, my world, change if you and I were able to live our lives from a less dogmatic, righteous, "religious" attitude?

We are never free from influences, from the moment of conception to the moment of death. But, if we are aware of where we are inside ourselves and what internal god is the source of our worship at the moment, we may be able to more intelligently choose which influence to worship.

Control and Influence

A number of years ago, I had surgery for which I agreed to a spinal, rather than a general, anesthetic. In the recovery room, I lay on a bed looking at my legs. I had the strange feeling that I was alive, warm, supple from my waist up. Below that, there was a sense of something like stone. The lower half of my body was dead weight. There was no sensation other than a sense of extreme density and immovability.

A nurse now stood at the end of the bed and asked me to wiggle my toes. I looked at her. Then I looked at my toes. Then I looked back at her. "How do I do that?" I asked. I had no idea how to move my toes! I could not move my toes! But if I had no idea how to move them now … how had they ever moved before? "Don't worry," she said. "When you can move them, call me." Then she left.

I continued to stare at my feet. I could feel a first stirring of anxiety carrying the potential to grow into panic. This must be what it is like to be paralyzed! … No! … It isn't like being paralyzed. I am paralyzed! Now I truly understood the term "dead weight." How could something so incredibly heavy be moved at all, much less by a thought or a wish? Or does it move itself and I only imagine I am doing it directly? I can't make the chair move by itself by asking it to, but I can move my body by intending to do so. But right now, I could not move my lower body regardless of wish or intention. What would life feel like with my lower body immobilized in a wheelchair, unable to lift myself, totally dependent on others to move and care for my body? It would feel just like I was feeling now! I knew the paralysis was supposed to wear off, but this taste of a different, potential reality was truly heart-stopping and mind-freezing. I was, for a short while, sharing the world of others much less fortunate than myself in this way.

I intentionally relaxed … at least the top half of my body … and directed my attention away from the fear, back to this interesting question. "If I don't know how I move my body, then how has my body been moving? I knew enough anatomy to understand how the brain, spinal cord and the rest of the body were wired with nerve pathways ferrying electrical currents throughout the machinery. I knew the anesthetic had interfered with the signal between my lower and upper half.

Was the electricity no longer flowing? That did not seem likely. Were the signals not being received at their appropriate locations? Were the wiring and current still operating correctly, while "I" was blocked from interacting with them? If "I" was blocked from sending and receiving signals from my lower body, then what was "I" in relation to my body? I thought in this way as I waited for sensation to return.

In time, my legs began to feel warm and I sensed a stirring in my toes. They moved! I now tried to direct my *intention* for them to move ... and they moved again. Had I made that happen? How was what I was doing now any different from what I had tried to do before they moved? Had I only encouraged them to move? I could not see a connection between the intent in my mind and the movement down at the far end of my body. Had I made a non-verbal suggestion to my toes? How would a suggestion work? Are my toes separate entities that can listen to and choose, or not, to obey my wish? Are other parts of me, like my hands, separate entities? They clearly seem to have a life of their own, moving all day without my attention or direction ... even talking for me through gesticulations that I am usually oblivious to ... although they do perform the movements, I wish for them to perform when I want them to.

My body obviously has a life of its own for which it does not require my participation or even awareness. My organ's function, my blood components stay within required limits, food is digested and eliminated, lungs breath, heart pumps ... and perhaps tens of thousands of other metabolic and maintenance activities down to the cellular, the molecular, the atomic, and perhaps, the quantum level, carry on their responsibilities in a near infinitely complex, interactive, multi-dimensional programmed system. Where am *I* in all this?

As *I* lay in the recovery room, experiencing life returning to the missing half of my body, my meditation continued.

Feeling out of control .... Realizing I had no influence ... ... I have no personal control over what will occur ... I will just have to wait and see what fate brings to my doorstep. All this applied to my mental-emotional state during this event. Realizing I had no control over half my body at the time, I relaxed and watched the drama unfold with interest.

Up until this event, I could "control" or influence the movement of my large muscles if the signal from my brain was not interrupted. I could walk and talk and perform activities within the parameters of my body's capacities. But as regards all my internal mechanisms ... I could indirectly influence them for good or ill with diet, exercise, relaxation, meditation, positive thinking, good maintenance ... but much more was beyond my influence ... even beyond my awareness ... much less, control. I could only act responsibly towards my body and hope for a long run of good luck.

Surprise Collapse

Writing about this memory today, I am now, by association, recalling an event that happened many years later. I awoke early one morning and went to the bathroom sink. Suddenly, I felt really, really awful in a way I have never experienced. I have no words to describe it. I stumbled out to the hallway and began to tell my companion that I did not feel well. I was aware my body was stooped and at an odd angle. My next awareness was of lying on my back on the floor. I had no memory of falling. I realized that if I had fallen to my right instead of my left, I would have gone down the stairs. An ambulance was being called. I did not, or could not, move. I clearly recall my inner state at this time. I was relaxed, unafraid, curious, amazed and philosophical. I understood I had no control over what was happening in my body. Nor did I have any intention at this point in trying to influence what was about to happen to me. I surrendered to the experience.

At the emergency room, I was tested, hydrated and a few hours later sent home. Apparently, my kidneys had been "damaged". This was my first warning of a medical condition that, so far, has been well managed. What was most interesting to me was how effortless it was for me to collapse and need medical care. It had happened on its own, on its timetable, indifferent to the needs or schedule of my personality. I realized, with interest, rather than fear, how easy death could be in the end. It is its own process and occurs in its own time frame. Previously I had known, with my intellect, that this was so. Now I understood it with all of me. The emotional taste was sobriety and interest. In a strange way, there also appeared a sense of freedom. Death was something I need not worry about. It was not my responsibility. My responsibility was to help my body stay as healthy as possible as long as possible. Nevertheless, it would decline, either through time, illness or accident. Over the process of life's trajectory, I had some influence but no ultimate control.

Equanimity in the Face of Death

This memory now reminds me of another. I was talking to a dear friend and the great spiritual mentor of my life, who had recently returned from hospital after a coronary incident. I was asking him about his apparent equanimity in the face of his body's decline. He said to me, "There is nothing to dying. I've died a couple of times already and they brought me back. It just happens. Nothing to be concerned about. I didn't even know I was dead." He maintained this impartial attitude until his last breath. The day before that final moment, which I was privileged to share, he had said to a small group of us, with some difficulty as breathing was now exhausting for him, "Pay attention! Remember … all of you will some-day be where I am at this very moment!".

Flashes

As I am exploring this subject, I see in my mind flashes of interactions with people over many years. There are situations I wanted to have un-fold in specific directions, but that met resistance or outright denial from others. The love interests that were not reciprocated. The business plans that did not receive support from those who had indicated willingness to help me or the potential customers who did not show up. When I was a young man, I had to accept that my body was not talented in the ways that would allow me to perform athletically at a competitive level. I was nat-urally gifted academically in some ways and disinterested or unskilled in others. No amount of tutoring in French could help me learn that language in school.

Credit or Luck

When I look back over my "achievements" in life, I recognize that much effort, considerable luck and the help of others, combined with some natural, inherent talents in communication and reasoning, were necessary for me to gain a professional degree that matched my skills and temperament. As I look around, I realize that I found a niche where I could grow and thrive. I realize that I am unequipped, by inclination and natural ability, for most societal roles so much better filled by others.

What can I take credit for? I did not create my body or a healthy ner-vous system or the type of brain I carry around inside my skull. I had no choice over my genes. I did not (as far as I am aware) choose the place, time or family of my birth. Each of these factors came with advantages and disadvantages. For most of my developmental years I followed the suggestions of adults and flowed along the life structure I found myself occupying. As I grew, choices began opening for me, but all within the basic framework accompanying my place in the life around me. I suppose

I could give myself credit for listening to some advice, occasionally making reasonable choices and being a fairly responsible, diligent student. But those qualities may also reflect my basic character. Could I have really done otherwise?

We have all heard some people say, and perhaps we have thought so ourselves, that, "If I can do it, anyone could do it." But is that true? How many variables of innate skill, or lack thereof, chance encounters, the luck of the draw and timing have combined into the shape of my character and life?

I can give myself credit for developing some interests and skills that I seem to have been born with. I also have to take responsibility for not developing others, allowing them to lie fallow due to demands of life, insecurity, finances, lack of support from others, laziness or timing. I think now of life as being like a game of cards. We are each dealt a hand. We can make a few exchanges within the rules of the game, but we have to play with the basic hand with which we began. We can try to be creative about what we have, we can calculate and play the odds and hope for good luck, but our possibilities are not limitless. What can I do with what I have been given? What am I willing to risk? Yet, even risk-taking may be an inherent predisposition, greater for some than others. Can I take credit for a quality that came with me at conception?

This reminds me of the several variations on a parable about three servants, each given one "talent" by their master who is leaving on a trip. When he returns, he asks each to account for what they did with their "talent". The first reports that the talent was invested and returned ten-fold. The second reports an investment that returned a five-fold profit. The third servant hands back the single, original talent, saying that he did not want to risk losing it. The master rewards those who made something from what they were given and punishes the one that took no risk by leaving him with nothing.

The River

At this late point in my existence, the sense of life now feels more like a river, a flow of momentum which carries me, sometimes slowly, sometimes rapidly, sometimes smoothly, sometimes turbulently, always moving… moving … continually without ceasing. What can I control, what can I influence, in this impartial current that carries not just me, but us all? I have learned to be able, most of the time, to keep my head above water. I've learned to be able, at times to float on my back and watch the scenery. If I am aware that some whitewater lies ahead (and I am often taken by surprise), I can try to maneuver around or through it without swallowing too much water.

Yet, there has been something else at work. There are interests and inclinations that have been part of my subjective world since childhood. My idiosyncratic attraction to mystery has sensitized me to certain qualities in the water that carry the taste of this interest. When encountering "molecules" of these qualities in the current, I have repeatedly swum towards them and allowed them to carry me into eddies and side-flows in the river. These repeated inclinations, probably determined by my inherent nature, have altered my path from the main channel, deviating over a lifetime, from other possibilities that would have produced a different life.

This river, in addition to all the idiosyncratic possibilities that lead to so many different types of lives for different people, seems to fork in a fundamental way that diverts those it carries towards different destinations, not just lifestyles. The vast majority of people seem carried towards lives of external focus, building achievements or failures in social, financial, political activities. They may mark the places they have been, the adventures they have had, the people they have met, the wonderful meals they have consumed at wonderful restaurants as the milestones of their lives.

If inclined to review one's life, most ask, "What have I done in my life? Where have I been? What have I seen? Who have I known?" The questions, "What have I learned? How have I been changed? Have I a sense of purpose about my life?" are of a different nature. The former highlight external activities. The latter focus on internal meaning.

The type of questions asked and the type of milestones one marks on the calendar of one's life indicate which fork of the river one is carried within. The lesser branch carries its passengers into a life focused more on exploration of the subjective internal world. Interest is more focused on the pursuit of the meaning of existence, both personal and in general. Swimmers in this channel are drawn to exploring the mystery of their inner experiences rather than seeking fame or fortune in the world.

To enter and remain in this branch requires an objective, rational confrontation with imaginary wishes for control and certainty and with illusions about one's capacity to influence people or events in most situations

... and have the outcome be what was wanted ... and without unexpected collateral reactions.

Loss of Illusion

Accepting an unwanted reality is a difficult meal to swallow. It is a type of death ... the death of a belief, a hope, a wish. The pattern of acceptance follows a basic format regardless of the loss being grieved. It begins with a long period of *Denial*, followed by intermittent, shallow, intellectual recognition of the problem, but still with a continuing attempt to cajole and manipulate life into correcting course back towards one's aim. In grief counseling, this stage is called *Bargaining*. When it becomes apparent that the "plan" is not working, that one cannot exert effective control, the mood will alternate between stages of *Sadness* and *Anger*. People can get trapped in any of these phases or a closed looping back and forth without resolution. The resolution lies in the fifth stage, called Acceptance.

Acceptance does not mean one likes the outcome. The outcome may range from disappointing to terribly painful and life-shifting. Rather, it is an acceptance of reality. This is the hand I have been dealt. I wish it were any other hand but this, but this is the one I must play, as best I can. Many people will take a shortcut into *Resignation* and believe they have accepted, but this is a deception. *Resignation* is tinted with sadness and anger. Acceptance has more the taste of sadder but wiser, or relief that the ordeal is over, or to discover oneself finally with an answer as to why one's attempts to control outcome failed. They failed because the event could not be altered. Or, even if maybe I could have said or done something to change it, whatever that might have been, it did not happen. So, this is what I have now, whether I like it or not. It cannot be changed. Our choice is to live in acceptance and make the best of it or to live in denial and continue to suffer a Quixotic mission in futility.

Which Branch of the River?

Which Branch of the River is carrying me? Well ... what motivates me? We can talk about people in general, but the location of any real potential efficacy lies within each of us. So, as I do with myself, I ask you, dear Reader, to explore along with me this question of external and internal efficacy, its implications, its limitations and what its pursuit may distract us from confronting.

Ask yourself, "when, in my life, have I had the desire to control people, events, activities?" All right. That obviously would be far too long a list for most of us to compose. How about two or three (or more if you wish) memories of situations where you tried, or always try, or at least wish, to make certain of the outcome? In reviewing these memories, now hopefully with additional understanding, ask yourself:

What was I trying to control?

How many components, people, timing, unforeseen factors would I have had to have complete mastery over to exert control?

Was control possible?

Perhaps you would say, "No. I wasn't trying or expecting to control. But I did want to influence the situation so that it would turn out the way I wanted it to." All right.

What was your plan for influence?

How many variables would have to fall into place for your influence to be accepted and the outcome conform to your vision?

If you were only trying to influence and not control, what would you have rated the likelihood of success ... 80%, 20%, 10%?

How disappointed were you at the time when things didn't go as you hoped? If your answer is any more than "mildly," I would suggest you were hoping for control and only pretending to yourself that you would be satisfied with an attempt at influence.

As you look back now on your examples, ask yourself if there was a degree of wishful thinking in your estimation. What role did luck, the always present wild card, play in the outcomes?

If things did work out as you planned, did you give yourself credit for this accomplishment or did you thank your good luck that everything, including how you approached the situation, worked out as you had hoped? Sometimes it does and sometimes it does not. What makes the difference?

The Role of Fear

Take a moment now and recall the experience of feeling out of control ... realizing you have no influence ... recognizing that what will happen depends mostly on chance or other people's choices, that you have no personal control over what will occur ... that you will just have to wait and see what fate brings to your doorstep.

Why do we all seem, innately, to fear what we call "loss of control"? What is so disconcerting in realizing that we may, sometimes, have degrees of influence, but can rarely force an event, or person, or relationship ... or myself ... to conform to what is wanted if there is resistance.

The first and natural reason is that we are programmed to try to survive. All life is programmed to survive. Survival must be long enough in duration for a creature to produce a copy of itself. It must avoid death until its first re-creation can occur. Then, its primary purpose completed, the organism continues to eat, sleep and procreate until its functions weaken and it stops living ... or it is eaten by something else in need of food so that it can also survive and procreate. The energy transformed through eating and then redistributed through elimination is the currency of Life, the continuous feast of energy exchange that powers the activity of all Life.

To survive, the organism has to negotiate its environment, the supports and the dangers. To protect itself, it is born with programmed strategies to increase its chances of a favorable outcome, moment to moment, for as long as possible. Does it have control, mastery, absolute power over the dangers in its surroundings? Of course not. It must depend on its built-in strengths and a great deal of luck. In fact, Nature overproduces the amount of new life because of the astronomical attrition rate. Just like the one sperm in tens of millions that fertilizes the egg, only a few of the vast many survive to adulthood and breeding capacity.

As we have bodies, and our bodies are animals, this built-in survival program also comes with our original programming. Our autonomic nervous system produces hormones that activate or relax our animal-body so that it has the necessary energy to fight, flee or rest as the situation requires. Of course, we would want to control the degree of threat and maximize the pleasurable experiences for our body. "No means no"! "Yes. Scratch a bit to the left, please."

If our body functions properly, we can make it move where we want to go, to carry us around the landscape and perform tasks, with its hands, arms, legs, that we, our mind, wishes to accomplish. We can "control" our movements dependent on our strength, coordination and physical training. But then, there are times this is less so, i.e., when tired, distracted, weak, clumsy, ill. For many of us, our body will, at some time, break a bone, have an organ malfunction, have a stroke. Then, where is our "control"? How could I have controlled my body before and now I cannot control it? What has changed? Perhaps, I never actually controlled it but rather influenced it, when possible, to follow my wishes. Perhaps my relationship with my body is not the master-servant arrangement I believe, but rather a symbiotic partnership between two very different entities intertwined with each other in order to become more through the blending than either can be by itself.

Control

Originally, the word "control" meant to "check or verify accounts." This original understanding suggests the quality of attentive, impartial observation, not the implication that the "controller" should tip the scales to force the accounts to be what is wished for. Over time, this word has transformed, as indicated by some of its synonyms: power, authority, command, mastery, supremacy, domination, regulation. It is this current transformation of the concept that we torment ourselves and others with today.

How does one obtain such power over others or over events or natural occurrences? Obviously, in relationships determined by fear, violence and intimidation, most will often choose the path of least resistance and fall into resentful or fearful compliance. This kind of control can be exercised over people … but isn't acquiescence still dependent on a surrender, a willing compliance, even if one is giving up in despair? History, both communal and personal, is filled with stories of those few who refused to submit and were either destroyed, escaped or formed a rebellion. So, the person with the capacity to use force only gains control through assent, even begrudged and compelled, whether it is given by an individual, a small group or an entire nation. Realizing that this type of control must be maintained by sufficient fear to sap any active resistance, this power possessor is always afraid of losing control, losing the ability to frighten and coerce others … pushing them to the point of having nothing else to lose. This produces a spiraling descent into more and more desperate measures to crush the soul and will of others to prevent them from rebellion or escape or suicide.

What about wishing to be able to control events that are not dependent on the activity and choices of people? If I have a machine that I understand how to operate, I can control its functions … until it stops working. But it was designed for me to be able to control. It is not "natural." What is left then but Nature and random luck? Can we control, totally "master," random events to force them to obey our will? This was the hope of less technological cultures who prayed and sacrificed to the gods for fair weather, good crops, the destruction of their enemies. Perhaps if one's tribe had a seer who could foretell events, better choices, better bets on the future could sometimes be made. Many today retain private rituals or prayer or affirmation or good luck charms to soothe and serve the same purpose. The activity of human-kind can alter climate and landscape, river channels can be dug to redirect the flow of water, but does this give us control over the seasons, storms, earthquakes, volcanos, tidal waves, the coming and going of comets, eclipses, falling meteors … or the un-foreseen consequences of felling the forest or altering the river? Do we have protection from these phenomena or are we hoping to chance that we, personally, are not in the way when they manifest?

Well, what about "self-control," total mastery, complete command of my moods, my thoughts, my reactions and impulses, likes and dislikes, habits? Do I never find thoughts or music in my head that I did not invite and do not welcome, but that will not go away when commanded? Do I never fall into moods, get caught up in attitudes, have mixed feelings? Where is my control in the emotional-psychological realm? How easy is it for me to permanently change a habit by willing it so? I can, if I choose to, focus my attention for a time on something of my choice, but this effort needs to be continually maintained as attention is flighty and easily drifts. If I can't even control my mind and moods, why am I even using this concept, this word, "control."

Influence

Perhaps a more reasonable aim might be to acquire "influence." Where the word "control" is hard, rigid, fixed, the word "influence" is softer, more liquid, more flowing. In fact, its origin from 14th century Medieval Latin is *"influentia"* meaning an emanation of power from the stars and from Latin, *"influere"* meaning to flow into.

Influence implies a connection, a channel between parties, where at least one of them is open to the emanations of the other. In allowing you to have influence with me, I am opening myself to your suggestions, ideas, motivations and moods, because I respect you, or fear you, and value the emanations towards me from your inner world. I am hoping that by being open to you, you will in return be open to me, or I am afraid of the consequences if I don't accept what you want of me. If I don't value or trust you or want what you are offering, I am not open to your offers of influence and there is nothing you can do to force me without doing violence.

Influence seems much more realistic as an aim. I can try to cultivate influence. Everything and everybody are a part of one larger Whole. To one degree or another, everything and everyone is entangled in the web of existence. Can I flow with, flow through or around, people and events instead of trying to push, shove and steer the currents? Do I have the courage to just attempt to steer myself rather than try to force a resolution, to renounce the fantasy of security stimulated by the illusion that I can control life?

Reflection

I am now reflecting back over my life. Were there any people, or circumstances, which had absolute power over me? Of course. When I was a child, my parents, guardians and other adults could, potentially, do with me anything they wished as I was small, weak and without their mental, emotional and physical capacities. We all start out this way. Whether our experience is wonderful, benign or negative, will be a strong factor in our attitude towards the goal of control.

In particular, negative experiential qualities from childhood may increase a need to maximize a sense of influence, if not control, later in life. Or, instead, we may develop a defensive sense of futility to protect us from the pain and humiliation of crushed hope.

A number of years ago, I realized that if I had had a different personality, I would have experienced a different childhood, even with the same parents, sibling and outer structure. Why? Because different personality types tend to make different interpretations of the meaning of events. By nature, an accommodating type of personality, my experience with power, control and influence has been ambivalent. So, I ask you, dear Reader, to imagine yourself with a different personality, more or less assertive, more or less risk-taking, more or less inquisitive, more or less sensitive, more or less introverted or extroverted .... how would this change have influenced the way you have experienced life ... and yourself? How might these differences have changed the way you relate to the wish for control or influence?

Conclusion

What, who, do I want to control? What can I control? What can I influence? Why do I feel authorized to make such efforts? For what reasons?

What can I take credit for? What do these "credits" get me? Do I store them in a vault? Do I cash them in? What is this credit currency? Who is the audience for my credit … others? … my - self?

What is the fear in back of my fear of not being in control? Is it fear of loss of prestige, personal or political power (is there a difference)? Is it fear of unwanted changes in my life pattern, in relationships? Do I believe I can ward off illness, aging, dying?

Where are such attempts useful and natural? Where are they invented and not part of nature?

To believe we can control, completely, continuously, correctly, without anything unexpected occurring is a delusion too far. We tend to deny that we have such fanciful, illusionary thinking.

However, our reactions of hurt, surprise, disappointment, irritation that well up with the frustration of thwarted plans reveal the reality of our subconscious hopes and fears and belie our rationalizations. Our reactions when things don't work out as we wished demonstrates a failure to recognize that nothing and no one happens in a vacuum. Everything is part of other systems larger and smaller, each of which is also entangled in other systems larger and smaller. To believe in ultimate, frictionless control is to fail to recognize that any attempt to control or influence occurs in a field connected with other fields. There are many other things in these fields than my agenda. When I move my attempt to control into a field, I meet everything and everyone else there who may be unaware of, indifferent or hostile to, my attempts. Every action brings an equal and opposite reaction. Whatever was neutral in the field before my effort began may become active when touched by my effort. Its effect might be supportive or unsupportive of my intent. It must be accounted for. To believe in control over life is to deny that resistance is a natural part of the give and take of existence and will appear whenever touched by the pressure of an effort to change something.

The reality is that we did not create ourselves. We find ourselves awakening inside vulnerable biological bodies that will inevitably suffer from illness, injury, death. All the people we love and cherish and want to keep safe and with us forever … are living inside vulnerable, temporary bodies also. Each moment is on loan to us. There is no certainty other than fluctuations in pleasure and suffering and then eventual death. We all hang by a thread through each passing second. To find an attitude that will allow one to flow with the current of life, enjoying the joy and grieving the grief, without self-pity, self-recrimination, without anger or fear, would be to practice the art of living while allowing the river to carry us to an unknown destination determined by whichever branch we have followed.

Wish, Hope, Expectation and Reality

"I *wish* he would finally show up on time."
"I *hope* he finally shows up on time."
"I *expect* him to finally show up on time."

"I *wish* there were something I could do to help save the world."
"I *hope* there is something I can do to help save the world."
"I *expect* there is something I can do to help save the world."

"Let's *wish* for a better future."
"Don't worry. I have *hope* future progress will solve our problems".
"Relax. I *expect* the future will be better. Things couldn't get worse, could they?"

What is a wish, a hope, an expectation? On what are they based? Do they all have the same level of certainty? When I use these words, how do I know which one to select … or do I use them interchangeably? Why is this even a question worth discussing?

These are emotional verbs oriented towards the future. They are incantations to assuage the gods to bring to me the results I want to have. They are a little like prayers uttered to soothe my apprehensions. They also are like bookies, oddsmakers. They predict the degree of likelihood for a favorable outcome. But do we use them accurately?

These are dangerous words. Misusing them can lead to ill health, emotional and mental distress, damaged or destroyed relationships, a life of unnecessary, yet recurring, suffering. On the other hand, under favorable conditions, they may actually lead to a life of relative equanimity, imbue the holder of the feelings with a positive attitude which, itself, may become a helpful variable in the dynamics of the situation. Being "positive" is universally proclaimed to be more likely to bring desired results than carrying a negative attitude. Confidence is a powerful ally. On the other hand, they are often casually employed to excuse inaction today in the wish, hope or expectation that some tomorrow, at some point in the future, will see a resolution to our problems. They have the potency to change our attitudes and manifestations. They should be handled with care.

When I wish for something, do I have the same feeling for the outcome as if I expected to have it? If I have hope, is that hope stronger or weaker than a wish? How is expecting something different from hoping for it?

When I was first exploring these questions, I tried to find the "taste" of each of these emotional states. What is the feel of wishing vs. the taste of hope or the experiencing of expecting?

I could feel a different degree of "density" for each one, with wish as the lightest and expectation as the heaviest. I could immediately see that I could wish for anything, possible or impossible ... it was only a wish and I didn't actually believe there was much if any, likelihood that the wish would come true. It would be wonderful, of course, but highly un-likely. I had a preference but not much investment in the outcome. After all, it's only a wish.

But, when I hoped, then there was at least a real possibility that it could happen. It wasn't totally out of the question. The percentage for success was sufficiently above zero for me to entertain a hope that, if I were very lucky, my hope would be vindicated. But would I expect that success was the only option and nothing could interfere with things going exactly my way? Of course not. I had a hope it would happen, not an expectation.

My personal definition of the word "expectation" is a demand that my fantasy come true. When I expect, it is almost like saying the check is already in the mail. On what basis am I so certain? What is the level of predictable probability to support such certainty? I can expect that Tues-day follows Monday, that eventually rain will fall, that the sun will come up each morning (if I am not living near the poles). These are cyclical events that are controlled by forces beyond me. There is sufficient human and personal experience to justify my expectation that these things won't change. But can I expect that the rent will be paid on time, that George will remember my birthday, that my son will fulfill his promise to mow the lawn today? Can I reasonably expect that patterns that have been con-sistent for a sufficient period of time will always continue to be so? What could go wrong? How about expecting politicians to keep their promises or that I will never again forget where I left my glasses or that the people I care about will change and become the persons I want them to be?

The Moment of Truth When Reality Meets Fantasy

Eventually, the anticipated moment arrives to reveal the answer to my emotional prayer. What happens inside of me, physically, emotionally, mentally, if what I wished, hoped or expected does not occur?

If I had only wished, then the response is a sigh, perhaps even an amused sigh, "Oh well. It was a nice wish while it lasted. Now, on to other things."

If I held a hope, a real hope, then the response is sad disappointment. "I'm disappointed. I so hoped. I was so close. It could have been, might have been, but it just wasn't to be. Just the luck of the draw."

But if I expected it to happen … and it didn't happen … then something must have had gone wrong. "This is not right. Whose fault is this?" Now I am angry, upset, disturbed and my reaction is likely to upset and disturb others, especially if I blame them for derailing what I, with all self-justification, expected.

These words are tone filters through which my subjective reality is constructed. The tone chosen for this event influences my interpretation of it, including the odds of success I envision.

The clash of energy when anticipation meets reality is a moment of great danger and great opportunity. The danger lies in the strength of the emotional reaction to disappointment. Typically, whatever the outcome, I am taken first by reaction, my automatic response to success or failure. There is not much danger if I am happy with the outcome other than my momentary intoxication in the happiness of having events turned out in my favor. If my reaction is negative, my body's stress hormones turn on and I am filled with uncomfortable sensations, which may provoke a negative response of frustration or anger outward. "Who or what is to blame for this?" Or my reaction may turn inwards. "How could I be such a fool … again!"

A healthy understanding of reality would help moderate or even eliminate these reactions and one would be able to remain emotionally stable in the face of disappointment.

It is useful to recall that a realistic answer to the question, "What can go wrong?" is, "Lots of things can go wrong" … flat tires, illness, bad timing, bad luck, weather, forgetting. If we are realistic, we already know from experience that this is a very long list. What helps maintain balance is an understanding of probability and the acceptance of random interactions of unrelated events bumping into each other for no reason other than accident.

Given the ever-present variable of chance, we would be on safer grounds to briefly review the odds from one situation to another. If they are so long as to be unlikely, like winning the lottery, then a wish is understandable. If the stated odds of drawing a winning number is one in five, then a hope is not unreasonable but obviously not certain. If you have been tipped off that you are the leading candidate for the position, then your hope might be stronger. But can you now expect, with surety, that your name will be called? If I have always been reliable, can you expect that I will be so again this time? That is probably a safe bet ... but unexpected factors may intervene.

The Inevitability of Friction

There is something deeper here. By Nature, our biology is literally programmed to make us uncomfortable in difficult situations so that we will, like any animal, move away. We will know we are safe again when our body releases chemicals that make us feel relaxed and comfortable. So, of course, our body will react with distress when a hope or expectation does not work out. But it is reacting because of the emotional predisposition we brought to the question as to its likely outcome.

I can counteract my biological machinery by using my reason. If I can really accept that Nature also has a law of unpredictability, of chance encounters and misses, that a quality of hazard is built into everything, then I can be more tempered in my predictions of the future.

A wider view of how things actually work would reveal that everything is in motion. The world outside me, my thoughts and feelings inside me, down to the molecules and atoms that make up my body ... all are in some degree of motion all the time. Nothing is absolutely still. Since there is motion, there needs to be sufficient or appropriate space for that motion to move through. But that space is also filled with other things in motion. Inevitably, things, whether ideas, wishes, bodies or events, will interact and unpredictable results will occur. Sometimes those chance encounters blend, and things go smoothly, sometimes they clash, and things go "off course" (off my preferred course), sometimes they pass through each other without interacting and I personally take credit for having made things work out as I wanted.

"For the want of a nail a shoe was lost, For the want of a shoe a horse was lost. For the want of a horse a rider was lost. For the want of a rider a kingdom was lost."

The Challenge to Our Wish for External Control

This viewpoint is inherently uncomfortable for it reminds us of the fact that we have virtually little to no control over nearly everything in life ...at least in our outside life. Emotionally accepting that we all hang by a thread at all times is a difficult state to achieve. In traditional cultures, divinities have been evoked to help calm our fears about this fact. In our modern secular culture, we turn to aphorisms, hopes and expectations, stress management and relaxation training, psychotherapy, bliss meditations and exercises and, of course, that universal salve, mind and mood-altering chemicals.

There seems to be, for many, a belief that if they are doing everything correctly, no friction, stress, disappointment, loss, tragedy will enter their lives. If such unpleasant events arise, they believe they have done something wrong ... or someone has done something wrong. Although secular on the outside, such beliefs are still religious on the inside.

In my role as a psychotherapist, the clients it was most difficult to reach were those who had been "fortunate" enough to have encountered very little suffering in their lives up to the crisis that brought them into therapy. Our body develops resistance to illness by exposure to germs. In order to produce antibodies to protect us later, we need to become sick first. In order to become strong in character, resilient in the face of inevitable, periodic difficulties, we need the experience of periodic suffering. How else will we learn how to cope with difficulties?

A degree of naturally occurring friction is not only necessary for a mature psychological development, but it is inevitable. It is built into life. Just as our bodies build muscles through working them, our character builds strength through dealing with frustration and adversity. There is no escape from external friction. How we cope with its frequent appearance offers continuing opportunities to deepen our understanding of the complexity and unpredictability of life and our really insignificant place in the larger scheme of things.

Internal Resistance

However, our problem is two-fold. In addition to external opposition, we have internal resistance, internal frictions. For example, I make a pledge to overcome some habit and backslide quickly. Or, perhaps I want to practice being more open-minded with people who have a different viewpoint, but then I find myself uncomfortable in that conversation. Convinced I am in the right, I stop respecting and listening to the other person ... again!

We create most of our suffering because of how we have been emotionally and intellectually programmed by our family, our ethical upbringing, whether traditionally religious or secular, our education, our politics, our peer group and so forth.

It seems as if we are making our own choices and have "free will," but this is not so. The vast majority of our thoughts, physical behaviors and emotional reactions have been conditioned into us by the interplay between the lessons both deliberately and accidentally pressed on us from outside life and our automatic reactions of comfort or discomfort, fight or flight, programmed into our body at conception.

Degrees of Freedom

It is possible, however, to find a psychological posture that has the potential for more degrees of freedom from this matrix of controls implanted in interaction with life. We all experience a small degree of this potential in those moments when we taste what ordinary language calls "self-consciousness." We can "catch a glimpse" of our self and then experience an emotional reaction depending on whether that glimpse shows us a person who does or does not conform with the image of who we wish ourselves to be ... or who we are pretending to be and want others to accept. The difficulty in these moments is that we become focused on, identified with, our reaction, which is also automatic given our programming ... rather than seeing the significance of a state of awareness in which I see myself, and I simultaneously also see that some part of me is having a reaction to the self that I am seeing.

For a moment, part of my consciousness has separated and is looking at the conditioned program I usually call "myself." What, who, is this other "self" that has stepped apart for a moment and is watching? It is this semi-independent aspect of our psyche that offers the doorway out of internal as well as external reactivity. With appropriate training, usually through some forms of psychotherapy or certain "schools" of spiritual development, this capacity for "self-observation" can learn to be less reactive to the concerns of self-image and grow the capacity to become increasingly quiet and calm.

When my expectation hits reality, which part of me will be present to assimilate the shock? Typically, it will be the conditioned part of me that believes in the efficacy of wishes, hopes and expectations, the part that believes it could or should be able to control life to meet its preferences, the part which must cling to that fallacy for fear of facing its true insignificance in the face of the complexities of existence.

If I can remind myself that wishes, hopes and expectations are not reality, but only emotional postures, then I can wish or hope for a favorable outcome, but more as a game. Maybe it will happen, maybe it won't. I know what I wish. Now, let's see how it actually turns out. I can make life into a movie, or a novel, allowing for the possibility of surprise. If I feel an expectation taking root, I can challenge it. On what is my certainty based? Is there a chance, no matter how slight, that something different may occur? That possibility could make life more interesting rather than frightening.

Most of all, if one develops this practice of impartial self-observation, many surprises become possible, including surprises about who and what I am, what life may be about at a deeper level and where I may fit into the larger picture in which my life is but a tiny drop.

Desire

C an I desire what I have never known? Can I desire something if there were not already a resonant receptor within me corresponding with what I desire? A sense of lack represents longing for relationship, connection with the "something" missing in the moment. Whether this object of desire is something tangible, i.e., material artifact, an accomplishment, a person, or whether it is an abstraction, i.e., to be a more compassionate person, or to serve God, or to know myself, the emotional experience of longing represents a sense of a lost or a wished-for future connection. I can feel its strong pull upon me intellectually, emotionally, physically, or any combination of the three. In another sense, that relationship must already exist. The longing is the thread that attaches to me at one end and what resonates for me at the other end but out of reach.

We don't doubt the existence of tangible desires. What about the intangible objects of longing? Do they also have an "existence" in a dimension of potentiality somewhere beyond four-dimensional space-time, in which are encompassed all the tangible goals I wish for? If the intangible realm did not have an "existence," a "reality" somewhere, if it did not have the potential to be fulfilled, then why do I have a receptor within my emotional/psychological structure arranged specifically to long for and receive what is wished for?

In an instinctive desire for air, water, food, the bio-chemical-neurological machine is pre-wired to seek the quality of molecular vibrations necessary to sustain its functioning. Nature is not going to program an oxygen-breathing organism to seek methane for its breath. At the moment of conception, the pathways to connect with life-supporting aspects of the environment are encoded to develop for the specific purpose of seeking their appropriate counterparts.

Wouldn't that process work in a resonant way in my emotional and mental "bodies" so that they are programmed to seek what will nourish their life? Emotional desire seeks fulfillment by searching for an experience of the right quality to satisfy the vibration of its wish. How do we know what to "long" for? Is it an intellectual choice or a "felt" need? We recognize what we call emotions as "feelings," literally a type of inner touch, vibration, movement, fullness, emptiness. We feel *something*!

Something in us is reverberating in response to…what? If we are feeling the lack of something and desire it to appear, then we are in relationship, in that moment, with a memory of something experienced that we want repeated or something not yet experienced that we wish to actually connect with.

My wish reaches out along the invisible thread that searches for an image of that which it believes would satisfy its hunger. The fact that the image, or sense, of this object of longing appears in the mind of the wisher, triggers a resonant biochemical reaction in the emotional part of a person, suggests that something in the emotional part was pre-wired to react to the wished-for image prior to the appearance of that image.

The same reasoning would hold for intellectual and conceptual functions. When a new idea appears in my mind, an idea or connection I have never seen or thought of before, where did it come from? Where was it the moment prior to my finding it in my mind? When the first human realized how fire could be tamed and used, where was the understanding prior to the thought appearing in the mind of the discoverer? Certain brain structures exist to facilitate abstract reasoning. Why would those structures have developed if there were no abstract understanding, a priori, waiting for a brain to find it?

When I experience desire, some part of me is longing for something it is currently missing. There is already a relationship between what I lack and what I long for. This desire can represent either very high or very low interests and motivations within myself. I need to know the difference so I can learn to discriminate the direction upwards towards my higher wishes and thus strengthen the pre-existing connection with my higher potential. Then, I must learn to hold the two, both higher and lower desires, in heart and mind simultaneously, recognizing that both represent parts of me that have their own lives on their own level. Both must be respected and fed appropriately. The effort to find this perspective and the state that allows for its manifestation represents an impartiality that does not itself have a desire for a particular outcome. It only sees what is there and accepts the Truth of that. Conditioned preferences of like and dislike, longing, and satiation may continue to be experienced inside me, at the level below impartiality, but when my consciousness is in that higher state, I accept what the situation presents and respond to it as best I can according to my understanding of what is appropriate and helpful at that moment.

So, dear Reader. I wish for you that the desire of your mind and the desire of your heart may find each other and become one. They are waiting to be discovered in the dimension of possibility ... waiting for each of us to open the door to the level just above our ordinary awareness.

"All that desires seeks to make a connection with what it lacks, something that is not present at the moment ... here is undoubtedly a striving, an urge to satisfy a need not immediately present; the fulfillment is not immediate, as is the case of reaction." *

---

* J.G. Bennett, *A Spiritual Psychology*, Coombe Springs Press, January 1974

The Shape of My World

What outcomes in my life do I wish to be able to determine: relationships, conversations, business opportunities? In all honesty, are there any outcomes at all that I do not wish I could determine? Attempting to shape our physical and emotional environment is a logical strategy based on the foundation of a biologically driven, instinctive program for safety and survival.

However, when this built-in orientation is captured by our wish for "success" in the psycho-social world of our human culture, we often bring to bear the same life-or-death pressure, natural to the body's programming, making and applying that intensity to our self-image as a shield, a defense and a weapon to help establish our place in family and society.

When the outcome we hoped for is at least somewhat in the vicinity of our original aim, we give ourselves credit for the achievement of having made it happen. When, as is more often the case, we are partially-to-completely thwarted in our plans, frustration or pessimism are among the frequent reactions. Why is my reaction so often negative, as if I expected I should have been able, with sufficient effort, to make reality conform to my wishes? If this does not happen, have I failed? What might I not have taken into account when assessing the possibilities of success? Have I ever thought about what factors are at play besides my own intentions and efforts when I set a course in life?

In my personal experience, I ask myself, and I ask you, dear Reader, to inquire of yourself also ... when I look at, when you look at, where I am, where you are, at this moment in life's journey, what could one, personally, take credit for? How do I understand why my life has taken the shape and texture I find myself living in today? How to explore this question?

Social scientists have observed that our view of reality is initially determined by our subjective experience of the aspects of the world we encounter during our first ten to fifteen years of life. Our primary perspectives, understandings, attitudes and conditioned reactions are programmed during this period depending on what we are exposed to. Obviously, this can change when we leave our home environment, encounter other viewpoints, other cultures and have new experiences outside the realm of what we were used to. However, the bedrock of our first decade remains, either as guiding attitudes or as a fulcrum to rebel against. It is the "reality" in which we marinated as children.

My World

I am now, at the moment of writing this, 78 years old. My earliest memories are from around the age of 3, so I have been cognizant for three-quarters of a century. The world I grew up in no longer exists ... for both better and, in some ways, worse. Events in history that fill my understanding do not exist in the psychological universe of most people I speak with today.

For me, subjectively, I feel both that I have been alive a long time and that my life has gone very quickly. How could so much time, so many events, so many people, so much happiness and sorrow be crammed into such a short time ... or is it a long time? It feels different depending on how I look at it. I am recalling now that, as my father lay dying at age 98, my mother, age 90, looked up at me with enormously sad eyes and said, after seventy years of marriage, "I always knew this day would come. I just never knew it would come so soon."

As a psychotherapist, I once worked with a man who struggled with a personality of persistent rigid tendencies and attitudes. Flexibility was very difficult for him. We searched his youth for factors that may have contributed to this pattern, but to no avail. One day, I asked him to bring pictures from his childhood and old family albums. Such images often inspired family stories that could be revealing of the origins of behavioral and attitudinal patterns. Among the artifacts was an old, stylized nineteenth-century photo of a soldier in a rigid posture, filled with pride and full uniform regalia. "Who is that?" I inquired. As my client responded, he drew his body upright, pulled in his stomach, pulled back his shoulders, straightened his head and said to me, firmly and proudly, "That is my grandfather! He was an officer in her Royal Majesty, Queen Victoria's British Indian Army!" My client was carrying in his mind, feelings and body, the memory of a time, place and world he had never personally experienced but had somehow incorporated as part of himself.

My life is not just my own experiences. Still, today, in my mind, I can hear my maternal grandmother's favorite song from the 1890s. From my father's Russian side of the family, I recall occasional references to the coming of the Cossacks, familial memory traces of pogroms and persecution in ancestral Ukraine, told to them by their parents and grandparents. I can imagine that my great grandfather had an influence on his son, my grandfather, who then had an influence on his son, my father, who then had an influence on me, his son. Beyond that, our family trail is lost. Yet … there were earlier generations that influenced my great grandfather and all the others prior that influenced them …. How much is my seeming "individuality" shaped by all these unknown forces?

Hanging by a Thread

How much does the element of Luck play in shaping our life? When I begin where I am now and look backward to how I got here and then how I got to the place that got me here and then to the place that got me to the place that got me here … there is a string of events, choices, accidents that brought me from the situation I was born into, nearly eight decades later, to my current state and status.

Am I living, designing, shaping, creating the life around me?

Am I being moved from situation to situation passively, wondering why things do or don't happen to me?

What keeps me breathing, my heart beating, my mind producing thoughts … wanted and unwanted?

Did I create myself? Did I create the people around me? Do I have control over what they say and do?

How much control do I have over what I do and say?

What is the Life energy that quickens me each morning and carries me through the day? Do I control that?

I need to think and feel into this much more deeply. If I don't control life, and often myself, if I don't control accident or fate, if I don't control life or death … then I, and everyone I care for, hangs by a thread every moment of existence.

I can increase my chances if I look both ways before crossing the street. In that way, I can reduce the risk of an avoidable accident. But that won't protect me from the unlikely but still possible clamshell dropped from an overhead seagull, hitting me on the head and causing me to fall down in the middle of the street. That would seem more like fate rather than accident, as it could not be foreseen. My luck just ran out.

Hanging from a thread, perhaps it is best not to make sudden, violent movements.

What can I control, hanging by a thread? Probably, beginning with relaxing and taking a deep breath might be a good start. A sudden wind buffets me and my thread begins to swing wildly. Will it break? Will it cause me to bump into someone else's swinging thread? The wind dies down and I am now spinning in tighter and tighter circles waiting for the momentum from the wind to unwind. My body might have become anxious or frightened or irritated, but I realize that if I keep my attention focused on relaxing and watching what happens next, including what ideas or behaviors may come from me next, instead of adding unnecessary tension to the thread, I can influence forces from my interior that could slow the thread down, even though I cannot control the forces that impinge on my thread from the outside.

Living on the Thread

Perhaps the secret of living more fully is learning how to live conscious of the thread of life from which I hang, but also of all the threads of accident, coincidence … and perhaps fate or even destiny.

But, is my personality, the creature of all these factors, all there is to me? What about the part of me that began this exploration? What about the part of me which wants to be in control and imagines it should be able to always direct events to my advantage? Can this part accept the reality of the intermeshing factors outside my sphere of influence and understand that it is trapped inside a matrix of forces? It is a part that wants to be able to shape its life and experiences by exerting its will on the world outside. It does not understand that the world outside has its own agenda. When it aligns with my wishes, I am fortunate. When it doesn't align, I am not lucky. If I am honest, I see I can sometimes influence events, but not always … and then, not always in the way I imagined.

But the world outside is not the only place where a life can be led. Everything I experience as being outside in the world is actually being experienced inside my brain … like a virtual reality game or a movie. Of course, my house and car and dog exist outside me, but I see the image of my house, I hear the sounds of the car, I smell my dog … it is these experiences in my brain that I call reality … and all are interpreted from my experiences of electrical and hormonal activity in my brain.

Also going on in my brain are my interpretations, associations and reactions to the images, sounds, smells, tastes and sensations that I am watching and experiencing in my brain as the reality-out-there. If my interpretations change, if I experience different associations, then the reality-out-there will shift for me. This shift alters the shape of life as I am experiencing it. When I view my life in the theater of my brain, I now see a different perspective.

I discover there is another type of influence that is very different from control. It arises from a shift in understanding, a shift in attitude and viewpoint. I am not totally helpless in the face of circumstances because I can influence my mindset directly. A change in viewpoint, a change in attitude, changes my experience and alters the shape of my life in that moment.

If I can be gentle with life and curious to see what crossroads it takes me to, I may be awake when choice points are encountered. Then I can occasionally choose a direction. Once on the new path, I am again carried by the flow in this channel, still conscious of the thread that helps me keep afloat but no longer fearful for its fragility. I can embrace it with appreciation and with gratitude ... even reverence ... and most appropriately, with awe.

Imagination: A Double-Edged Sword

I was deep in daydream. The story was stimulating my body with sensations and emotions connected with the imagery. Then ... I began to reawaken to a sense of myself, while still in the midst of the living-movie in my head. A moment prior, I had been totally "lost" in the dream, enjoying the excitement. As the audience, I was vicariously feeling ... as the audience for the dream ... as if the story was an actual event happening to me right then.

Now, I became aware that "I" was "in" a daydream that I had initiated ... and was enjoying. This dawning recognition did not immediately stop the continuation of the inner movie. Even while the daydream continued, another part of me was experiencing astonishment at the complexity and realism of the created images ... and how my body could not distinguish them from outer reality, was responding as if the dream was reality. In fact, there was no outer reality at that moment. All that existed for me was the daydream. As I awoke to what was happening to my attention, I saw again how inner reality could produce reactions as intense as, if not more than, the "real" world outside. A strange question then appeared.

A Strange Question

I wondered whether I was actually creating a small segment of a different "reality." A small segment, like several feet of movie frames cut into a short film. ... and .... these "people" in my created splinter-reality ... did they have a life of their own for the short duration of the dream? Were they experiencing what I was directing them to do in my inner production? Probably not ... but the strange question made me consider how I might feel if I was aware of how others were imagining my image in their daydreams. Yet, the question remains. Clearly, their images in my mind were affecting me. And I know that what I imagine about others can influence my feelings and behavior towards them. Perhaps I do have a responsibility for what my imagination creates ... and not only to myself.

At the stimulation of this strange question, which I had never before thought about, I turned my attention back to the daydream. I felt a reluctance of some part of me to stop the show because "he" was really enjoying the stimulation in his body from the story. I also felt the power of the images begin to wane as they started to fragment and dissolve under the gaze of my more awakened attention. The energy or motivation (are they different?) to maintain the daydream had disappeared with my awakening frame of mind. The bewitchment, the enchantment, was broken.

The Power of Imagination

All that I have described above probably took no more than a few seconds. But it made me wonder about the power of images and thoughts to evoke emotions and the power of emotions to evoke images and thoughts. If images and thoughts could stimulate strong sensory and emotional reactions ... and hypnotize me so that I forgot I was the audience looking at the equivalent of a movie or play on the screen in my mind ... then ... depending on the type of story, different emotional states could be evoked, different physical sensations aroused, both of which would add to the reality of the dream.

I am recalling now what I experienced during a movie when, with my heart pounding and breath stopped, I realized that my body was responding to the frightening image on the screen. Of course! Why else do people go to scary movies other than to vicariously experience an emotional intensity that they don't get or may not want to get in real life? In that moment of recognition, I realized I had agreed to have my biochemistry manipulated by the filmmaker to evoke an experience I was not enjoying. I took control of myself, stood up, and walked out of the theater. I have avoided films of this type ever since. If I try to keep bad people and events out of my life, why would I want to bring such impressions into my mind through my imagination?

I have been interested in the power of images ever since, whether in advertising, politics or entertainment. Notice, dear Reader, how little public discussion there is about the substance of political policy in the US but, instead, how political candidates create negative advertising with images and music to stimulate the emotional responses in viewers, which will increase the likelihood of frightening their target into voting for them, the "safe" candidate who cares about them and not the other "scary" candidate who doesn't care about them. This is always a dangerous pact with the devil. Once emotions are aroused and attached, first to a particular issue or person, and then grafted onto the self-image of the target of the manipulation, it is very difficult to de-condition the linkage. Once I attach my opinion or viewpoint to my image of myself and assume this validates me as a good and righteous person, detaching me from that opinion feels like a diminishment of my self-worth. Then, I become the opinion which I may have been manipulated into accepting as an intrinsic part of my righteousness. Stimulate enough people and you can produce mobs and even revolutions. All demagogues, advertisers and propagandists understand this aspect of psychology.

An Experiment

Dear Reader, you could begin to explore this right now if you wish. If you don't want to try, just skip this paragraph. If you want to try, then read to the end and then return here … and relax your body. Follow your breath. After a short while, close your eyes. When you feel really relaxed, find a disturbing memory or upsetting image. Look at that for a short while. ….. What has happened in your body? If you have done this correctly, your body is no longer in the state of relaxation it was when you began. Now …. take your attention off the disturbing memory or image and turn your attention again to relaxing your body and following your breath. When you feel ready … find a wonderful memory or image and stay with that for a while. ….. How does your body feel now? Try switching back and forth between the two memories, all the while noticing how your body reacts to each image.

Our bodies are highly reactive to images. The emotional quality of what our imagination is producing will influence the body to release either stress or pleasure hormones. Our body does not know whether our brain is presenting to it material from the world of the senses or from the world of the imagination. Always a good servant, the body responds in varying degrees of fight, flight, relaxation, pleasure or excitement, depending on what is happening in the image-making machinery in the brain. This brief experiment should be all that is necessary to recognize some of the power and danger of imaginative processes.

Now, use your imagination, dear Reader, to envision a future technology that would allow us to experience the feelings, sensations, smells, touch and emotions of the characters in a movie. That leap of realism would exponentially increase the depth of the trance of entertainment beyond the effects of just vision and sound. This new technology is already under development, driven by the virtual reality gaming and pornography industries, and will then find its way to the military to increase the realism for training and the entertainment industry to bring more people to their shows. This will make us all increasingly vulnerable to mental and emotional manipulation by advertisers, politicians, governments, corporations …anyone with a wish and the means to shape our thoughts and reactions. This does not sound like a good societal direction to me.

And yet, isn't this exactly what happens when I intentionally daydream … or … find I have been "captured" by my imagination without my realizing it? In the former situation, I choose specific images and themes in order to activate a capacity that requires imagination … such as arithmetic or planning … or to produce a particular vicarious experience in myself, like visualizing going down a ski slope or practicing for an interview … or, perhaps, to work through a problem with someone, or plan a trip, or to entertain, or excite myself with a distraction in a boring moment. So, there are obviously different motivations for intentionally stimulating the imagination, stimulating the parts of our brain that produce pictures and stories. The only difference between imagination and virtual reality technology is that, in the latter, someone else decides and programs into me the dream they have designed, and which then, I have agreed to ingest.

In the situation of the capture of my attention, the daydream begins and runs on its own, stimulated by something in the moment, internal or external, that I may not even be aware of. Now I am the passive receiver of whatever the images are showing me … until I wake up and realize what is happening. Then I have a choice of continuing to watch or, turning my attention away. Prior to that, I had no choice. My attention had been kidnapped and I didn't realize it.

If what the imagination is producing is a conspiracy theory or is interpreting what you just said to me as disrespectful or is daydreaming while I am talking and mixing the content of the two together or is ruminating about how I should behave when my conscience is telling me differently, then whatever I am imagining or interpreting, becomes my reality. What else can I base my reactions upon other than my sense of reality at the moment? To do otherwise would seem insane. And yet, the content of my imagination is often limited or incorrect, thus throwing into question what I feel and believe is Reality. Its contents leave traces even after I have woken up. These lingering traces eventually become involved in my interpretations of what is happening. Even when I am awake, imagination, in the background, in my subconscious, out of sight of my attention, may select and arrange the impressions I am experiencing in that moment.

Brains as Search Engines

All brains are hard-wired to look for patterns. Some patterns are implanted at conception to facilitate safety and increased chance for survival at birth, like birds programmed to recognize the shadow of a hawk. Patterns are also created by life experiences. Touch the hot stove once and there will instantly appear a recognition pattern that will last a lifetime. Psychologically, a cruel act or deed, or a wonderful word or deed, can likewise imprint a pattern on the neuronal network of the brain. These patterns will then resonate whenever anything or anyone evocative of the original person or event comes along.

In addition, there is also an imaginative process at play. The neuronal stimulation by and of these patterns will resonate in other parts of the brain and stimulate sounds, images, thoughts, feelings which then stimulate the network of memory and associations with any linkage, even remote, to the feel of the original resonance. All these associations vie for presentation to the pattern-searching mechanism. All sorts of dots begin to appear. How do they connect? Are there different ways to connect the dots? Am I missing any dots? Are there any dots here that don't belong? Do I ever think to ask myself these questions when I am reacting to someone or something?

Combine the automatic pattern-search engine built into the brain with our memory and imaginative capacities ... and our creativity can form beautiful, complex, sophisticated theories and interpretations of meaning and significance. Most unfortunately, the dots are not always accurately connected, or the pattern seen is only one of other equally reasonable conclusions based on the angle of viewing of the other participants. The action that follows is often based on sincere but incomplete or erroneous assumptions and beliefs.

The majority of reported daydream content includes planning ahead, interactions with people, positive or negative, or dreams of success or worries of failure. There are also varying amounts of sexual fantasy dependent on age, sex and situation. The prime question here is, "Am I using, or allowing to be used, this mental energy to create scenarios in my mind in a responsible way ... doing something constructive with it that may lead to a change for the better such as practical planning and problem-solving... content that may lead to an improvement, something with more potential?" If I am using it to worry, to regret, to plan revenge, to call myself or someone else names, is this what this instrument was designed for? Is this a waste of this precious, mysterious energy? I certainly have a responsibility to my body to protect it from wasteful reactions to frightening or worrying daydreams.

What is the Purpose of Imagination?

"What is this imagination mechanism designed for?" That's an interesting question. Most obviously, it enhances its owner's chances of better decisions and better chances at survival if one can imagine threats that have not yet arrived. This is as true for modern humans in their social relationships as for cavemen or animals in the wild. Whatever keeps us safer, more comfortable, happier, is surely something to plan and watch for. But imagination obviously has exponentially greater possibilities for humans. Certainly, if we were not supposed to use it, we wouldn't have it. What is its purpose in humans beyond learning from the past to avoid problems in the future?

When I think about this question, I also reflect on what is known about how thoughts or images or memories appear in my mind without stimulation through my outer senses. The biological geometry of the pathways that electrical currents follow to different areas of the brain when these functions are operating, is fairly well calibrated now. But, actually, how pictures, words, stories, form in our mind from the stimulation of electrical and hormonal action in our neuronal network is a total mystery … as is how "I" can activate these functions, at will, for the purposes explored above … as is the mystery of how they operate on their own and capture my attention when I am trying to focus it on something else.

The Meaning of "To Imagine"

"Imagination" is an interesting word. It is defined in the dictionary as "a visual representation, a likeness," and in contemporary culture, a picture produced on an electronic display (such as a television or computer screen). The latter is particularly interesting because this seems what is happening on the "screen" of our mind as the electronically stimulated displays flash on and off. In this exploration, I suggest we expand the definition beyond just visual imagery. An image is also a symbolic representation of something … this something's image projected outside itself. It may be symbolized in sound or touch or sensation as well as a picture.

Our words are symbolic sounds that stand for ideas, concepts, feelings, instructions, anything that can be conveyed by words. Thus, when considering the realm of our imagination, all mental activity of this sort may be utilized in the mental process that creates, from the stimulation of its electrical neuronal structure, internal symbols, visible, or knowable, only to oneself, which represent reactions to and interpretation of events past, present and even future, both real and not real, both possible as well as impossible.

An idiosyncratic play on words led me to think about Image-Nation. And, in reality, it is a world, a nation, a universe of pictures, words and sensory memory, most accumulating from actual and vicarious experiences in life, but some of which pop into our minds unbidden, never before thought or seen, sometimes wanted but often very unwelcome. Since images, pictures and thoughts can influence emotions dramatically and then lead to behavior patterns based on the images believed to be the ultimate truth of a situation, we have to be very careful where we travel in this psychological region, this nation of images.

I must literally "keep my wits" about myself when swimming through this internal ocean of symbols and images. I must try to remember who I was just before my attention entered this theater of the mind.

Imagination as a Dimension

Another question arises here. How exactly is it that we "travel" or "move" in the sphere of our imagination? We don't have a physical body to carry us around when we are in the mental realms. Can I think about Attention as the vehicle? I know in the dimension of imagination, I can travel via the direction of my attention into the past or the future, or fantasy worlds that can never exist and I can have experiences in the world of images that change me both in the moment and perhaps into the future.

The heights and depths in the nation of images range from the monstrous to the sublime, with most of the activity of a harmless but usually repetitive nature. At an ordinary level of psychological functioning, I always feel safe playing with imagination. ... yet there is great danger when I do not understand the subtlety and power of these images as ... "Here be monsters" that lead me into fearful, resentful, negative attitudes and behavioral responses! But in the upper levels of this world is also the realm of inspiration, revelation, creativity of the most sublime qualities. When understood and visited responsibly, it can be the realm of angels

This higher image-making function allows entry to the world of creativity, the dimension of possibilities, to the doorway of epiphany and occasionally divine inspiration. Why do we have this capacity in our brains? My type of reasoning suggests that this capacity has developed within the human brain because there are higher levels of "creative energy" with which we are designed to be in contact. It suggests that the "progress" of mankind in science, philosophy, art, medicine, and all that is constructive, which goes into a developing civilization, has its source in the realm of the image-creating machinery of our brains. A part of our mind then receives these interior impressions, has the possibility of evaluating them and deciding which to bring out into exterior existence in some form representative of what we saw, or heard or felt in our mind's-eye ... an image of the image, which itself, was an image of the original idea that touched our mind.

Gift or Accident and Personal Responsibility

Given this way of looking at the mystery, it begs another question. Is this creative energy, this god-like capacity to create an idiosyncratic local reality and use it to explain and guide my life, this capacity to Will images to appear and move with a life of their own in my mind ... is this function a gift given for a purpose, or is it an accidental neurological development which I can and should play with as I wish with no responsibility to myself or others for what I am doing in my secret place?

There have been moments in my life when I found myself constructing long speeches as if I were President or telling certain people off or defending myself or making imaginary presentations on subjects of interest to me. There have been long, scintillating oratories that I truly enjoyed thinking up and listening to in my head ... even when I did not initiate the daydreaming. On realizing they were happening, I would often voluntarily re-enter them for their entertainment value.

This can be a deeper problem if what is being rehearsed or relived over and over again, are grievances, hostilities, painful losses. Not only will this content put my body, feelings and mind in a collective negative state, but because my attention is lost inside of them, they are experienced as if real! And when they become real to me, I may act out material from the state created or energized by the imagination ... like a sleepwalker. If someone is acting out a terrible inner state, they are likely to hurt themselves or other people, sometimes physically, more often emotionally and psychologically.

Think about, dear Reader, some of those moments in your life when, after your emotions calmed down, you felt real regret, even surprise that you could have said or done what you said or did in that stressful moment. What were you imagining was the situation such that you felt justified in your reaction at that time? If you don't feel that way now, what has changed? Do you now imagine something differently?

Imagination is the equivalent of Nature's virtual reality program ... and I don't need to wear a headset! In a literal sense, when we are daydreaming ... we are dreaming ... during the day ... with our eyes open ... often while in an activity ... but our body is on autopilot while our attention is lost in the daydream. We are probably lost in the same or similar bio-psychological activity, which we call night dreams, but we are not safe during the day as we are, at night, in bed. Rather, we are sleep-walking through our lives, saying and doing based on what we may be imagining is the reality facing us.

One of the easier to see examples of this phenomenon often occurs when driving a car, when I suddenly "come back to myself" and realize I have gone miles without any subjective memory of the road because I was thinking or daydreaming or listening to the radio or music or absorbed in conversation with my passenger, instead of continually being aware of myself in the driver's seat, my hands on the steering wheel, watching the road and the traffic around me. I have on occasion gone right by my exit and had to make a lengthy detour.

Who was driving my car while I (my attention) was elsewhere? Who avoided the other cars, changed lanes, slowed down or speeded up? Do I only "zone out" in this way when driving? Are there times when my attention is lost in imagination while I am in motion, walking, talking, relating to people ... and on "coming back" to the conversation or the situation, I realize I have "lost time" and don't know what has happened during my absence?

As often as not, I find that when my mind is daydreaming, I did not initiate the activity. This is very interesting. When I am intentionally creating a daydream, it feels as if I am the writer and director of the story. But, who ... or what ... is the writer and director when I did not initiate the daydream? It appears that this creative activity, whatever quality of psychological energy is able to literally create the pictures and themes, voluntarily or involuntarily, has a life of its own. I can use it, but it operates even when I don't initiate, even when I am trying to focus as hard as I can on something else but am continually distracted back into the unwanted or inconvenient fantasy.

Three Components

So ... there are three factors ... some kind of creative energy ... my attention ... and then an experience in my mind and/or body and/or emotions as a result of my attention joining itself to the product of this creative energy. Sometimes I intentionally direct the creative energy to produce a daydream for a specific purpose, whether practical or pure entertainment. More often, I wake up in the story and realize I never noticed entering it.

What chooses the story for me? From the outside world, a sight, sound, a taste, a smell may set off a conditioned association that stimulates a memory. This memory may then stimulate an emotional state resonant with the memory. Or I awaken in a mood and wonder about how I got there but may not be able to locate the intervening trigger. Or I may be experiencing a particular emotional state and my daydreams conform to the quality of the emotion by producing images resonant with it. They seem mutually interactive. Where is my intellect in all this? It seems to be the audience, either passive or active, in its relationship to attention.

I see that this image-making capacity is a very powerful ... something. It influences my physical body, my emotional state and what I think about. When I am in imagination, particularly when I have lost touch with my sense of myself as the viewer of the daydream, I am at the mercy of the content of the images and storyline. If they relax me, this does little harm and may do good ... unless I am in a situation that requires vigilance to the immediate context. If they make me tense, or excited, or afraid or angry, they stimulate the release of stress hormones which can damage my body, corrode my emotions and distort my thoughts. Whatever this something, this creative capacity is, it needs to be handled with care and awareness.

Ever since that moment described at the beginning of this exploration, I have become more aware of daydreaming, more cautious about what I allow (when I am aware enough to be aware of the dream) and more interested in how this phenomenon works, what it is for, who is operating it.

The Power of Belief

In my psychotherapy practice, I repeatedly saw the power of belief.

Our assumptions, interpretations of meaning, our belief systems about ourselves, others and even how life is supposed to work all have their roots in our imaginative capacity. To try to put myself in someone else's place requires an act of imagination. If I were that person in that situation, what would that feel like? Compassion means co-passion, feeling together, experiencing what the other is experiencing. How can I try to practice the Golden Rule if I can't imagine how my words and behaviors and moods influence other people?

Yet, because we live every moment with this capacity to build worlds ... from nothing ... worlds which we then have to live in without realizing they may not be what they seem ... we don't realize the power that imagination has over us ... if we are not careful. I now recall a phrase I heard somewhere during my years of therapy practice. "Neurotics build castles in the air while psychotics live in them." A variation I recently discovered repeated the phrase but added at the end ... "and my mother cleans them!"

Most cultures extol "imagination" as a universally good quality. We are encouraged to "use our imagination." It becomes for us a tool to help us solve problems, take another "look" at a past event to learn from our revisit, to plan for the future and also entertain us. It is one of the capacities to appear with development of our frontal lobes. Although other animals behave in ways suggesting limited, practical planning, the human capacity can build spaceships, design governments, invent theories and speculate on the meaning of life.

Our imagination is our private place, a place no one else can see into. There, we can act out our secret desires, wishes, fears, hopes, longings. In this secret location, I can be whomever I wish to be, do whatever I want to do with whomever I want to do it with or to have experiences I have no opportunity ... or perhaps courage ... to actually try to experience. Try this, dear Reader. Give yourself permission to imagine something you would not want anyone else to know that you have in your mind at this moment. Take your time with this memory or fantasy or image or thought ... whatever has appeared in your inner sanctum. You can do whatever you like in here. You are safe from any outside knowledge or interference. But ... are you safe from the effects on your body, your emotions, your thoughts, your moods, your reactions ... from what you are presenting in your mind for you to experience?

In this secret place, I am a god. I say, "Let there be that memory from last week." And Lo! ... there is the memory for me to revisit. Or, I say, "Let me see numbers so that I can calculate in my head the amount I will need to withdraw from the bank." And Lo! There are numbers in my mind which I can manipulate with thought. Or, I could say, "Show me what it would be like to have a relationship with that person over there." And Lo! Here is a very interesting fantasy to absorb my attention. How are you doing that? Is this a case of "wishing makes it so?"

But I am often an absentee god. The machinery of imagination operates on its own and captures me, who a moment ago thought himself a god ... then captures and pulls my attention into whatever show is currently playing in the theater of my mind. If I don't make the decision to use the imagination-machinery intentionally, the decision will be made anyway, but automatically or accidentally by the machinery itself.

Having the imagination function within our minds is like having a tiger by the tail. Worse, it is like giving a child a weapon to play with ... and without an operator's manual! How can I learn to operate this power responsibly? I would have to begin by having an open mind about this idea that my imagination was a place of potential danger and then intentionally begin to study what was happening in my mind.

Studying My Imagination

When I began to study this phenomenon in myself, I soon realized that being asleep in imagination had a different feel, a different taste to it when compared with the moments when I felt awake and aware through my senses. I saw that I never realized my attention had left the outside world for the inner world that imagination was presenting to me ... until I realized my attention had left the outside world. I noticed that I could be aware of the world around me but also remember what I had been imagining a moment before. Why? Because I could see my imagination as just that... imagination ... when another part of my attention remained attached to my body and the world it lived in.

I saw that this was the key to studying how imagination worked without immediately having my attention captured by it. I began to practice trying to sense and feel more deeply the physical reality of my body, first one limb at a time, then several and finally the whole body. And, when practicing this, I also tried to be aware of the world around me as well. When I was able to be simultaneously aware of the sensation of my body and what I was experiencing around me, I tried to expand this. While sensing the reality of my body's existence, I would intentionally activate my imagination to view a scene from my past. I tried to make this split attention last, but saw it was continually interrupted by another association or sound or thought or even an itch would break the hold of my attention on my practice. But, in those short moments of simultaneity, I began to learn about the interaction of imagination with the other parts of me.

An Experiment: Split Attention

Dear Reader, you can easily experiment with this double-viewing right now... if you wish. Try this, but read it through first. Close your eyes. Find a memory in your mind right now. It doesn't matter what it is. You may see an image and/or remember sounds or tastes or feelings associated with the image. Study the memory while trying to also be aware of your body's posture and state of tension or relaxation. Now, open your eyes. Continue to feel the solidity of your body while you take in the sights, sounds, smells of the location of your body as you read this. Try and keep your attention in contact with both the feeling of your body and the experience of the room around you.

When you realize you have lost that connection, just re-establish it again ... over and over and over. Now, close your eyes and repeat your visit to your memory ... or a different one if you wish ... but try to hold onto the sensation of your body. After a while, open your eyes and look around, again practicing holding onto your body as the grounding point for your attention. When you feel ready, try to look inward at the memory with your eyes open and continue to remember to feel your body's solidity. With practice, most people are eventually able to be aware of both ... the world around them and the world inside them that may be responding, in that moment, to the external situation ... or may be off on its own adventure or complaints and oblivious to the outer world.

Activating Attention

How do you activate your imagination? How do you enter the world of images? Try this now, dear Reader. Close your eyes and remember your childhood home. In your mind's-eye, take a walk through the home, room by room, looking carefully to see what your memory brings up in response to this request. Take your time. Let yourself be surprised. Perhaps you will turn a corner and meet a family member or friend or your dog or cat. Now … try to see how, exactly, you have created this internal picture show. If you are a person who does not see images but remembers and thinks in sounds, feelings, words or some other modality, then, of course, use whatever tool your imagination has provided for you. In whatever way your imagination operates in you, try to see how this happens. What are you doing to bring up visual, sensory, auditory or other impressions? All of these phenomena are resonant images of something. An "image' is any symbolic representation. It does not have to be a picture.

Taming Imagination

In Greek Mythology, if you looked directly at Medusa, you would be turned to stone. In our psychological world, if we look directly at imagination, our attention becomes frozen and a slave of the emotional power of the imagination. Perseus was able to slay Medusa because he looked at her through her reflection on his shield. When we make the deliberate effort to find the sensation of our body and breath and still watch what is happening, this quality of more detached attention becomes our shield. We can watch the content of imagination without our attention becoming trapped.

Developing this capacity to be aware of what is happening in your mind without losing contact with your body in the outside world brings a degree of both safety and freedom from the dangers of imagination. With this capacity, imagination can become a truly creative tool to benefit me rather than a tool on autopilot that uses me and leaves me vulnerable to the manipulations of others.

Knowledge and Understanding

Have you ever felt the distinction between "knowing" and "understanding"? Far from a semantic difference, I find the quality of subjective experience between the two is profound. Let's examine the experience of knowing. It occurs in one's intellect as a thought or theory or idea. "I know the names of all the oceans" ... or ... "I know my multiplication tables" ... or ... I know the capital of Armenia ... or ... I know the way to San Jose". Knowing is the acquisition of information, whether valid or not, information about the material world or the mathematical world or names and dates of historical events and the theories and opinions about what they meant for humankind. Knowledge is the outcome of the acquisition of information ... bits of data.

I can read about the Battle of Waterloo. I can memorize the names of the participants and learn of opinions about the reasons for the battle being won or lost and its impact on the history of Europe. But I wasn't there. I did not actually meet the protagonists. I have never personally experienced any type of warfare, much less cavalry charges with lances, bayonets and cannons. In that sense, what kind of "understanding" can I have of this event?

The State of Understanding

The state of understanding, as I have come to discern it, is the result of adding actual, direct experience to my mental knowledge base. A personal example ... my first time at the ocean off the Maine coast. I had grown up on Long Island, New York, and my beach experience was in the warm Gulf Stream. One of my fond memories of youth was a summer body surfing along the south shore of the island. This was the experiential understanding that I had of ocean swimming up to that time. I had heard about, acquired a knowledge of, Maine and its waters, from conversation and reading, so I knew the waters were said to be cold. That was an intellectual particle of knowledge my mind had picked up prior to that first day along the Maine coast.

It was a bright warm day with brilliant sunlight. The sand was hot under my feet. I ran towards the water and kept running another ten or twenty feet until the water reached my crotch. I gasped, and without missing a stride, my body reversed itself, on its own, without an intellectual decision by my reasoning mind and ran backwards out of the water and onto the beach. Those few seconds had transferred my knowing into an understanding. Now I understood that this section of the Atlantic was not the ocean of my boyhood. I now understood the meaning of cold water in a way I could never have discerned from acquired knowledge alone.

What had changed to add additional dimensionality to my knowledge? Obviously, my body and its senses were now active participants. This was no longer a fact that others had told me about. Now, I had become one of those who could speak about this phenomenon from personal experience. But there was more. This was not only a sensory event. It was also an emotional event. I now had feelings about this body of water. I did not like the cold. I had always been ambivalent about the ocean. It is very deep. It isn't solid. It moves up and down … sometimes very much up and down. I can't breathe under water. There are creatures in the ocean that would eat me. But now, the enjoyment of comfortable water for surfing was no longer available in my new home.

As I recalled, by association, this event from many years prior to coming across the distinction between the two experiences of knowing and understanding, I now understood that understanding is a combination of knowledge and experience.

In later years, as a psychotherapist, I periodically had as clients, commercial fishermen. Their stories of adventures and near-death experiences on the ocean were often accompanied by a fatalism about the severity of the water temperature. They knew they would not survive more than a few minutes of immersion. Some never even bothered to learn to swim. Some were even disdainful of "survival suits" that would prolong their life if they went overboard. They had an understanding that far exceeded knowledge.

I recall a lovely autobiography called *The Tracker* by Tom Brown. The author relates that as a young boy living adjacent to the New Jersey Pine Barrens, he was befriended by a local Native American who taught him the art of tracking. A line from the book has always stayed with me; "To know, you have to go."

Implications

This difference in quality has become increasingly helpful to me in both evaluating my own opinions and beliefs and those I constantly hear around me from acquaintances and the surrounding culture. At the funeral service for a beloved friend, his son added some levity to the eulogies by recounting that his father had often told him when challenged in conversation about something expressed, that he knew a great deal of facts and that they were all backed up by his opinions.

This difference is not academic. Human relations, decision and policymaking, conflict or peace, are based on peoples' evaluation of the "facts" they believe and the opinions they hold based on these facts. How many of these opinions are based on personal experiential data versus knowledge of what other people have said about a subject, a person, the implications of a government policy? How many of us actually try to confirm, for ourselves, the reality of what we hear? Because of our need for social approval and our laziness to do our own research, we all tend to believe what we hear from people we consider to be "like us". Most likely, they also have heard it somewhere from someone who heard it from someone … and so on.

Find Out for Yourself

Dear Reader, you could try an experiment right now. All these words carry information about my understandings. For you, they are facts about what I say are my understandings. You cannot verify my memories. But you can explore your own distinction between information and understanding.

Let your mind open to associations and memories on this subject. Recall times you were certain about something only to later receive information, or have an experience, that either reversed or deepened your initial assessment. When you realized you had been wrong, what was that experience like inside yourself? Were you surprised, shocked, embarrassed, angry, happy, sad, interested?

This will often happen with new data. Until recently, we had been told by astronomers that life could not exist on Venus. Then there were reports that a gas, associated with life forms, had been discovered. Was there life on Venus? Then, further reports suggested that this was unlikely. For me, this was an experience of knowledge about what others said they were discovering. It was a fact that this knowledge had been acquired. What it meant was a matter of interpretation. But what did I understand? I have no personal experience with Venus or non-Earth-based life forms … and

I wasn't any good at Chemistry in school. This is knowledge about the natural world that I can accept as information, with the proviso that I always keep my mind open for more information. But, if "to know requires that I go," that is not going to happen.

Conflict between people, either individuals or groups, and even nations, is based on assumptions about the intentions of others: are they a threat or an ally? This assumption both precedes and then maintains conflict. It is a phenomenon that demonizes, alienizes, the "Other." They are stereotyped by their group, labeled by race or political orientation, so that individuality disappears, and all are judged the same. These assessments are claimed, by their adherents, to represent their knowledge of the facts about the others … but what is understood? Conflict resolution depends on both sides having first-hand, person-to-person experiences with representatives from the other side. When I can experience another person as similar to myself, as concerned with their family, with well-being, with fairness, with wanting to feel respected, then I experience our common humanity. I can then feel, sense, see our commonality. Under these circumstances, I not only have the data from my thoughts, but I have emotional and sensory impressions as well.

I have been fortunate to have traveled to other countries, learned a little bit of other languages and customs. I have friends now around the world. What I noticed on returning from a new location was a new feeling of interest and concern for the people of that region. I began to be aware of news from that country and what was happening to the people I had met there. Because of the experience of the sights, sounds, smells, tastes of the place and the real people with real families, wishes, hopes, fears, I had an understanding which now enriched and brought new dimensions to my prior knowledge.

Two Different Levels

"Understanding" is an interesting word. What do I stand under? To what beliefs, principles, experiences, codes of ethics do I pledge allegiance? If I say that I understand, on what experiential data am I basing this assumption? Do I really have personal experience to back up this claim, or am I basing it on opinion?

Knowledge can be shared. Knowledge is data. Data are units of information. Information is potential energy. These data units are transferable by mental activity and through the use of the mediums of sound-words-language and images. Among members of a group with shared language and symbolism, the knowledge can be transferred with considerable agreed-upon accuracy.

Knowledge acquired only in my mental apparatus is cut off from the experience of life. My body senses and my emotions feel life. They are in contact with a larger reality that my mind only conceptualizes but does not directly experience. I only have to touch the stove once to understand the meaning of the word "Hot." "Broken heart" transforms from a literary phrase into an incredibly painful experience when it happens inside of me. "Now I understand what that means!" Now I understand what they are talking about, what they have gone through because I have had a taste, an experience with that quality of energy also.

Whereas knowledge is only mental, understanding brings the information only acquirable through direct experience of the heart and body.

What would I discover if I reviewed all that I believed I knew and asked myself how much of what I thought I knew I actually understood? Regardless of whether we agree or not on the meaning and implications of an experience, we cannot deny the facts of sensation and feeling. They may be harder to capture in words than ideas because they flow more like water or air. Words are blocks of meaning. Feelings and sensations are non-solid carriers of mixtures of meaning. But, if I feel hot and you feel cold, or I feel happy and you feel solemn, those are experiences, not ideas.

All the ideas about what it is like to feel loved cannot substitute for the experience of feeling loved.

Do you understand?

I Have A Body But I Am Not My Body

Perennial Wisdom tells us: "You have a body, but you are not your body. You have feelings, but you are not your feelings. You have thoughts, but you are not your thoughts."

How strange. What would be left of "me" if this were true. How could this startling declaration be validated? To begin, as the statement is addressing me ... and you too, dear Reader ... it is making this assertion about my body, my feelings and my thoughts. The only direction I can look to investigate this is at my body, my feelings and my thoughts. Since it is inside my body that I experience its sensations as well as mental and emotional activity, I will have to direct my attention into myself.

Am I my body? Or ... do I have a body which I inhabit? If I was unfortunate enough to lose a body part, say an arm or a leg, ... would I still be me? What about people who have lost all four limbs and are only a trunk and a head ... are they still not themselves ... just minus major body parts? Suppose that such a truly unfortunate person went blind and deaf ... would they still not be themselves, only with catastrophically diminished functional capacity? What about people who are totally paralyzed but still able to communicate by blinking their eyes? Journalist Jean-Dominique Bauby was able to dictate his memoir after a massive stroke that left him with the horrific condition called "locked-in syndrome." Was he not still inside his body, which he could no longer control except for blinking his eyelids?

I am obviously inside my body and intricately connected with its sensations and feelings ... but is the "I" that is aware of being inside my body ... that experience of being aware of myself ... is that the body, or is it me being aware of being inside my body? Take a moment now to a look inside yourself, dear Reader. What is your impression?

What do I understand about this body I claim as my own ... as if it were my possession? Wait ... as if it were my possession ... my personal property? That verbal formulation suggests that subconsciously I do realize that my body is my personal property. I want it respected by others, not hurt or endangered. I know I should be more respectful and attentive to it myself ... diet, exercise, stress management, care and grooming, regular dentist appointments. I must take it to the doctor when it doesn't feel well. It won't take itself. In a way, it is like a farm animal that must be taken care of so that it can do the work I require of it ... from carrying me where I want to go to performing the actions that I need it to perform in order to manifest my intentions out into the world.

Verification

Let's repeat the experiment offered in an earlier reading that will also be helpful here.

Maybe dear Reader, you might like to try it? Place your hand in your lap. Look at it. Now, in your mind, think of the word "rise". ... What happened? ... Now look at your hand and, aloud, say to it, "Rise!". ... When I try this, my hand continues to rest in my lap. Obviously, the word "rise," whether silent or out loud, is not what makes the hand move. Now, look at your hand again and allow it to rise. ... just let it happen. ... As you watch it move off your lap, try to see how this actually occurs. Did you make it happen? If so, how? Or perhaps it just seemed to happen when you accepted and allowed the intention for it. In a way, this phenomenon of physical movement appears to fill the requirements for the presumed psychic ability of "psychokinesis", the capacity to move objects with your mind. As our body is an object, this seems to be proof of this hypothesized capacity ... at least, in regard to the physical body.

My Body

So, what do I actually know and understand about this body I inhabit? I am not a physician ... probably you, Reader, are not either. Do I, do you, understand how the body actually works ... all the thousands, perhaps tens of thousands of biochemical processes, interconnected, on-going at all times from the moment of my conception to the moment of my death? Can anyone artificially make a body? Science may be on the verge of growing life in the laboratory, but this would represent discovering how Nature has always done it. It is not our invention. So, even if you are a physician or a biochemist, or a geneticist, you are not the creator. You are learning how the body is constructed and operates. It was already created before science began to study it.

All bodies, from single cells to plants to the largest creatures, contain an awareness that is, at the minimum, sensitive to its environment. My body contains an awareness that is cognizant of much more than sensory impressions from my surroundings. This awareness also contains thoughts, feelings, memories, hopes, fears from my internal psychological world. I cannot live without my body, but my body can continue to live without my awareness … such as when I am asleep, unconscious under sedation, or in a coma, but there is obviously much more to me than just my body.

Feelings

What about the statement that I have feelings, but I am not my feelings? Is this true? Don't my feelings come from my heart? Aren't they the true expression of who I am? How can they not be me? What examples can I find to support this proposition?

I am well aware that I experience different moods. When I am feeling happy, confident, optimistic, the world seems brighter and I feel lighter. When I am feeling down, depressed, insecure, unloved, angry with myself, the world seems darker and I feel much heavier. Since I very much prefer the up moods, why do I ever spend time in the down moods? Some psychologists may suggest that I am subconsciously punishing myself … but even if that were a factor, I am not intentionally choosing to do so … and, in any case, how would I do that? Do I know how to regulate my moods and the biochemistry that goes along with them?

I know I can influence my body depending on what I think about. I could intentionally dwell on unhappy thoughts to try to induce a miserable mood. But why would I intentionally do that? For much of my life I have done just that, all too often. For many of us, there is often a compulsive attraction or sense of self-affirmation in negative moods. If you also recognize parts of yourself in this description, dear Reader, then this is a useful question to challenge yourself with. When this has happened to me, the experience was more like I couldn't help myself. Attention was repeatedly drawn back again and again to the sad or distressing thoughts.

Yet, even in this situation, there arises a question. Do my unhappy thoughts bring about a down mood or does the down mood trigger the unhappy thoughts? If I am my feelings, I ought to be able to control them. Yet, I am often taken by surprise to discover a feeling of envy or jealously, or insecurity or affection or excitement. Why didn't I see them coming? Why are feelings always shifting, so distracting, often unwanted? If I am my feelings, why don't I just will them to change when they are inconvenient or uncomfortable? Better still, why don't I just never allow bad feelings to occur?

I certainly am aware of feelings because they constantly manifest as sensations in my body and often interfere with my ability to focus and concentrate my mind. But ... if I am aware of them ... and if I can't consistently conjure up and maintain specific feelings on demand ... or easily change moods when they appear ... then I can see why the Ancient Wisdom may say that I have feelings, but I am not my feelings.

I seem to be the awareness that becomes aware of the feelings-sensations in my body which then influence my thoughts and moods.

Thoughts

Well, what about my thoughts? Clearly, I am the one who is thinking my thoughts. There is nobody else in my head to think them for me. Didn't Descartes, when he was pondering this same question, come to the conclusion, "I think, therefore I am"? I need to think about this. Is Descartes suggesting that I am my thoughts and the fact that there are thoughts in my head proves that I exist?

But, as I try to think about this, searching my memory bank for associations that might be helpful, I notice my attention has to fight off other, non-related associations. "Why hasn't that return phone call come in yet? If I can't get my new phone to work, I'll have to return it and order a new one. That will really be annoying ... wait ... what was I thinking about? Ah yes. I was thinking about whether I was my thoughts. But now I hear an argument in my mind that is accusing me of wasting time on such an impractical question. I have a list of chores to do today and it is getting late ... now that itch on my back has returned ... wait ... what was I thinking about? Now my wife calls to me from the other room and I momentarily turn my attention towards her. Now, my attention is free again. What was I thinking about thinking?" And so, it goes.

If I am my thoughts, why can't I control them? Why are there often thoughts in my head that I did not invite and do not want ... thoughts that worry me or frustrate me or distract me? What about that song that keeps playing in the back of my brain and is driving me crazy? Or that disagreement that replays over and over and over in my mind, upsetting me with each repetition? Or that lovely daydream about last winter in Costa Rica.? Why do I keep forgetting where I left my glasses? Why can't I control the focus of my attention better? If I could control my attention, maybe I could control my thoughts.

There is that interesting thought again. I also noticed that same thought a few minutes ago in regard to thinking about my feelings. If I wish I could control my distracting, ruminating and upsetting thoughts, then that would suggest ... that I am not my thoughts, but rather I am aware of them and can, at best, momentarily influence but not control them.

Your Mind

If you are still dubious, dear Reader, try this experiment.

First, clear your mind. That, itself, is a fascinating phenomenon. What exactly do you do to *clear* your mind? Aren't you your mind? When you speak of your mind, to what exactly are you referring? You are clearly more than just your thoughts, just your feelings and just your sensations. Perhaps, a simultaneous awareness of all these three functions would constitute mind? But we are often aware in a given moment of sensation and, in another moment, we are "lost" in feelings or later "lost" in thought. So, our awareness can be narrow or broad and deep. Do we mean by the term "mind expansion," the enlarging of our field of awareness?

Have you noticed that our language keeps bringing us back to personal pronouns ... we, me, us, I? The language intuits that "we" or "I" am more than my functions. Perhaps mind refers to the activity of sensation, feeling and thinking, in addition to the awareness of their process and content. This seems more inclusive.

But there is still a problem. If I can change my mind or clear my mind, what is the "I" that is making this effort, how is it making the attempt and what is it that becomes changed? Can I change my mind at will ... or do I notice that its viewpoint or attitude about something, or someone, has altered when I wasn't looking? Is there something more to Mind than these four components?

Let's return to mind-clearing. I suspect most of us understand this to be a re-directing of attention away from thoughts that I do not want to be thinking about. If I make my mind a "blank," how do I experience that? No thoughts? No awareness of feelings or sensation? What am I eliminating and clearing away to leave my mind "empty" and ready to accept a new impression? How long can this state last before something else enters it? When it is "clear" for a few moments, am I unconscious ... or is there awareness but without thought processes ongoing?

So, let's try this experiment. Clear your mind ... Now, try not to think about a pink elephant. Do not think about or see in your mind an image of a pink elephant ... and do not have a reaction to this suggestion. Now, remember to try not to think about this silly image. Try this for a minute. .... What happened?

If you want to explore this phenomenon further, try to guess what you will be thinking about exactly two minutes from now. Write it down. Set a timer for two minutes. Then continue to read this paper. When the timer goes off, what were you thinking about? Was it what you predicted?

So, dear Reader, whether at this point you are convinced or not, through your own inner exploration of this ancient proposition, let's suspend disbelief a little while longer to explore the implications of our reasoning ... and our experiments above.

Who is Looking?

In looking at the question of your body ... and the question of your feelings ... and the question of thinking ... who was looking and questioning? Who tried the experiments offered above? Who is agreeing or disagreeing with the proposition outlined here?

If I am not actually my body, feelings or thoughts, it would seem that the term "I" would best be applied to the Awareness which is interested in this question, has read the paper up to this point and tried to sincerely engage in the suggested explorations above. In religious, philosophical and spiritual disciplines, this awareness has many names: Observer, Witness, Spirit, The God-Within, the Third Eye, the Soul, "Real I," Son-of-God, Son-of-Man, Higher Consciousness, Higher Mind and others. The word-label is not important. What is important is the quality of the awareness that includes itself as well as the content of sensation, feeling and thinking (here defined as automatic associational trains of words, ideas and images in response to either outer or inner stimulation).

To discover this higher conscious potential, I must be open to the possibility. If I have never heard of it or never noticed it in myself, then the question of possibility does not exist for me. But, if I am curious as to why so many intelligent people over so many thousands of years have talked about, and testified to, the existence of this possibility, then, perhaps I might keep an open-minded attitude and go seeking, within my-self, for this rumored treasure.

What will happen to me if I confirm this statement and claim it as my own? At the very least, it will produce a change of mind. With a changed mind, my world, and my sense of myself in it, will undergo a transformation.

If it is true that I have a body, but I am not my body, that I have feelings, but I am not my feelings, that I have thoughts, but I am not my thoughts … then … my experience of life will become very, very, interesting in ways I could not have anticipated.

What Do I Understand? What Do I Stand Under?

When I give my attention to anything that interests me, that interest will energize me, stimulate me, motivate me into motion. It is as if it has fed me its energy and fused its Will with mine. From an ordinary viewpoint, something is imbued by my interest in it. I place meaning into it even if others do not. From another viewpoint, that something was inherently of interest to me even before I discovered it. It held energy in potential, waiting for me to notice it, feel my attraction with it. We are attracted to each other. We are in a relationship, my interest and me. I need It to energize me and It cannot fulfill Itself without my joining with It, taking It inside myself to add Its energy to my smaller, initial interest.

The attraction of joining myself with something larger than myself allows me to drink from the greater energy of that something more than just myself. We can experience this in everyday life when we turn our attention to anything of great interest to us, whether it be politics, sports, hobbies, my work, certain people. My political causes, my local sports team, my hobbies, my work, my friends take my attention and galvanize me. Because they are aligned with my interests, they attract my attention towards them. Then they absorb my attention, and I am "lost" in my interest. When we say we are "plugged in," we are not just being metaphorical. The energy flows both ways. I become powerful, sometimes even drunk, on the surge of energy pouring into me. But the price is that my attention is absorbed into the greater flow and, unless I am able to keep some attention on myself in the midst of passion, I lose myself in the greater ocean of energy. Depending on the source and quality of that energy, this may be a wonderful or a very terrible surrender.

People become fanatical about politics, sports ... whatever their particular passion may be. In extreme cases, it makes people careless, then violent, even homicidal. It can become the mass psychosis we call War. People become enthused, infused, mentally, emotionally and even physically, when they become connected, even involuntarily, with a source that can command, whether through fascination or fear, their attention. We don't have to like the stimulus, we may even be repulsed, but if it is compelling or if we are compelled to give it our attention, the process of energy transfer occurs in either case. Of all human interests, the most potent is sex, the energy of creation itself, as experienced in my body.

The pornography industry is one of, if not the most profitable industries, generating billions of dollars per year. Even the thought or image of something of interest may animate not only my attention but also my emotions and my body.

What attracts me to something is the *feel*, the actual *experience* of the *energy moving inside* me when in contact with … or even thinking about … what attracts me.

Where does that energy come from? It appears inside me with contact, whether physical or mental. So, the energy must come from the attraction. Attraction itself must be an energy … maybe something psychologically equivalent to gravity. Like attracts like. What resonates at my frequency will set me resonating in synchronicity with it. Its vibrations stimulate me so that I then begin to vibrate. This is energy transfer.

I ask myself, "What type or quality or taste of energy do I want to experience?" Then I take myself, either literally or in imagination, thought, daydream, to where I can feel the energy of attraction. I am feeding like a bee, tasting the nectar of attractive resonance and flying my attention from flower to flower, carrying the pollen of experience, memory, sensation, feeling as I continually search for the stream of attraction to orient me in my search for stimulation. Stimulation is induced by vibration. Vibration is a manifestation of energy. Again, what type of energy do I want to taste, to eat, at the moment? There are many varieties of taste. What type of energetic experience, physically or emotionally or intellectually, do I want at the moment? Which have I found attractive before? Can I have a choice in what quality of energy I am eating? If I follow my interests, is that the same as feeding myself vibrations of the correct quality for me? Which me? As there are different levels of me, each level may have its own preferred taste in energies. Which of my levels do I want to be feeding? Can I have a choice?

What is my understanding at this moment? What knowledge or experiences or theories or principles do I stand under? Whatever I stand under, or stand for, is larger than myself. Therefore, in connecting myself with what attracts me, I will carry much more energy, energy to excite, energize, stimulate people … perhaps very many people … into manifesting what the energy is directed towards. From this perspective, we are being used by the energy of attraction to manifest Itself out into the world through some combinations of our idiosyncratic ways of manifesting from our inner world … talking, writing, painting, moving …

The greater energy which then moves through me gives a momentary capacity for expression or enjoyment or creativity that I would not be experiencing without having connected my attraction to its Source. Then, for as long as the connection lasts, we are joined. It can flow through me because I have aligned my interest with Its interests and I can join my little will, my limited capacity for consciousness and creativity with the larger reservoir of this something greater than myself. Then, briefly, in a way, as I join It, It is joining me, and we become One. I am infinitesimally tiny ... and It is infinitely large, I have very, very, little energy compared with Its endless universal capacity ... and yet ... somehow ... we are the same Something.

What I stand under represents my Understanding. My Understanding is the source of an energy greater than my own. An understanding is an idea that has ripened through actual practical experience. The original thought is now infused with confirming experience. Within me, it is now more than it was the moment I first saw it in my mind. Experience has brought me into contact with my feelings and body. It has grown down into me, from my head to my heart and into my body. The idea now fills me and has transformed into understanding. I now truly stand under the understanding, bathed in its light and able to embody manifestations resonant with Its level of energy.

Ideas are seeds, carriers of information seeking fertile soil in the minds and feelings of humans. The seeds need good soil. The soil is fallow without the seeds. This is not only an energy transfer; it is an information transfer from a level above to a level below. Perhaps, like rain, like cosmic waves, always flowing, falling upon, whatever it encounters, whether fertile or not.

If a new idea enters my head, where did it come from? Who had to think it first to then transfer it to me? But ... how would it have gotten into the other mind to begin with before it was transferred to me? Or ... maybe .... the idea pre-exists human minds, waiting to be discovered ... perhaps over and over again.

To stand under an idea such as this would give enormous energy. To actually Understand an idea like this would transform my understanding of myself and of the very nature of existence.

Emotional Transmission

A long-forgotten memory of a strange experience appeared, by association, in conversation with my wife this morning. We were talking about the mystery of how people become emotionally connected, how they can feel inside each other, intuit each other. We wondered about a type of energy that we radiate that can be experienced by others and the quality of which can set the mood for our interchange.

The energy represents a frame of mind ... an attitude. The attitude determines the interpretation we make of the meaning of the situation in front of us. That interpretation is what I accept as "reality" at that moment. I manifest into my surroundings based on my belief in that reality. Then, the other person experiences the flavor of the energy that is coming from me and undergoes the same sequence of internal steps to come to an interpretation of the meaning, but from their perspective ... and then their responsive manifestation appears and begins its influence on me.

At that moment, I recalled a strange experience when I was around 17. I was at a school basketball game with my girlfriend and my best friend and his girl. I was relaxed and enjoying myself. Suddenly, I felt gutted in my solar plexus. A gaping hole had opened up. It was icy cold, pitch black and filled with a deep, hopeless despair. In that moment, I could understand suicide. I was stunned and baffled and afraid. The experience lasted only a short while and was then gone. It has never returned ... thank God. I don't want to ever feel that pit of despondency again. I had had periods of depression off and on in my life, but nothing remotely like this horrific taste.

I related this story to my wife ... and as I was telling her, another event came to mind as if to answer the unspoken question about the initial association. I was a school psychologist in my mid-thirties. The principal asked me to interview a young female student who the teachers had expressed concern about. She was brought into my office and I introduced myself. Suddenly, I felt as if I had been slammed in the chest by a force, followed by a wave of energy I can only describe as hatred. We looked at each other and I knew it was coming from her. I intuitively understood that she had not been told who I was and the reason for the interview. She felt set up and directed a blast of hatred through me. Needless to say, the

interview ended within moments of its beginning. She refused to participate and left.

I had no doubt at the time that it emanated from her. Why was this
memory appearing now? Then, in my mind, it connected with the event
at the basketball game, which I could never find a way of understanding
because I had no experiential context in which to place it. Seeing, now, a
potential connection, outside of time, between these two memories,
opens a possible way of thinking into it. I now wondered if someone adjacent to me in the crowd had been carrying this suicidal feeling inside
themselves and I had inadvertently tasted the emanation from them?

The two events, separated in outside-time by many years, now felt
somehow connected in the world of inner experiences. Wherever they
had been "stored" in my memory library, they were now adjacent to each
other on the same shelf. Time had been "folded', bringing different past
events together and transporting them, into their future … my present. I
had done nothing. This process of mind-changing had occurred on its
own and then showed me a new pattern.

We all know, from our ordinary lives, that moods, ours and others', can
be "infectious." We have phrases acknowledging this phenomenon, such
as, "She is such a downer. His spirits lift everyone around him. They are
truly inspiring. She has such great energy; I always feel better around her.
When I walked into the room, you could cut the tension with a knife".

How does this happen? How is it that we feel "moods"? How do we
"pick up" other peoples' "feelings?"

The experience of what we call "mood shifts" or "mood changes" has
a biochemical basis. Anti-depressants, anti-anxiety medications have
brought relief to millions not possible until recent times. By introducing
certain molecules into our nervous system to influence the balance of
their naturally occurring internal counterparts, we are trying to reprogram
the software that runs our emotional functions. Feelings are not thoughts.
Feelings do have a sensory component in that we experience them, or we
feel the shifts in levels and quality of functions in our body that these
molecules regulate. But feelings have their own world.

Just as thoughts are carriers of information, so too are sensations and
emotions carriers of information. Thoughts carry facts and theories. Sensation brings information about the physical state of the body. Emotions
carry information about … how we feel. But what do we mean by this?
Our body is very sensitive to our thoughts and feelings. But, an experi-

ence is more than an awareness of changes in the body's response to mood shifts. Emotions also carry information ... about my preferences, my attitudes, my attractions and interests, and the "atmosphere" of my heart in a given moment.

Our emotional state is influenced by both our head and our body, but so too are our body and head influenced by emotion. The three functions are mutually interacting parts of a larger whole. Often one or two are in conflict with the other one or two. The state of experiencing balance and agreement between the three is a less frequent occurrence for most of us.

How does our emotional state influence other people? How do we know what another is feeling? Obviously, they can tell us in words. They can also show us through their tone of voice, body posture, quality of touch (or lack of it). Social scientists believe the large majority of our communication is through these non-verbal channels. There are two obvious channels of exchanging this information between people.

First, your eyes and ears can perceive another persons' posture, degree of anger or affection in their voice, recognize their level of muscular tension or the expression on their face. Unconsciously you may pick up something in their scent, pheromones, perhaps, that brings information on a channel hidden from consciousness. Your mechanical associational processes then instantly compare your interpretation of what you believe the other person is feeling, based on your previous experiences with these cues, both in other people as well as the person in front of you. This interpretation in you then stimulates in your body a shift in the balance of emotional hormones based on that interpretation. Now you are feeling something, also in response to the other person. Information has been transferred into your brain and nervous system through these sensory signals. Whether your interpretation is correct or not, and therefore your behavioral response appropriate or not, are different questions. A transfer of hormonal information has occurred, mediated by your senses and previous mentally associated experiences.

Sometimes this process is visible to your inner eye, either at the moment while in process or later on reflection. Often, it occurs out of sight of your awareness. Then, psychologists call it sub-conscious or un-conscious. This process of signal reading, interpretation and biochemical and behavioral response seems independent of our choosing. You may be able to manipulate or hide your outward behavioral manifestation ... if you are aware of your feelings in the moment ... but you don't choose your reactions or easily control them. The fluctuating intensity and quality of feeling states will show themselves through, or emanate from, the body and be picked up by others sensitive to their expression. To the extent the receiving person has similar patterns and is aware of some of them in him/herself, the interpretation of the meaning of these signals may be fairly accurate. We all know that the longer you know someone, the better you can "read" them. When you can't find points of commonality, there is no resonant harmonic, and so your interpretation will likely be off, sometimes disastrously so.

We can see the thread of interaction. For example:

– A thought appears in the mind.

– The emotional implications of the thought produce a reaction in the body.

– The body, believing the accuracy of the thought, responds biologically to the mind's suggestion by rebalancing hormones connected with moods that would match what the mind suggested to the body.

– Now there would be experienced a feeling about what the mind suggested, as well as a physical response.

– As the mood changes, the mind now makes a new interpretation influenced by the alteration in mood ... or ...

– Before the mind even becomes aware of the hormonal shift, the body has noticed and responds with muscular reactions of relaxation or tension.

– Any of these three functions can initiate this interaction.

To the degree my mind is aware of its interaction with emotion and sensation, balanced and reasonably good interpretations can be possible. To the degree my mind is not aware, then these patterns are outside the sphere of my awareness ... and thus, not consciously available ... but nevertheless potent and influencing ... some may say running ... my life.

Implications

But, what of these two unusual experiences I recalled at the beginning of this exploration? I was in eye contact with the young girl who hurled a thunderbolt of hatred into me, but I felt the impact without any initial sense of her physical posture or voice. I was just beginning to look at her as I introduced myself. She never spoke. If my experience of her hatred had been initiated through her non-verbal cues, I would have registered her physicality first and then registered the wave of revulsion. But I felt the collision first. That is what got my attention. Then I looked at her. She had said nothing. As I began to take in her face for the first time, I saw a look of hatred in her eyes. In my recollection, the impact came first, not the outer generated visible signals.

In the other event, there was no awareness of another person. The feeling appeared inside me instantly, lingered and then disappeared. There were no visual cues to begin this process. It was internally generated. As I had never experienced that feeling before and I have never since, it is difficult to rationalize that the feeling came from me. Thinking on that possibility and remembering the feeling of total hopelessness gives me a feeling of why some people would kill themselves rather than live in that pitiless state.

Clues from Science

Recent research has demonstrated that every one of the currently estimated 73 trillion cells in our body generates a small electromagnetic field. Each of those 73 trillion EM fields, tiny electrical generating cells, overlap ... and overlap ... and overlap ... until they collectively form an organ. Every organ then generates an electrical field that overlaps with the fields of all the other organs. This coalescence produces an electrical field permeating and surrounding our bodies. The heart's electrical field is reported to be more than 100 times greater in strength than that generated by the brain ... and extends three to five feet from our body. Interestingly, most people report that their sense of "personal space" with strangers extends about three feet around them and decreases as comfort level with the other person increases. The image that appears here is that, like cells and organs, every human body radiates around itself, in a three-to-five-foot diameter, an electric magnetic field. This field carries information about worlds inside a person's body and mind.

Since the molecules of our emotional life are also generators of electrical fields, their information will be included in the blended fields and their vibrations will set up a resonant response in the other person. It seems reasonable to assume that the EM field of each body overlaps with the fields of every other body that comes within three feet of it. Then the fields would blend, and information would become mixed together. That shared information from the other person then may influence your mood

… and vice versa.

Intercourse and Energy Transformation

There is a greater importance to conversation than sharing of information and opinions. In doing so, we are literally sharing the invisible inner world of our thoughts and feeling with others. It is interesting that conversational exchange is also called "intercourse," recognizing the commonality of penetration, release of information and the conception of something new that can grow and develop a life of its own. Whether a new biological life or a new idea or a new attitude and perspective, all information/energy exchange is a creative process.

Through the resonance of our words and stories, we stimulate responding words and stories from our companions. The vibrations from these resonances represent electrical stimulation of the neurons in our brain. We are sharing electrical energy with each other when we interact. If you are not physically present, I can interact with the imprint you have left in my memory, but then the only new input comes from my interaction with your image, so it is a form of self-stimulation. If we are physically together, our fields can interpenetrate as well. When together, we each contribute new input with each new impression we create within each other. We are sharing a meal and each of us is food for the other.

Under the best circumstances, that food is nutritious for both. Often, one may experience indigestion. If what is being shared comes from the darkest regions of human feeling, the meal will be poison, if not fatal.

We live in an ocean of continuous vibration over an enormous scale of potential. Like all wave phenomena, in places they coincide and increase energy by pooling their coherent energy. In other places they clash and create chaotic patterns that eventually resettle into new forms. In yet other places, they cancel out.

If we can develop the ability to monitor the interactions between our thoughts, bodies and emotional responses, we have the possibility of moving towards a personal inner harmony. This internal stability and awareness can then absorb and re-regulate the emotional energy coming to us from others so that we are energized if it is coherent with our own and we are not dis-harmonized ourselves if it is not.

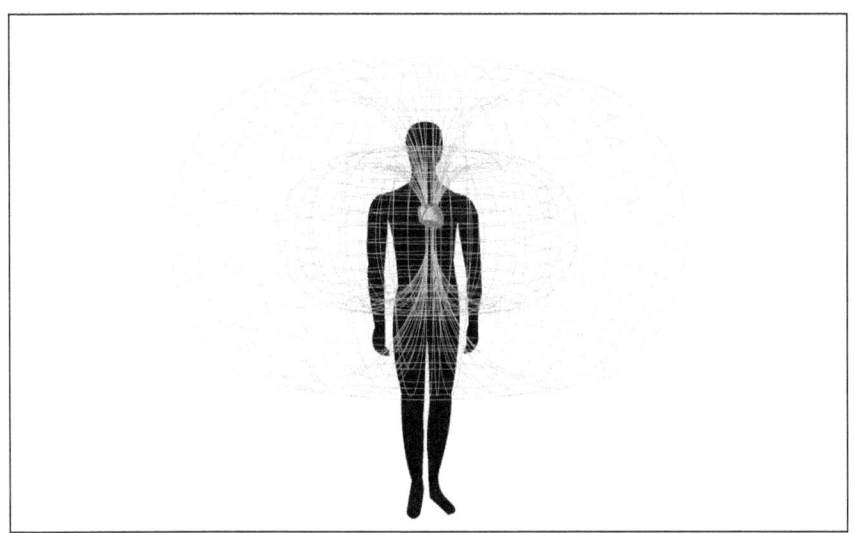

Figure 5. The Electromagnetic Field of the Heart*

---

* The illustration is based on the image from *https://en.wikipedia.org/wiki/ Magnetocardiography.*

Unnecessary Suffering

There is so much suffering in the world. When I allow myself to think about it, I feel a pain around my heart. I recall the saying attributed to the Buddha on his Awakening, "Behold, the world is monstrous suffering ... and ... it is also Nirvana." It is this dual possibility that is the most heartbreaking.

As a human being, I have experienced a normal share of suffering, physical, emotional and mental, during my life. I recognize now that although some was inevitable ... some was not.

I realize that, even with caution, I have suffered before, and will suffer again, pain in my body, illness, fatigue ... along with periods of health, energy and comfort. I have been fortunate that the latter have predominated, but I know the taste of the other side of the continually fluctuating flow of "seasons for everything under heaven."

As I get older, I feel my body slower, less pliable. My doctors tell me that a couple of my essential body parts are beginning to fray. It is only a matter of time that the inevitable other side comes around once more. I can prepare my body for some of the oncoming stress with exercise, good nutrition, minimal self-induced or environmental pressure... to the extent I can avoid the latter ... but in the long run, I am elongating what I have, not changing its eventual fate. I can improve the quality of what I have but not alter the inevitable.

Since my body has a life of its own, which neither needs nor takes much direction from me, I am mostly along for the ride. I can accept the responsibility for overseeing good maintenance on my body, but it has its own programming and sense of direction that I am not privy to. I get to sense and feel what it senses and feels because I live inside of it. This elemental, sensory suffering is a component of life. All life, to a degree, is sensitive to its surroundings in order to survive, to know in which direction lies safety and in which lies danger. We cannot avoid experiencing sensations in our physical body.

Periods of unpleasant sensation from an ill or injured body are inevitable according to the laws of Nature. So too are challenges to my emotional and intellectual comfort. How I learn to endure unpleasant experiences is the domain of unnecessary suffering. The key variable is my attitude, the mental and emotional perspective I bring to interpreting the meaning of my experience.

Self-Imposed Suffering … Personal Examples

When I was in high school, I felt self-conscious and shy around girls I was attracted to. I was also very near-sighted. As I did not like the way I looked in glasses, I only wore them while in the classroom. During breaks and changing classes, I would remove them. I used to joke with myself that the only way I knew approximately where I was in the school complex was due to the walls being color-coded. Otherwise, everything was blurry. At the end of my senior year, I learned to my disbelief that several of the girls I had been attracted to had also been interested in me and had spent a long time trying to get my attention. They eventually gave up, deciding that I must not be interested in them! As I pondered this unbelievable … and, in hindsight, tragic information … I realized that of course I didn't notice. I could not see the expressions on their faces because I had removed my glasses for all school events other than classroom time! But then I also realized that even if I could have seen, one of three results would have followed.

One: I would not have noticed their attention because I was too em-barrassed to let them see mine and risk their shaming me for it, so I would have avoided direct eye-to-eye contact.

Two: if I had seen them being flirtatious towards me, I would have assumed it was someone behind me who had their attention, and I would risk embarrassment if I showed that I had assumed I was the object of their interest.

Three: if there were no one else behind me, I would have believed they were just being polite and would not have risked assuming anything deeper.

As a result, I suffered from my misunderstanding, my misassumption about both myself and them. This was during a period of depression, loneliness and self-abnegation that, viewed with hindsight from a more accepting sense of myself, was not necessary. It was the result of a mind-frame that rendered me unable to make a different interpretation. That unhappy interpretation felt like reality. In fact, it was the reality of that particular mind-frame and it determined which alternate actual reality would occur, that is the girls and I never connected with each other in the way each was interested when with a different attitude, another entirely different reality would today be part of my life story ... and, by implication, theirs as well.

Now, many years and many experiences later, I live within a different perspective, and so I live in a different reality. In this current reality, the suffering that accompanied that insecure, youthful mind-frame does not exist.

Several years ago, when I lost my wife to cancer after a three-year struggle with the disease, I suffered more deeply because I castigated myself for not having recognized the significance of a request she made of me, a short while before she died, and which I did not act upon at that moment. I did not realize that it could be her last request. As time passed, I came to understand how my pain and denial of what was happening right in front of my eyes had blinded me to the reality of the situation. It has taken a long time to begin to forgive myself for missing the signs. Losing her was an inevitable suffering. Helplessly watching her pain was an inevitable suffering, but the suffering I experienced from blaming myself was not inevitable. It was the result of my mindset at that time.

I blamed myself for not emotionally understanding, for unconsciously avoiding the reality in front of me, in order to dull my pain, although in hindsight, this is understandable and all too common for surviving spouses and family. Today, I still carry sadness but less self-blame.

Shifting Perspective

As a psychotherapist, a primary object of my work was to help my clients find a different mind-frame. I am not suggesting that rose-colored glasses are the recommended state. I am suggesting that there are different ways of "looking" at situations, different frames of mind with which to extract a sense of meaning and direction from a situation.

Some suffering is unavoidable and out of our control ... illness, death, loss, injury, accident, random-poor-luck. This is part of the experience of being alive. Time flows always. Life relentlessly moves on, carrying me with it, through good times and not so good times. As I am part of the tempo of life, I am also carried by the rhythm.

But there is more to me than my physical body. Brains are programmed to search for meaning, to try to connect the dots so that I can understand the larger picture and be better able to predict the future. This ability to learn from the past to plan for a projected future is an amazing gift, but with a potentially fatal weakness. In its programmed drive to connect the dots, it will find dots to connect regardless of whether those connections are, in actuality, valid or not. Once the connected dots form a discernible image, my mind accepts that image as ultimate reality, believes it is the truth and acts on it. This is a primary reason human interchanges are often filled with conspiracy theories, hurt and offended feelings and misunderstandings ... all of which typically are blamed on the other person. Rarely do we look at ourselves as contributors or initiators of the reactions confronting us.

Suffering from Learned Beliefs

One of the predominant types of sufferings I encountered in my therapy practice was a person's belief that there was something fundamentally wrong with them, their fear that they would never be able to be "good enough," the exhaustion this caused them and the problems this assumption created in their relationships. Where does such a belief come from? We are not born with it. Our genes don't program for specific beliefs.

We learn these beliefs about ourselves when very young. Sometimes, they are implanted in us by actual cruel words said, or cruel acts done to us by others which we have taken in and accepted as true indicators of who we are. More subtly, there may be deeds done or not done, that seem to imply a message about underlying motivations of others towards me. And there are also words with which we may learn to accuse ourselves, sometimes with little or no outside help. Believing cruel inner voices is painful.

It causes suffering, mental and emotional, from ruminating, worrying, reviewing rejections and reliving painful events or personal failures or imagining angry confrontations in my daydreams or unpleasant fantasies about the future. My belief in these derogatory messages about myself causes suffering in my body from the stimulation of stress hormones and muscle tension ... and, perhaps, injury due to distraction caused by the chaos in my head and heart ... or I may unconsciously act out in a way that injures or endangers me. Often people will become trapped or addicted to self-destructive patterns, which become a form of self-punishment and confirmation for their negative self-assessment.

Suffering and Meaning

The suffering experienced from the effects of painful memories, trauma, lost longings or inner self-criticism is real. My mind, my emotions and my body do suffer. But the origin of this type of suffering often comes from how my mind has connected the dots, and even which set of dots it is using, in its attempt to find the storyline, the explanation, the reason for what is happening and why.

But it is not just my intellect that is involved in creating and maintaining either a positive or a negative mindset. It is also the memories stored in my body.

Much of the "learning" trained into my body occurred without my awareness or permission. My body is filled with conditioned reactions to different stimulation and situations depending on what made an impact on me, mostly when I was young and developing my preliminary mindset, but also any time life presents a trauma, my central nervous system may realign itself. Situations associated with very pleasant or happy times will stimulate my parasympathetic nervous system and release hormones that are experienced as pleasurable and relaxing. They will also cause me to seek out those situations again.

Situations associated with very unpleasant or unhappy times will stimulate my sympathetic nervous system and release a variety of stress hormones that alter my body, feelings and thoughts. Typically, this will condition me to try to defend against and avoid any remotely similar situations …. but not always. For other reasons, I may actually intentionally, or unconsciously, continue to replicate situations reminiscent of the trauma in an effort to finally learn how to "get it right" or because this is what I am used to, what my nervous system believes life is supposed to feel like. I may even believe that it is what I "deserve." This is how our personalities, attitudes, strategies and defenses, form.

Voluntary Suffering

Sometimes, we submit ourselves intentionally to a form of suffering in order to achieve something we value or feel we must try, perhaps without a guarantee of success, such as volunteering for the challenges of physical sport or adventure, or taking risks in relationships, or stretching our mind, or accepting the discipline of the armed forces or of a highly structured workplace.

This type of "suffering," dedicating oneself to achieve something only available through long, hard effort, is voluntary, and we accept it as the price to be paid for the outcome we hope will ensue from the effort. Yet, why should we experience, as "suffering," something we have chosen as the necessary path to a goal? It may stress me, exhaust me, stretch me ... and that may all be uncomfortable and even physically painful ... but why would I think of this as suffering? But ... I would not consider it as suffering ... unless I *thought* of it as suffering! As Shakespeare observed, "There is nothing either good or bad, but thinking makes it so."

"To Suffer"

The Latin root for suffering comes from *"sub-,"* meaning "below," and *"ferre,"* "bear." Suffering is something pressing you down that you have to submit to and bear, carry.

I recall a social psychology study from many years ago which concluded that ethnic groups differed in their reported experience of pain depending on how they understood the meaning of their pain, emotional or physical. One group might see suffering as a test from God that must be endured in order to mature. Another group might see suffering as punishment for things done or undone. Some groups are more stoic, some more melodramatic. One group reported less distress when they understood the reason for their suffering compared to when they did not understand.

Everyone experiences illness or injury at one time or another. Everyone eventually loses someone important to them to death. How we think about these events, what sense we make of them, whether our conscience is guilty or not .... and many other factors ... will influence the degree of additional suffering we will experience on top of the normal grieving process.

Resilience

One of the mysteries encountered in the practice of psychotherapy is the phenomenon called "resilience." I have worked with people who experienced unbelievable levels of trauma in their childhood, yet some of them continued to struggle to free themselves from their emotional scars while others collapsed from the pain and remained trapped in their conditioned patterns. The level of trauma is not a clear indication of which group a person will fall into. Some people with objectively less exposure to trauma may lack the resilience displayed by some with much grosser injuries.

Part of the reason relates to attitude, to how a person thinks about themselves and what happened to them. Negative self-attitudes, looking for scapegoats, anger over unfairness, worries about a future yet to reveal itself or regrets over a past that cannot be re-done, are all bad habits mostly taught and modeled for us by others. This additional layer of blame, regret and continual replaying in one's mind of painful pasts and frightening futures adds an additional, unnatural and unnecessary level of suffering.

Someone once confessed to me, "Dr. Aronson. I finally see what I am doing. I am imagining all the dreadful possibilities that might happen so that I can protect myself by planning for them … just in case they happen. I line them all up on the mantlepiece in my mind and try to decide which, of all these awful possibilities, if it did occur, would be the worst so that I can start my planning with that one. Then I take it off the shelf and put it in front of me and dwell on it. I realize now that I am "borrowing my woe" from a future that doesn't exist now and probably won't in the future because I have to admit that the future never is exactly what I predicted and often totally different from what I anticipated."

Another client put it a bit differently. She wasn't so much anxious as she was angry. One day she said to me, "I just realized that what I am doing is like drinking a cupful of resentment every day to keep me strong when it is actually a poison that is making me sick."

It is this interpretational psychological level, imposed over natural grieving and sadness, that is unnecessary and destructive. It also seems to me to account for a majority of human suffering. Most humans who are suffering will withdraw in their pain, and in the process may abandon those who need their attention and affection, thus recreating in those left outside their defensive circle, the sense of inadequacy and emptiness that the sufferers, themselves, are trying to avoid by withdrawing in the first place.

Others, in their pain, will lash out, creating difficulties for those around them who then, in their turn, suffer as a result of how the first person is handling their suffering. We are all interconnected. If you pull on one piece of the psychological-social fabric, other parts are affected and will pull on yet others in their reactions to the discomfort initially caused by the person who is manifesting their suffering in a way that affects others.

Unavoidable Suffering

The most tragic and difficult situations to heal are those caused by trauma provoked by others, such as violence, rape, sexual abuse, the loss of a loved one, a broken family, the bizarreness and unpredictability of drug-addicted or psychotic or sociopathic caretakers, or simply someone's carelessness. And, of course, the worst of humanity's psychological perversities, war. These are all very bitter pills to swallow. They often require grief or trauma counseling to heal.

Nevertheless, part of the suffering which must be addressed, beyond the necessary grieving, is this additional layer of psychological interpretation which can manifest as understandable hatred of those I hold responsible for my suffering or, often, guilt, shame, survivor's guilt, a sense of responsibility for what was not my responsibility ... and self-hatred if I believe I am the cause of the abuse or neglect manifested towards me by others. Often victims are blamed for the hurt done to them by others, thus exponentially adding to their pain. It is this self-blame that is typically taken on by the child who blames him/herself for what they suffered at the hands of others.

For those who suffer silently or only hurt themselves, this is often a private tragedy, perhaps shared only by close friends or family. ... if they are aware. Those who turn their suffering into anger and blame can affect many, many people. History provides endless extreme examples of mass murder, terrorism, political leaders starting wars and revolutions, which result in untold suffering and death for millions.

Fortunately, the majority of people are spared these society-wide horrendous experiences by a mixture of geographic location and luck ... and yet, there is widespread unhappiness even among those groups and individuals who have escaped the effects of wars and catastrophes in their lives. How can we understand this?

What causes the most unnecessary suffering for most of us, most of the time, are the interpretations that we make about our suffering. So, most of the traumatic acting out in the world of humans is not directly caused by the unavoidable suffering that comes through no fault of our own, which, like Job of the Old Testament story, we must periodically endure, but rather, it is our interpretations of the *meaning* of our suffering that add to our personal pain and may subsequently lead to collateral damage if we act out our pain on those around us, thus adding to the suffering of others as well as our selves.

Another puzzling phenomenon encountered in the therapy office is the resilience of painful interpretations and "stories of myself" that people cling to despite the harm these thought-forms and attitudes are doing to them and those around them. In a way, the last thing we seem unwilling to let go of is our story of who and what we believe we are, especially the suffering we have endured.

A need to understand who we are and to find a meaning for our lives seems to be built into many of us. When we are children, adults tell us who we are or who they believe we are, or should be, both directly and indirectly. We are raised in the story of our family, or our group or our nationality, or our ethnic origins, and the historical resentments and achievements, accumulated by the group over time. Some communities have oral and written history going back hundreds or even thousands of years and expect each new generation to honor that history as if they themselves had actually lived it.

We are asked to accept the story of others as our own. How we then interpret the meaning about ourselves from our own subjective experiences with peers, teachers, coaches, strangers and things that happen to us is often interpreted through the lens of the group history and combines to produce my story of me. Whether I like the story or not, whether it reflects well on me or not, is irrelevant. It is my belief in the reality of who I am, told to me by others and then confirmed through my self-reinforcing idiosyncratic interpretations of what I, myself, actually experience in life. How can I argue with "reality"?

This is a source of unnecessary suffering for humankind. It only seems inevitable due to insufficient awareness of the process I am trapped within, and which, if not understood, condemns me to endless repetition.

When crimes are committed, police search for the motivation, the belief system of the perpetrator. Was the suspect paranoid? Did they have motivating political beliefs? Had they felt abused by those they attacked? Was it a crime of passion? Were they hungry and desperate? Did they act carelessly but without intention?

When wars happen, historians and analysts ask, "Why did country X attack country Y? Was it over food, land, resources? But countries don't attack other countries. The leaders of countries mobilize their people into agreeing to attack, or forcing them to attack, the people of another country. People make these decisions for other people, sometimes over a personal sense of insult of the ruling class against the other ruling class. Was it due to misunderstanding each other's motives or was it due to outright greed of the power-possessing leaders?"

Hidden psychological attitudes are important because each suggests a different type of response and potential resolution. All events have as the source of their inception the belief systems, the mindsets, the attitudes of those who inflict their manifestations onto others, often many others, who have nothing to do with the pain or distortions in the inner world of the perpetrators. Often, this aggression or coercion of others is justified by the perpetrators as being for "their own good".

All manifested behavior is the result of internal psychological processes in the actors of the drama, the kind, helpful, even angelic, along with the uncaring, cruel and even evil. People generally don't act out in negative ways unless they themselves are filled with a sense of dissatisfaction with themselves or their lives. If one is not the type to naturally look inward, rather than looking for the source of their pain in themselves, in their history, in their unconscious defense mechanisms, then one will project personal distress outward and initiate conflict with others whom they blame for their own inner dissatisfaction.

It is rare in life to have the good fortune of totally avoiding contact with sociopathic, narcissistic, paranoid, and sadistic personalities. Assuming most people will play by our rules, we often don't recognize what we are up against with these types of people and are thus left defenseless for lack of understanding. With the exception of the sociopath, who appears deficient in the production of stress hormones and thus may not feel fear as ordinary people do, the other distorted personalities do experience suffering of a sort from their own perspective.

Avoidable Suffering : Indifference of Others

I am recalling now a story told to me many years ago by my mentor. He presented a situation then current in the news. There was an African country experiencing famine. The world had responded by sending food and supplies which had been sitting on the docks waiting to be loaded onto vehicles that would drive them into the country's interior to feed the starving people. But this was not happening. The food sat spoiling on the docks. There were no trucks to transport it. "Why is this so?" was the question asked. We came up with many variations on logistical problems of transporting the life-saving parcels. Finally, we recognized that the reason for lack of delivery to those in need was not a logistical issue. The fact was that the local government did not care. It was not in their interest to feed this group of people.

The resulting unnecessary suffering was due to an attitude and political calculation, not to lack of vehicles. The suffering this caused to those left helpless was immense. Perhaps some of them harbored understandable resentment. Their resentment, although natural, was an added layer of suffering which may, in time, breed a group of people bent on revenge ... and so, the cycle continues. Each act of revenge leads to the rationale for more retaliation which leads to more revenge which leads to more retaliation for the revenge attacks.

Imagine what our world would be like if all children were raised with love, acceptance and kindness. Most of them would, in turn, be able to do the same for the next generation because they did not, themselves, carry unresolved pain which would be projected onto others. What would male-female relationships be like if no man abused a woman or vice versa? What would the world be like if members of groups stopped blaming members of other groups for the outrages done by long-deceased members of either group on each other in the distant past? What would the world be like if people with different opinions or goals did not personalize those differences and make enemies of those who held different viewpoints, but rather looked at the differences as just that ... differences in opinion. How or if those differences could be resolved for the greater good would be secondary to neither side demonizing the other. What keeps us from living in this type of world?

Who is Responsible?

The ultimate tragedy is that, in a way, it really is nobody's fault. It all just happens because the majority of people are unaware that their sense of themselves has been programmed through the stories told to them by others ... and also by idiosyncratic interpretations invented by them, themselves. Our world is the way it is due to the collective consequence of all the distorted inner worlds, all the inner psychologies mechanically conditioned by the interpretation of the meaning of all the events that have happened to us and all others remotely associated with us ... and even stories of people in places far away whom I will never personally know.

The solution lies with each individual person to be curious enough to suspect that a large portion of their suffering is internally driven and fortunate enough to find someone or some therapeutic or spiritual system to show them how to escape from their unconscious programming. If we all changed our minds, our world would change.

Here is an inner soliloquy demonstrating a moment of real-life inner exploration.

I know I have to repair my broken heart. Do I need grief counseling? I feel like I am in mourning. How do I put my sadness down and stop carrying it with me everywhere? Am I carrying others' grief and confusing it with my own? Maybe not all this sadness is mine. I'm beginning to believe that a percentage of this suffering I harbor did not originate with me; it is, in some strange way, within me but not mine.

What of this suffering do I feel belongs to me? If I can admit to it, it is the pain of a little child; actually, a young part of me, unseen and scared and alone and then hurt, abandoned and finally angry.

What is alienated inside me? The little child who's never good enough? "If only," I keep telling the child buried inside of me, "If only you were different.

If only I had called John, been smarter, been more hardworking, been more like Ellen ... been kinder ... or less judgmental ... or ... or ... or .. or or ... ."

I can see that I sometimes project my self-feelings onto others. I make judgments about faults in them and then react to those assumed faults. But, when I am really sincere with myself, I have to admit that I am most irritated by my perception of faults in others of which I, myself, am often guilty. I can see that what I criticize in myself, I also sometimes do to others. I sometimes wonder if I am sensitive to characteristics of others that remind me of what I don't like about myself. Is it possible that what I do to myself inside, I do to those around me? Is that what is happening when others offend me? Are they projecting their inner world onto me?

I seem addicted to a world of either-or, right or wrong, perfect or imperfect. Part of me has no tolerance for my being anything other than "perfect" and "in the right." I know that this form of rigid thinking is a strangling type of poison. It is bile. I wonder ... instead of continuing to criticize myself ... and through projection, others... could I find a way to transform this bile so that it no longer makes me sick? Can I change the way I think about myself and my suffering or will l remain stuck on this attitudinal plateau forever? Is this what will heal my heart so that I can accept, maybe even love, myself ... specifically the sad little child I've carried with me since my youth?

But ... I am not perfect, have never been perfect and it looks like I will never be perfect. There are situations in my background that were very painful. I did feel unloved and unwanted and inadequate. I must have assumed that if I could become perfect, then I would be lovable, wanted and adequate. Was I actually, in fact, unloved, unwanted, inadequate ... or did it feel that way to my child's understanding?

If I was, in actuality, unloved and unwanted, was that my fault as an innocent child or was it an inadequacy in the emotional world of my caretakers?

Those who raised me were also once children. Did they feel unloved or unwanted or inadequate, were they abused as children? Did that leave them feeling inadequate as adults ... as parents or guardians? Did their parents, my grandparents, feel inadequate as children? Did they inadvertently pass that on to my parents, who passed it on to me ... ? There are apparently different ways of viewing this situation and they lead to very different ways of feeling about myself and what happened. Which is true? Can, in some way, both be true?

But now, I notice that the thought of a different way of looking at my suffering also brings resistance. If there is a choice between suffering and not suffering, why would any part of me hesitate?

What wants to keep my heart in pain also seems terrified to let go. Is it the sad, frightened, hurt, angry little child inside me? As I listen to it, I learn the following:

– *It has dedicated its life to figuring out what was wrong with itself. It cannot imagine letting go of its life-long quest because it believes that, if it does, there will never be any hope of escape from the pain.*

– *If it should let go, I would have to grieve the years wasted chasing a mirage. That would mean that even my search for salvation was inadequate ... thereby confirming the initial, disabling interpretation.*

– *If the alternative is considered from a higher perspective—that my pain is the inevitable result of my childhood interpretations of the meaning of my responsibility for painful experiences inflicted on me from my environment—if it is in fact, just emotional and mental bile, the release from pain could be instantaneous, provided I chose to believe this aspect of my suffering was due to a misinterpretation made when I was very young.*

– *The young part of me has also been afraid to let go because it believes that the only way to get free is by effort. If the type of effort I have made all my life to be perfect enough wasn't necessary, then I will assume I have "failed" ... yet another misinterpretation.*

It seems that, actually, if I have been carrying this type of pain, the only way to get free of my self-negativity, or resentment, or anger ... is to let it go. If I am carrying something very heavy or very hot, all I have to do is open my hand and it falls and I am free of it. In this way, the attainment of freedom from the suffering could be instantaneous.

Actually ... now that I am thinking about this ... I have not been immersed in my suffering every moment of my life. There have been many times when I was distracted from it or in another frame of mind or a different mood and ... the pain wasn't there at those times. Maybe, I feel the pain when I am reminded of it, when I remember it. Obviously, I will be reminded from time to time, but maybe when that happens ... if I think about it not as a personal failure, but just something unfortunate that happened ... it still feels sad, maybe very, very sad but I don't feel inadequate or unloved or imperfect, if I can see that it was something that just happened and not something I intentionally, deliberately made happen.

From one viewpoint, of course, I am imperfect. From another, higher viewpoint, my inherent imperfections are irrelevant because nothing is perfect.

If there is a higher perspective that releases me from some degree of pain and a lower viewpoint that adds to or locks me in pain ... what is keeping me in the "basement" of myself?

I need to heal my heart and alter my assumptions by changing my perspective on the inner "program" that was conditioned into me in childhood.

Self-Assessment

How about you, dear Reader? Can you separate the inevitable suffering that is out of your control, which life periodically brings to your doorstep, from the additional suffering you pile on top with your interpretation of the meaning of why this is happening to "you ... of all people!" ... as if it doesn't happen to others as well?

What is it that prevents us from seeing this distinction? In a paralyzing but understandable way, we often prefer the sense of security of the suffering we already know rather than risk the possibility of the suffering we don't know, even though a different interpretation of meaning could ultimately bring the freedom of relief from pain. It requires a leap of faith and the courage to take that leap to look again from a different perspective.

This blindness to other interpretations is the primary reason why the last thing most people will give up is their suffering … and that is the most painful tragedy of all. Looked at one way, we do not need to add to our suffering, but from another perspective, we have no choice because we cannot see through our limited, self-oriented view of reality. In this way, much of the world's suffering could instantaneously disappear …but it won't.

Yet it can disappear for individuals, if not the majority. It can disappear if I can separate the wheat from the chaff, the mis-assessments made by my imaging additional, unnecessary layers of self-assigned suffering from the real inevitable suffering that awakens me to the mystery and vulnerability of life, diminishes my egoism and quickens my appreciation for those I love. As an individual, my suffering could disappear … or at least be reduced … if I let it go. Will I? Do I want to? What is keeping me from letting go?

In a larger sense, if "suffering," whether emotional, intellectual, physical or spiritual, is the subjective experience of tension between what I wish and the reality of what actually seems to be, then, unless I am satisfied with what the moment brings, there will always be a discrepancy. It is also clear that what we mean by "to suffer" is relative.

Remorse

The suffering I feel, if I do feel this quality of suffering, between my ideals for myself and the reality of my daily level of manifesting, can be a productive tension, a source of helpful energy … if I know how to appropriately use it. Ordinarily, it is wasted in shame or guilt, shame that I have "let others down" or guilt that I "let myself down" and am, therefore, inadequate, lesser or bad. These are socially trained attitudes that judge me based on the standards of others (shame in front of them who are judging me) or based on those standards that I have applied to myself as signs of my "goodness" or "worth" (guilt) and I become judge and jury of my worthiness or I accept the judgment of others. Both are related to my relationship with my community, so its roots are outside me.

Remorse is a different state. It is the state of seeing that I have fallen short of standards I have established for myself, separate from, and sometimes different from, those set by family and friends ... but as a regrettable fact that energizes me to try again .... and again ... and again ... as I work towards my own inner gold standard. Remorse, the taste of the Truth, is itself, the punishment ... a slap on the face, a word in my ear, a sinking feeling in my stomach. The Truth does not require shame or guilt. It requires acceptance of fact and acceptance of responsibility to continue on the straight path of my inner aim. Whether I ever, permanently, attain that state is not central. What is essential is that I use this inner aim as a guiding star to help me lead my life in a way I deem responsible. The taste of "missing the mark", as in archery (the original meaning of the Greek verb "to sin"), although often bitter, should be recognized, and gratefully accepted, as a warning indicator that I momentarily fell "asleep" and lost the path, and it encourages me to try again. It becomes a motivating reminder, not the self-imposed punishment of shame or the societally-accepted punishment of feeling guilty.

Remorse is the voice of true Conscience. It requires courage and tolerance of a special type of pain. It is an objective reminder of a truth. It does not seek to hurt through guilt or shame. It shows us our location in relation to that truth. When understood in that way and accepted as a guide, it has the potential to mature and transform me into a quality of being that is my birthright.

In addition to self-inflicted suffering, there is physical suffering, emotional suffering, intellectual suffering. There is spiritual suffering. There is voluntary and involuntary suffering. There is willing suffering for a higher aim and suffering imposed upon me by outside circumstances.

Suffering and Identification

Whether I define my experience as suffering or something else also depends on whether I identify the whole of myself with the discomfort or pain. Changing the definition can subjectively alter the quality of the suffering. The reality is that if I hurt my leg, or someone hurts my feelings, the experience will be different depending on whether I believe that I, all of me, is suffering or whether I recognize that only my leg hurts, or I am aware of sad or angry feelings in my chest ... but I do not need to conflate myself with my leg or my feelings of the moment. When I identify myself with anything, whatever the power imbedded in that something, it will energize my sense of self so that my sense of self merges with it. Then, subjectively, I am the pain; I am the hurt feeling. I have lost track of the rest of me. Without the perspective of seeing the discomfort as *part* of my experience, when I identify myself with it, I develop tunnel vision and all that I am aware of is the part of me that is suffering. Then the experience is very much more intense.

Life is always in motion. Time continuously flows. For everything, there is a season. The inevitability of impermanence can be a form of suffering. But suffering is also idiosyncratic and definitional. If I dedicate myself to a life of service to something greater than myself, then suffering "for the greater good" is yet another category.

In the end, whether I feel I am suffering or not is, in part, a subjective interpretation of the meaning of my relationship to what I must endure at the moment because that is the reality in front of me.

If we all changed our minds, our world would change.

Perils of Perfectionism

W hat is wrong with striving for perfection? Aren't we encouraged to strive to do our best, to always improve, to learn from our mistakes, to try not to commit the same errors a second time?

The Problem

As a psychotherapist, I recognized that one of the frequent sources of stress, anxiety, sometimes depression and a tendency to find faults in oneself and others was a felt requirement to be "perfect." The inability to achieve this unblemished state was an underlying source of self-recrimination for many. The fruitless striving to meet this standard often resulted in anxiety and self-reproach. The quest is a double-edged sword, both a blessing and a curse.

Two Sources: The Curse

The primary, outer-directed source of a drive for perfection seems to have its roots in the dynamics of personal relationships. Somehow, during the developmental years, the idea of "perfect" became associated with feeling accepted by others. Often, a child, when listening to adults trying to instill a sense of striving and responsibility for hard work, interprets these admonitions as a stipulation that "success," as defined by the adults, is synonymous with being respected or loved. The striving for perfection then becomes a defense mechanism to ward off criticism and gain acceptance. Children rarely voice their interpretations, primarily because they don't realize they are interpreting but rather believe their feelings and thoughts to accurately represent reality. As a result, adults may be unaware that their well-meaning intentions are being subtly misunderstood.

It may also happen that one or more significant adults in a child's life do make this link intentionally. Parents and teachers often tell children that they are "proud" of them. The wish behind expressing this sentiment is encouragement and pleasure for the child's success.

Some children, however, may ask themselves a related question. "If you are proud of me when I succeed, how do you feel about me when I fail? If this concern is put directly to the adults (which it is typically not), the adult response is usually self-correcting. "We are proud of you whether you succeed or fail. We are proud that you try". Again, some children may then worry about whether they are "trying hard enough." This pressure may be just as harmful as the quest for achievement. How does one prove, to oneself or others, that one has tried *hard enough*? The only proof would be a manifested perfection, thus trapping one in an endless loop.

And some adults believe that the use of negative reinforcement and withdrawal of love and approval is a good motivator for children. This approach is typically a disaster for the inner world of the child. Some adults, insecure and resentful, may actually sabotage their children's efforts at success just as the ancient gods who devoured their own offspring.

It may also happen that the adults influencing the child have unresolved issues of their own with performance related to their own self-worth. They may have been conditioned to this way of thinking by those people who raised and educated them. In this case, they may raise or teach children consciously or unconsciously, with the same set of standards that they brought with them out of their own childhood. They may believe this is the right way to shape a child since it was done to them. They may be unaware of, or not believe in, other approaches. Thus, they parrot the manifestations of their elders from many years ago.

It may also be that an insecure adult, with their own perfectionistic issues, sees the child, not as an individual with a life separate from themselves, but as an extension of themselves by which they fear they, the supervising adult, will be judged by others. After all, "perfect people should be perfect and perfect people raise perfect children." If their child may not be judged perfect by others, that becomes a personalized reflection on themselves. Thus, the child is pressured to perform for the sake of the adult's self-esteem. In this case, the child's interpretation that they are only loved and valued if they live up to the adult's expectations is actually accurate. Such a child may either rebel and deliberately fail to assert their independence or become a defensive perfectionist like the adult they are trying to keep pleased.

If the latter is the outcome, such a child often grows into an adult who, themselves, project their perfectionistic standards onto those around them. "If I am to be perfect, then you should be perfect also, especially if people associate you with me." Then, in my mind, your performance becomes a reflection on me, and I impose my need to be perfect as frequent criticism of others who, in my opinion, are not. This obviously creates tension and unhappiness in relationships, which is itself a sign of imperfection, thus increasing the pressure for myself and others connected to me to look perfect.

If sufficiently conscious of their inner world and capable of a degree of self-honesty, the person striving for perfection typically knows they are not perfect. They then have to lie to themselves or others to pretend that they are. No mistakes or errors are allowable. If insufficiently conscious to recognize their own inconsistencies, they only see imperfection in others. Such people appear as "control freaks," narcissists and hypocrites to those around them.

Two Sources: The Blessing

On the blessing side, the longing for perfection may represent an inherent internal striving to literally be the best I can be ... for myself. This standard does not compare results with others, nor is it contingent on recognition by others. It seems to be a feeling-knowing that I have more potential than I am using or have developed. I may experience a sense of obligation, even if I don't know to whom or to what, to live up to the potential I believe I was born to grow into. This can become a guiding life principle, but one for its own sake, not for recognition, although that may occur from the outside world. In current language, many refer to this as striving for the "personal best."

Where then is the problem with this second source? It is the assumption that the goal is achievable in the way I image it and that my worth, in some way, is dependent on achieving my aim. In a way, internally-directed perfectionists are visionaries. They can see into the dimension of The Perfect, but they mistakenly believe that the Perfect can exist in ordinary life.

What is "Perfect"?

What do I mean by the dimension of The Perfect? Webster's dictionary defines *perfect* as "being entirely without fault. "Ask yourself if you have ever envisioned the perfect day, the perfect moment, the perfect outcome, the perfect relationship, the perfect life? Where do you go to find the image of this ideal? You go to your imagination, the image-making capacity in your mind. Our brains allow us to form pictures and thoughts and to use those pictures and thoughts as guides to our manifestations in the outside world. In this visualized dimension reside all possible idealized* images of what could be, and often of what cannot, in actuality, exist in our material world.

In the realm of ideal images, circumstances are always ideal. They are ideas† in the mind.

In the arena of my mind's eye, everything is represented in its theoretically perfect, ideal form. This is the nature of this dimension. This is the source of inspiration and creativity. The images "seen" here are perfect because there is no wind, no rain, no time. There is no erosion. Nothing can change because it is already fixed in an ideal form.

Bringing these images and ideas into the actual life I am leading encounters difficult problems in translation. Artists are universally frustrated during this process as the world we live in is not perfect. To paint what I see there in the dimension of the ideal or score in music what I hear there, or to construct the perfect relationship or to create the perfect image of myself I imagine there, requires dependence on the natural or trained skill in my body and the tools and material necessary to reproduce the ideal which I have envisioned if it is to take a manifested form.

If it has to do with idealized non-material qualities, that translation is dependent on the development and stability of my Being, my emotional and psychological capacity to express, without deviation, my sense of the ideal. If I am trying to impose my standard on others, they would have to be willing to conform to my vision of their ideal self and then meet the same barriers to consistent manifestation of the ideal.

Resolution

To be an internally-driven perfectionist requires that I find a way to accept the limitations on re-creating, in this world, what I have seen or sensed in the higher world of ideal possibilities. The acceptance of this limitation is usually a long, painful and confusing process to the extent that I feel like a failure (less than perfect) if I continue to believe that I should be able to recreate on Earth what I have seen in the Heaven of the

---

* The dictionary meaning of ideal states, "existing as a mental image or in fancy or imagination conceived as perfect; existing only in idea.

† The word "idea" is a late 14c concept meaning "archetype, concept of a thing in the mind of God ... pure immaterial pattern, of which the individual objects in any one natural class are but the imperfect copies ... a concept of what ought to be differing from what is observed."

Ideal templates.

Ironically, the perfect solution is to accept imperfection as a law governing the level of our life on Earth. Here, things are always in motion. Other people have their own ideal images that they pursue and which are not necessarily mine. Typically, there are many different ways to solve a problem, create a work of art, have a relationship. Which is the perfect? Have you noticed that as you have grown older and have had more experiences, your understanding sometimes changes? To period-ically review how your perspective has altered over the years is an il-luminating exercise.

I encourage you, dear Reader, to explore yourself in this way. You will often find that what seemed perfect in the past may not seem that way now. The Ideal is fixed. Reality is fluid. So, what has changed? Have you changed? Are you the same person now that you were in the past when your understanding was different?

Acceptance of reality as it is, does not mean I need to like it! Ac-ceptance does not mean I cannot try to shift conditions to more approxi-mate my image of what would seem best to me. But I also need to distinguish wishes from possibilities and possibilities from impossibilities. I must find an attitude that allows me to disengage my sense of personal self-respect from my achievements, whether real or wished for.

In a real sense, the part of me that strives for perfection is that very young child who first made this interpretation. It is the young child who first felt the call to be my "best" to achieve something in life. An adult body has grown up around it, but it still remains, struggling in the Sisyphean attempt to achieve the impossible. If that child had someone to correct its misunderstanding, someone who would encourage its searches without linking outcome to the child's worth and love-ability, I would not be suffering from perfectionism today.

That "someone" could be yourself. The past is not dead. It is alive in you right now. You could, in this moment, talk with, reassure this child inside yourself that their wish is noble, but their perspective represents a misunderstanding. You could try to show the child how to separate its sense of self from its achievements.

The contemporary field of psychotherapy and personal development offers very practical models for helping this younger part of me disen-gage from an addiction to perfection. It is perfectly valid to seek relief from stress and have a more balanced personality. However, most of the great spiritual traditions offer disciplines that can take one much deeper than a more balanced personality. They offer freedom from attachment to what you have been conditioned, since childhood, to believe is yourself.

Which direction you may wish to take, if this is a personal issue for you, depends on the depth and direction of your desire; relief from stress or release from an idealized image of your*self*. These practices, whether psychotherapeutic or spiritual, take time and effort, sometimes years of work, depending on how deeply the conditioning is embedded in your neuronal network.

As an immediate exercise and a taste of the possible freedom to come, you could read this essay aloud to the part of you that struggles with the question of perfection. You could imagine this younger you, sitting in front of you … right now. Have a conversation, in your mind, out loud or in writing, with this struggling part. See what happens.

In the process of learning to guide this younger, pressured part of me, I grow towards a more accurate understanding of reality and my place in it. I can also then become more compassionate and forgiving, not only towards my child but to the "children" inside all those other adults around me.

To Forgive Myself and Others

E ckhart Tolle writes, in the introduction to *The Power of Now*, of his transformative moment when he realized, in the depths of depression that: "I cannot live with myself any longer."

And he then reflected, "This was the thought that kept repeating itself in my mind. Then suddenly, I became aware of what a peculiar thought it was. Am I one or two? If I cannot live with myself, there must be two of me: the "I" and the "self" that "I" cannot live with. Maybe, only one of them is real."

To Forgive My Self – When Anger is Directed Inwards

How do I come to wage war on myself? The predominant cause in the majority of situations begins early in life. Long before a young child develops the abstract conceptual capacity to have the question "Who am I?", the circumstances and people around them are providing on-going stimulation that the young child experiences along a felt continuum of pleasant or unpleasant, comfortable or uncomfortable, feeling safe or un-safe, loved and liked or unloved and un-liked.

These feelings stimulate the built-in survival instinct in the nervous system, which is designed to automatically move us towards safety and comfort and away from danger and discomfort. Long before a child's mind develops ability for language, and therefore the ability for thinking in words, the body and feelings are learning what and who, in their world, is associated with good or bad feelings. As our bodies are programmed to find ways to avoid danger and move towards safety, through trial and error, the child unconsciously develops strategies towards this end. For example, if allowed to cry alone without being comforted, a child may learn to hide feelings and pain, growing into isolation or stoicism without any awareness of the origin of these patterns. Or a child may learn that they can get attention by crying. Thus, reinforced in the formative years, a habit of manipulating their environment through displaying weakness may develop and become fixed in personality.

For each of us, the "world" is what we personally experience. A child who grows up feeling safe and accepted experiences the world in that way. To a child who grows up feeling un-safe or un-loved, the world is un-safe, potentially dangerous. These determinations are based initially on feelings and sensations, not on thought. They shape the nervous system to form habitual reactions in response to the "felt" nature of the surrounding world. This is the way all life learns to survive and adapt.

When capacity for language begins to appear, the child learns by mimicking the sounds spoken by others, eventually learning to assign meaning to these sounds. Long before the philosophical question of self-concept arises, children collect labels, directly and indirectly, from people and events around them, i.e., smart/dumb/, pretty girl/ugly girl, good boy/bad boy. The child automatically begins to use these labels to build its primal sense of self. These labels become the foundation of how one talks to and thinks about oneself.

Not all labels are given by others. Our brains are programmed to look for patterns. We cannot avoid that. Whether the perceived patterns are valid or not is another question. As the capacity for theorizing develops, the child will explore explanations for why their world treats them as it does, makes them feel as they do. For example, angry, tired, irritable, distracted parents, or competitive siblings or a mean teacher or cruel school ground bully will compel the child to search for a way to relate to their world that, they hope, will make people behave differently, feel kinder, more interested, more accepting towards them.

The perfectly logical initial hypothesis is that there must be something that I can do to make the situation better. This response is more likely to be intuited initially and only put into words much later, if at all. Whether these attempts to discover adaptive responses to the type of world I hope to change are successful or not, the assumption is egocentric: "I," myself, must be the cause of how the world treats "me." It must be something about me that makes people angry, impatient, hurtful.

Adults often initiate or reinforce this belief by directly linking the child's manifestation to approval or disapproval. On the one hand, how else would one socialize a child? On the other hand, the problem is that children will tend to globalize the criticism of their own behavior or attitude with their worth and love-ability as a person. Angry or emotionally immature adults, or adults who were abused themselves and repeat those patterns on children now in their care, may directly feel and convey that their love is conditional. Then the interpretation is correct. "I am not lovable. I know because they told me so."

Of course, a child's behavior interacts with the reactions from others. Good child-rearing focuses on behavior, without attacking the quality of character. "When you behave that way, this is what will happen as a consequence" is not inherently belittling or hurtful to self-concept. The problem lies in any real or perceived attack on the child's inherent worth. If the environmental reactions raise this issue, then the logical assumption by the child will be, "something in me is not right, is missing, isn't good enough."

These are the type of thoughts that begin to appear in the head to try to explain the uncomfortable feelings and sensations in the body. These thoughts may be kept quietly to myself, leaving others unaware of my reactions or interpretations and thus unable to correct them for me if, in fact, I have misinterpreted events and the motivations of others. Or these thoughts might be overtly reinforced by actual cruel or insensitive remarks or behaviors addressed to me. In either case, the result is the development of a type of psychic auto-immune response where I come to believe I am the primary, if not sole, cause of the pain in my life. I may believe that the people who hurt me are doing so in response to the hypothesized bad or inadequate part of me that I believe is the cause of their manifestations towards me. For example, "if I were smarter, my father would respect me" or "if I were more athletic, I would be more popular" or "if I didn't ask so many questions, the teacher wouldn't be so annoyed with me," or "if I was a better son, my mother wouldn't drink so much."

These thoughts and self-attitudes become hard-wired. As years go by, they persist, whether reinforced from the outside or not. Worse still, I may not be able to come up with an explanation, other than there must be something wrong with me and then assume that I am too dumb to figure it out, or change it, thus adding to my self-criticism. There may also be any number of life situations where I wished I had responded differently. Regret and guilt may come to haunt me. Under these conditions, how can I forgive myself for being inadequate for life?

Often, this sense of inadequacy may become a self-fulfilling prophecy. Expecting that I am condemned to mistreatment by the world, I may repeatedly find myself in abusive relationships that are similar enough to my childhood experiences so that this pattern of negative self-assessment is continually reinforced. Since my world has always felt like this, it seems normal. My tendency will be to interpret events to fit my assumption so that even when I am accepted, I don't feel or believe it.

Or, I might behave in my relationships so that people who are not abusive become frustrated and may be provoked to react in ways that I can experience as the rejection I expect. In this sad situation, my negativity becomes contagious and may stimulate negativity in others. In a strange way, I may be so used to my "suffering" that I cannot imagine, indeed am unwilling to even try to imagine, a different way of viewing myself.

If I reconsider my understanding of myself, I may have to admit I have wasted my life up to this point. For some, this prospect is so painful that they will cling to their suffering because they are used to it. Letting go requires a long grieving process which seems, at the outset, more painful than my self-abuse. I may feel "safer" with the suffering I know than risk the suffering that might come with re-evaluating my life and relationships. Also, there is safety in being the one who administers suffering to myself. If I begin to hope for better treatment, the disappointment, when it doesn't appear, will be worse than what I do to myself. Better the devil I know than the devil I don't.

This pattern can also play out for people who are, by nature, perfectionists. The drama of the perfectionist appears because such people are visionaries. They can "see" into the world of the Ideal and recognize how things could be in a perfect situation. The problem arises when "could" changes to "should." Now, it is imperative that perfection occurs and, once established, never deteriorates! If I am what must be perfect in order to be good enough, loved enough, then I am trapped in an endless quest for what cannot exist on the material plane. In the world of the Ideal, nothing ever changes. Life is not like that. Life is not frozen. It flows like a river, with rapids, still places, eddies. Nothing stays the same. Can I forgive myself for not being perfect? Who said I was supposed to be, needed to be, could be? And ... whose definition of perfect am using as my model?

Levels

The foundational spiritual commandment of the world's foremost traditions is, "Love God, love your neighbor, and love yourself." Embedded therein is an "I-Thou" relationship between "myself" and God, between "myself" and my neighbor and between "I" and my "Self." The mystery of how to relate to "my Self" lies, I believe, in the understanding of relativity and *levels*. If I view the relationship between my different, often conflicting, psychological moods and reactions on a horizontal axis, as if they were all on the same level in terms of quality, maturity, understanding, then how to love "myself" seems like a paradox. If all is on the same level, what can judge or forgive from a different perspective?

If I recognize different levels and qualities within my psychological experience, some representing left-over conditioned reactions from earlier years and some representing differing attitudes and viewpoints from accumulated experiences later in life, some imprinted when I was very young, others acquired when I became mature, some which are still open wounds, some which have healed, some which were never damaged at all, then a different relationship becomes possible.

In the psychotherapy of "recovery," the utilization of these more mature parts to re-educate and re-condition the less mature and less conscious parts is called "re-parenting the inner-child" or finding the "higher power." This reframing of perspective is the basis for current cognitive-behavioral treatment approaches to curing many neurotic reactions. In spiritual work, it has names like the "Higher" and the "Lower" or the higher Self and the ordinary self, or "Father-Son-Holy Spirit," or the "Christ Within."

The question has additional nuance. If I wish to forgive myself, which parts of me must learn to forgive what other parts of me? Who is the part of me that is judging? On what basis is the judgment made? What parts of me are being judged? Are there parts of me that do not make judgments about my worth or competence.? How many "parts" of "me" are there?

Where do my judgmental, unforgiving parts come from? Often, they are like recordings of the words or tone of voice of those who originally hurt me. They have been recorded inside me and turn on to criticize me in a similar way to how I was initially criticized. To hurt myself is a way of saying, "See. I know I am not good enough, so I will punish myself on my own so that you (others) don't need to."

I also need to understand that anger is a secondary response, a defense against the primary feeling of pain. What parts of me are in pain? Are anger or criticism helpful in healing pain? When I am in a judgmental state, I believe I represent the "good" and what I am judging represents the "bad," and there is no commonality between the two. I am stuck in a black and white world where there are no shades of gray. This applies to when I am judging others and also when I am judging myself.

However, it is possible to learn to discern differences in quality, appropriateness, health, maturity without judging from a position of moral authority. Judgment, in the sense of discernment, is not the same as being judgmental. In a state open to discernment, I can see and feel into both sides of an issue. There is understanding and compassion for each. Nevertheless, if a choice must be made, it is made on a much deeper, more sensitive foundation.

The origin of the word "forgive" comes from the concept "to release from debt." When I feel I am owed, that a wrong has been done and must be righted, then I am in an attitudinal position that keeps me waiting for resolution before I can let go and move on. I feel like a victim at the mercy of the wished-for resolution, waiting, …waiting … waiting … for the corrective change to occur before I am ready to let go of the past and see what can now be done with my new and unexpected future. I have become the prisoner of the desired result. I remain in a trap created by my attitude.

Forgiving "myself" can be a challenging problem if I believe I am unworthy and will not become worthy of forgiveness unless I make certain changes in myself or undo some action taken or untaken in my past. But this is a circular argument. I can't forgive myself until I change myself, or the past, for not being what I, or someone else, believes I should be. But I can't change myself, either because I can't make myself what I am not, or, I don't know what is wrong with me but believe something must be wrong if I am not what I believe I should be.

So, I can't forgive myself until I change but I can't change until I forgive myself!

What if forgiving myself is the change!

The underlying philosophical belief here is that "I" should be, or could be, perfect, or at least much, much different in some important way. Where did I learn this assumption? How did I come to believe that I am not good enough? In what way and for whom am I lacking? How do I respond to the voice that repeatedly asks, "What's wrong with me"?

To free myself from this reaction, to find a way to let go of my tight grip on self-negation, I must discover where, inside myself, the resentment is coming from. But it is painful to explore what I consider my negative qualities. Why would I be willing to dig deeper into myself if I truly believe I am correct in my negative opinion of myself? If I am willing to look deeper, part of me is already free, or wishes to be free, of the reaction and is reaching down to the rest of me to show the way to this freedom.

If I carry a low self-esteem and assume that my perceived weaknesses are the trigger for attracting hurtful behavior from others, then a hostile or dangerous situation becomes, to my way of thinking, somehow my fault. I may then lash out at others in my pain or, if I keep my pain inside, I then attack, hurt and abuse myself as the cause of the problem. In terms used by psychologist Eric Burns, "You're OK but I am not OK." Since these reactions are dependent on my assessment of the situation, they are neither inevitable nor necessarily permanent. More importantly, they may not be accurate. A change in perspective will inevitably lead to a change in response to a newly perceived situation.

Mechanical Nature of Negative Reactions

One result of inner psychological work of the type promulgated by G. I Gurdjieff is a recognition that my body is a biological machine with thousands of programmed reactions and responses, most of which occur outside my awareness. For the most part, my body runs itself. I can influence it to some extent, for good or ill, but most of its functioning is out of my direct reach. I am carried along through life inside my body and its programmed reactions, like a passenger in a car. To the degree the "car" has capacity, sufficient fuel and roads are available, I can steer its direction to some extent, but it still runs itself according to its own design.

I also come to realize and accept that the vast majority of my emotional reactions have been learned, many unconsciously, through life experiences, both direct and indirect. Without studying the roots of my reactions, I believe that they are my choice, rather than responses imposed on my nervous system from without, most accidentally, perhaps some deliberately. Most of us recognize that we typically do not have control of our feelings and often discover ourselves acted upon by them whether we wish this or not.

I may also come to realize and accept that the same is true for the origin of most thoughts that come and go in my mind. Most of us rarely challenge a thought or wonder where it comes from or whether it is even true. If it appears in my head, I assume without question that I must be the one thinking it and, therefore, it must represent me accurately. But is this so? If I watch inside my mind, I often notice that I don't know why certain thoughts are in my head. I didn't ask for them to appear. I may not even want to be thinking in this way.

Yet, here are these habitual thought patterns, inner dialogues, chains of associations about self-criticisms, painful past events or worrisome future possibilities constantly hijacking my attention and stimulating my hormonal system to produce sensations that I experience as "emotions." So, maybe I am not the one "choosing" the thoughts, but only suffering from them as they come and go. Maybe I've just noticed that there is "thinking" going on. I didn't initiate it. I don't even want it present. I must be observing the thought process. That must mean that I am not my thoughts, but rather I am the part that observes and registers them!

The Beginning of Freedom

This change in perspective can alter how I think about my thoughts. I am now in a position to examine my thoughts, including the complaints against myself. When I look at my grievances towards myself, I can see that this inner self-criticism is often directed at parts of me that are embarrassing to how I want to be seen by others or how I think about myself. At the moment, I don't see them as only parts, fragments of me floating in my head, but rather, I become identified with them so that they seem to be all there is of me. It seems like these problem parts of myself are a danger to me.

For example, I am angry about my shyness, or my memory, or my weight, or my inability in an area that seems important to me, or to other people who are important to me. I believe these deficiencies must be the problem in my life. Therefore, I am the problem in my life because parts of me are not fulfilling the image I want myself and others to have of me. Thoughts appear that judge and criticize the whole of me because of the perceived weakness that I believe makes me insufficient or un-lovable. If I believe I am my thoughts and feelings, I believe I am un-lovable and insufficient. Why do I believe this? I believe it because I feel badly as a result of these types of thoughts stimulating my sympathetic nervous system and the unspoken assumption about the cause of these bad "feelings" about myself is confirmed by "my" thoughts.

If I recognize that self-thoughts, feelings and criticisms, may not necessarily be true, I can now begin to challenge them and question their accuracy. I can back up a bit inside myself and look at this self-directed negativity, which globally judges the whole of me because of aspects of my personality and reactions that I wish were different. Does that make the entirety of me unacceptable, un-lovable, incompetent? My inner judge will say so. The "judge" is all or nothing. Any perceived or assumed deficiency ruins the whole.

What about the part that wants to change? Is that bad also? I can also question why I believe these qualities need to be different. Who told me they do? Who have I been comparing myself to? Is it my fault I am not attracted to or not very good at math, or I am tone deaf and can't sing or less "smart" at something or less attractive to some people's taste than some others? I wasn't born with these ideas about myself in my mind. How did they get into my head? Do I take personal credit for my strengths or the things people like about me? Wasn't I conceived and born with different potential capacities, some which have worked in my favor and some not? Did I create these qualities and potentials and place them inside of myself at conception? Perhaps, I can take credit for developing some of my qualities and responsibility for not developing others, but my negativity did not arrive with me at birth. It unconsciously developed as a coping mechanism, shaping itself to challenges of different life situations during my developmental years.

Am I responsible for the existence of these defenses? I may be responsible for how I try to deal with their influence on me, but I did not intentionally create them. If I did not create them, then how can I judge myself for them, even if others appear to do so? I can see them as my responsibility to deal with, but not my fault that they were conditioned into me. If this is the case, can I release myself from the debt of being who I actually am rather than who I have learned to believe I should be? If I'm not "good enough" for some people, does that mean I am not "good enough" for anyone? And ... while I am thinking about this ... why do I want to be in relationship with people who are not accepting of me? What is the point of that?

And how did I come to give these negative people the authority to define me?

The Care and Feeding of Negative Thinking

If I learn to watch my self-mitigating thoughts with interest and curiosity, instead of agreement, from a small distance inside my mind, I will begin to see some repeating patterns. I will discover that the negating inner thoughts often use rigid, demanding, pejorative words like "should," "ought," "must," "have to." These judgmental thoughts leave no room for any result short of perfection. They never cut me any slack. They are often accompanied by self-destructive statements that I am not good enough, that there is something wrong with me. This voice disguises itself by whispering into my inner ear something that has a bit of fact, i.e., there may be something wrong with me or I am not good enough. Indeed, I may not be as skilled at some things as others or falling short of standards I wish to uphold, but the voice takes that fact and spins it further by adding an interpretation and a prediction, i.e., "because you are not as __x__, therefore you are no good at anything, nobody wants you and you will end up in some terrible, un-redeemable situation." It is the negative twist in meaning and the prediction of disaster that drives my negativity towards myself. As long as I believe that these words are true, I accept the never-ending criticism as valid.

To persist, thoughts require a kind of "food." This food is of two qualities: *attention* and *belief.* Thoughts that are not interesting, thoughts that don't feel to have meaning or importance, tend to drift in and out of my mind without capturing my attention for too long. Neither do they have much emotional power, so I tend not to believe them or spend much time with them. But thoughts that I *believe* have great emotional power precisely because I believe them! I give them power through my belief and acquiescence to their presence in my mind. My body's survival mechanism either relaxes or goes on alert depending on the perceived meaning of the thoughts.

If I decide that I want to understand the origin and evaluate the accuracy of my thoughts, I can practice bringing an attitude of *interest* and *curiosity* to observing them. Doing so allows a degree of separation between myself as the viewer of the thoughts and the thoughts themselves. This questioning of their accuracy can begin to weaken my automatic belief in them. This lessening of belief then makes it easier to shift attention to more productive thoughts, such as "what are the roots of these thoughts, how far back in my life do they go, how old was I when they first appeared? Did someone tell me this about myself or make me feel bad about myself? Did I come up with this theory about myself as a child? Was it accurate then? Is it accurate now?" The gradual withdrawal of belief and attention begins to starve these conditioned thought patterns and thus to weaken their hold.

Which "Self"?

So, which "self" needs to be forgiven by which other "self"? As our fundamental habits and reactions are shaped from infancy through childhood, is it reasonable to blame an innocent child who is trying to learn how to grow into the life in which it accidentally finds itself? Does this younger version of my current adult self owe my current self an apology or compensation for how it was raised? What is the "debt" my child-self owes to my adult-self? What is gained by holding onto the sense of debt? Has holding a grudge against "myself" all these years helped my younger conditioned self to change its patterns? What could help a child learn to accept itself as it is, develop its interests as best it can, and not feel personally responsible for not having been conceived in the womb with qualities envied in others? Is criticism and shaming a healthy learning environment for such a child? If I continue to believe and give unexamined attention to these chronic inner criticisms, how does this help?

I could let go of the sense of debt. I could say to myself that I wish I could sing much better, but I could take singing lessons and see how far I can come. We all have limits. I could be content to explore mine rather than nurse anger at myself for having any limits. If I free myself from the necessity to be perfect, or at least close to perfect, my whole experience of myself and my world can change.

To Forgive Others – When Anger is Directed Outwards

The projection of anger and judgment outward, in most cases, is a variation on the defense of self-image and typically has the same causation in the early developmental years. Think about the people or situations in life that acutely stir up emotional reactions within you. We have all met many different types of people in the course of life and everyone suffers disappointment, betrayal, hurt feelings at times. This is part of the life experience, along with pleasant and rewarding situations. Life contains a huge continuum of experiential qualities. Why do some bother us deeply, even to the point of lingering throughout time and coalescing into grudges and resentments? Also, what bothers some people does not bother others. What is behind the individual pattern of likes and dislikes and why do some of the dislikes lead to extremely negative, often sustained, feelings of victimization?

The distinction I wish to draw is between intellectual disagreement and strong, visceral, emotional dislikes and rejections. It is the latter that lead to enduring resentments and violent verbal or physical reactions. The issue of forgiveness is not triggered by disagreement alone. Whatever the disagreement, it must be intense enough, go deep enough, to trigger a long-standing, unresolved issue in my life. If not, I would not take the situation personally, be personally offended. After all, as mentioned above, each of us has a different pattern of situations that deeply bother us. What is my pattern? If I make a list of things that really, really bother me, events that I just can't let go of, why does my list take that form? Why do other people's lists take a different form?

There are a couple of factors to consider. Unresolved personally traumatic events leave deep imprints on our nervous system. The sense of humiliation or fear or shame I felt that time long ago can be re-triggered by any current event, even remotely similar in form or nature or timing. These painful reactions are conditioned into our nervous system in the same way Pavlov discovered "conditioned" responses in his laboratory dogs. In Dr. Pavlov's situation, he discovered that his dogs began to salivate when he entered the lab at the beginning of the day in *anticipation* of being fed. He then rang a bell before feeding them. They then began to salivated to the sound of the bell. Then he paired other irrelevant stimuli to the bell and then to each other to produce a string of stimulants unrelated to food, but each of which produced salivation.

Whatever is paired with a potent stimulus takes on that potency. In this way, we can become reactional to events and situations not bearing direct connection to the original event. For example, why does a song, or a beam of sunlight, or a time of year or a specific smell, or a certain look on another person's face produce an emotional response and perhaps evoke long distant memories? Because these unrelated events have become paired in a string of conditioned associations.

This is an automatic, instinctive process to help protect us in the future from similar painful events. But it can't protect us when the triggering events take us by surprise or are only tangentially similar, yet similar enough to evoke its echo in our nervous system. Often, I don't know why I have such a strong reaction. There may or may not be a real offense coming from the outside. If I am hypersensitive to criticism, for example, I may hear it where it was not intended. Or I may accurately hear it but "overreact" due to my sensitivity. In this case, I develop a grudge against another because they inadvertently triggered an ancient, deeply buried unhealed wound in me.

Can I forgive them for bumping this sensitive place in my psyche? Did they do it on purpose? Even if they know my sensitivity and provoke me anyway, they are not the one who created this vulnerability in me. If they are not the person who caused it, why am I holding them responsible for the tender spot I need to heal in myself? If they are the person who caused it, I need to re-evaluate my relationship with this person who does not wish me well. I can safely assume they have their own demons and are projecting them onto me.

Projection

This phenomenon, called "projection," works this way: there is some-thing in my character that I am certain would embarrass me if others no-ticed ... or perhaps I don't want to admit to myself ... or which was very painful and caused a wound that has never healed, so it erupts repeatedly when triggered. It is common that I would try to distance myself from these uncomfortable inner facts by strongly disagreeing with or even at-tacking anything that reminds me of them when encountered in others. Psychologists label this phenomenon "projection." It works this way. The faults of my own that I won't acknowledge to myself, or the faults I try to hide from others, will cause a powerful emotional, even violent and self-righteous reaction in me as a defense to distance my sense of myself from these parts of me when I believe I am seeing them in others.

There is a line in Shakespeare's *Hamlet*, in which Queen Gertrude comments "The lady doth protest too much, methinks." Proclamations of innocence, when gratuitously offered, suggest insincerity. Why is she proclaiming her innocence when one has not yet accused her of a crime? In the days when pornography was censored, why were some of its most vocal critics the first to volunteer for censorship committees to screen the offensive material from the eyes of others? Why would some men go out of their way to attack homosexuals who are not bothering them?

There are instances of deep psychological insight in the Bible that illustrate this point. In the King James Version of the text, we find the following: "First, remove the beam out of your own eye, and then you can see clearly to remove the speck out of your brother's eye."* or "He that is without sin among you, let him first cast a stone at her."†

Canceling

Maurice Nicoll, student of Carl Jung, P D. Ouspensky and G. I. Gurdjieff, recommends "canceling" as a cure to one's own hypocrisy. When noticing a strong emotional judgment towards another, such that you are feeling superior and entitled to issue judgment, and perhaps even punishment, ask yourself the following. When have I ever done anything remotely like this either to another or to myself? Am I totally free of any

---

* Mathew 7.5

† John 8.7 ASV

prejudice, any intolerance, any error? Have I never forgotten something important or said something in anger, accidentally or even intentionally hurt some?

If I am honest, I can always find a connection. I could become curious as to why I have such a strong reaction when I do not have such an intense response to so many other things of which I dislike or disapprove. My resentment can subside or even disappear when I realize that all of us are subject to these issues, including myself. At that point, I may find my way to a perspective that allows me to forgive others because I recognize they do not really know what they are doing, as I realize that I don't recognize what I am doing when I am lost in negativity.

The cure for lack of forgiveness towards myself and others is the recognition that states of negativity are signs of waking-sleep, Gurdjieff's "second stage of consciousness." Escape from projection and negativity begins the process of "waking up", the freeing of attention and belief from illusion.

A client of mine once said to me, "Dr. Aronson. I see what I have been doing to myself all my life. I have believed that drinking a cup of resentment each morning kept me strong. But I see now that resentment is a poison. How can drinking poison daily make me feel better?"

Summary

In forgiving my conditioned parts for their unbecoming manifestations due to their not knowing what they do, I can also forgive others for not knowing what they do. Forgiving transforms through understanding. Understanding does not require agreement but rather the discovering of a reconciling context that demonstrates the inevitable suffering which we will all encounter in life. Suffering is a natural part of living. It is like a law of Nature. The law operates differently at different levels, with greater degrees of freedom from some forms of suffering higher up, fewer degrees of freedom lower down.

Buddhism calls the prison of the lower levels of understanding the "Wheel of Suffering." If my heart can break for my own suffering without falling into identification, self-recrimination, or self-pity, I am freed from the chains of unnecessary and imaginary suffering. If my heart can break for all of us, all those trapped on the Wheel, with no understanding of how we got here and no way of recognizing the path of escape is through acceptance of reality, without looking for compensation from a sleeping humanity or an indifferent, impartial Mother Nature, then I can accept without personalizing, without identifying myself as my suffering, whether caused by myself, my fate, amoral people or the unconscious projections of others.

Fear and confusion are usually our companions along the way for a long time. As a deeper understanding begins to mature, it starts to encompass the conditioning factors received from ordinary life. They are not automatically de-potentiated outright, just because I begin to see their origins and how they influence my experience of life. These patterns may linger because many are strongly imprinted and continue to stimulate thoughts and reactions even as the quality of inner presence increases. Trying to neither run from nor identify with these continuing automatic tensions represents, for me, a quality of understanding, the experience of "conscious labor" and "intentional suffering."*

It helps me to think of these uncomfortable and frightened emotional/ psychological reactions as belonging to the layer of childhood memories and understandings that persist inside the maturing adult. Can I find an attitude that tries to comfort the "child" inside rather than frighten it or join it in its fear? When I am afraid and insecure, defensive or angry, how would I want to be approached? I would first of all want to be heard. I would want to feel that someone was more interested in understanding my distress than in lecturing or judging me. Can I bring that attitude to-wards the parts of me I consider problematic? Can I bring that attitude towards others whose manifestations "offend" some sensitive part of me?

To achieve the possibility of manifesting the state of "doing unto others as I would have them do unto me," an attitude of understanding of the multi-leveled aspects within my psychological world must appear. As I come to recognize and accept that my own personality has unstable aspects due to no fault of my own, I can recognize and accept that this is true of others as well. We are all stuck on the mechanical, automatic, mindless wheel of suffering. Only by accepting that fact and learning not to personalize "my" suffering can I learn to feel and respect the pain of

---

* "Conscious labor" and "intentional suffering" were terms used by the spiritual teacher, G. I. Gurdjieff, to describe an attitude that could lead to freedom from conditioned reactions. Since life is filled with labor and suffering, we can complain, space out or learn how to be aware of ourselves inside the activity. This subjective sense of the separation of the psychological Observer from the reaction being experienced is a doorway to the dimension where there are no opposites, but only different parts of a larger Whole.

others when they behave in ways I do not like. Their behaviors may be very disappointing, hurtful, damaging ... but are they *personal*? To be truly personally directed at me, the other would have to really know me, to the core. Otherwise, they are projecting onto me as a screen that in some way triggered their own discomfort. Closer to home, do I know myself well enough to accept the unpleasant manifestations of my conditioned personality to my preferred self-image without taking these parts of myself personally?

In other words, am I willing to consider releasing myself, and others, from the debt of being imperfectly conditioned by life forces, over which none of us had any initial control and, perhaps are only now, deep into life, beginning to discern, along with the many "mistakes" made because of that impersonal conditioning? Only when I begin to recognize the coils of conditioned, programmed attitudes in which I find myself trapped can I begin to become responsible for managing the damage. With inner sincerity and compassion, I can become a person of deeper being, sadder but wiser and, paradoxically, filled with the joy of freedom from the narrow world of opposites.

Reconciliation

Not unlike many fathers and sons, there has been intermittent tension between my son and me since he became an adult. The why's and how's of the situation are not important to this story. The situation wasn't terrible, as it can tragically become for those less fortunate than me, but it left both of us often frustrated and sad. Several months ago, we again found ourselves in a situation of this tension. I noticed the same responses coming up for both of us and the same inevitable stalemate and period of wounded feelings. I had thought about our situation often over many years. I did not know how to shift our foundation. I sought advice from others and attempted different approaches, but nothing changed the dynamic between us.

Then I realized that I was not practicing with him, what I was practicing with others ... and had advised my clients to do in their relationships. Despite our periodic friction, I was too emotionally close to him to be able to find perspective.

For years I had tried to look at the world through what I *imagined* were his eyes to understand him better. From my perspective, I could readily see the impact that the divorce between his mother and me had had on him at a critical time. I could see how circumstances unfolded over many subsequent years in a way that periodically left him with confused and hurt feelings. I assumed that our current difficulties all stemmed from those unfortunate earlier situations, leading to a sense of guilt and responsibility on my part to try to protect him from more pain. But despite my intentions, I was not successful. What was I missing? What could be done?

Then, one afternoon, on a telephone call, without warning, it was happening between us again. This time, as the energy began to sour in the way typical between us, I realized what was happening. I saw my habitual tendency to explain to him that the hurt he was feeling was because he was misinterpreting me and if he would only listen to me and recognize his error, his pain would go away. I humbly use this as an example to demonstrate that a good therapist needs to undergo the fire of his own difficulties to know what others are feeling and facing in their own situations. This understanding includes how one can be highly functional in most areas and relationships but can also have blind spots where one's own wounds lie. The difficulty of seeing my part in this situation was my reluctance to let go of the past and look at what was happening now as perhaps a contemporary phenomenon and not a direct influence from past events.

As I listened to him talk about how I had hurt his feelings, I saw my own frustration that I was also not being understood begin to well up. At that moment, I stopped my defensive response and redirected my listening to him. I then had a memory of my frustration trying to get my own father's attention and respect. Several examples flashed into my mind in a split second. I decided in that moment to let go of any attempt to explain myself or correct his "misunderstanding." Instead, I listened to him, with my feelings (since they were now freed from an occupation with myself) and not just my thoughts.

I felt his frustration and pain over his interpretation of my behavior. I felt him as a man with a career and a family and responsibilities, doing the best he could ... and sometimes becoming very frustrated with his father. His father believed he was helping his son become more independent, but this was not the message being received. If the message is not being received, the fault is in the transmitter for not finding a frequency that the receiver is able to receive. I had been trying to communicate on the wrong channel. Using my imagination, I put myself into his feelings as he spoke them out. The emotional taste I then experienced felt like what I had experienced with my father. The vibration was the same. My son's pain with his father was making my pain with my father resonate.

I said to him, "When I really listen to you now, I realize that, while trying not to, I have inadvertently created in you the same feelings toward me that I felt towards my father. And ... I am very sorry." He felt heard and thanked me.

I have seen this pattern in many people and families over my years as a therapist. I had spent twenty years in my own therapy, both as part of my wanting to be a good therapist as well as working through neurotic conditioning from my childhood. Both aims turned out to be the same. Yet, despite all these years of working on myself and others, in my persistence in wanting to be the type of father I wished I had had, somehow, I had become my father to my son. It is sad and powerful that I remained blind to this until I became an old man.

Over the few months since this revelation, I have noticed my acceptance of this reality. The pain of this seems to keep me awake to my-self when I am interacting with him. It helps remind me to focus on his reality and approach him from that position. Then we can begin to meet on his ground once I give up the insistence that we meet on my ground. Perhaps, once secure on his ground, we may someday drift towards the middle. But that is not important. I am happy to meet him on any ground. Our interactions now feel more relaxed and warmer.

Theme of Reconciliation

The longing for reconciliation, not just in my personal life but between any and all people, has been a very strong theme for me since an early age. I first noticed the emotional tendency when I was in my early teens. Stories and themes about reconciliation, emotional healing, reunions be-tween people long lost to each other, the healing of old wounds, the end of wars would cause me to cry. I am recalling now a night in 1972 when the "official" end of the Vietnam war was to start at midnight. I left the house a few minutes beforehand and walked down the dark street of the little coastal Maine town where we were living. At midnight, church bells began to ring. Without warning, I began to cry … and cry … and cry. All that needless suffering and death were over and the time for "healing" could now begin. As my life has worn on, this tendency never abated and is with me today. Just last evening, I watched a film with this theme, and I cried at the presentation of re-uniting. I have wondered what this longing is about. Why does it touch me so deeply?

What is this psychological-emotional state we call reconciliation? The dictionary tells us that to reconcile means: "restore friendly relations be-tween, cause to coexist in harmony; make or show to be compatible, balance, attune." Conciliation is the "end of estrangement and the action of mediating between two disputing people or groups".

The existence of this attitudinal state and the difficulty of achieving it begs for exploration. There is no need for reconciliation unless there is a conflict in need of it.

A more nuanced viewpoint I have developed in the later part of my life is the recognition that "cause and effect" is not as simple a relationship as it sounds. If we don't notice an effect, was there a cause … of the non-effect? If there seems to be an effect, can we be certain of the cause? Was that initiating "cause" the effect of another preceding "cause"? There are always things in motion. Objects move through "space" and memories are carried by the river of Time. Ideas penetrate minds and infiltrate populations. Rumors move through crowds like infections. Feelings flow. The force exerted by moving energy, material or psychological, inevitably meets an energy of a different quality. That difference produces the phenomenon we call "resistance." The word "resistance" often carries a pejorative sense to it, as if something is wrong if there is resistance. This reaction is itself resistance to the reality of inevitable qualities of "resistance" to any initiatory movement.

Obviously, the first factor, or force, is movement of some sort. For movement to be possible, there needs to be space to allow the movement. In that space will be the results of past and current, moments and movements. Into this space, something new enters. The movement will meet whatever was already in the field of potential action in which the initiation is trying to manifest. What happens when they meet ... the movement and its field of possible manifestation?

For example, I've noticed that my friend might have forgotten something. Believing my assessment, I offer help. To my surprise, I am met with an unexpected and indignant reaction. "You think something is wrong with my memory? Well, there isn't! I can handle this." I had sent my offer of help into her psychological field where, unbeknownst to me, it collided with a lifetime struggle with a controlling, critical parent. My offer bounced off her defenses and could not come into manifestation. Nothing changed.

There are a number of variables at play. The force of the initiation, the movement, may be strong or moderate or weak. The direction it takes when trying to manifest will vary. The angle of approach will influence what is encountered in the field of action and, thus, what may or may not result. For example, should I be direct or oblique, forceful or soft, authoritative or deferent? The content and shape of the field it is moving through will also offer varying degrees of "resistance," from strong rejection to passive acquiescence to enthusiastic reception. Typically, resistance, or incompatibility of the space and the movement to accommodate each other, will result in either a clash or ... nothing happens. In either case, nothing new appears. The initiation is un-realized and the field remains unchanged. The initiatory impulse could not bear fruit due to lack of harmony with its space of possible interaction.

"To Resist"

What do we mean by "resistance"? The term comes from late Middle English: from French *"résistance,"* from late Latin *"resistentia,"* from the verb *"resistere"* "to take a stand, to stand firm." The field, which is being penetrated by a moving impulse, must find a way to accommodate it, to take a position in relation to it, and if not, to reject it or ignore it. So, to re-sist is to take a position, again and again, whenever something enters our material, emotional, intellectual, psychological field of awareness. It is not a choice. It is a lawful dynamic. How we handle it, however, is modifiable depending on our wish and understanding.

For example, I've again noticed that my friend might have forgotten something, but I have tried to remind her before and met with rejection, so I am more cautious. I begin to say something, but my voice is soft and hesitant. She doesn't respond and I suspect she either did not hear me or is choosing not to respond. I am relieved and don't repeat the offer of a reminder. "It really is her problem, not mine," I tell myself.

The Elusive Third

For the two factors to appropriately blend, a third factor must be present to reconcile the differences. This third factor represents a different field of possibilities that can encompass both of the original fractious factors. It may be most easily understood as a different perspective, a different attitude that allows for a viewpoint larger than the *either-or* opposites that dominate when the third factor is missing. Philosophically, both the initiation and the resistance are part of a larger Whole. They clash or ignore each other when they are not related through a larger Whole. The third, or reconciling factor, brings a viewpoint from the realm of a larger, uniting reality. Its perspective literally originates from a higher psychological state than the *either-or* position.

In contemporary life, we have seen remarkable examples of people who were able to "rise above" the natural desire for revenge. The "Truth and Reconciliation Commission" in South Africa following the fall of Apartheid sought to heal the society by providing a forum for victims to tell the stories of their suffering to those who caused it. The perpetrators received amnesty by acknowledging the pain they caused and asking their victims for forgiveness.

In 2006, ten young Amish girls were killed in their one-room schoolhouse in Pennsylvania by a deranged young gunman. The community responded by comforting the family of the killer. I heard a story years ago about a war in Africa in which, as a nun was being raped and eventually killed by a soldier, she said to her killer, "I forgive you." The young soldier was transformed by the event and, after the war, became a Priest. I also recall hearing a story about the Dalai Lama debriefing a Tibetan monk after his release from many years in a Chinese prison. When the Dalai Lama asked him if he had ever been afraid, the monk replied that, yes, he had once been afraid that he was about to become angry with his captors. In 2015, nine members of a Black Church in South Carolina were murdered by a gunman. At his trial, a number of surviving victims and relatives of the slain told the killer that they forgave him, and the community was solicitous to the killer's family. During my psychotherapy practice, I learned of an international group of Jewish children of the holocaust helping to heal the guilt-ridden children of Nazi perpetrators. Themes of charity and mercy abound in all cultures, as suggested antidotes to the corrosion of resentment, which metastasizes the curse of victimhood, and if not attenuated, will continue violence and hatred into generations to come.

I am recalling now one of the first couples I saw as a marital therapist. She was pouring out her feelings and he was responding defensively from his head. Finally, she said to him, "Look. There is more going on here besides just the two of us. There is you, me and there is our relationship. We have to put the relationship before our individual feelings." She wanted him to focus on the larger picture and not just his personal preferences. She wanted him to be willing to sacrifice something he wanted for the greater good, for the commitment that had melded them together into the larger Whole of marriage. Without wishing to serve, or feeling that we are part of, something larger than our self, there is no third viewpoint.

The prefix "*re*" means to repeat. Etymological dictionaries note that "conciliation" originates from the 1540s, "the act of converting from jealousy or suspicion and gaining favor or goodwill," from Middle French "*conciliation*," from Latin "*conciliationem*" "a connection, union, bond," figuratively "a making friendly, gaining over," stem of "*conciliare*" "to bring together, unite in feelings, make friendly, assimilated form of "*con*" "together, together with."

"Bringing together and uniting in feeling" indicate that "re-concile" implies that there had been an original "togetherness," a larger combined state that has become fragmented and requires a putting back together in its original, blended form.

Self-Discovery

This brings me back to my personal sensitivity to this theme. As a psychologist as I studied myself and many other people. I have discovered that our sense of being "one" person is an illusion. Within us are many disparate patterns, some conditioned into us by life and some tendencies with which we were born. Sometimes I feel generous, sometimes not. Sometimes I am annoyed and unforgiving, while at other times, I am the reverse. Sometimes I "act my age," and sometimes, I react like a child or teenager. Sometimes I remember a promise I made and, at other times, forget all about it. In both a metaphorical and literal way, I am many different people living in the same body, each taking its turn from time to time being the one in charge of my manifestations. Later, all my parts have to pay the price for what some fleeing mood has wrought on myself and others.

To reunite all these parts in a common, shared awareness would move me towards being the Whole, Individual person I only imagine I am but do have the potential to actually be ... if I can acknowledge the reality of my fragmentation and work to understand the many sides of my personality. If I am willing to engage in this self-study, I may come to recognize that if I am like this, then so are others. If I can be reconciled with my contradictions, it becomes easier for me to be less judgmental with others for theirs.

Thus, the state of Reconciliation itself is deeply moving to me. To search for the wish brings me into a "higher" location in my inner world. My level of consciousness is broader, deeper and higher than when I am trapped in the state of either-or, right-wrong, agree-disagree. In this state, I am reminded, indeed I re-experience, the reality of a psychological position that is free from the negativity that accompanies the tension between an initiation and a "non-cooperative" field. I am temporarily reunited with the reality of a larger Whole context into which the two sides, the initiation and its field, are both a part. The difference between them is seen as an illusion created by a limited viewpoint that cannot see the larger picture.

I believe now that my sensitivity relates to a couple of factors. Personality research has demonstrated the usefulness of recognizing different personality types. These types represent differences in the conditioning effects of life and the development of survival strategies resulting therefrom, and our underlying "essence," the temperamental qualities

192

and potential talents we were born with before they were altered by life experiences." The former is learned and can be modified. The latter seems inborn. The Jungian idea of "Archetypes" refers to the type of human we represent out of the pantheon of possibilities.

There are several archetypes I emotionally resonate with when I read about them. The Wounded Healer archetype implies an intimate understanding of *agony*. Sometimes the Wounded Healer is able to heal his/her own wounds and use this knowledge to help heal others. Other times, the wounded healer uses his/her own suffering to open a space of compassion for the other to enter. This energy can cure.

Compassion for Others and Self

No one can lead another to a destination they have not reached themselves. The basis for "compassion," literally to *feel together*, comes from a shared sense, a shared experience, a shared understanding of suffering. Co-passion comes from the psychological level above the common state of division. It produces a union of experience. The fact that someone actually knows how I feel, because they also have felt what I feel, and they tell me there is a way to heal, produces a state of confidence and hope of a much deeper quality than working with a technician who intellectually presents strategies without the shared emotional quality. In a state of compassion, I am not alone. I am in a shared psychological space with another human who personally understands my suffering. Sharing this space together is a transformative experience. The energy from this higher, unified state can bring fractured parts back together and make them whole again.

The *Sin Eater* archetype originally used ritual to clear the dying of their sins. Our modern sin-eaters are counselor and psychotherapist, the new secular priesthood, the carriers of secrets, pain and suffering shared with them in the modern "confessional" of the therapy office. While the traditional religious understanding of sin means an offense against religious or moral law, psychotherapeutic healing uses the original Greek and Esoteric understanding of "missing the mark," as in an archer's arrow that misses the target. In this sense, to "sin" is to make an error in aim, understanding, judgment. There is no "moral" implication if the "sin" was not an intentional attempt to hurt.

The modern Sin Eater carries the knowledge of the client's "sin" in the non-judgmental realm above the psychological level of "right-wrong."

When the whole person is considered, their past wounds and defenses, their conditioned ways of interpreting and reacting to events, then the understanding of how the "sin" occurred, how the "mark was missed," can come into view. By accepting knowledge of his/her "sin" without judgment by the therapist, the client is able to move their own sense of self from the rigid judgmental level to the more nuanced, non-judgmental level above. This doesn't mean that reparation or repair work is not required with those others who may have been hurt by the client's inadvertent manifestations, just that the "sinner" can begin to understand himself or herself in a broader, deeper perspective that diminishes futile self-flagellation. The "sinner" has been re-united, re-conciled with deeper, subconscious parts of him/herself. When the light of awareness and understanding illuminates what was not available to regular consciousness, consciousness expands with the addition of new information and understanding.

The Prodigal Son is one of my favorite archetypal parables. This theme of *re-unification* of what belongs together goes much deeper in me than the ordinary wishes for a closer relationship with my biological father. The experience of this higher state of consciousness, the place that can see what unites rather than only what divides, is a psychological experience that I wish to dwell in. I feel more "real," more "whole" in this state. When in this state, I can experience again and again the confirmation of a higher "reality." In that state, one is open to the creative impulse that may bring a perspective that can heal, that can re-establish a solidity that had been fragmented. It can create a new possibility that did not exist before and could not come into existence in the limited space of the clash of un-reconciled impulses.

Reuniting the Self

I believe now that this compelling yearning on my part to facilitate reconciliation originates in my essence. I believe that humans come into life not only with different genetic patterns but also with "spiritual" patterns, energetic patterns, particular designations for an archetypal role, a representative from the pantheon of universal roles, required by the human community, both for community living as well as connecting humanity with the patterns underlying humanity as a species, not just individuals.

Those of us haunted by the question, "Who am I?" wish to be re-united, long to be reconciled with the answer to this question. There is a nagging feeling that, perhaps, I once knew the answer … perhaps before my conception into a body. There is a sense that my real "home," or real purpose in life, is related to this answer. This is the theme of many ageless fairytales and parables. The creators of those stories knew about the journey towards this mystery and left us their understandings in story form.

I have discovered that, for me, the doorway to this exploration begins with entrance into this higher psychological state of reconciliation. It is a state where the apparently un-reconcilable opposites are held together in an open-ended wish to discover a commonality that can unite them. This unification will create new conditions and new possibilities. When I experientially enter this attitude, I become changed. I become different. I become something new, more than I had been.

A favorite fairytale of my daughter when she was a little girl came from Norway. It was called "East of the Sun and West of the Moon." It recounts the theme of a young bride who must undertake a long journey to find her groom. She is told to look for a land that lies "East of the Sun and West of the Moon. It is a long and perilous journey", she is warned, "but if you can discover it, you will find a welcome within.". In recent conversation with my daughter, she talked about finding herself in a psychological space where she could see the unifying possibilities around her, but her friends and colleagues were often lost in the land of Yes or No. She had discovered it through her own inner journey to a more mature level of consciousness. I reminded her of the fairytale and welcomed her to the kingdom. "There are not many of us here," I told her, "but you are not alone."

Names, Stories and The Location of Memory

I was hiking through a forest along the Maine-New Hampshire border with an old friend on a warm autumn day. On the way to the trailhead, we had passed over a bridge with a name placard attached to it that read "Nathan Desjardins," which I assumed commemorated a revolutionary or civil war area resident. Knowing my friend valued local history, I asked him about the name. Thus, I learned instead a contemporary story of a local young man who wanted to be a police officer. He died on his first day of duty in an auto crash on the way to a reported drowning. The veteran officer driving was said to have been speeding unnecessarily, and this resulted in the young man's tragic death. To honor him, the town had put his name on this isolated bridge. Then there was the attached detail of a woman drowning, which had been the cause of the police dispatch. In my mind's eye, I briefly saw a body in the water and wondered about her identity, her family, what had happened. Then we were over the bridge and my mind turned back to the beautiful scenery and a palpable feeling of love for the northern New England terrain and architecture.

A short time later, we were walking through an area named "Bog Pond" along a path called "Fiddlehead." I stopped by the marsh, listened to the breeze nudge the trees, took in the autumn colors and began to feel a previous mental knowledge deepen into an emotional understanding. The former now felt shallow compared with the depth accompanying the feeling of the reality of what I had previously only known with my thoughts.

I experienced the reality of the fact that when objects or places in the landscape are given names, in a way, they have been sacralized. Something from the experiential world of people has been affixed to this place or object. The name carries, attached to it, a story of people and events, usually connected to the location but sometimes far distant from the geographic locale. It is a way of depositing a bit of the lives associated with the name.

Psychic Footprints

Names are not just location markers. Names are also story markers. They mark a "location" in someone's life, a "place" in the flow of their time where they had an experience which they wanted to convey, long into the future, into the minds of people whom they would never know. People who notice names and are curious, as I was about the name attached to the bridge, understand that something from the psychological experience of others, often long dead, can be transferred into the space of one's own experiential memory.

The names are psychic footprints, giving a life of meaning to the physical place. Lying dormant, contents coiled tightly within their letters ... waiting ... patiently ... waiting ... to catch the attention of a passing mind which would take them in, would open them up, digest them and bring their story to life once again. A mental image appeared in my mind of Memory clinging to a location like a cloud, waiting for a receptive mind to walk by, notice and ask, "What happened here that someone would make the effort to attach a name?"

Memory Clouds

Later in the day, we returned to my friend's farmhouse. This old farm, and the surrounding landscape, is a sacred place to me for many reasons that I might explore in another reminiscence. (Until that time may come, it will remain within only me and unavailable for others to digest.) For now, as I was walking along a path towards the back of my friend's barn, I passed by a particular location and I "saw" a memory image, in my mind's eye, of my friend and me with another man we used to spend much time with. The three of us were walking in this very spot and talking. The memory was nearly forty years distant. The old conversation came back to me and I laughed, recalling the humorous episode. Then I reflected back on my impressions about names, locations and memory. As I had been pondering earlier in the day, I now began to look at the experience I was having at this present moment through the lens of that deeper perspective.

This particular reminiscence seemed "attached" to this specific spot where it was originally recorded. At first, it seemed as if I had walked into the "cloud of memory" which had been waiting, for one of the three of us, to walk through it. Of course, only the three of us carried this event in memory. No one else in the universe had this recollection and my friends might recall it differently, making it a different event, or may have forgotten about it, turning it into a non-event. The event, when it had happened, obviously made an "imprint" on the fabric of my memory, which had just now been "awakened" by walking past the location. (In actuality, both other men recall the moment as I do.)

When I moved beyond the place on the path where the event had occurred, the memory became less intense. As I continued around the corner of the barn, I began encountering other "clouds" of *memory... memory* connected to these other locations, which started to crowd the first one out.

I recalled what I had heard about the ancient native Australians who had been affixing experiences and stories to nearly every rock, hill, gully, stream in the Outback and passing this oral history along to each generation for perhaps 10,000 or more years. These people were literally walking through the lives of their ancestors as they moved through their own. For them, it was not just an intellectual remembrance of a myth but an emotional and physical re-experience of literally walking through living history. Wherever they went was part of their collected remembrance. It was all "home," in a sense, even if this was the first time their personal body had walked through the area.

Their mind had been there already, sharing a dimension of psychological remembrance spanning thousands of years and many hundreds of generations. The experiences of each of those ancestral minds had been pooled together. Different aspects of the gigantic psychic tapestry had been woven and affixed, pinned to different landforms. As centuries and then millennia went by, the fabric would be woven again and again through words spoken to each generation. When people traveled, went on walkabout, they would encounter the locations told to them in the story and the "book" would unfold for them in their mind, their heart and in their body, which was now sensorially experiencing the location spoken of from story. But the events were not only in the past ... in a way they were also now, being relived in the mind and emotions of the new experiencer, now.

The area around my friend's farm is like that for me. The area around each of my homes, places I have traveled to, all contain yeast for my remembrances attached to that location. Isn't this why we take photographs of people we love, places we have traveled, events we have attended? "A picture is worth a thousand words" is probably an understatement. Moments of our lives are embedded in the image, waiting to be relived again when our attention falls upon them. Photographs, like names, are also footprints through the landscape of our experiential dimension.

But is it only the story that contains the memory? What of the countless reports of locations having a "feeling" about them? Throughout history, there are tales of places cursed and places blessed, where people unfamiliar with local history claim to have feeling reactions to the location

Memory and Time

When we remember, we are remembering now. In the present moment, we are having the experience of re-experiencing what we remember now. When I think of the past, I am thinking about it now. When I think of the future, I am thinking of it now. When I recall my history, I am re-experiencing aspects of it now. While some individuals can recall entire conversations, verbatim, and some have an eidetic or photographic memory, ... for me personally, I cannot capture the entire sensory-emotional-intellectual experience at the actual time of the formation of the memory ... but rather, a picture of it, some conversation fragments, what I was feeling and thinking about at the time of the experience, a remembrance of the feeling tone of that situation. Sometimes, the memory will revive the same emotions I had experienced in that distant moment.

These were imprinted onto the canvas of my feelings, into the cells of my body as sensation, and into words and ideas in my intellect. If the recollection is strong enough, my attention and awareness might temporarily leave the current location of my body and be transported back in time into the memory to re-live aspects of it again. After a while, I "snap out of it" and am perhaps surprised to find myself teleported back into my body and out of the world of memory.

What has happened? Where have I been? Where is this place where memory is stored? Speaking just of myself, it feels to be somewhere in my brain and/or my chest and /or throughout my body ... sometimes all three locations simultaneously.

But, what of the memory encoded in the names on the ponds or crossroads or waterfalls? For example, if you have been to the coast of Maine, you might ask, "who was the young woman who fell from Maiden's Cliff in the town of Camden in 1864?" What happened in "Squaw Hollow" near Ashford, Connecticut, in the early 1800s to warrant this name? Near where we were walking is a place called Lovewell Pond. It was the site of a critical battle in 1725 between settlers and local Indians. The militia from Massachusetts was led by a Captain Lovewell, who died in the fight. It was so important at the time that it was celebrated in story and song for more than 100 years. Reading the accounts of it now, viewed from today's social perspective, reveals an all too familiar tale of clashing cultures, each defining itself as in the right. It is a story of tragedy, suffering, meaningless death. As told by the mentality of the storyteller, it was heroic. Viewed from today's understanding, it is heartbreakingly sad. Today, few know or care except for local historians. They are the repository of local oral history. In this way, memory lives through the collective minds of many people over long periods of time and is carried into humanity like bees carry pollen. Where is this place of collective memory located?

Stories other than human can be read from the outer landscape itself, by those who speak the language of Nature, stories told by tree growth patterns, rock formations, animal activity, the changing course of a river. But the human story lives in the landscape of memory, invisible to the unenlightened mind. Those who wished their experiences to be remembered by unknown generations to come told their stories and then pinned them to parts of the landscape in a name. The name could not be avoided in times to come. People always use place names to locate themselves. Anyone passing through the area or looking at a map would see the name, might remember and repeat the name to others. Most never wonder about the meaning of the name, but a few do. Then the story re-emerges again from the vault of living history and transfers a particle of itself into the newly initiated listener.

Memory Matrix

How many memories are attached to a location? There are as many memories as there are people who have had experiences in that place, or have heard about them. Countless memories accumulate and give birth to stories, which, in turn, give rise to other stories that become attached to the place. As one story is pursued and reactivated, attached to it are potentially other stories about other people in adjacent areas or connected with the person who placed the name.

To look out over the garden in my backyard towards the forest brings the question. How many other people have been in this place, lived here, walked here, had experiences here ... but did not attach a name ... at least not successfully? Names, if not posted, only survive as long as the last person who remembers them. This is a reason for the importance of passing along our stories.

Why do we continually tell our stories to our friends and relatives and to ourselves? What is this compulsion to share experiences? "Let me tell you what happened this morning." "What did you do today, dear?" "What happened to you?" "It's a long story. Where shall I begin? I think I was five years old." "Never forget the story of our people." Most of us have an intrinsic need to connect our subjective world with the subjective world of others. We want to be seen, to be known, to be respected, to be understood. Connections between bodies can go no deeper than sexual contact. But what of the connections of the heart and the melding of minds? How deeply can we feel about each other, feel into each other, care and love each other to the point of sacrificing our self for the other? What happens when two minds resonate with the same idea and energize each other in a brainstorming frenzy of creativity? In a way, through the process of sharing our experiences, our feelings, our thoughts, we interpenetrate each other's psychological worlds. Two material bodies cannot occupy the same space at the same time, but feelings and ideas are not material. Feelings and ideas can blend, like gases, overlapping and interpenetrating each other.

Just as the atmosphere around us today is saturated with inter-penetrating radiations of radio, television, cell phone, internet … not to mention all the natural radiations flowing through us … so too are the saturating psychological experiences which happened around us. Natural sources of vibration originate and can be measured in the outside world surrounding us. Reverberations of history and story ripple and flow in waves through the interior dimension of psychological experience. The realm of psychological experience resides not only in individual minds but represents the collection of all possible human experiences combined. We can access this unimaginably vast library when listening to or reading the words of others or looking through their mind's eye into the paintings, photographs and videos they created so that we could share in a part of their world. The oldest cave paintings found to date are esti-mated at over 60,000 years. In them, we can see and feel images from their prehistoric world, its animals, their lifestyle and perhaps religious beliefs. It is a portal into the mind of our pre-historic ancestors. Other than our superior technological and scientific knowledge and their superior practical knowledge of how to survive in the wild, how are we different from them?

Words are the technological breakthrough that allowed early groups of hominids to form societies of people who could share their knowledge, their experiences and stories. This accumulation is "immortal," relative to the short lifetimes of all the individuals who deposited (or uploaded) their personal life's material into the library of collective memory. I can today read the words of Plato or Cicero or the Buddha. By adding my attention and stirring with interest, the "freeze dried" ideas of long-dead individuals come to life again. They enter my subjective psychological space as a blending of dead minds with the living. But, if they "come alive again" when I blend them into my mind, can I say their minds are dead? If the vibrations of their thoughts live again in me, perhaps the lifetime of a "mind" depends on the transmission of its stories. As I absorb their perspective, these thoughts from long ago use my mind as a carrier.

Qualities of Memory

But, what of the quality or usefulness of these stories? Some represent timeless wisdom. Some are attempts to immortalize heroics or sufferings of others ... as in, "Never forget." Some may have had a local purpose at the time, which is no longer recalled or of use to anyone living ... but lingers in the name.

Communities will change some of these names in later epochs for many different reasons. When the old name is removed, in time, its story will become forgotten and it disappears from the active, accessible arena of the communal mind of humanity. With no one to remember it, not even its name, it becomes a ghost wafting in the shadows, no longer accessible to modern minds. The magic of archeology is its ability to locate objects that can still tell a story about the people who made and used them and the gift of deciphering ancient languages to allow their stories to live again long after the last speaker of that tongue has vanished from the Earth.

Stories hold people together, for good or ill. As a boy, I recall the tradition at Passover of retelling the story of the Exodus from Egypt. It was told as if it had happened to each of us today, in the present, because it had happened to us, our people, the people that I "belonged" to, the people who claimed me as one of them. Their story was also my story and was to be incorporated with my personal sense of myself.

I have read that Sunni and Shia Muslims are in conflict today over a succession conflict that occurred fourteen centuries in the past. Since your people did such and such to my people a millennium ago, then we must carry on family tradition and avenge the old wrong by fighting each other, now, today. The stories of the lives of the saints, martyrs, founders of great religions are told and retold as living examples of how to conduct oneself and what to believe … as are the stories of conquerors, human monsters who killed masses and destroyed cultures for the glorification of their name. The disruption and distortion of historical memory is a favorite and devastating tool of dictators and conquerors and politicians who wish to brainwash those under their control into believing that the leader, or current dominant group, defines the beginning of Time.

In a strange way, such thinking is both true and untrue. It is true that the culture in which I am raised (conditioned) shapes my thinking, my values, my behaviors. What is moral and ethical in one time period may be considered immoral and unethical in another. How I think about myself, what options in life are open to me and which forbidden or discouraged by my cultural indoctrination are all determined by others and implanted into me as a child. To have a civil society, this is all necessary and many traditions are practically useful and can promote the development of good character.

On the other hand, am I only my cultural training? Did I bring any seed of individuality with me at conception? Did I, personally, escape from Egypt? Did I, personally, kill your ancestor a thousand years ago? One can see how this type of conditioning through story can function as a hypnotic suggestion, enthralling people into living in a way that reflects experiences they have never themselves experienced … living as if they personally had suffered or experienced defeat or victory in a land and time far, far away. This can give one a sense of rootedness in history. It can also distort the judgment that might be needed in a moment that could be interpreted through the lens of different stories. It is said that history is written by the victors, but the victims keep their own history in stories whispered in the night when the victors aren't listening.

"What's in a Name?

For many, their name and the name of their family become like a sacred totem. "We are Johnsons! Don't ever forget that." "Don't you know who I am? I am Paul Martin Duckworth IV!" "Don't ever call me that name again!" "Congratulations. You are now an American." How do I come to believe that I am my name, my designated label? Listen to how Shakespeare has Juliet challenge this belief.

"'Tis but thy name that is my enemy;

> Thou art thyself, though not a Montague.
> What's Montague? It is nor hand, nor foot,
> Nor arm, nor face, nor any other part
> Belonging to a man. O, be some other name!
> What's in a name? That which we call a rose
> By any other name would smell as sweet;
> So Romeo would, were he not Romeo call'd,
> Retain that dear perfection which he owes
> Without that title. Romeo, doff thy name,
> And for that name which is no part of thee
> Take all myself."

When I was a child, I would sometimes repeat my name over and over until it was just a meaningless noise. In that moment, I had a taste of the arbitrariness of the sound affixed to me to carry as a name throughout my life. People often change their names, traditionally women at marriage, children at adoption, people wishing to hide their identity ... and sometimes in the belief that if I call myself by a different sound, I can escape the psychological-emotional history associated with the original word assigned to my person when I was born.

I don't know the name assigned to my father's family in centuries past. As with many immigrants, on arrival at Ellis Island in New York, local officials could not pronounce the foreign name and so asked, "What is your father's first name?" As the response was, "Aron," my grandfather Joseph became "Aronson." I have heard a pronunciation of what a cousin remembers as the original name, but we have no way to translate the consonant rich sound into English other than phonetically. Attempts to trace the family prior to this name change have been futile. Therefore, on my father's side, I am Stephen, son of Bernard, son of Joseph, son of Aron from the city of Minsk around 1900 ... after which the trail goes cold.

But why should it matter? On the positive side, identifying who and what I am with a name and story gives a sense of grounding. I can locate myself in history and give myself a definition, a role and perhaps a purpose in life. In a recent film of historical fiction set during the period of Danish-Saxon wars in Medieval England, the central character identifies himself as "Uhtred, Son of Uhtred, heir to Bebbanburg." He wears this identity as a uniform. Because of it, he feels compelled to make choices that move in the direction of what he considers his "destiny," as defined by the title he affixes to his sense of self. Women who love him either urge him onto his destiny, reminding him that he is supposed to be a "King" (perhaps in the hope of appropriating the title "Queen," for themselves) or plead with him to just be a man, husband and father and not risk getting killed in attempts to live out the story he assigns to himself … although as he sees it, he has no choice but to fill the tragic-hero archetype he believes himself to be. Another character is surprised to discover that he has been named as a King and struggles to fulfill the assigned role, which he has no training or temperament to occupy.

We may believe we lead more prosaic lives, but is that so? Names are important to us to the degree we use them to define ourselves. What role does who I believe myself to be, play in my life choices? What opportunities have I said yes or no to because of how I defined myself and the manner in which I am supposed to lead my life? Why was my name chosen for me? Does it carry a family story? Has that story influenced me in any way? Not only do I have a given birth name, but I carry the name of a nationality, perhaps a religious community, a name for the role I play in society: doctor, lawyer, craftsman, blue-collar, pink collar, white collar, rich, poor. Do I identify with a political ideology or party? Do I identify myself as a fan of a particular sports team, or city, or movie star?

We are always labeling ourselves to signify our affiliations. Other people will also label us from their own perspectives and motivations. Look how sensitive we are to racial, religious or sexual slurs. We have the historical phrase, "Those are fighting words!" "Take back what you called me, or I will …." We cling to our names and labels because they allow us to identify our location in the collective mindset of our culture and community. People want to know "where I stand" on issues, which groups I identify myself with. Without a name and label, how would I respond? How would I know my "place"?

In Genesis, we are told that on the third day, "God called the dry land "earth," and the gathering of waters He called 'seas' " and that "man gave names to all livestock and to the birds of the heavens and to every beast of the field." Naming is a creative function that man is said to share with the Universal Creative Impulse. In one sense, it is a costume to be draped over my naked personality when I am a child so that I, and others, have a way to place me in the concentric circle of groups that will become the external form of my life. But, is the uniform I wear appropriate to who and what I may be in my essence, the shape of my inherent talents, potentiality and typology? Is there more to me, something essential but hidden underneath the weight of names, labels, roles and inherited stories? Is there a deeper level in the dimension of psychological-emotional-motivational phenomena than names and labels, another level underneath the collective cultural stories?

Names affixed to locations and names affixed to people serve the same purpose. They are markers for hidden stories archived in the invisible dimension of collective experience, themes of which the living person carrying them may or may not be aware. Is it possible to see past my name, past my story? My parents could have chosen any of thousands of other names. If I had been born elsewhere, I would have been given a different story. If I had interpreted some events differently, I would have constructed a different story … and a different form of life.

Who am I, separate from my name, separate from the stories I have been given … stories I claim as my own, whether I personally experienced them or not? Who was I actually designed to be?

That may be a different story.

The Many Versions of Me

Who was I before this moment? This strange question arises because I am just now recalling a time 30 years earlier in my life. This memory resurfaced because I was, just last night, having dinner with the friend who is referenced in the below story. I had taken my son, David, to visit this friend who owned a small hotel on the shores of a Maine lake near the Downeast coast. In my mind's-eye, I see us there, my son and me. I see the landscape, the interior and exterior of the buildings. I see my friend and his wife and some of our interactions. Now a mental side-door opens into an adjacent memory. I am taking my son, by canoe, out onto the still dark waters just before sunrise. The air is cool. The call of a loon occasionally breaks the silence. The air brings us only the sound of lapping water and a mild breeze through the treetops of a deep pine forest. There is the slightly brackish smell and taste of cool lake water in my nose and mouth. The sun begins to rise, and I look at David, hoping he may be experiencing, as I am, a taste of the mystery and heartbreaking beauty of the moment.

Now, three decades into the future of that event, the recollection returns to me. I watch it. I see myself in the scene. It is a younger version of who I am today, now in my late 70's. The understanding, emotional development and perspective of this earlier "self" were both similar to, but also very different, from this current version of "my-self" today. If "he" had had the understanding and perspective that guides my mind and feelings now, how different would have been the quality of his life back then … if he had known what he would experience, waiting ahead of him in time? How much of his later suffering can now be viewed, in retrospect, through the lens of age, as unnecessary … if only he had known then what his older version knows now? How many regrettable choices, ensuing from that more limited viewpoint, could have been avoided?

But, if they had not been experienced, digested and learned from, would I be today the man that is looking back at his younger self with compassion and much deeper wisdom? There is now another image appearing in my mind of a ladder, perhaps a rung for each year, stretching downward … downward … now nearly eighty rungs … back to the moment of my first awareness. It seems a very, very long way down.

The First Version of Me

I had been conceived just before my father left to join the army at the beginning of World War II. He was stationed in London for the next three years. I lived with my mother and her parents during this time. I am told, that when I began to talk, I asked, when a man I did not recognize came to the house, "Is this daddy?" My first memories involve my father, so I can assume I began to awaken to my existence during that third year. I recall a coming home party for him. I am in the living room of my grandparents' house, then also my home. I can still see the image now, a forest of legs stretching above me, the people on top of the legs talking grown-up talk.

I am next to my father's legs. I am asking him to play with me. It is a game he must have played with me earlier, although that memory is not available. I have a clear sense that I wanted him to do this again. He agreed, although I do not recall that moment specifically, but I am now bending over and sticking my arms backwards between my legs. He stands behind me, takes my hands and pulls upward so that I flip in mid-air and then land on my feet. I ask again, and we do it again. I ask a third time, but he replies, "No. Not now." and returns to his conversation. I feel hurt. I also remember watching from my bedroom window on the second floor as he washes his new, 1945 blue Buick. I clearly recall the day my parents brought my sister home from the hospital after her birth. I can see the room I was in, the furniture, my parents standing at the door holding a baby in a pink blanket. I was three and a half years old.

Who was I then, this small, dependent child, wanting his father's attention and feeling, even then, a sense of protectiveness and affection for my sister? The awakening entity in my little body was conscious, in those moments, as I have come to experience the meaning of that term today. He had within him the seeds of sensitivity, affection and desire to understand a world, a universe, whose existence he did not, at that time, even know existed.

Another Version of Me

An example of this comes to mind at this moment. I am five or six years old. I am on the playground behind my school. I see in front of me the fence running along the edge of the playground facing the side road. I am slowly walking towards the fence and I am thinking … actually beginning to ponder. This seems to be my first recall of this quality of mental inquiry. I am turning over and over in my mind a rumor I had heard that day. I do not recall where I overhead this amazing, hard-to-understand information. What I was pondering was the rumor that there was a *second* ocean! I lived at the edge of the Atlantic. I knew the ocean, but I did not know it had a name. It was simply "The Ocean." So, I asked myself, "How could there be a second ocean? Where would you put it? How could there be room for another?" I suspect this memory has always been available to me as it represents an early moment of awakening consciousness and the stirrings of critical thinking. This quality clearly links that little boy with the older man writing these words. He was like the seed pod from which the more mature versions of me would later emerge.

The Ladder

As I follow the train of thought I am experiencing in this moment, I can see the toddler down near the bottom of the ladder, the middle-aged father halfway up and my current self near the top. I say "near the top" for the logical reason that I still live. How many more rungs are there above me? I am hoping for ten or even twenty more before the top, but I can only look down, not upward.

How, in the past, could I have not known what I know now? Today, what I have learned is obvious to this version of myself. But it was not obvious; it was not even visible to my earlier versions. Where was this deeper understanding back them? Where was it hiding … waiting … patiently waiting for me to discover it and add its quality to the composition of my Being?

When I look at photographs of myself over my life, I see physically different people. I "know" these images are "me," but they are not images of the physical "me" today. We all look at photos of our younger selves and comment on "how young we looked," but we don't feel, don't taste, don't experience the profundity, the implications of what we are looking at. In some ways, these images are of the same basic body, the same genetic material, but in another much more obvious way, they are showing a different physical body that no longer exists. Its form has altered. Its functional capacities have changed. Its organs have grown older. Every cell in this body, except for the neuronal cells in the brain, dies and is replaced, depending on the organ, every few days to several years. Bodies literally change over time because the constituent parts that make up their form are continually changing. Are the forms of me on each rung the same person or are they each a similar but not identical version?

The question becomes more profound if I examine the content and understanding of the psychological perspective of each of those versions. Haven't we all looked back and wondered, "How could I have believed that? How could I have been blind to that? If only I had known then, what I know now." A child's understanding is different from that of a young adult. Hopefully, the middle-aged person no longer thinks as they did when young. The potential wisdom of old age is built on the learning of each previous version below on the ladder of life.

"When I was a child, I spoke as a child. I understood as a child. I thought as a child: but when I became a man, I put away childish things."*

The Library of My Life

Looking back on all these previous versions of my current operating system, I am now focused on the differences between these men, below me, each representing a stage in the unfolding of what I have become today and may become in what remains of my future. What holds them together? They all share access to the same line of memory. The recording of the experiences of each man is deposited in the same library. Over the portico to this library is carved, "The Memory Library of My Life." Each version of myself has wandered the hallways and reading rooms of this library and re-lived the impression of his former selves.

Although, I must admit that, for the most part, I revisit the same rooms over and over. How to gain access to deeper recesses of the library is a mystery. I find that if I allow myself to wander the corners of any memory room, doorways of associated memories may open ... sometimes several at a time. I cannot explore them simultaneously. I have to choose one in the moment and follow it. Along this new path, other memory portals may open into an expanding connection of associations. Sometimes they interconnect and I find myself back where I started. Sometimes they branch and branch and branch, leaving me wondering how I got to this location from where I began ... if I can even recall where this line of remembrances had started. No wonder it is difficult to build a map of the library. The sections open and close, disappear and reappear depending on their associational links. There also feels to be enormous areas that are in perpetual darkness, their memories apparently un-retrievable. What parts of me lie there, out of reach of my conscious mind?

---

* *1 Corinthians 13:1*

This continual line of enlarging stories, this library of impressions grows, as a body grows and carries its passenger, Consciousness, with it in its daily rounds through the life that has developed around this person. The capability to access this labyrinth of impressions is dependent on the functional capacity of the organic material in the "head-brain "of the physical body. Yet, the library must remain somehow independent of the capacity of the librarian. How can I know this? How often have I "forgotten," "misplaced" a memory, only to have it "return" to me at a later time. We joke that memory sometimes hides "on the tip of my tongue." People with dementia may at times "come back to themselves," "become themselves again," and for a while have access to parts of the library. Victims of trauma who have "lost" memory for the events may sometimes retrieve them through therapy or hypnosis or a sudden shock that opens the door to the hidden room of suffering. Sometimes a dream will lead to the recall of a long-lost experience, even perhaps, to be "tasted," re-lived in the dream itself.

Growth of Understanding

As both the physical and psychological bodies continually modify on the journey up the ladder, in a way, the "world" in which my awareness lives is also continually altering. My understanding changes with new experiences, new thinking, new ideas. As my perspective shifts, it alters my experience and interpretation of the world around me. Does anything remain the same? Is there any continuity?

My awareness, or sense, of myself as The Consciousness, the Observer, inside this continually altering matrix of mind, feeling and body, does seem the same today as in my earliest memories. The taste of being present to the existence of myself at age five and then at age fifty is the same taste of being present to myself now as I approach eighty. This sense of "observing' my thoughts and feelings inside the body and its outer physical manifestations have not changed. This sense of being aware of being present as a Witness to the unfolding events of my life always carries the same taste, the same quality. Sometimes it is more intense, sometimes less so. It is the experience of myself having the experience of thought, feeling, body sensations and interactions with the people and world about me. With a very intense memory, I can say, "I remember being there, feeling and thinking this, while the event unfolded around me. I can say, "I remember being there," because I *was* there, *consciously awake* to my thoughts, my emotions, my behaviors in that moment. Perhaps my memories are imprinted in varying strengths and depths due to fluctuating degrees of conscious awareness of myself as the Observer who is witnessing, and experiencing, the event.

What is this "sense of myself" that feels to be the common thread connecting each rung of my life? Looking at all the prior versions of me, how they have changed physically, emotionally, mentally, attitudinally, perhaps the only aspect that represents what I am in essence, what does not change throughout life, is what I call my consciousness, my attention, my awareness of myself living a life from inside a body which walks the surface of the planet we call Earth.

Yet, how can I truly call it my own? Can I take credit for these phenomena? Do I, does anyone, have any idea what this energy is that gives the experience of existing? Do I own my consciousness, attention, awareness? Or do I share in it as I share the air of the planet? Doesn't everyone else seem to have degrees of awareness also, some more, some less? Even animals seem to be keenly aware, certainly of their surroundings, even if not objectively capable of the abstract experience of self-awareness. Perhaps, this sense of myself is a level or quality of experience shared in different ways with life itself.

Whatever I am, whatever we are, does not seem to be a constant, but rather a "something" or a collection of "somethings" constantly in flux, nothing to which we could really ascribe materiality, other than the physical body.

How interesting that my remembrance of canoeing with my son at sunrise on a Maine lake thirty years ago has today become the doorway to a meditation of the mystery of myself. If I am willing to take the time to wander through the library of my life, who knows what new connections, new insights, new understandings and perspectives lie waiting for the light of inquisitive and open-minded attention.

I'll have to remember that.

The Mystery of Feeling

T he music sounded "soulful." I'm feeling "melancholy." That is really "irritating" me. I feel "hopeful." I really "wish." I am "lonely." I feel "grateful." I am in "awe."

How do I Know What I Feel?

How do I know what I feel? How did a particular feeling get its name, its label? How do words describing invisible, subjective states arise in a linguistic system? How can a feeling-state be verbally shared? Are we truly sharing experience just because we agree on the word?

Reader! Look inside! Think about and picture a few situations where you had strong feelings, both negative as well as positive. What feelings describe each of these experiences? Now, how do you know to call these sensations or emotions by specific names? What exactly do you experience before you put this label on it?

There seem to be two different qualities of experience that are both called "feelings" or "emotions" in our ordinary language. The origins of one category are known today, while the other somewhat understood, while the other category is an overlooked mystery of deepest implication.

The sensations we experience as a result of molecular hormonal changes in our physiology are well understood. It is these sensations of physical arousal that represent one of the categories we call *feeling* or *emotion*. Our flight or fight instinctive response system, when noticing perceived threats to safety or invitations to pleasure, triggers subjectively recognized changes in biochemical balances. A sense of danger triggers the release of stress hormones, i.e. cortisone, adrenaline, norepinephrine, which alter heart rate, breathing, shifts of blood volume from interior organs to muscles and brain, muscular tension, among other effects so that we can respond aggressively or defensively to the perceived threat. The threat can be real or imagined, directed towards my body's integrity, or my image of myself or my safety in a relationship. These sensations tend to be uncomfortable and promote a search for paths of escape. When escape is achieved, the body relaxes its tension and reduction in discomfort is the reward. This is the work of our so-called "sympathetic nervous system."

So-called "pleasure hormones," dopamine, serotonin, endorphins, oxytocin, make us feel safe, comfortable, euphoric and give an experience of "pleasure" and attraction towards the apparent source of stimulation. This is the work of the parasympathetic nervous system. To re-experience the pleasant sensations, behaviors develop to stimulate them repeatedly. This built-in mechanism promotes movement towards safety and continuation of the life of the individual and species.

Both these mechanisms together make up the Autonomic Nervous System, a hard-wired, instinctive program, totally mechanical and functioning at an unconscious level. They work by facilitating the release of different combinations of hormones that control reactions in the body in response to stimuli interpreted, by the body or feelings or mind, as dangerous or attractive.

Hormones are arrangements of molecules. The body seems so designed that continual fluctuations in the release and balance of different molecules correlate to these subjective experiences and objective reactions. How and why they should do so is mystery sufficient to cause stunned amazement if we can overcome a sense of familiarity with these every-day experiences such that we are habituated to seeing the wonder of this process built into the basic operating system of all animal life, including ourselves. All species are programed for pain and pleasure to facilitate movement towards and away from situations that either threaten or increase survival chances for the individual and the species. All mammals and birds to varying degrees, share an emotional world of play, nurturing, affection, cooperation and affinity for members of their group or species and, in many cases, between species. As mammals, we share this emotional world with many of our companions on the planet ... and it now seems with some cephalopods as well.

There are three basic survival strategies demonstrated by life: flight, fight or playing dead responses to danger tend to produce observable outer manifestations from the body, muscular or vocal expression, tone of voice, movement towards or away from the perceived stimulus. We humans can talk about these experiences with each other with some considerable degree of agreement as we all have the same basic physiological responses.

When I say I feel "angry," "afraid," "excited," I can pinpoint specific sensations in particular parts of my body. Although individuals experience variations in how, and maybe where, these hormonal changes are "felt," there is a discernible change in subjective inner experience. If asked, I say I know I am angry because my jaw is clenched, my fists are balled tight, I feel flushed, my voice is faltering. I may describe "anxiety" as a rapid heartbeat, shallow breathing, shaking limbs, a sense of "doom" (another interesting word). When excited, I may feel some of these same changes but interpret them differently because the situation seems positive rather than negative. There is research suggesting that how we interpret the meaning of these subjective experiences depends on how we interpret the meaning of the situation. For example, if called to the boss's office, I may interpret the "butterflies in my stomach" as apprehension, but if these same sensations are experienced at the beginning of a situation promising something potentially pleasant, like meeting a prospective love interest, I may label the sensations as "excitement."

The second quality of "feeling" or "emotion" is far more subtle and individualized. These are experiences of "quality" relating to the world of values, not physical survival. What am I subjectively experiencing that, by association, brings to mind words like "soulful," "hopeful," "longing," "remorse," "appreciation"? What am I experiencing to cue for me a label describing different qualities? How do I know I am experiencing gratitude, awe, inspiration? How do I know the taste of conscience? What is the subjective experience of being touched by the Divine? How does the thought of a spiritual life create, if I am that type of person, a feeling of wishing for contact with something greater than myself? Is there a biological underpinning for the taste of a wish?

Known from the beginning of humankind, certain chemicals and plants contain molecules that clearly stimulate experiences of "expanded consciousness" and altered perceptions. These experiences often lead to alterations in values and beliefs. Do the molecules pre-determine what is altered in the user's perspective or do they create changes in perception that then lead to change in understanding and valuation? Why would we have receptors in our nervous system to receive these mind-altering molecules? Why would these molecules have such a profound effect on us, changing the direction of a life and sometimes a society?

The Autonomic Nervous System has a clear reason for existing. It facilitates organic survival in the most basic Darwinian manner. Does this other system of "feeling" also have a built-in reason for existing in us? Are we also programmed not only to survive physically but also to develop higher sensitivities and reasoning? And what of the unexpected moments of altered consciousness not associated with the ingestion of these stimulating molecules? Does our body produce them at random intervals or in emotionally charged situations? The vast majority of these experiences of value and meaning are not associated with any outside stimulant.

The world of value and meaning may overlap the pain-pleasure survival mechanism at an instinctive level, but its larger field of action extends into the realm of philosophy, belief, concepts, principles, even when the roots of the feeling cannot be pinpointed. Meaning and value can be talked about because they involve an intellectual, symbolic component. Thus, these components appear to limit this higher level of subjective experience to humans due to the addition to our brain of the frontal lobes as the arena of conceptual thinking and perceiving.

So, how do I know what I value? Why would I go against my flight or fight response and face discomfort or danger for a matter of "principle"? Why would a mystic intentionally undergo discomfort and deprivation in the search for an invisible, theorized connection with a "higher" power? Why would I risk or even knowingly sacrifice my life for "something I believe in"? Such responses go against "Nature" and, in that sense, are "unnatural."

In the case of survival-enhancing reactions of attraction and repulsion, the shifts in hormonal balances are programmed into the organism to involuntarily produce the behavioral response that will increase the likelihood of living another day. The sensations of comfort or discomfort will automatically create the urge to move towards or away. No "thought" process is required. The fact that this protective system has been in place since life appeared clearly indicates that life forms have built-in receptors sensitive to these hormonal fluctuations. They come with the development of the creature in utero, or egg, and are ready to function at birth.

Are there built-in receptors for the experience of value and meaning, waiting for certain types of situations to trigger their awakening? We know from studies in developmental psychology that some value-appearing reactions occur in young children, such as empathy or sharing, although they may appear at different ages for different individuals and may not appear at all in some. With many children, they seem to need to be taught or modeled. The discovery of "mirror neurons" would seem to suggest a built-in mechanism for reciprocal sharing of basic emotional states relating to comfort and discomfort in others. They are a likely candidate for a biological basis for empathy.

The question of value and meaning requires a degree of understanding of, or intuitive feeling for, underlying principles, or laws, in order to become generalized to situations far removed from the initial incidents that originally stimulated them. Learning the "letter of the law" would seem to be based on reward and punishment, which is the basis of the survival principle. It can be learned and practiced without deeper understanding of the underlying reasons for the law. The "spirit of the law" requires an understanding of the meaning and larger principles which give birth to the law as their practical expression.

Material science has confirmed that certain molecular formations, which are themselves temporary combinations of certain atoms, which themselves are temporary combinations of sub-atomic particles, which themselves are fluctuating mixtures of the underlying energies which shape and direct the structure and functions of the universe, interact with built-in receptors that trigger sensitive responses in life forms, which are designed to facilitate their survival and procreation. It appears clear that the material of biological life is intimately connected and responsive to certain universal energies which seem designed to support the activities of that life. Organic life is connected to the underlying structure of the universe. Is our emotional/psychological existence also connected to the underlying structure of the universe? If not, what is it connected to?

What can we reason about non-mass-based subjective psychological phenomena like valuation, meaning, conscience, spiritual aspiration? If there are, so far, undiscovered molecules associated with these qualities, they also, logically, would be built into the fabric of universal energies. As the survival mechanism serves the greater purpose of Nature, the existence of these more subtle, inspirational "feelings" must also serve something, perhaps something higher than the biological needs of the Earth.

However, our thinking, reasoning capacities, although influenced by underlying biochemical imbalances, appear not to be primarily hormonal in nature. Our nervous system runs on electricity as its foundational energy. Electricity in motion generates magnetic fields. Our psychological functions appear to represent the functioning of electromagnetic field phenomena. Electromagnetism is currently understood to be one of the four "Forces" that hold the universe together. It has recently become increasingly acceptable for researchers exploring the nature and origins of subjective "consciousness" to speculate that our psychological life is an aspect of the quantum realm rather than the biological level.

How then do I know, so that I can label it, what I am experiencing when I refer to questions of value and meaning? Am I "sensing" fluctuations in the sub-atomic world inside myself that correspond to and stimulate an awareness of these "higher" feelings that can function separately from, and at times at odds with, the biological program for survival of my material body? This logically implies that "I" have mechanisms, some built-in and perhaps others that require further development, for experiencing both biological and quantum fluctuations.

What then does this imply about the nature of "I"? The "place" of experiencing the subjective world of psychological and "higher" emotional experiences appears to lie beyond biology. Following the logical progression, the home of "I" must lie either within or beyond the quantum realm, its sensitivity stretching from the world of matter to non-material dimensions not measurable by material science.

How I know what I am feeling now seems intimately connected with the mystery of what I am at the deepest level.

The Mystery of Talking About Feelings

Humans have built-in mechanisms for verbal, symbolic speech that are lacking in other life forms. To be sure, other life forms have "language" but not the ability to conceptualize and vocalize those concepts beyond modeling behavior for the young of their species. Clearly, some creatures use tools and problem solving, but they don't write books or produce teaching videos for later generations. They have the beginnings of culture but are limited by the structure of their programmed brain and nervous system.

There is a great range of conceptual and verbal capacities among humans, just as some animal species appear "smarter" than others and individual animals within a species seem more intelligent than others. Some of these capacities can be developed by education and practice if the underlying potential exists in the person, but not beyond the ceiling determined by the health and structure of the brain of the individual. Just as we all have different potential physical functioning depending on health and genetics, this appears to hold true with emotional, intellectual and conceptual potential functioning as well.

Given our special capacity for inventing sounds and symbols to represent things and experiences, another question arises. It seems logical that sounds assigned to material objects and observable behavioral manifestations could be shared and agreed upon. At some point in time, an ancestor picked up a solid object and made a sound. A companion, hearing the sound, mimicked it. For example, in English, the guttural sound, "r-o-c-k," became the agreed-upon sound denoting this object. As time went by and the development of the hominid brain continued, more and more sounds could be assigned to and agreed to represent the material world and observable activities of fellow hominids. What we would later call "verbs" rather than initial "nouns" could appear to represent movement. "Go," "come," "leave," probably initially accompanied by arm gestures, would expand communication possibilities.

The human brain is wired for language. The capacity is built-in. Infants begin to learn language from within the womb, listening to the vibration of the mother's voice and perhaps voices around the mother. After birth, the child will learn whatever language is spoken in its presence. It is taught to use labels for things. Later, it is taught words for feelings and emotions. Grammar is a built-in process. The child will mimic what it hears until the neural pathways associated with the particular language have become myelinated (hard-wired), so the language can flow automatically without thinking. We can see this process halt when we have to "search" for the right word.

How then could we explain the expansion of language for non-observable, non-material reactions? Experiencing the biologically based sensation from the pleasure-pain system, the autonomic nervous system with its parasympathetic ("it's safe, come closer") and sympathetic ("danger, run away"), how could we understand the development of sounds to indicate what is being experienced inside at the sensory level? An early man feels a surge of adrenaline at the sight of a mammoth or relief that he has returned to the cave with enough food for the clan. How, and why, would he search for a sound denoting this state of inner experience? Where is the external agreed-upon object to which to attach the sound? There is nothing to point to.

Much more mysterious is the question concerning how labels could have appeared and found agreement for subtle feeling states such as those relating to value, belief, meaning. I suspect we all know the confusion of trying to find a word to describe a novel experience. "How can I say this?" "I don't have words." "I can 'see' it in my mind's eye, but I can't talk about it." "A picture is worth a thousand words."

These kinds of unusual experiences, perceptions, insights, epiphanies require a poet or mystic or storyteller to try to find a way of combining words so that they *point* to the experience, even while knowing that the pointing is not the experience.

The listener, if the description does not evoke in them a resonant association from their own experiential library, will respond, "I don't understand what you are talking about. I don't resonate with what you are saying." If the listener has had a related experience for which the speakers' words do resonate, the reply can confirm a potential experiential overlap that could lead to the perception of mutual understanding. We can understand another person's inner world of thoughts and feelings only to the degree to which those experiences resonate with our own. We can feel their experience inside ourselves because we have that experience in us already. It is our experience we are tasting, only having been stimulated by sounds from the speaker's mouth, sounds we call words.

Since the development of this linguistic capacity has evolved over time with homo sapiens, it logically must be part of the built-in programming within which we find ourselves living. Since traits and capacities that have utility survive, and those that do not tend to atrophy and eventually disappear over time, reason suggests that our capacity for language has served to facilitate our physical survival in a world of stronger creatures and biological hazards. By extension, the mysterious capacity to develop a language for subjective experiences must have arisen to help us learn to explore, learn from and become knowledgeable about our other "home" in the invisible, non-mass-based "world" of our hearts and minds.

In this world, we do not need verbal language for our experiences. We "feel" our way. We "sense" our way. See images in our "mind's eye" that produce non-verbal understanding. If we are present as an observing Awareness, then we may search for "words" to describe to ourselves and others what we have experienced. Why the drive to communicate? Are we not searching for confirmation, affirmation that I am not alone in my view of reality when we ask questions like these? "Have you had a similar experience or am I alone? Am I crazy or are there really other "realities" behind or interpenetrating the outer world of my senses? What in the world am I? How can any of this be happening? What is really going on here? What does all this mean?"

In the end, it comes down to meaning. Perhaps the search for meaning is what our linguistic and conceptual capacities are designed to serve. Who or what is using us to search for meaning?

Relativity of Language

Many years ago, mid-way through my first marriage, my wife and I had an argument. Once again, she was complaining to me that when she felt ill, she also felt neglected, not "taken care of," by me. I had often used the same words in complaining to her about the same feelings in me. This mutual complaint had gone on for years. Neither of us could understand why the other could not understand. Then, in the midst of another one of these repetitive disagreements, an idea appeared in my mind.

I then asked her, "When you say, 'take care of,' what exactly do you mean by 'take care of'?"

"What do you mean, what do I mean?" she replied with irritation. "I mean, I want you to take care of me. I take care of you when you don't feel well!"

I was very surprised. "What do you mean when you say you "take care of me"? I don't feel taken care of."

"I do take care of you. I leave you alone and don't bother you unless you call", she defended herself.

"Wait a minute," I exclaimed. "Leaving me alone unless I call is … taking care of me?

"Of course, it is," she said.

"O.K.," I replied. "I think we are using the same words to mean different things. Leaving me alone until I call for help is not my definition of taking care of. I want you to check on me often, bring me soup, play cards with me, keep me company. That's taking care of from my point of view."

"God! No!" she said with force. "That would be hovering, like what my mother did to me."

And there you have it … years of disagreement, hurt feelings and lost opportunities for helping and bonding … all over the meaning of three words … "take care of."

There are many factors that make relationships between people difficult at times. The relativity of language is a major issue. We all assume that if we are speaking the same language, our words will be understood and we, certainly, will understand what is said to us. The single above example demonstrates the fallacy of this viewpoint.

Ask ten people … or five people … or even one or two … to define "love" or "success" or "appropriate" or "do the right thing" or "fair share" or "God" or even "sex," for example. Actually, dear Reader, this would be a very interesting experiment for you to perform in order to gauge the accuracy of the concerns expressed in this exploration. Assuming that if we all are speaking the same language, whether English, Russian, French, Spanish, Mandarin, we all are operating from the same definition for our words, is a dangerous and sometimes fatal misunderstanding. Anyone with any experience trying to translate from one language to another immediately recognizes that the same word or concept or nuance in one language may not have exact counterparts in another language. What takes one word to describe in one language may require several words or a phrase in another.

Vocabulary and Understanding

The extent of a person's vocabulary also sets a limit on conveying understanding and subtlety. As a student, I read in Sociology 101 that Innuits had over twenty words for snow. A recent search on the internet tells me that Swedish Lapland has 200 words for types of snow and Scottish 421 for the substance. I could not imagine the differences in snow that would account for this number of variations as I could think of no more than a few words from my actual experience. When I began to ski, however, I quickly added to my vocabulary, as I was now paying attention to snow with a motivated and discerning eye for skiable conditions that I never had a need to look for prior to changing my relationship with the frozen white stuff.

Words are sounds that have agreed-upon symbolic meaning for concepts, feeling-states, opinions, suggestions, requests, directions. Words allow communication between people who have never met and may even be separated by thousands of years. Words allow us to express our subjective, idiosyncratic experiences to seek confirmation as to whether others have personally had our experience as well …. or whether we are alone in our corner of reality.

Take a moment now, dear Reader, and reflect on times when you have searched for words to describe an experience and were left saying something like, "I really don't have words to describe it." A greater problem is believing that our words do describe our thoughts or experiences accurately and assuming that the people we are trying to share with have had the same experience, which they may not have, or the same thoughts, which they may not have, or would use the same words to describe their thoughts and feelings, even if similar to our own.

An additional problem is that, for most of us, images often appear in our mind accompanying our words, or our experience appears to us first as images and then we have to search our vocabulary library to find words that best describe the image. Look at all these words I am utilizing, as author, to try to communicate, with accuracy, the subtlety of this question to readers I have not met and probably never will meet. Will I be able to find the words that best represent my vision, with minimal error in understanding on the part of you, my unknown Reader?

Common sense and experience recognize that "A picture is worth a thousand words" … and sometimes many more than that are required to paint a verbal image of the complexity of that which we wish to convey. And, even more problematic is the fact that each of us may have different images which arise through association with the same words, depending on our individual exposure in life. Mention the word "soil" to a farmer and a city shop owner and the level of information and detail forthcoming will be very different. The world of a life-long urban dweller will have words and experiences alien to that of a life-long rural dweller and vice versa. These different environments produce different societies with different dialects, different vocabulary, attention to different details and even different viewpoints on life itself. Unfortunately, our conditioned tendency is to assume that our understanding and definition of a word or phrase is always the same understanding and definition used by the other person.

Thinking in Images

Just as our definition of words may vary, the pictures accumulated in our minds that often accompany ideas and feelings are idiosyncratic to our personal life experiences. For example, the word "home" may bring up warm, grateful and happy feelings and images to one person, but the word "home" may bring up a cold, unhappy, fearful, resentful feelings and images to another person. Less dramatically, many people have never actually seen or experienced snow. How could they then visualize the finer distinctions of those whose lives depend on recognizing such differences?

I once had the wonderful experience of introducing a friend from the midwest USA to the Atlantic Ocean. She had read about oceans. She had seen pictures and movies. But she had never actually experienced the ocean. I recall blindfolding and leading her to its edge. When her eyes were freed from their restraints, she was literally speechless. All she could say was, "Oh my God. It's so big. It is so big."

I still recall the emotion I often felt as a boy looking at stars through my telescope. The experience included a sense of infinity, of timelessness, of absolute cold, of total silence, of unspeakable loneliness, of unfathomable distance, of the sparkling brilliance of each star-point piercing the blackness. What is the word for *that* experience? Awe? Stupefaction? Terror? Spellbound? Mystified? If you have not had this particular experience, dear Reader, how could you think about or talk about it? If you have had this quality of experience, what words would you choose to use … and who do you suppose would actually understand what you were talking about?

As a novice learner of Italian many years ago, I quickly came to realize that the same sounding word had different meanings depending on context. I take this for granted in my native English and rarely notice unless a meaning is questioned. In another language, the possible social faux pas are inexhaustible. I also learned this about body language in a small restaurant in Tuscany when I gave a hand sign, which in the English-speaking world means "excellent" in response to the waiter's inquiry about the quality of the meal he had served us. A companion quickly pulled my hand down, explaining that what this sign meant in Italy was not what it meant in the USA!

It appears to be a common joke in many cultures that there are too many lawyers. What do all these lawyers do besides complexify life … unless they are my lawyers? Most of them construct laws and documents by crafting the words to create contractual agreements that either have very specific meaning or are flexible enough to allow loopholes, depending on their aim. Much legislation creates additional difficulties because the language is imprecise and needs interpretation by a court, which itself must guess at the initial intention, poorly crafted linguistically, behind the legislation. An American politician recently epitomized the absurdity possible in these situations by employing as a defense the legalism that, "It depends on what the meaning of the word 'is' is." He explained that if "is" meant "never has been," that is one thing; but, if "is" meant "there is none currently," that is a different thing."

Assumptions and Relativity

When we use words atypical for our normal speech, we may be more sensitive to the need to explain or define. A problem stems from our habitual use of common words, such that we take for granted that everyone understands in the same way we understand. In addition, we rarely listen to ourselves talk and typically don't hear what we are saying or how we may be saying it.

For instance, let's take a well-worn example found in many philosophical writings. What is the meaning of the word "world"? Are we referring to the specific planet Earth or any of the planets of our, or any solar system? Or do we mean the Western world vs. the Eastern world, or the First world vs. the Third world or my individual world of family, friends, work, hobbies? Perhaps we mean the world of life vs. non-living, material forms or animals vs. plants or the mammalian world vs. the world of reptiles or birds. Maybe we are thinking of the academic world or the world of politics or the world of sports. Often in psychology, the term is used to represent different experiential levels of reality as in the outer and inner world.

Obviously, this exploration could go on for some time with just the word "world." When we speak, we ought to consider the scale of possible meanings for the words we choose, often dependent on context, prior history, shared values and interests. Words also can convey different meanings depending on the other words used with them or the timing of their delivery or the tone of voice, the situation in which the words are employed. All these variables are subject to the idiosyncratic interpretation of each party involved in the attempted communication.

For example, I have often been either amused or at times alerted by the word "Sweetheart, _____," used to begin a statement by one lover or spouse to the other. In a given context, it may be simply a heart-felt expression of affection, or it may be used as a defensive preamble to soften the reaction of the suggestion or criticism that follows, or it may be used sarcastically as a weapon. It is all in the tone, timing and context … as well as the historical interpretive memory of the listener.

Experiment: Try This With Your Friends

If you would like a sobering, or an amusing, experience, dear Reader, ask yourself for your definition of "love," "responsible," "fair," "equality," "on time," "thoughtful," "loyal," for example. Use any words or terms that interest you, or perhaps seem to be frequently employed during misunderstandings, or escape from people's mouths during emotional complaints or disagreements. Later, take your list and ask other friends and family for their definitions of these terms. Try to encourage yourself and them to be as precise as possible, such as, "Yes, I hear you felt offended. But how exactly did I hurt your feelings? Was it something I said or did or did not do, or when I did it? How did you understand what I said? It may not be what I meant."

The Devil is in the Details

"The devil is in the details" is an expression that applies in these situations of misunderstanding. The first place to look, and the easiest problem to fix, is in the relativity of the words being used whenever there is disagreement, emotional reactions, confusion or any failure to recognize a common understanding. If the differences in definitional understanding can be clarified, a sizable number of relational difficulties disappear, and the "World" (at least our world) runs a bit more smoothly.

Without recognizing the fluidity and idiosyncrasy of our words, we are often trapped in a Tower of Babel, believing that we are agreeing, when, in fact, and unbeknownst to us, we are not in agreement … a fact that will eventually emerge and often result in accusations of deliberate deception, falsehood and cheating. … when the problem was due to a misunderstanding of terminology, as in my opening example. Or we may believe we are in disagreement when in fact we are not but rather are using different words or concepts to describe our goal or justification for our method of achieving it. A current and perennial conflict in many communities is the question of a "fair" taxation rate. Probably most people would agree on the aim of "fair" distribution of financial responsibility in a society. No one ever argues for unfair taxation. It is the definition of "fair" that produces conflict.

Talking to Myself

This problem becomes more critical when it is myself that I am talking to. How I define a problem for myself, what I believe could be a solution, my justification of my actions … or lack of action … will be based on a blending of emotional feeling and conceptual framing. If I do not challenge myself to clearly define the words which I use with myself in my own head, I may be leading myself and others astray. If I decide I am a "victim" rather than a person dealing with the complexity of life, the outcome for myself and others will be dramatically different.

An antidote to this phenomenon is to approach communication with awareness. I need to watch the thoughts formulate in my head and listen to my voice when I speak. To speak without listening to my thoughts and my voice is like carrying a loaded weapon without a safety ... or training. Sooner or later, someone is going to get hurt.

To sidestep my mental conditioning, I can incorporate the following questions into my reasoning, both for my own thinking and to what I am trying to understand others wish to convey to me.

Ask myself:

What do I mean when I use the term ....?

Why have I chosen this phrasing rather than an alternative?

What are alternative words and phrases that could describe my feeling or decision?

What are specific examples to illustrate what I am trying to say?

Ask others:

What do you mean when you use the term . . . ?

Why have you chosen this phrasing rather than an alternative?

What are alternative words and phrases that could describe your feeling or decision?

What are specific examples which could illustrate what you are trying to say?

Many difficulties people have with each other could be reduced or eliminated with an interest and attention to the relativity of words.

Habituated to the Mystery

We take words too casually. We are so used to talking that we have habituated to the mystery of what is happening. My eardrums are picking up vibrations from pressure waves of air colliding with them from the outside. These pressure waves were emitted a moment ago, by that person over there, through the vibration of air in their vocal cords and shaped by their tongue, teeth and lips on the way out of their mouths, to produce a vibration which, they assume, will carry the essence of the thought or feeling, which they wish to express to you. This vibration, from their voice, now resonating in your eardrums, stimulates an electrical current in nerves that run, like telephone wires, into your brain and terminate in the area that translates (somehow) thoughts and feelings into mental words, which then stimulate other neurons which carry an electrical current out to your voice box and diaphragm that, in turn, sets the tensions to produce the modulation in vibration that will be carried on your exhaling breath to be shaped by your tongue, lips and teeth into the vibration that will flow towards your listener in response.

How does the mind activate speech? You can explore this right now, dear Reader, by trying this experiment. Put your attention on your vocal cords. If you cannot sense them immediately, try humming or speaking a few words or sounds. Feel the vibration in your throat. Now, stop breathing for a few moments. Talk to yourself in your mind. Content doesn't matter. If you cannot find thoughts to think, then try counting "aloud" in your head. While you are thinking words or numbers in your mind, sense your vocal cords. With practice, you can become sensitive enough to feel them moving in response to the thoughts. All that is missing is the breath. Thinking activates our vocal cords even when we are not speaking … this small bundle of muscle can "read" our thoughts.

When these vibrations, called words, enter into me, they start a cascade of activity that ends in an interpretation, in my mind, of what these words mean, based on my personal history with them. The information these vibrations carry is blended into my fabric. The thought transferred, the opinion offered, the new information imprinted, now becomes part of me. Any emotional influence connected with the word, any pleasure or pain, gratitude or resentment, confidence or fear, is now a part of me. Unless I am known intimately, the speaker of these words will likely, have no idea where in me this information, these transferred feelings will be stored, what they will stimulate from my past, what defensive or open response they will elicit from me.

And, I have no idea where in my listener, my words will lodge, what ripples they will create, what they will merge with inside the mind of my listener, awakening old pain, perhaps changing them in some way.

When I speak, anyone who hears my words, both my intended audience, as well as innocent bystanders, becomes impregnated by the entrance of my words into their nervous system and brain and by their interpretation of what they believe I am saying to them. We are feeding each other, infusing each other with psychological and emotional material from our invisible interiors. How often am I paying attention to what I am eating and what I am dishing out?

Responsibility

The utterance of words is a huge responsibility which we rarely consider. We don't consider because we are lost in our own thoughts, our own interior words, to the extent that we may ... perhaps ... see the other person, but we do not *feel* them, do not *resonate* with them. Nor do we recognize the mystery or power of the sounds vibrating, rippling through us, from person to person.

In the pre-scientific age, people perceived a similarity between the mystery of a universe, the origins for which cannot be found at the level of its existence, and the mystery of words, themselves formulated in a hidden world within a heart and mind, riding the exhaled breath to express themselves in, and shape the world beyond, the invisible place of their origin.

The impression was that the universe was breathed into existence on the breath of "God" (one of many words used to symbolize the hidden energy behind all other energies). God breathed out the Word, and from the darkness, there came light. God breathed again and more words resounded forth to create and name "day" and "night," "land," "waters" and "heavens." When man was created, he was given the privilege and responsibility of assigning names to all the animals.

Today, science gives us, as a rational counterpoint to the unscientific poetry of past ages, this story of the "Big Bang." Long, long, long ago, there was Nothing ... nothing at all .... not even Space ... and then "something happened"... and ... a "particle" of energy, very, very small, maybe the size of a grain of sand, ... or a billionth the size of a grain of sand ... or maybe even much smaller ...suddenly "exploded" and began to expand. It carried within it all the material and laws necessary to establish and regulate our universe. Today, everything in the universe exists inside that still expanding particle ... which is, itself, always larger than the universe it contains. What it is expanding into is unknown. But, since the universe contains all there is, it must be expanding into the Nothing that preceded its appearance. Everything came from nowhere and popped into existence. The forms and laws we see in the universe today are the expressions of that original impulse from a place unknown and outside the universe, we see now.

To some, the universe appears to be a very, very large machine whose working parts can be explained, measured and tested. This machine, with its infinite number of forms, functions in consistent and predictable patterns. Because the underlying workings of the machine are discoverable, this is interpreted to mean that the Universe did not have an initial designer but constructed itself according to the governing laws which guided the construction of the machine. The guiding laws themselves have no source other than themselves. They are also mechanical. Thus, there is no plan, no purpose, no meaning and no designer. It is all the result of a random accident ... or something else ... which started the process.

This secular, materialistic viewpoint is dominant today among many scientists. Their response to the eons older perspective is generally dismissive to derisive, calling it superstitious or supernatural. As the eyes of the materialist look outward and see nothing behind the materialized pattern, the response is ... if it cannot be seen, weighed or measured, it is not material and therefore not real. Ironically, they are looking outward from the invisible interior of their mind, a dimension that cannot be weighed or measured. It can be seen ...if one can see oneself. If not, we are invisible to ourselves and by current scientific definition, we, who are holding these firm opinions, do not actually exist.

To others, the universe appears infinitely intelligent. If it is not a random, cosmic accident, then it is an expression of whatever established the laws which govern it. "Supernatural" is not a pejorative term here. Since the Laws of Nature are among the secondary laws of the Universe and were not in manifestation in the early Universe for a very long time, any cause beyond the arena of Nature's activities would by definition be, above or beyond Nature ... and thus super-natural. The super-natural is a location other than what we define as Nature.

In Hebrew, the word "*Ruah*" means breath or spirit. St. Paul wrote, "All Scripture is breathed out by God."* In Hindu, breath is called "prana." The focus of the Upanishads is the Self, the Supreme Self and prana. In Sufism, the mystical branch of Islam, "Breath is not synonymous with air, nor with oxygen. Breath is that which emerges from the divine origin and has as its essence the temperament of the celestial" In the Qur'an, the breath is related to the physical and spiritual life of the human being.

Our questions, our fears, our hopes, our humor, our anger live in a world of vibration so much finer as to be non-material when compared

---

* *2 Timothy 3:16*

with the world of matter. To enter the outside world and be communicated, their meaning, their intention, must be transferred to the breath and released on the exhalation so that the vibrations of our inner psychological world may ride from human mind to human mind on puffs of air.

The capacity for language to express the subtleties of feelings, and the complexity of conceptualizations, gives humankind the power of a god. Humans can share the invisible world of the mind with other humans, both present and past, local and distant, known and unknown, alive now … and not yet born. This is a magical process as mysterious as the creation of the Universe.

The material Universe is the outward manifestation of its invisible, underlying laws. Words are the outward manifestation of invisible, underlying thoughts and feelings. As the thoughts and feelings, in order to convey themselves, design the words which will carry them through the air, they become the guiding laws for what we say and how it is said.

Fairness and Justice

O f all the forms of psychological/emotional negativity we tend to carry with us through life, it is our outrage over what we consider "unfair" and "unjust" that burns the hottest. From the long-standing grievances of persecuted minorities to personal feelings of "being owed," "waiting for justice," " waiting for an apology," this sense of violation is particularly intense and tenacious. It is a bitter taste, something that can literally "gnaw" at our insides. It seems impossible to resolve without adequate compensation for the un-justice done to me, or my loved ones, or my group, or my nationality or my personal sense of values, or my …… there seems to be no end to the type of grievances human beings can hold against one another.

We may say we cannot understand why other people would cheat or lie or steal or break bargains or change their mind when they promised not to. These are wrongs. These are violations of the rules. They are outrages against fair play … particularly when done to us and ours!

Ironically, and tragically, we are typically blind when such violations against mutual understanding are committed by me or mine against others outside my community. If I cannot see my own contradictions, it will be easy for me to criticize others for not seeing their own.

Responsibility

Take a few moments, dear Reader, and review for yourself some of the times when you broke your word, forgot a promise, did something you typically criticize in others. These discrepancies between my view of myself and the reality of my behavior at times typically escape my attention, are ignored or rationalized as necessary or even excused as "retaliation" or "revenge" justified by what was previous done to me or mine by others. For many people, the concept of fairness applies more to others relating to them than it does to them relating to others. It is certainly much easier to judge and condemn others rather than to critically examine myself.

Fairness as a Construction

Where did this concept of "fairness" or "justice" come from? Obviously, to have stable, organized communities and relationships, there must be sufficient agreement on issues important to the participants of the compact. In small groups or clans, rules of conduct are agreed to by consensus and are eventually codified as the community grows in size. When the group is small, and all individuals know each other, the "rules" can be simple and few. People can communicate directly to work out disagreements. Whatever roles are required to maintain the group life are filled by those recognized in the community as most competent for that particular role.

Because leadership tends to be based on agreed community needs, maintaining those roles depends on performance to continue community support. Necessities tend to be equally shared and, in that sense, equalized. The number of necessary roles is limited; food gathering, food preparation, toolmaking, child-rearing, clothing production, camp construction and divination. Historically, because of biological differences such as strength and childrearing, these roles naturally evolved to be filled in part by these considerations. Yet, there is evidence that some Neolithic women hunted alongside men and that elderly or injured individuals would be taken care of and assigned useful roles which they could perform. Probably, most members were what would today be called "cross-trained," being able to share many functions when others were unable to do so.

As communities became larger, the management of group life grew increasingly complex. Specialized roles developed to handle these complexities. Some roles were obviously more critical than others, such as engineering canal construction or training an army vs. spinning wool or digging ditches. These practical differences inevitably led to social differences and the emergence of a power structure. As societies began to sort their members into different strata based on these differences, some groups rose to the top and some sank to the bottom of the social ladder. The elite level began to accumulate more of whatever passed for wealth, be it cows, bushels of corn, rare rocks that we call "jewels," slaves (members of other communities captured and forced to serve against their will), or anything that could be exchanged for goods and services between the classes. Having more "currency" (whatever the community considered valuable) equated with more prestige and the power to make decisions and impose "rules." Inevitably, the temptation to make, or manipulate or violate the rules to favor those with the power to make and enforce the rules, became part of the history of humanity.

When these differences become too stark, when those possessing power become too greedy, too haughty, too cruel, too indifferent to the difficulties of their community, conditions are right for an overthrow of leadership. The question of how to maintain the balance of power between the "rulers" and the "ruled" has been the subject of experimentation from the beginning of recorded history. Absolute rulers, chieftains, kings or queens, in order to maintain power, must either sufficiently supply the needs of their population or rule by force, intimidation and fear.

Power-sharing with the population has gone through millennia of exploration, from one-person rule to experiments with republics and democracies. This recognition of the need for balance between leader and led has been encouraged through time by philosophers and spiritual leaders as well as enlightened despots. History records the names of many leaders judged to be "lawgivers" from Hammurabi in ancient Babylon, to Moses, to Confucius, to Solon, to Mohammed. The "Law," a codified set of rules for making cooperative community living possible, will maintain social stability if it is seen to apply equally to the top as well as the bottom of societal strata, to minority communities as well as the majority.

If that minority is enslaved, they are under a different set of laws. (It may take slaves a longer time to rebel than free poor people, but history records the inevitability of slave uprisings.) When the agreed-upon rules, whether mutually accepted or enforced from above, are broken, mechanisms for resolving the problems caused by this violation of public understanding must be devised, whether a trial by ordeal or a trial by superiors or by peers, or armed enforcement. Penalties for violations are specified as part of the growing "body of law."

Between private parties, families, marriages, friendships, additional agreements and understandings develop based on mutual agreement, assumption and custom. Tyrannies obviously can and do exist in such small, small private groups. Whether this is acceptable or not in the larger communities in which these smaller units exist depends on the values of the larger community. In some cultures, male dominance is still the accepted norm. The paterfamilias with the power of life or death over his family members did not disappear with ancient Rome but is still alive in many traditional societies. Revenge killings, arranged marriages, honor killings of those who "dishonor" the family are events still making the news in our so-called modern era.

Obviously, the abstract concepts of fairness and justice are critical for social harmony, particularly for those who look to these principles for protection against the strong. When the rules are applied equally to all, the requirement for justice is met, the equal application of the law to all, regardless of role, position, power or wealth. Knowing that violators, including the elite, will have to make restitution under the law allows the weaker party to feel respected and be less fearful of the more powerful.

Without this reassurance, greed will feel more confident to assert itself among the strong and fear and resentment will infuse the weak. When the weak reach a breaking point, violence will erupt. When the strong feel threatened, violence will be their solution. A sense of living in a fair and just world instills trust in all parties. The sense of living in an unfair, unjust world breeds despair, cynicism, disrespect for the rules, anger, rage. Clearly, my interpretation of whether the world, an event or another person has been fair or just will determine which world I experience and how I will respond.

Although the application of law by government is a major source of difficulty in many places, the vast majority of difficulties from feelings of unfairness stem from disappointments in personal relationships. "I trusted him not to tell!" "It's unfair for her not to reimburse me!" "They were supposed to have shared the inheritance with me, but they kept it all for themselves!" "I can't forgive her for what she said." "Why does he always get more than me? It's not FAIR!" "You cheated on me!"

Each of us has a list of past or current complaints of this sort. Often, the holding of this feeling influences relationships, sometimes over generations, and usually not for the better.

Defining Our Words

Something I discovered in my psychotherapy practice, particularly working with couples, is that we never stop to actually define the words we are using. For example, what is "fair" to one person may seem "unfair" to another. Some people insist that everyone must have their "fair share" or "pay their fair share." Communism and socialism have this conceptual framework, but no one ever defines the applied, practical meaning of the concept "fair share." Attempts to do so result in arguments over who has the correct formula for "fairness." Much of historical and contemporary political friction stems from this question.

To work our way into this exploration, I ask you, dear Reader, to take a few moments and bring to mind past and/or current feelings you have

236

about the experience of fairness or justice in your own life. What are your grievances? Who, or what circumstance, has been unfair to you? Of what have you ever been accused unjustly? What is the taste of that feeling? Can you feel it now?

Once, in looking for a way to explore this painful subject with a client, I saw, in my mind's-eye a baseball field with its boundary lines marked in white chalk. I recognized that, under the specific rules for baseball, the ball was "fair" or "foul" depending on which side of the line it fell. There was nothing personal about the call of fair or foul. It was simply a fact. That's what the umpire is for, to impartially determine the fact according to the law of the game. Why was it a fact? It is a fact because that is the rule in this game called baseball. In a different game, there would be different rules, the lines would be in different configurations and there might not even be a ball. Nevertheless, in that second sport, there would still be idiosyncratic rules that established the parameters of that particular game. Different games, different rules. The rules determine the architecture of the game. Without rules, there is no game, only random, chaotic activity.

In this sense, in order to have a shared culture of fairness, everyone would have to agree on the rules as well as the game being played. Arguments I have heard and sometimes participated in: "I didn't agree to that!". "YES, YOU DID." "You're not being fair!". "You're the one who isn't being fair. We had an agreement. You said 'OK' when I asked you." "That's not what I was agreeing to. You always set me up like this. You're the one who isn't fair!".

After hearing a number of these types of conversations, I began to wonder if the participants were playing the same game … or even on the same field. This is a good question to wonder about anytime there are these types of disagreements. Ask, "What does "fair" mean to you in this situation and why?" If I take the time to listen, without trying to defend my position, I will frequently hear myself responding, "Wow …. that's not how I think about "fair" in this situation."

If both parties assume that they are on the same page when, in fact, they each have a different understanding, everyone feels treated unjustly. One way to diminish the number of grudges I carry is to take the time to explore why someone else feels the situation unjust when I do not … why they do not feel it is unfair when I do. I don't need to agree that, from my point of view, it seems unjust to me if it does not, but I know, from my own experiences, the feeling of unfairness, how it stings. I don't need to defend my position. What I do need to do is be willing to explore two different understandings without either one being right or wrong, but just different viewpoints. Having established that, there may still be a practical problem to resolve, but the differences don't have to be experienced as personal betrayals.

Communicating Through a Fractured Personality

Another factor that raises the feeling of unfairness is the lack of recognition by most of us that we do not have one stable personality, one stable emotional state, one stable set of responses for all situations. When a friend makes a statement or a promise in one frame of mind, why do we blindly expect they will remember it or actually go through with the agreement when they are in a different state of mind or emotion? Well ... if we have known them a long time and they have displayed a capacity for consistency, then it is not unreasonable to assume that they will do in the future what they have done in the past. Does that guarantee that they will do so?

Ask yourself, dear Reader, have you always been 100% consistent on everything you have promised, agreed to, given your word to? Take a few moments here and think about those occasions when you have not been reliable. Do you understand why ... not the rationalization you may prefer ... but the real reason?

If you are not always trustworthy, why do you expect this from others? We can hope and we can expect ... until proven otherwise. We can extend the benefit-of-the-doubt and we can be disappointed if it doesn't occur ... but why do we expect fairness and call for justice when it doesn't appear? If we understand that even the best people, including ourselves, are not always consistent, then we understand that the definition of "fair" and "just" cannot be that things are going my way without any surprises.

Then there are circumstances when something is promised in good faith at the moment of the promise but proves undoable at a later time under unforeseen circumstances. A number of years ago, a friend of mine asked me to loan him a good sum of money which he would repay in a short while from the proceeds of a pending business deal. I had known this person for a number of years and knew he was often on thin ice financially. I did not want to embarrass him by probing about his difficulties, especially since he asked me not to mention this to any of our associates.

I assumed, for no verifiable reason, that he might be having tax problems. A while later, a mutual friend came to me to discuss his discomfort with this person asking him for money, which he also gave without question. My second friend told me that he had been asked to maintain secrecy. He was uncomfortable as our debtor was a leader in our community.

A short while later, my debtor asked me for additional funds of a considerable amount. Now I asked what type of situation he was in and found out he was involved with a well-known scam. When I told him this, he denied it and defended himself and demanded that I owed him money since he was my elder. I declined. Then I discovered he had done this with two other colleagues for considerably greater sums and asking each of us not to tell anyone else. I also subsequently found out that not only had he been warned by his wife, by his bank, by his attorney, as well as public information from the F.B.I. and ignored all the warnings. Then I discovered that he had done this in a different community from which he then had to flee in disgrace.

It is very interesting what we may not know about each other even after long years of close association.

Subsequently, he promised to repay me but stopped after the second installment. From this incident, I learned never to "loan" money but rather to either "gift" it or decline. I also realized that from a normal viewpoint, his treatment of me, and the others, had been unfair and unjust.

However, as I thought about what I knew of his personality and what he had to deal with in his life, I realized that he really believed in the legitimacy of his "business deal" and believed he could repay his debts. From his position, he had not been unfair to me or our colleagues. He had been sincere but had, himself, been deceived. Well … that was true. He had believed the scam. So, in such a situation, where would I go to find "justice"? I had a choice of deciding I had been cheated and was due compensation or I could decide that I had made an understandable and principled error in judgment. Who was to blame here? What were the circumstances in the life of the person perpetuating the scam? Does it matter?

Deliberate Deception

But this does bring our exploration to the situation in which we are deliberately deceived and manipulated. I, myself, many years later, fell for a similar scam. Looking back afterwards, I saw how I had missed the warning signs, but nevertheless, I had been badly duped and truly naïve. I damaged no one but myself, but it caused me to remember my poor friend and his willing suspension of disbelief. What a crushing disappointment he must have experienced on realizing he had lost all his own and his friends' monies ... again. He had been an easy mark due to his need and his blind naïveté. Any of us could and probably has been taken advantage of by a more cunning person. Take a moment, my Reader and review your own life experiences. If something like this has never happened to you, you are the exception.

Now ... ask yourself if you have ever intentionally taken advantage of or manipulated someone to your advantage and against theirs? Again, if nothing comes to mind, then you might want to take more time ... or maybe you, yourself, are again the exception to the rule.

Nature is populated mostly by herbivores with a smaller population of carnivores. Carnivores circle the herd watching for the weak, the distracted, the ill, old and young, to drift from the safety of the herd. It is no different in the human herd. Cheats, thieves, sociopaths, sadists, watch for those around them who don't see them for who they are. When we are blind to this type of predatory personality, we are easy prey.

Is this fair? Not by the rules I play by! But the human carnivores don't play by my rules. They are playing an entirely different game in a different league. As long as I am blind, I don't see them. They are expert at hiding themselves from the naïve. It is not a fair match. It is more like leading a hypnotized lamb to the slaughter telling it you are taking it to a green pasture.

Again, from my personal point of view, is this fair? Of course not. Is it just? Of course not. Can I bring my deceiver to justice and get compensation for my loss and enjoy seeing them punished? Maybe ... usually not .... and it may cost more in time, money, emotional and mental energy to make the attempt with no guarantee of success.

Using our carnivore analogy one more time, is it unfair that the weak and the slow become sustenance for the carnivore and its family? Is it unjust? Or is it the way of things, a law of life?

Life is full of danger and unpredictable possibilities. Staying as safe as possible, staying within the lines of relative safety, is generally an act of intelligence. However, it only improves our odds; it does not guarantee that we won't find ourselves the victim of something or someone not playing by the rules we expected. Whether due to inattention, naïveté misunderstanding, poor luck or deliberate deceit, we cannot protect ourselves at all times.

Since unpredictability is a law of life, and since people misunderstand each other in life, and people make mistakes and change their minds in life, or occasionally break their own self-professed principles, and some people make a living out of deceiving trusting people, why would we expect ... even demand ... that everything be fair? How could the subjective viewpoints and feelings of different people line up so perfectly that there is never disappointment and let down ... or cheating?

Conclusion

Fairness is a concept. It is not a thing. It does not have a material existence. It is an idea, a principle for people to follow, as best they can, from moment to moment, mood to mood.

Fairness lives in the minds of people as a concept which they hope will be an operating principle for everyone they engage. Fairness is an aim, an aspiration for certain people who wish to develop within themselves the capacity for such consistency that they can fulfill the values which they have chosen to follow as their guide. For such people, the aspirational principles provided by the ageless wisdom of the Golden Rule and its many offshoots are a beacon by which they attempt to guide themselves. Not everyone makes that choice with that degree of seriousness, many may wish to but do not have the consistency, and some have no interest in such an encumbrance on their egoism and passions.

Does fairness exist in Nature? Do animals worry about justice? They live in a sensory-emotional world, not a conceptual world. Their relationships and survival are governed by physical factors which enhance their chances to live long enough to reproduce. The strong, healthy and smarter animals tend to survive longer. Animals are not programmed to worry about whether that other animal in the clearing is thinking judgmental thoughts about them, but only, "Is that food or a mate? Is it safe or dangerous? Those are the rules of that world. The rules apply to all in that world without prejudice. There is nothing unfair or unjust about the Laws of Nature. They apply to all without discrimination.

What is "Justice"? The concept originated in an Old French word, "*jostise*" meaning "uprightness, equity, vindication of right, administration of law," If one of the laws of Nature is that some beings are carnivores and most are peaceful creatures, then there is nothing inherently "unfair" about some people breaking their word, forgetting their promises, cheating, lying and sometimes intentionally deceiving. This, too, would be a law of Nature. The Laws of Man attempt to temper the manifestation of man acting out his animal nature, but they cannot prevent it.

Literal justice is the impartial following of the rules, the laws … no exceptions. In being blind to partiality, the rulings of justice will often go against what we wish could be the outcome.

Since the word "fairness" comes from the Old English "*fæger*," meaning "pleasing or attractive," it is no wonder that the application of blind, impartial Justice would often be experienced as unpleasing and unattractive … and thus, unfair.

In our human world, our behavior is generally motivated much more from our psychological world than the natural world that governs our physical bodies. Mentally and emotionally, we recognize another concept … that of "extenuating circumstances." The law may say that if you steal a loaf of bread, you are a thief. But, if you stole the loaf of bread to feed your starving child, we generally recognize that your action does not necessarily imply bad character. It may actually imply the opposite. That we are able to make the distinction between the spirit and the letter of the law is a result of our higher conceptual capacities. It is an example of including the larger context as the third element in deciding what is fair and just. What were the circumstances? What was the motivation? What is the past history? Without balancing the rule, the deed and the situation, human law can become as impersonal as the laws of Nature. We would certainly consider that unjust.

Heroes, Archetypes and Personal Destiny

W e often ask children: "What do you want to be when you grow up". Occasionally, we also ask other adults: "What did you want to do with your life? Do you ever wonder if there is a purpose to your life that you should discover and fulfill?"

On the one hand, we might ask ourselves: "How would anyone really know how to answer those questions?"

And, yet … most will have some specific response at one time or another. Out of all the opportunities that life provisionally offers (if we are fortunate enough to live in a situation that does offer more than basic survival options), why do we choose only a few, or sometimes, only one? Or, why do we sometimes avoid a conscious, deliberate choice and allow ourselves to drift with the tide, living the life chance brings?

Resonance

If I survey what interests me, or moves me emotionally, in activities, in people, in subject themes, I will notice a pattern. As a child, I may have wanted to become a fireman, a teacher, a farmer, an athlete, a leader, a mother or father, an explorer. Why do my imagination and emotional interest gravitate in certain directions and not others? Who have been my heroes, my role models? Who are my heroes, my role models today? What type of people am I interested in reading about currently or in history, or following in the culture? Is there someone I wish I could change places with or a lifestyle I imagine would make me feel fulfilled? If money and time were not an issue, to what would I like to devote my life?

Although, to our common perception, our bodies and the world around look and feel solid, engineers, scientists, musicians who study the laws of frequencies understand that everything vibrates because everything is made of atoms and their sub-atomic components, all of which are vibrating. These infinitesimal energy packets, tiny building blocks, are the material from which everything is made and their functions determined. Different rates of vibrations determine what will blend and what will not, what makes one form and what makes a different form, what facilitates one type of function and what facilitates another. Different

243

vibratory rates either attract or repel each other. When resonances blend, we could expect a harmonious potentiation in energy or possibility. Where they do not blend, we get a clash and disharmony. Sometimes, the vibratory waves cancel each other out.

In studying the body, it has been discovered that molecules are able to carry and exchange information and energy with other molecules because they are designed in a lock and key type of arrangement. A molecule of a certain configuration will seek out a receiving molecule with a specific configuration to match. If there is no match, they don't "dock" and cannot "unlock" the coded message attempting to be transmitted. We are discovering, in environmental research, as well as medicine, that all of life and the functions of our bodies and the planet we live upon are interwoven into a global whole. If something is disrupted, moved into a location it was not designed for or removed entirely, the harmony of the whole system is affected.

How everything developed to have its specialized location in the larger whole is a question for another time. Whether one is a devout Darwinist or whether one sees a pre-determined architecture unfolding, the ob-served interconnectedness of infinitely, differently, designed parts is incontrovertible. Square pegs are designed to go in holes that are square, not round.

In my years as a psychologist, studying both my clients and myself, I realized that this principle of fit, of harmonious resonances, of lock and key, also functions in the psychological world of thought and feeling. Our language recognizes, through feel, what our rational minds often over-look: "We resonated." "She gives off good vibes." "We are in harmony." "They are a perfect fit." "The experience was jarring." "The tone was off." "It didn't feel right." "I get tingles up my spine whenever that hap-pens."

Each of us is attracted or repelled by certain people and situations even while we are generally not dramatically reactive, or are even indifferent, to most. A classic reason for some depressions, anxieties and difficult life situations is an individual either not being sensitive to the pulse of what does and does not resonate with them or being unable to follow the more harmonious path due to fear or obstructions from their environment.

Our individual patterns of attractions and repulsions follow the lock and key model. For someone or something to attract or repulse me, there must be a resonant receptor already in me, waiting for the stimulus from outside to cause it to vibrate in response. Aspects of my inner world are entangled with aspects of the outer world.

There are two factors that determine these patterns. I may want to become a mechanic like my father because I want to please him. Or I may want to become a mechanic like my father because I am a physically oriented person who loves to work with my hands and figure out solutions to practical problems. I may want to become rich so people will envy or accept me, or I may want to become rich so I can fund charities and help many people. Some of the pattern comes from my personality's desire to increase or fashion its self-image for people outside itself. Some of the pattern comes from a deeper inner desire which may have nothing at all to do with the people or environment around. "I wanted to be a musician, but my father insisted I enter the family business." "I didn't want to stay in my hometown, but I didn't want to disappoint my parents, so I declined the job offer from away." "I always wanted to be an entertainer from the earliest time I can recall, even though no one in my family can carry a note or tell a joke. They all think I'm crazy!" "I felt a call to the ministry from the first time I attended church as a child."

The interior-generated pattern is reflective of how one is programmed at conception. It is the lattice of strengths and weaknesses, affinities and dis-affinities that make up who I actually am "designed" to be, what shape I am designed to take in relationship to life, the role in the larger whole that my type of person is to play, the shape of my key and where in life I will find the lock into which I am designed to fit.

The outer-generated pattern may accidentally, and happily, be resonant with the inner receiving location or, it may be a partial fit, or it may be totally dis-harmonious. It is the latter that leads to much frustration and suffering in the world.

I trained to be a psychologist because it fit my personality and because it offered flexibility in the type of work I could do since most jobs do involve people and people inevitably have problems that can be addressed. It was actually suggested to me as an option that fit my profile on a career matching test. It also provided the monetary stability that comes with a professional degree in my culture. It wasn't initially a passion. There was much about the training and many job settings that were not attractive. I now see this practical career choice as representing my conservative nature, my preference for predictability and security. But I was by nature a good listener. I was deeply moved by themes of healing and reconciliation. And I was interested in people. Some other professions attracted me but felt riskier, and I did not choose them for that reason.

My true passion ignited, years later, when I met, within weeks of each other, both the teachings of G. I. Gurdjieff and Jungian analysis. They opened me experientially to verification of alternate realities as well as providing a practical way of exploring the invisible world of the psyche. I awoke inside the life I had been leading for thirty-eight years and found myself in front of a doorway opening to my heart's desire and the vocation I had been born to fulfill.

Finding the Way Home

Looking both forward and backwards from that time in my life, I can clearly see the "trail of breadcrumbs" I had been dimly following to bring me to this place of discovery and which have now consciously guided me to my present location in myself and in the new life that has developed around me. The theme that wound its way through each stage of my life was an intuition that there must be more to reality than what my senses showed me. Its manifestation was an enduring attraction to mystery. Following any line of research or investigation or reasoning, when applied to Life and Consciousness, inevitably led to other unanswered questions. Each discovery, whether by science or my own endeavors, led further into the mystery but always came to the edge of a cliff, beyond which lay more mystery. I love standing at the edge of that abyss and feeling the mystery calling me from beyond.

Writing this, I am now remembering an image that came to me during my Jungian analysis in which I was standing next to a campfire surrounded by impenetrable darkness. I felt that what I was searching for, what I desperately needed to understand, lay just beyond the edge of the circle of light. I piled more and more wood on the fire to enlarge the circle, but the expansion of light only pushed the edge of darkness further away. The mystery remained in the shadows, continually retreating just beyond the firelight even as the illumination grew in diameter. That image captures the feeling of my search up to that point.

I recognize now that, along with my attraction to the relationship of mystery and the question of other realities, there were themes governing what I liked to read, what excited me to talk and think about: science fiction, lost cities, parapsychology, UFO's, history and science. And there was a pattern to the heroic figures, real and imaginary, that interested me. I loved the story of King Arthur, but it was Merlin I wanted to be, never the King. I wanted to be like Saint Francis, not the Pope. I wanted to be a mystic, not a theologian. I wanted to be an adventurer, an explorer, a discoverer, a teacher.

I have an innate timidness about physically risking my body, but I was fearless about delving into the realm of mind and feelings. Although I have allowed myself some physical adventures and learned much from my body, my chosen field of exploration was the psyche. I wanted a life full of meaning, not one that often felt as spiritually nutritious as cardboard. As a Jungian, I recognize myself in the Tarot card XII, the Hanged Man. I discovered that some ancient mystical symbolism and art resonated in me when others left me unaffected. I came to experience the reality of fairytales and parables as symbolic representations of psychological realities, an ancient language passed from generation to generation to teach, by *feel*, different aspects of the inner world in order to bring it into the light of the listeners' awareness.

When in mid-life I discovered the system of psychological transformation brought to the West by Gurdjieff, I felt I had "come home." I discovered that I, myself, was the mystery I had been searching for and that attention and consciousness were aspects of myself directly relating to the questions, "Who am I and what is my purpose on Earth?" These were questions that I could study directly since they were inside me. None of these directing interests originated from the world outside my skin. Typically, they found no resonance in my family and friends.

An evocative area of study has appeared in the past few decades. We are all familiar with how iron filings will arrange themselves into the shape of the electromagnetic field generated by a magnet. If loose material, like iron filings, or salt or sand or even water, is exposed to vibrations of different frequencies, the material will arrange itself to display the pattern of that particular vibrational resonance with that particular material. In this process, beautiful forms appear, many of them complex mandalas, some recreating archetypal symbols. Recently a researcher claims to have been able to produce three-dimensional reconstructions of vibrations.

Looking at these images produced by this method called "Cymatics," I immediately associated to Plato's hypothesized World of Forms. I could see that forms must represent a materialized representation of a basic pattern, the continual resonance of which holds the form together. When the resonance weakens, the form begins to dissolve. This viewpoint is also reflected in the controversial theory called "Morphic Resonance."

Patterns of Attraction and Repulsion

It occurred to me that the form of thoughts and feelings must also follow this principle in their own "world." The pattern of my attractions and repulsions formed a map. What generated and maintained the patterns were attitudes, understandings and the program conditioned into my nervous system both by heredity and environment.

All the observable behavioral and emotional manifestations of life forms originate in the invisible, internal, subjective sensitivity and patterned reactions *inside* the organism. In the world of man, that external pattern is what makes and destroys all human endeavors from civilizations to relationships.

As a psychotherapist, my work was to find the invisible, underlying mental and emotional "frequencies" that produced the behaviors and feelings in my clients that were diminishing their lives. When those frequencies could be changed through insight, emotional healing or behavioral re-conditioning, the outward manifestations altered, thus also changing the response to them from their environment.

Studying the ideas of Gurdjieff, I found confirmation of my therapy discoveries in his description of the process whereby different qualities of influences resonate in different individuals according to whether or not they have within themselves what he called a "magnetic center," attraction for a particular kind of influence. He suggested that ordinary life mechanically produces influences such as sports, entertainment, politics, business. These types of influences related to the ordinary life outside, he called "A" influences.

People with a built-in affinity for the inner world of the psyche, that is, for a spiritual search, and were less interested or invested in everyday life, were differentially sensitive to what he called "B" influences. The suggestion is that B influences were not accidental but were deliberately released into the stream of ordinary existence by individuals who had found liberation in an inner life impartial to the pull of ordinary circumstances.

These special influences were intentionally placed in the world by such liberated people to serve as help, as directional beacons, for those who could feel the difference between these vibrations and those produced by ordinary, random, external conditions. Feeling the difference, those seekers would orient towards these "higher" influences in their own investigations for something real to help with their own search. Examples of B influences are enduring parables, fairy tales, myths, sacred music, dance, architecture which could change the emotional state of those sensitive to their resonance.

Regarding the topic of resonance, I am now remembering the moment I was learning to tune a guitar. I had no musical training when young and this was unexplored territory for me. I subsequently discovered that there is a musical affinity and degree of native talent in me that I have not developed. Now, as an older man, its small, fractured exploration has been a delightful surprise. This first time with a string instrument, I was learning to bring the strings into "tune" with each other. As I listened, I experienced the notion of "flat" and "sharp" as a felt reality.

"Flat … tighten … flat … tighten … no … now too sharp … loosen … loosen … oops … flat … tighten … THERE! The vibration fell into a slot! I not only heard and felt the slot, but I could see the slot in my mind's eye. In that moment, I understood this application to feeling one's way through life, both inside and outside one's mind. In a way, it should be like the child's game of hot and cold". "You are getting warmer, warmer … no … now you are getting colder". I understood the guidance offered by resonance as a compass or gyroscope that can lead us to who and what we were designed to be.

Even if I am not that fortunate to construct an outer life that accepts my inner world, I can place my center of psychological/emotional gravity in the exploration of what most energizes me inside while playing outside the role the world demands of me, economically, socially, regardless of the restrictions imposed by circumstances. If I play the role consciously as a necessity but reserve my energy for my internal interests, then I can still find resonance with my essential nature.

If very fortunate, I may escape the fate of having my life controlled solely by outside conditions. If even more fortunate, I may find my destiny, a compatible blending between the place in my interior of my interests, talents and passions with the shape of my outer life.

I have come to see that the heroes and archetypes we are attracted to are the equivalent of our end of the lock and key in search for the role we were created to occupy in the greater whole of Life, Nature and, perhaps, the Cosmos. Destiny, if anyone has one, must be an expression of finding the individual place of harmonic resonance between my essential psychic-physical architecture and the roles which life needs filled.

When my inner life of attractions, dreams, longings does not match the role I am playing in the world, I will be unbalanced, out of harmony with myself .... unless ... I can discover, and respect, what I feel most drawn to and find a way to satisfy this internal call, as best as possible, given whatever the inescapable demands of my outer world. Then, regardless of outer difficulties, my inner world can be alive and fruitful.

Conservation and Wastage of Psychological Energies

I am sitting at my computer, looking not at the screen but inside my mind as my fingers move across the keyboard. I am looking inside to see if I can notice yet, the outline, the tentative map for me to follow into this extraordinary, complex, subtle, and mysterious question which I want to explore. I also want to explore it not just for myself, but I hope to find a way to express what I am finding in this search so that you, dear Reader, can follow my journey with me … until you notice your own path opening up.

I recall several conversations with electrical engineers and physicists. I always asked the question, "What, actually, is electricity? What, actually, is "energy"? The reaction was always the same. Back to me came a definition of what energy of any type can "do." I would ask again, "Yes. But what exactly is it"? Back would come a reframing of what "it" could "do" with a description of how it was generated and directed. I would ask a third time, "Yes. But what exactly is it"? Back now would come a blank look … silence … and then the admission, "We don't know. We actually have no idea. We just know how it works."

Recent discoveries have brought the exploration of the source of energy down into the sub-atomic realm of the "Planck" level, currently understood as the smallest possible measurable quantities. Even here, at the deepest levels of the sub-atomic world, is eternal spiraling vibration. This universal eternal vibration seems to be closest to the source of all observable energy. Technically, then, the answer to the question, "What is energy?" is that energy is vibration. And yet…the cause underlying this universal vibration is left unanswered. Thus, ultimately, the response to the original question also remains a mystery.

We all talk about "energy," we use "energy," we want more "energy," but in actuality, we have no idea what we are talking about. IT … energy … just is.

Moreover, we are all aware of energy in different intensities, levels of power. What is most obvious is the energy of natural forces, then the energies that power our machines and inventions. Then there is our own body. Who doesn't always long for more physical energy? The ability of energy to create movement and change is most obvious in the world around us … weather, wind, earthquakes, volcanos, rivers… the Sun. We have learned to harness some of this energy, direct it through our inventions to do work for us, typically faster and better than we can ourselves. Then there is the living world around us, filled with life forms that move, hunt, mate, play, live in communities.

What powers these biological machines? There is an energy at work here also. We call this form, or quality, of energy "Life." Ask a biologist, "What actually is "Life"? The answer will be a definition of what living forms can do. Ask again, "Yes, but what actually is "Life"? The answer will be a description of how life operates. Ask again, "Yes, but what is "Life" actually? There will be a moment of silence … followed by, "We don't know what "Life" actually is. It must be a type of "energy."

Even if we don't know what energy itself is, we can trace the word's appearance and changes in meaning. In Late Latin "*energia*," from Greek "*energeia*" activity, from "*energos*" active, from "*en*" in + "*ergon*" work. Used by Aristotle with a sense of "actuality, reality, existence (opposed to "potential"), but this was misunderstood in Late Latin, and afterwards, as "force of expression," as the power which calls up realistic mental pictures. It wasn't used scientifically until the early 1800s, which brings us to our current usage: usable power (such as heat or electricity) also: "the resources for producing such power." But it still retains its origins with uses such as "dynamic quality, narrative energy, the capacity of acting or being active, intellectual energy, and a usually positive spiritual force, the energy flowing through all people."

Before energy became a scientific word, it was used synonymously with another word that is still with us, "Spirit." The dictionary defines "Spirit" mid-13c "animating or vital principle in man and animals," Old French "*spirit*" "spirit, soul" and 12c Modern French "*esprit*" from Latin "*spritus*" "a breathing respiration and of the wind or the breath of God, inspiration, breath of life, esprit." It also has been used to mean a "supernatural immaterial creature, invisible corporeal being of an airy nature."

In the early 14c, the meaning moved toward the realm of mind and psychological experience. Alchemy used it in a scientifically metaphorical way to talk about a "volatile substance; distillate … then Mid 14 c "character, disposition, way of thinking and feeling state of mind," followed by Late 14 c "divine substance, divine mind, God and extension of divine power" to "an inspiration" and 1580 in a metaphorical sense "animation, vitality," "*spritus*," "a breathing."

As the Enlightenment moved further away from religion to establish itself in the realm of reason, the "animating, vitality" and "spritus" was transformed into a more "rational" word, "Energy," even though both words originally were used to point to the same mystery. "Energy" at this point sounded less "spiritual" or mystical or religious. "Energy" was a "something" that could be studied and utilized. "Energy" could be measured and directed. "Energy" was real and of nature ... not super-stitious like ephemeral "Spirit."

Yet, whether we use the word "Spirit" or "Energy" to refer to what makes anything move and live, we still have no idea what we are talking about other than the observable effects of Spirit/Energy.

Studying Energy

G. I. Gurdjieff recommended that if one wanted to understand the Universe, one should study man and, if one wanted to understand man, then one should study the Universe. Like others before him, he suggested that since we are made of the material and energies of the Universe, then the "Universe" is part of us and ... we are part of It. Thus, we could come to understand more about It by going into ourselves, since the Universe will be found there as well as out in the Cosmos or down in the infinitesimal dimensions of the cells, molecules, atoms and sub-atomic particles ... from all of which we are composed.

Much has been discovered about how Energy moves, directs, creates, destroys and transforms matter ... in the material world that surrounds us. Our scientific instruments can look out to the edge of the physical Universe and peer down into the quantum realm, out of which the material Universe appears. But there is a third realm that our conventional instruments cannot penetrate, and without knowledge of which, no complete understanding of existence is possible.

What is looking out through the telescope at the stars? What is looking down through the electron microscope at the atomic structure of crystals? What imagined, designed and built these instruments? What conceived the questions the instruments were designed to answer?

Actually, since we, ourselves, are at this juncture in our exploration ... what is looking at these words on this page? What is interested enough to still be reading this slowly unwinding essay? The answer to this question would be ... you ... my dear Reader. It is the mind, your mind, my mind. It is our minds that lie in the middle and connect the ends. Only the Mind can notice mysteries, ask questions and create ways of searching for meaning.

What is the energy ... the spirit ... that powers the mind, my mind ... your mind? This question has been pursued with amazing results, up to a point, by neurologists. One question that is debated and not resolved is, "Are the brain and the mind the same"?

Current estimates of the number of neurons in the typical human brain vary. One recent estimate was 86 billion ... but who's counting? Eighty-six billion in a three-pound lump of living goo? Whatever the actual number, we are dealing with very crowded real estate. Growing at the tips of each of these neurons are small branches like trees, each with multiple branches of their own. These are called dendrites. It is currently estimated that each single dendrite may receive signals from many other neurons. In the cerebellum, it is currently believed that each dendrite is in contact with as many as 200,000 other neurons!

What are these structures for? Functionally, they are the equivalent of electrical wiring.

In fact, they are biological conduits for electricity. At a fundamental level, my body, your body, runs on electricity. Of course, we learned this in school a long time ago. But it actually wasn't so long ago that this discovery was made. It also takes no time at all to habituate to the shock (no pun intended) of this fact.

The same power that lights the clouds during thunderstorms, that illuminates the polar Auroras, that lights our cities, runs our computers, that is the underpinning of our technologically based civilization, is the same "energy" that runs all Life ... and ... moving electricity creates the phenomenon of magnetism. Electromagnetism is currently understood to be one of the four, so-far-discovered, basic forces (energies, spirits) that created and maintain the Universe as we know it today.

The moving electricity in our neurons and dendrites creates magnetic fields around their movement. All of our cells, our organs, even our whole body is a blending of countless smaller electromagnetic fields. Inside our nervous system and our brains, electrical impulses constantly flow. These impulses stimulate the production and distribution of a vast number of molecular structures that guide and maintain the life in our body. It is the same inside our brain. The cessation of this activity is called "brain death." When the electrical current no longer flows through our brain, "we" are considered to be no longer there.

What else goes on in the brain? The electrical activity also stimulates the production and distribution of molecules, hormones from specific glands which manufacture these molecular combinations. Hormones carry information, instructions to different systems in the body through the blood, which flows through every cell in the whole structure. This information tells the target system to produce more or less of different substances, which then influence the health, capacity and functionality of the body.

Different combinations also contribute to different types of brain activity that then allow for different types and qualities of experiences. It is these experiences which we experience! From these experiences that we are having inside our brains, our impressions of ourselves, our lives, the world around us and the meaning of things, that our experience of being alive, of thinking and feeling and sensing, arises. From all this is born our sense of ourself as a living entity having experiences that we call "my life."

Psychological Energies

So, now we can talk about "psychological energies." "Psyche" is the ancient Greek word for "mind" and "soul." Its synonyms include "ego," "spirit," "anima," "subconscious," "character," "individual."

Electromagnetism runs the physical activity of the brain. Different qualities of brain activity create different qualities of experience for the experiencer. Hence, different states of mind lead to different perceptions, understandings and hence, meanings for the "experiencer."

But all life runs on electricity and magnetism in this way. What is different about human life? Do we have experiences and capacities that seem different from the animals and other life forms around us? Let's look into our minds right now. I am visualizing my childhood house … now my first pet … now my first kiss.

So, dear Reader, why don't you try this yourself? What do you see … right now? What memories are appearing for you if you take a few moments and look at the screen of your mind for the appearance of images from past chapters of "The Story of You"? Take your time. The following material will have more meaning if you can confirm its reality through your own experiences.

Are you experiencing any feelings with these images, or conversations or storylines? If so, how is that happening? How are you creating the image you are seeing, the conversations you are hearing again ... images and words which may stimulate emotions?

Where are you seeing these images? "In my mind," you might say. O.K. Where is your mind? "In my brain," you will probably respond. O.K. How are *you* creating these images or voices or recreated events so that you can re-experience them? And, while we are exploring this, where, in your mind, are you located while you create and view these images? How do you know you are in your mind? What do you mean when you say, "I must have been out of my mind." If you are in your mind, are you and your mind something separate? Is your mind something you occasionally inhabit? Are you and your mind the same? Are you your mind?

Perhaps right now, you are pausing to think about this experiment I have suggested. How are you making happen this activity that we call thinking? Are there words in your mind? Are you creating those words or are you hearing them... or seeing them? How are you actually performing any of these activities or are you following them as they unfold before your inner eye? Your ears and eyes point outward. How are you hearing thoughts or seeing images in your mind?

Looking inside, intentionally focusing, is tiring. My attention keeps drifting after a short while. I have to keep renewing the effort. It seems to take energy to make and continue this type of effort. But, I notice that when my mind is drifting, when I am not making this type of intentional effort to direct and hold my attention, that drifting does not seem to take much, if any, energy. There seem to be two different qualities of energy involved in this experiment.

After repeating this several times, I can feel or sense a different quality, a different type of pressure involved with a deliberate, intentional focusing of attention compared to the feel of my typical quality of attention, which drifts effortlessly, mindlessly, from one association, one thought, one activity, one memory to another. Only occasionally do I make the effort to deliberately take my attention by the arm and say to it, "Look there. Stay here. Don't move"! And then, I have to watch my attention to make sure it doesn't drift or run off with some distracting thought or the next movement noticed out of the corner of my eye.

We are all familiar with these qualities even if we have not stopped to study them. We all know the difficulty of focused attention for more than a short time. There is a third quality of attention which we all know, that combines the feel of the first two. Recall what your attention is like when you are reading a riveting book or watching a movie or sporting event or lost in daydream. There is no effort required here to hold the attention in place. In fact, it is difficult to break the hold of this type of attention and "tear ourselves away" from the object of our fascination. Our attention is mesmerized, captured and held by our interest, fascination, by a strong emotional pull of either attraction or repulsion. The new factor which has entered here is an emotional quality of interest or attraction. When fueled by the energy of emotion, attention can become extremely powerful.

Qualities of Attention

So, from observation and direct experience, there appear to be three qualities of attention.

Our general predominant, undisciplined attention that automatically, mechanically, moves from one stimulus, one thought, one feeling, one daydream to another over and over until something "calls our attention" to refocus in a new direction. If what called my attention has an emotional component, it may now hold my attention indefinitely, but without much, if any, effort on my part.

At some point, the trance is broken. Let's say I hear my name called. I "wake up" or "snap out of it" and deliberately focus the beam of my attention to the source of the voice. I sense concern in the voice. I am aware of myself moving towards the call and responding, "I am on my way." I find my friend needing to talk. I put everything else out of my mind and focus my attention on her words, her face, her tone. If my mind begins to drift, I immediately bring it back into focus on the conversation. The degree of my caring and interest help to fuel my ability to remain focused.

We could say that there is a quality of *body attention* that automatically scans my environment, outside and inside myself, just as any animal is programmed to watch and sense their environment for purposes of survival and safety. There seems to be a quality of *emotional attention* that can focus and hold our gaze, inside or outside, often with a tunnel vision that precludes all other possible sources of stimulation. Then there seems to be a quality of attention that comes directly from *willed intellectual effort* to choose, hold and continually refocus attention on something of the intellect's choice. Attention itself must be a quality of energy with at least three levels of intensity within its range.

As we are exploring different qualities of attention, we are also talking about different functional capacities in the human being. As with all life, we have energy that fuels our bodies. Whatever this energy is, it must be very fast ... and very intelligent ... as it is monitoring, adjusting, directing and maintaining countless interacting chemical and electrical reactions in our multi-trillion-cell organism. We often give this energy the name instinct. When it "runs low," we become fatigued, or weak, or ill or we die. We rest and sleep and eat to replenish this energy.

We also know that energy fluctuates in our feelings. We talk about being "energized," "pumped up," feeling "high" with excitement. We also talk about "emotional exhaustion" and experiencing "dulled" or "dead" feelings. Nothing drains our emotional endurance more than the negativity of anger, anxiety, depression and fear. Clearly, there is an energy that fuels our emotional world.

Of course, we are all familiar with the experience of a mind that feels "sharp" and one that feels "dull." We can focus on intellectual activity only for a period of time before our "mind gets tired" and we "need a break." Perhaps after doing something physical for a while, we again find we have "energy to think" with. Perhaps you, Reader, might want to take a break from reading this material if you find yourself "losing" the emotional energy we call interest.

Fluctuating Energy

Just as all energy moves in waves, the rise and fall and rise again of physical, emotional and intellectual energy in cyclic patterns creates an experience of continual energetic movement for the experiencer ... myself. The difficulty of finding the right type of energy for the moment at hand ... and sustaining it ... can be contributed to, in part, by the frequency and rhythm of this energy moving through us. We may not actually be in control of these fluctuations. Wasting this energy results in the experience of greater turbulence and eventual depletion. Conservation results in diminished fluctuations and thus an increase and duration of capacity.

Are these three different qualities of energy ... physical, emotional, intellectual ... or is it the same energy-producing different experiences in different locations in our physical-emotional-intellectual structure? This is a theoretically interesting question but not one with a clear, practical implication. What is clear, if we pay attention inside ourselves, is that we can discern fluctuating qualities of attention in body, emotion and intellect.

Why is this underlying energy fluctuating? Is there a large generator somewhere sending out pulses that pass through us, lifting or dropping our "energy level"? Are there "accumulators" in our three parts, intellect, feeling and physical, which collect and hold energy until needed but then need to be refilled when drained by too long a stretch of a particular activity requiring that quality of energy?

We know that the energy that runs our bodily functions, including our brain metabolism, comes first from photons. Photons are "packets" of light. They are continually streaming from the Sun in all directions. Some are intercepted by the Earth and fall upon its surface, where they are absorbed by plant life to make chlorophyll. Plants are eaten by insects and animals. Insects and animals then eat each other, thus sharing in the energy from the Sun. We then eat the plants, animals … and sometimes the insects … certainly honey and all the plants pollinated by insects.

We absorb sunlight directly through our skin to maintain the necessary amount of vitamin D. We also absorb photons through our eyes as they continually devour the reflected light which surrounds us. All life is powered through the absorption and digestion of other life forms, as well as sunlight and atmosphere.

So, we are back where we started. Life is fueled by Life. Is Attention fueled by Life? Is Attention fueled by more or higher qualities of Attention? Well, it is hard to imagine anything being aware if it were not alive. Is Attention a power that comes with the energy of Life, or does Life awaken or attract the energy we call Attention?

We all know that we can stimulate more energy in our body with appropriate food, rest and exercise. We know that harmonious and interesting situations and relationships generate energizing emotions and poor ones drain us. We recognize that the same is true for the energy required to think, reason, ponder. Over the course of a day, energy seems to "run down" and by nightfall, we become "sleepy" and need to "rest." We go to bed where our body becomes immobile and we lose consciousness for many hours. If we have "slept" well, we feel "rested," and our energy is refreshed again. If we have slept poorly, we wake up still tired and "run down."

Heart, Mind Body Interaction

We humans have been studying our physical bodies for millennia. We know a great deal about the gain and loss of energy for the body. We know far less about our emotional and mental life in these terms. We do know that they are affected by what happens in the body. The physical fight or flight response, hormones that stimulate pleasure and those that stimulate fear and anxiety, levels of health or ill-health influence the capacity of the brain to function and obviously influence our feeling and thinking functions.

What we are just beginning to learn about is how what we think, what we believe, what meanings and interpretations we place on events also have a large influence on the levels of appropriate energy we have to work with. It appears that meanings and interpretations carry energy themselves which can be endowed to us ... or they function like nerve impulses, stimulating the rise and fall in us of energy ... or like enzymes that stimulate the production of hormones that alter our conscious states... or perhaps all three.

These are phenomena of our inner world, the dimension of thoughts, feelings, hopes, worries, self-image. We can see the effects of our inner states on our outer behaviors, which then may leave their imprint on the outside world of people, objects and events. These phenomena cannot be studied in the world outside. We must learn how to direct and hold our attention internally, intentionally, on watching our emotional reactions and our thoughts as we encounter different people and events in outside life.

For example, dear Reader, have you noticed any emotional reactions inside you on reading these ideas? Have you noticed any thoughts, in agreement or disagreement, appearing and disappearing in your mind in response to the direction of this theme? Responses of interest or agreement will stimulate a certain quality of energy in you. Disagreement or disinterest will result in a different mental/emotional "taste." You can probably feel the effort necessary to split your attention, so that part is reading these words for comprehension while another beam of attention is trying to track your mental and feeling reactions. This is the intentionally activated quality of *directed attention* from your intellect, spoken about earlier. It is difficult to maintain. There seems to be little of this energy available and it is easily and quickly used up.

It is this quality of attention that will be needed to explore this question of the conservation and wastage of psychological energies. Since the energy that powers our psychology, the fuel for our "conscious" experiences, is inside us, that is where we must go to study it. How do we not waste this precious quality of attention? How can we collect more of it?

Capture and Imprisonment of Attention

The first and primary problem is a state of semi-consciousness, which Gurdjieff called "Identification." In order to understand and recognize this state in yourself, we will approach it from the other end. Reflect back over your life and look for moments in memory when you felt unusually alive, aware of yourself, inside your body, aware of what you were thinking and feeling, aware of yourself as an "actor" playing a "role" in the life situation in which you find yourself at the moment. These may be moments of great fear and danger when one experiences the thin edge between life and death, or they may be moments of stunning beauty, awe, gratitude, love, happiness. Sometimes the content is very ordinary, but the intensity of your feeling alive seems like a moment of Grace. A moment when everything, including the fact of your personal existence, was unusually vivid. Unfortunately, these are rare moments for most of us, but they confirm the possibility of a greatly enhanced sense of *presence*.

Now, compare the experience of moments like that with the "taste" of a typical day. How often in a day do you have moments of these qualities? If one honestly studies this question, you will notice that many impressions, visual, auditory, sensory, thoughts, feelings, images of other people and landscape float in and out of your field of attention. What is typically missing in your field of awareness is the actual, palpable sense of yourself as the viewer of the scene, the observer of the action, the witness to the internal reactions, the "experiencer" of moments of life.

If you are willing, you can try another experiment here. Try to sense yourself inside your body, looking out through your eyes at these words. Try to continue reading without losing this experience of yourself as the Reader. What do you notice in this attempt?

I recall with clarity a moment a number of years ago. I was driving home after a meeting with friends who shared my interest in these types of questions. As I watched the road, I was also intentionally making the effort to sense the physicality of my body, maintain some attention on my breathing while also being aware of my hands making small adjustments on the steering wheel to maintain my place on the road. My mind was alert and this division of attention into several parts was being sustained with minimal effort at the moment. I felt "Present" in the sense I was coming to understand this particular state of consciousness at that time. Nevertheless, I was also aware of a feeling that I had forgotten something. There was something else I needed to include in my sphere of attention. What could I have forgotten?

I reviewed my mental checklist. I was aware of the sensation of my body surrounding me. I was aware of the rhythm of my breath. I was monitoring my thoughts and feelings. And, I was keenly aware of the road, oncoming traffic and my body automatically operating the car. Nevertheless, the feeling of something missing continued to nag at me. What had I forgotten?

Then, I burst out laughing in the moment I remembered that I had forgotten to include myself in my field of awareness! This feeling of myself is much more than an intellectual concept or label. The actual state of consciousness that allows for the direct experience of myself as the very Witness to all the perceptions and efforts described above had been missing. Then it appeared ... and with it, the experience of myself appeared also.

To most people, this description will make little to no sense. "Of course, I am aware of myself at all times," they might say. I thought so also in the years before I learned how to study the question inside myself. There are many ways to verify this strange state of affairs. A simple one which you, dear Reader, could try if you are interested would be to intensify what you tried a few moments ago. Once again, look at your hands ... right now. Be aware of yourself ... inside your body ... looking out through your eyes at your hands. Experiencing "being in your body" is not a thought; it is the actual experience of the solidity, density, warm, tingling, pulsations, respiration ... the actual awareness of the sensation of your living body with you inside it.

With this enlarged experience of yourself, as a Watcher inside your body, look at your hands without losing this sense of yourself present in your body. Try to maintain this dual focus, part of your attention on your hands and part focused inside on this special awareness of your existence in this moment. How long will it be before your attention begins to drift and you find yourself distracted by a thought, or memory or random association? How long will it be before you literally "forget" the awareness of yourself? If your intention was to look at your hands without losing this experiential sense of yourself as the Watcher, how did you lose contact with it? Where did you go? Why did you leave? What caught your attention and kidnapped it from your intention?

Are You Always Aware of Yourself?

How would this type of effort be of any practical use? "I can remember myself in this way whenever I want to," you might say. "I can remember myself whenever I need to." But is this true?

Try to recall memories of moments when you lost your temper when you blurted out the words that you had promised yourself you would not say, when you forgot the reason you had left one room to go into another, when you realized you had no idea where you left your keys or reading glasses or the book you had been carrying around, when you apologized to someone by saying something like, "I'm sorry. I am not usually like that. It's not like me. I don't know what came over me". Or, waking the morning after too much drink and hearing, to your embarrassment, what your body did the previous night when you were absent from it.

Where do you go when you are not aware of yourself in the way being discussed? Why is attention so difficult to control unless it is in relationship with a strong emotion? And, in this latter case, we are not controlling our attention. It has been captured and is controlled by the degree of interest in what occupies the field of attention.

What are the typical strong attractors that pull my attention away from the inclusion of the experience of myself as the Awareness that is trying to experience my life? Not surprisingly, for most of us, the most powerful magnets for our attention are our concerns about what other people think and feel about us. As we are social and communal creatures, this is a natural concern. The problem is that, for many, this concern becomes a habit, often an involuntary obsession. Reasons for this are numerous and are readily available in any basic psychology or self-help literature which also offer a number of methods to help explore your own idiosyncratic patterns and ways to modify them. What is relevant here, however, is that this concern about what others think is a major thief of attention and energy … and with that theft, the cause of the loss of awareness of yourself. You are thinking about yourself, but you are unaware of yourself as you do so.

Awareness of Self-Image is Not Awareness of Self

As I write this statement, I realize the subtlety of what I am trying to express. It sounds paradoxical that in a moment of thinking about what others think about you, you would not be aware of yourself despite the concern about yourself and your image being at the center of the mental/ emotional concern of the moment. The quality of being aware of yourself is not a thought, a concern or a concept. It is a direct awareness of your consciousness being embedded in a body that breathes and has thoughts in its brain and feelings in its chest and solar plexus.

When I intentionally direct attention, simultaneously, into my mind, into my feelings (chest and solar plexus) and into the sensation of my body, I have attention grounded in at least three different locations. Then, in order to capture my attention and separate it from the experience of myself, the pull on attention from a thought or a feeling or a sensation or a memory or someone's comment must be strong enough to dislodge attention from the other parts of me as well. If I can recognize that part of me is reacting out of concern about others' reactions to me, I can re-ground most of my attention in some other location, typically my body, so that awareness of myself as the person who has just noticed this reaction inside me does not disappear as the rest of my attention rushes to wrap itself around that concern about what others think of me. The concern may remain, or it may weaken without the support of my full attention. Regardless, if my experience of myself does not disappear into the concern, I retain my abilities to assess and direct my reaction. Instead, if my awareness becomes totally absorbed into the thought or reaction, I have become identified, blended, swallowed, "eaten" by what has just captured my attention.

The Pull of the Body on Attention

Concerns and worries also naturally stimulate our fight or flight system, revving up the body to defend itself … although the danger is generally not to my body but to my self-image and sense of safety in relationships. The stimulation of stress hormones, or pleasure hormones, if my thoughts of others' reactions to me are pleasant, will distract attention and pull my consciousness further away from remembering itself as something separate from the reaction it is observing. Subjectively, as my attention flows towards the source of stimulation, its focus narrows until all I am aware of is the concern, or the reaction or the worry or the fantasy. When the focus of attention narrows, like the iris of a camera, what is left out, what disappears from my world in that moment, is this special feeling of my existence.

Our attention is continually "identified" in this way, all day long, day in and day out, year in and year out. Most people can live their entire lives in this diminished state of consciousness. Most of what captures our attention is mundane, whatever activity we are involved in at the moment. Our attention is captured both by events outside in the world and events, reactions, thoughts, daydreams in the psychological world inside us.

The events which produce strong emotions, passions of pleasure or negativity, anger, jealousy, resentment, fear, anxiety, are the largest attractors. With emotionally neutral material, the quality of attention is primarily of the physical, mechanical type, drifting from one thing to the next without a strong emotional reaction. Material that stimulates strong emotions, positive or negative, brings the quality and capacity of emotional attention, which can hold us spellbound, without effort on our part, for long periods of time and pull us back to it again and again when we try to break off the contact.

The Magnetism of Emotion

The question of wastage of psychological energy is most pronounced when attention becomes identified with feelings. But, wait a minute. What type of psychological energy is lost when attention is trapped in identification? Isn't it beneficial to find something of such great interest that one can get "lost" in it, "lose track of time," "lose oneself" and one's worries in hobby or pursuit? Well, it may be so. When attention is absorbed into something pleasant, this does trigger the parasympathetic nervous system to release pleasure and relaxation hormones. This is good for stress reduction. Stress reduction does save energy, physical, emotional and mental. As an obvious fact, relaxation of our musculature, as well as our emotions and thoughts, is a critical factor in conserving mental as well as physical energy. But, conserving the energy, we wake up with each morning is only part of the equation.

Is the primary purpose of having been born with such a complex brain capable of experiencing the reality of its existence and functioning differently with different qualities of psychological energies, to just manage my stress? And where is that stress coming from, if not predominantly from my negative concerns, which trigger the autonomic nervous system to release fight or flight hormones which then stress my body, mind and heart? If one stays at this level, then life is a continuous loop between pleasure and pain.

Intentional Attention

What of the third quality of attention, intentional effort that I deliberately Will for a purpose of my own in the moment. This is a use of attention of my own choosing, not attention involuntarily drawn from me by random associations or strong emotions.

If I want to find a way out of the cycle of mechanical-emotional attention, I will need to study how to watch the push-pull on my attention. I will need to conserve the more refined energy of intentionally directed attention from being drained by the emotional and physical-mechanical pull. The conservation and even the generation of this higher quality of attention is one of the aims of most meditation traditions. The use of a mantra or "ground" for attention allows the strengthening of Will with the practice of the demand to return attention to the mantra or ground over and over and over whenever the drift away has been noticed. This gradually builds a capacity, like building a muscle, to decrease the amount of loss when the mind is pulled to focus on things not necessarily of my choosing, particularly things that stimulate emotions which then increase the hypnotic pull. Eventually, one can divide attention, holding half of it on the mantra or ground, and intentionally direct the other half to watch the interplay between outside events and my internal reactions.

As this capacity to periodically make the effort to direct my attention in this way increases, what I perceive in this state of divided attention can become very interesting. But a new difficulty enters at this point. Much of what I begin to see of my own psychology is likely to present a different picture of myself than that which I have spent a lifetime cultivating as my "self-image." Some parts of me that are addicted to my self-image will have negative reactions to the deeper truth of my complexity when observations inside contradict my accustomed view of myself.

My attention just freed moments ago from some other identification is immediately captured by the reaction to what I have just observed. I will have to train my attention to be able to free itself from the reactions of offended parts of myself so that the study of my psychological world can continue at a more truthful level. It is a long process.

I mentioned earlier that emotion strengthens attention. If I truly want to know myself at a deeper level, to free myself from illusions and misunderstandings, then this search, although at times uncomfortable, can become electrifying. If I can minimize becoming identified with my egoistic reactions, if I can find the appropriate receptive and grateful attitude, then the new perspectives about myself that begin to appear can bring with them a surge in interest and begin to generate more of the higher-grade attention. At this point, I can begin to generate more psychological energy of the quality necessary for this search.

Splitting Attention

Another way of thinking about the process of attention and psychological energy can be illustrated by the example of looking at a house. I am looking at a house. There is the impression of the house. The light reflected off the house and into my eyes is transformed into electrical signals that then travel along my optic nerve to the visual cortex at the back of my brain, where they stimulate (no one understands how) the reconstruction of an image of the house. The light waves have literally made an impression on the sensitive receptors in my eyes, producing a series of electrical impulses which make an imprint in my brain, which I experience as an image of the house.

There has been a transfer of energy from the reflected light outside into my brain and mind on the inside. This stimulation keeps my brain humming. Sensory deprivation experiments demonstrate that diminishing or eliminating stimulation of our sense organs from the outside diminishes the production of energetic activity inside my nervous system. Deprived of the constant inflow of stimulation from the senses, brains begin to malfunction. In experimental subjects, sensory deprivation can lead to psychosis. Children and animals deprived of appropriate and necessary amounts of stimulation fail to develop normal nervous systems and suffer brain damage. Obviously, this continual transfer of energy is necessary to keep us powered up. When outside stimulation is curtailed, the only stimulation available comes from our inner world, where we tend to forever automatically circle around the same repeating thoughts and feelings. Our attention tends to orbit, like a satellite, around strong conditioned mental and emotional attractors.

When the core practice of learning to ground and divide attention is achieved, then the energy derivable from experience is potentiated. Instead of just looking at the house, I have an impression of myself, in my body, while looking at the house. In a way, the energy of impressions has doubled. The energy from the impression of the house has now been joined by the impression of myself as the viewer of the house. The inner activity of my inner world as I look at the house now is added to the enlarged picture of the moment. The moment becomes deeper, richer ... a new and more potent energy has appeared from this effort.

Energy is Food

In a literal way, in addition to food, air, water and sunlight as sources of energy for our body, impressions, both those coming from the outside as well as our interior, continually feed, energize our brain and our mind. Our physical bodies can live off accumulated and stored energy for up to six weeks without food. We can live for perhaps a few days without water. Our brain begins to die after four minutes without oxygen. It is said that we would die instantly if all impressions stopped. Without impressions to carry, our nervous system would have no source of fuel to generate the electricity that maintains our life.

What we call impressions are actually the impact on our nervous system of a flow of energy at a particular wavelength. It is the energy that impacts and initiates the cascading energetic reactions that lead to our experiencing something about that moment.

As we develop the capacity to watch, listen and sense inside ourselves while simultaneously being aware of impressions from the outside, we double the amount of energy available for paying attention in this way. In this process, we diminish the waste, sustain the conservation and even increase the amount and quality of psychological energy available to us.

The phenomenon of Attention appears to us to be a function of the Life energy. One capacity that separates life from non-life is a quality of attention we could call sensitivity. Sensitivity is a form of awareness that allows subjective experiences of aspects of the environment both inside and outside the life form. In simple life forms, that sensitivity is limited to variables like temperature, chemical composition of surroundings, the presence of other life forms supportive and dangerous. In more complex life forms, additional sensory organs begin to expand the scope of sensitivity to expanded areas of the electromagnetic spectrum. Vision, hearing, taste, smell, balance open new dimensions of existence to the awareness of creatures with more advanced sensory equipment. The ability for smell, sight, sound vary dramatically depending on the functions available.

For example, we have recently learned that birds can see the Earth's magnetic field and navigate by it. Some animals see in the ultra-violet range, while others see at night through sensitivity to infra-red. It is estimated that dogs possess up to 300 million olfactory receptors in their noses, compared to about six million in us. And the part of a dog's brain that is devoted to analyzing smells is, proportionally speaking, 40 times greater than ours. Our sense organs are far more complex than much simpler animals but far less efficient than in many other animals. Sensitivity opens up an interactive relationship between the creature and aspects of its environment to which it is sensitive.

To the degree that sensitivity is an experience, there needs to be some sort of "mind," or level of awareness, to have the experience. Obviously, the mind of an ant, the mind of a dog, the mind of a human have enormously different potentials. The more complex the mind, the greater is the sensitivity to greater ranges of frequencies in the electromagnetic spectrum. We are fed and sustained by the energy available at our level of the universal energy spectrum.

The electromagnetic spectrum represents the known range of frequencies and potencies of the energy of the universe. At the highest ranges, the quality of the energy would destroy all life and materiality at our level. At the lowest levels, the frequency waves have slowed down to such an extent that they appear almost flat and seem to have very little, to no, power. Interestingly, these extremely long frequency waves, (ELF) waves correspond to the frequency levels operating in our brains. Ponder that strange fact, dear Reader.

Whatever energy or spirit may be, it fills the Universe. The Universe is energy. Energy carries information decipherable by a corresponding receptor. Thus, different levels of energy carry different levels of information. Energy vibrates at different rates. The faster the vibration, the higher the frequency, the closer and taller the waves, the more powerful that level of energy. At lower levels of power, the vibrations are slower, the frequency slower, the waves lower and further apart. Everything that exists occupies a range of levels that support its existence. Everything lives in, is saturated by, is fed by, the energies available at their level. If a life form is exposed to levels of energy higher or lower than their tolerance level, they are destroyed. As water is to a fish or air to a bird, energy is the medium in which we exist.

Mind

What subjective experiences lie above the level of sensitivity? Obviously, sensitivity does not involve thinking as it is mediated at the sensory level. If an animal can visualize or think in some way, then these sensory signals stimulate a resonant representation of their meaning in the form of an image or thought ... if that creature has image or thought-making organs in their brain. Sensory awareness then seems to be the first and, in some ways, the lowest of the possible *psychological* energies.

Psychological because the energy is directly, *subjectively*, experienced. And to have an experience, there must be an awareness to experience that experience. Therefore, in a sense, all life has a psychology, a subjective world of experiences. Every living organism lives in a subjective-psychological world that extends outward and inward, dependent on the development and sensitivity of sense-organs and what levels, frequencies of energy they are designed to sense.

If you are still with me at this point, my friend, I ask you to look inside again and see what else is in there beyond sensation. What feelings, thoughts, images reactions are you aware of experiencing right now? The quality of these experiences is far deeper, richer, more subtle, and carries exponentially more information than just sensory input. This would seem to represent a level of psychological energy above that of sensation. What has been added here is an awareness of higher levels of energy, literally an additional dimension. Sensory information is carried at the level below. Emotional and conceptual information is carried on the frequencies of this next and higher level. This is the level of direct awareness of what the sensory level is communicating. This could be called Conscious psychological energy. This dimension and the sensitivity level are the bandwidth of psychological energies in which we spend most of our lives. These are the realm of physical-mechanical-emotional-intellectual-automatic-attentions.

A reason why we generally have such a limited quantity of intentionally directed attention may be that its source is above the normal limits of conscious energy.

Anyone familiar with the creative process will recognize where this conversation is going. As I write these words right now, for the first time on my computer screen, the experience for me is like watching fingers move and words appearing. It is as if I were taking dictation. Just as in this moment for you, dear Reader, I have no idea what is coming next. I am, as this is being written, reading it for the first time, just as you are in this moment. I do not yet know how this chapter is going to conclude. I am just watching the words appear. I try to see where the words are coming from. I am only aware of one or two words in my mind just before they escape through my fingers onto the screen. Clearly, I am witnessing this process, but I do not know how it is happening.

This is the realm of the creative process. This is the dimension, the level of energy, from which come new ideas, inspirations, epiphanies and the awareness of my existence in the moment. More than just conscious, this level is creative. It is a region of flexibility and surprise. Ideas, images, thoughts come into existence in our awareness from nowhere … nowhere that we are conscious of. Some of them are extraordinarily potent. They lead to the creation of buildings, airplanes, medicines, nations, religions, theories about the origin of life and the universe, meditation practices that can change one's understanding of existence. This seems to be a creative energy. This is where our mind can come alive and join an awakened heart. This also is a level in the universal energy field, what we scientifically call the electromagnetic spectrum.

Energy Waste

How could I possibly conserve or waste this quality of energy? Wastage of this precious quality occurs when I use it only to pleasure myself in fantasy or to take personal credit for the gifts that mysteriously appear in my awareness in a creative moment. If I don't recognize the privilege and mystery of discovering these amazing phenomena occurring inside me, in my very own mind, if I assume that I, myself, created them, then the energy runs out.

This is the reason behind so-called "artist's block" when the creative muse stops sharing inspiration and the artist can no longer create because the artist believed that the creation came from him/her, rather than him/her being a receptive conduit. This misunderstanding and misattribution of the creative process results in a squandering of the energy by de-potentiating it down to the lower level of ordinary conscious energy, where lives my ego, my self-image. This lower level of ordinary conscious energy becomes clouded with emotional reactions and mental ruminations. The door to the higher level of creativity closes.

Higher Psychological Energies

To access the creative level requires, in part, an attitude that accepts lack of control, humbly understands that it is privileged to participate in the creative action. It recognizes that its awareness is now in relationship with something infinitely larger than itself. It is like making love, allowing the energy to flow without attempting to control ... trusting and surrendering. Then the creative energy can participate with me, in a way impregnate me, with a new conception. Together, something new may enter into the world through me.

Beyond this level of psychological energy lies the realm visited by mystics and sometimes myself, yourself, in a dream, or near-death experience, or a sudden revelation which leaves me changed, but for which I have no words of description ... because it was an experience. I didn't think it; I experienced it! I was there! And that, there, is a dimension far above the here of my ordinary conscious level. The reports of people who have been there are incomprehensible to those who have not been. Typical are the reports of feelings of Unity that cannot be conveyed to the uninitiated. This would seem to represent a fourth level of consciousness from which the creative energy originates.

The Ghost in the Machine

Are Mind and Brain the same? When unconscious, in a coma, in dreamless sleep, my brain continues to function, but without my presence to experience those functions. It would seem that my Mind is something that appears and disappears from my brain. It is clear that my subjective awareness does not run my brain, although it can influence some of its functions ... and vice versa. The brain, as part of the body, is programmed to operate all its vital functions automatically to preserve the body. Its functions are immeasurably faster than my relatively slow consciousness could ever follow. It is like I, as Mind, occasionally visit my brain. Then I am aware of myself inside my brain.

So, either the Mind is as a vehicle to move its occupant (me) in and out of the present moment, into the past or into an imaginary future, to bring back to the present what I have found outside its minuscule boundaries ... or ... I am my Mind. Or, is that phrasing taking credit? My, personal, mind? Is Mind individual or universal? If Mind is energy ... how can it be divided? Energy is energy at different potencies. If Mind is Energy ... "If?" "What is the alternative?" ... Mind is Energy. Energy is Universal. If Energy is a One and Mind is Energy ... then all Minds are One and mine is a fragment? Am I Mind?

Ask a neurologist or psychologist, "What is the Mind?" What comes back is a list of the functions and phenomena that a mind can perform. Ask again, "But, what exactly is Mind?"

The response will be a description about how brain activity and mind functions interact with each other. "Yes," you may persist, "but what actually is this awareness which we experience as myself having an experience?" Typically, the response is a repeating loop of the first two explanations or an exposition on the "mind-body" question.

Ask a philosopher or mystic, "What is mind?"

The response might be, "The ancient energy principles of Shim(Mind)-ki(Energy)-hyul(Blood)-jung(Body) states: "Where consciousness lies, energy flows, bringing blood and transforming the body." This phrase implies that consciousness is the true reality behind the appearance of form. A simpler way of saying Shim-ki-hyul-jung is, "Energy goes where mind goes."

Recall one of the definitions of "Spirit"; "Supernatural immaterial creature, invisible corporeal being of an airy nature." "Supernatural" in the sense that its nature or origin is beyond (Supra) the current field of awareness of our scientific capacities.

How is this different from "Energy"; an invisible force which creates movement, evolution and involution of forms, processes and sustains life?

Does not our Mind, the awareness of ourself inside our bodies and brains, create movement, thought forms and images, evolve theories, transform understanding? Is it not invisible, even to us? We can see the effects of our Mind. Can we see our Mind? What is looking?

Physicists have led the way for some brain researchers to begin wondering if our Mind lies in the quantum realm, the dimension of sub-atomic particles which pop into and out of existence from the "quantum foam," the field of potential energy which fills the Universe. Come to think of it, we, ourselves, pop into and out of existence, for ourselves, as we cross the boundary between the levels of sensory-emotional attention and of conscious, self-aware attention. We only become aware of ourselves when we pop back into the conscious, self-aware level and realize that we had popped out back into the sensory-emotional level but were not aware that we had done so since we were no longer aware of ourselves when we popped out … until we popped back in.

Here is a description of the quantum realm: "Quantum physicists discovered that physical atoms are made up of vortices of energy that are constantly spinning and vibrating, each one radiating its own unique energy signature. Therefore, if we really want to observe ourselves and find out what we are, we are really beings of energy and vibration, radiating our own unique energy signature -this is fact and is what quantum physics has shown us time and time again." This sounds very much like "Spirit"; "Supernatural immaterial creature, invisible corporeal being of an airy nature."

Niels Bohr, Nobel Prize winner for his work in quantum theory, said, "If quantum mechanics hasn't profoundly shocked you, you haven't understood it yet. Everything we call real is made of things that cannot be regarded as real."

How are you, my Reader, coming to terms with the ideas expressed here?

If everything about ourselves that we call real is made of things that cannot be regarded as real, then what are we, what are you, what am I, that is discovering that we, you, I, fit the definition of an "immaterial creature, invisible being of an airy nature"?

To Eat or Be Eaten

Impressions as Food or Impressions as Carnivores

Our most precious attribute is our Attention. Attention is a vehicle carrying within it the "Mind's Eye" or the "Observer" of the information, brought through impressions to the Observer through the "medium" of Attention. In any given moment, the only "reality" I am aware of are the impressions (sensory, emotional or mental), that are contained in the "field" of what I call "my" Attention. When Attention shifts, what was in awareness before, now disappears from awareness and is replaced by some other impressions. What we call "memory" is a phenomenon that collects, collates and stitches together these separate moments into a storyline. I can then utilize Attention to review these disconnected internal impressions and reconstruct them in a way that maintains my "story-of-myself."

When, after a time, memory wants to visit these "recordings," some are available for viewing, but most have "disappeared" and seem not retrievable. There appears not to have been enough Attention to remember them all. But there may be a related reason that memories are not always strongly recorded. A special study of the quality and movement of Attention can demonstrate that the Mind's Eye is not always present in the field of awareness even though recordings are being automatically made.

There is something additional that can appear in the field of Attention that is usually not noticed. It is very subtle. Only by discovering It can one then notice Its absence. This fleeting something is the experience of myself being present as part of the field of attention. For those who have not noticed the fluctuations of this subtle distinction, the contents of Attention are the primary focus of awareness, but not the awareness of the user of the Minds' Eye. "Who is looking?" is not a question that arises.

We all know, from experience, that impressions have different "tastes", arouse different levels of interest, attract different parts of us. Some impressions attract intellect, some stimulate emotions, and many attract our body's desire for pleasant sensations. We all also know that the taste of impressions can be negative, positive or neutral. Obviously, some impressions have a strong influence on our attention, positive or negative, while others leave us indifferent. Some seem to bring us more energy of a certain quality, while others seem to drain us of energy. How can we gain more energy and lose less? Does this fluctuation in the "taste" of impressions have something to do with memory or moods?

What happens when the wave/particle beam of Attention notices something in the sphere of Its awareness? It moves towards the impression of greatest interest at that moment. When It touches that beckoning impression, It enters and is absorbed by it. Attention disappears into the impression. For a while, if the attraction is strong enough, everything else other than the impression of interest disappears. The sphere of awareness shrinks, like the iris of a camera lens. The whole world now consists of this impression... because my Attention is now *inside* the impression, *absorbed* by it, part of it. Nothing else is noticed or remembered because nothing else can be seen or sensed. Attention is isolated from all Its other collected memories. It even forgets about Itself.

A few moments later, I "snap out of it" and recognize again where I am, who I am with, what was happening. The iris has opened up somewhat and the field of attention is now holding more impressions again. It has escaped the confinement inside the previous impression and is momentarily freer. In a few moments, something else "captures" my attention, the iris narrows to "focus" on this new interest and "I" disappear once more down the rabbit hole and am absorbed into a new impression.

Who is this "I"? This is the Eye of the "Mind's Eye." This is the Observer, the Witness. What else could be using Attention to explore the outer world of the senses and the inner world of thoughts and feelings? However, it seems that the Observer does not have very good control over the "vehicle" of Its Attention.

To "do" something with my Attention, I first have to locate it. Where is it now? What has It been doing while I have not been attentive to It? Then I must "take hold of It" and point It at something. I then have to keep It from wandering away and unconsciously giving Itself to something else. I may have to repeatedly "bring my attention back" in order to maintain my "focus."

An incalculable help in learning to steady Attention is the practice of placing some of this Attention into part of my physical body. If I intentionally pay attention to the sensation of my hand or arm or leg, at the same time I am giving some leftover Attention to something else, I find that with the "split focus," Attention is a bit less drifty as long as I can maintain the dual contact. When untrained, Attention is like a puppy and the continuous flow of impressions is like squirrels. If I don't "leash" the Attention, it chases everything it sees. When I "ground" part of my Attention into the sensation of my body and work to hold it there, then I can direct the rest of it to examine the perception of my choice in the moment. In this way, the sensation of my physical body becomes a "mantra" to which I continually return my flighty Attention.

Working like this inside myself, trying to "exercise" my little Will, feels like work. It is a struggle. It feels like I am trying to develop a muscle. But, how often do I actually experience this struggle? Most of the time, I "notice" my Attention only after being "lost" in "paying attention" and then "returning." If I study this for a while, I notice that my Attention comes and goes, drifts, gets "stuck" on something and then drifts off with something else. I now understand the meaning of the phrase, "a train of thought." My Attention is continually drifting from one thing to another. Often those things it "a-lights on" are not necessarily interesting or pleasant. Sometimes they are actually upsetting. Why do I pay attention to them? Why can't I control my Attention better?

I "recall" now that there are times when I feel more in control of my Attention. The times I can decide for myself what I wish to pay attention to are the times I am actively engaged in trying to maintain the focus of Attention. Those are the times I am, at least somewhat, aware of myself as the director of the Attention. When I am aware of Myself as part of the field of Awareness, I seem to experience myself as more Present, more conscious, more far-seeing. And, I have much clearer memories for moments of this quality than on average. So, perhaps Memory and Attention, and being aware of Myself, are related.

If I want more "energy" in order to be aware of myself, I need to be careful about allowing my Attention to get kidnapped by an impression without my permission. Getting highjacked seems correlated with a loss of energy. Is this cause, or effect, or a combination of both? What kind of "energy" am I feeling? It seems connected to an intensity of Awareness, an intensity of consciousness … a psychological energy that interacts with what I am giving Attention to!

How am I going to free up more of this special energy?

Recognizing I am linked with my Attention, first, I need to study which impressions tend to kidnap me the most and keep me prisoner the longest. I next notice that most impressions are brief and temporary pirates. I recognize that there are some other things out in the world that fascinate me.

And there are some memories or fantasies inside me that I tend to keep re-visiting or dwelling upon. I need to study these attractors to understand their continual hold over my Attention. Why do I keep returning to them, either without a fight or willingly running into their arms?

What is particularly interesting is that some of these thoughts and reminiscences are negative in quality and get me upset. Yet, I still find myself their prisoner over and over again. When I am in their clutches, there is no recognition of myself in the narrow field of awareness in that moment. I have nothing beyond the circle of limited awareness to hold onto in order to pull myself out of the circle. I return to my awareness only when I "wake up" and separate, even briefly, from what had captured me. Now I have the "energy" to try to at least make a choice about redirecting my Attention. Whether or not I am successful is less important than that I have had another moment to practice strengthening the "muscle" that has the potential to control my Attention, and thus the place of my Awareness and my experience of "reality" at that moment.

Now I notice something else. My Attention is always getting absorbed, or "eaten," when It encounters a perception. The more Attention I give to something, whether fascinating or threatening, the more important it must be to me. If I didn't believe it was important to give my Attention to this, why would I be allowing this to happen? I don't have this much trouble with things I don't believe are important to me in some way. Maybe it is my belief that is part of the problem. If I didn't feel it important to give Attention to this, I probably wouldn't. It would be easier to control my Attention around it.

Now I see part of the reason my Attention so often gets glued to thoughts or moods or external interests that stimulate my emotions. I believe they are important to dwell on, either because of the pleasurable feelings they stimulate in me or because of the threat they pose (and I believe that I need to go over them repeatedly to defensively plan), or because they are a painful memory which I cannot "let go of" … the wording of which suggests that, for some reason, I am "holding on" to this suffering. The more Belief and Attention I feed to them, the stronger they get and the weaker I get! It is as if they are eating me! Worse, I am feeding myself to them!

Now I can begin to challenge my belief that this is an important impression to dwell upon. Where did this belief come from? Was it correct at some time but not now? Was it ever true? Who told me? How did I come to this conclusion? But also, when I am willing to challenge my belief, my Attention is briefly free to explore what the Observer is interested in, not what is automatically calling to the Attention. I am momentarily in charge and free from the seductive impression.

In this case, the Observer wants to study this dynamic in my psychological world. What is the relationship between my beliefs, my Attention and the ebb and flow of the awareness of my Self? I realize that when I am aware of my Self in the moment, I, as the Observer, can find the impressions in my field of Attention interesting without being "captivating." The energy that would have immediately and automatically flowed into the perception, and thus feeding It and strengthening Its hold on my Attention and eliminating my awareness of my Self, now seems to feed my effort to balance and maintain my Attention on observing this process.

It now seems that from moment to moment, my Attention is either automatically being eaten by the gravitational field of fluctuating impressions, or my Attention is able to "stand back" and look without falling into the impression. Then, objects that are of interest to the Observer are being "digested" in order to feed and enlarge the understanding of myself, as this Witness. As I appear to be the Witnessing-Observer, then I must conclude that from moment to moment, I am either digesting and deepening my understanding by "eating" the impressions of the two worlds that flow around and through me … or I am literally being eaten by impressions of both my inner and outer worlds … the two worlds I am trying to observe and study. Attention is the life "blood" of Awareness. If I am the Observer, then I am also Awareness. If I give away the energy of Attention too casually, I am feeding my Self to the world below when my true Home is the world above.

"The eye with which I see God is the same with which God sees me. My eye and God's eye is one eye, and one sight, and one knowledge, and one love".

~ Meister Eckhart

Waking Up

To wake up, we must stop dreaming the dream of who we believe we are. We want, we need, to believe we are our self-image, our personal history, our story as told to us by ourselves, by our family, by our community or nation. We have been conditioned to believe we must accept as true the personality attributes assigned to us by ourselves and collected from others, like burrs, as we've walked the path of our life.

The experience of being aware but without an identity is ... unthinkable. We literally have no way to think about that. If I don't have an identity, if I have no story, no labels, no image of who I think I am ... it would be like having total amnesia. I would be aware of being aware inside my body. But who would I be? What would I do? The thought is unnerving.

But, what's in a name? The essence of something is not the name, not the label.

My name, my label, my personality serve as anchors for what I believe is my "sanity." Without those anchors, I would be a disembodied awareness ... floating? ... suspended? ... embedded? ... where? ... attached to ... what?

To experience that would mean I had gone insane! Doesn't sanity lie in materiality and the sensory reality of my body, my feelings, my thoughts? All these phenomena must be me.

If I ever had the experience of observing my materiality, my sensory, emotional and intellectual reality ... and in that very moment realizing that I wasn't what I was observing, that I wasn't what I was seeing ... but, rather, I was what was having the experience of observing ... then ... I would experience myself as a disembodied awareness ... floating? ... suspended? ... embedded? ... where? ... attached to? ... what?

Everything is experienced in the brain by the Experiencer.

This Experiencer experiences from inside the brain within the body.

I, the Experiencer, am obviously in relationship with the body I occupy, but I don't need to identify myself *as* my body or its functions of sensing, feeling and thinking.

I seem to be the passenger, not the vehicle.

I can't think about this idea if I have no experiential references. What words and images could I find to describe something I have never experienced, something I have never seen, heard, tasted, smelled? Our ordinary thinking is a mental activity that automatically and mechanically puts words and memories into associational trains with a connecting theme and runs those trains through our mind ... whether we want them there or not. We see and hear the contents of the train and we call that thinking.

Some of us have very effective organizers of associational thinking in our heads. The faster we can associate, the more related thought forms we already have stored in our brains to work with, the more often our associations will have a practical impact on the situation at hand. We call this intelligence. What it is, however, is a very fast, very efficient computer program that recognizes patterns and can "connect the seemingly related dots." This doesn't mean the dots are connected correctly, but you become aware of the pattern being presented to you in your mind. Generally, if it appears in your mind, you tend to believe it must be true. We also call this thinking.

But there is a different type of mental processing that does not use words. This type of intelligence watches and observes what is happening in the world beyond the body and inside the ordinary thoughts and emotional reactions that continuously interact with what is perceived outside. It can understand and reason spontaneously without needing to use words to talk with itself. It is this higher-level mental consciousness that can experience an awareness of itself inside its body.

This is not so strange as it may sound. Most of us experience a few brief moments in this higher conscious state from time to time. Have you experienced beginning to awake from a deep sleep and realizing, for a few seconds, that you had no idea where you were or even who you were? Or perhaps in a moment of great surprise, or fear or embarrassment, your mind went blank; you could think of nothing to say, "tongue-tied," as they say. Or maybe you noticed something strange on the horizon and having no understanding of what it was until you were much closer? Or maybe you saw a shadow and had no idea what had cast it until the lighting changed. Or perhaps you had a dream full of complex imagery and plot lines which were unable to talk about even though you could still see it in memory? Or perhaps you once found yourself in a novel situation or somewhere you had never been and you felt an intense realization, in that moment, of your existence as if you had just woken from a dream. You were more fully aware in those moments … that is why you remember them now … but you were not in your typical intellectual mind where your words reside. Without words, you cannot talk with yourself of the story of yourself, your personal version of history or what you believe and think about yourself. That data is not stored at the higher level. At that level, one can see a different viewpoint on what we call reality.

What do we "wake up" from? We wake up from having our attention so completely focused on words, daydreams and sensory impressions that we lose track of an awareness of our self as the one who is having the experience. To wake up is to re-member, to put back together the experience of myself having experiences through sensory input, emotions and thoughts about what is being experienced. Any experience of less than that intensity is a form of waking-sleep. What we typically believe is the only real reality is actually more like a semi-awake dream state which appears very different in the state of Waking Up.

An Approach to Exploring the Mystery of Attention

There is a deep level of mystery that is discernible even in ordinary life. We can occasionally realize "what we are thinking," occasionally recognize we are "lying to ourselves," see our "daydreams," experience an insight that shifts our orientation.

Beyond Conditioning: The Mystery of Interior Sight

Something lies within our psychological experience that appears to operate from beyond the conditioned neurological- biochemical-material three "brains," or areas of functionality (intellect, feeling, sensation) within the body. This "something" appears unexpectedly for brief moments, offering the possibility of escape from the trap of a conditioned "mind."

Part of the illusion created by our programmed reactions is the belief that we operate out of this "freer" something on a regular basis. In fact, the moments spent in this "freer" state are rare and brief. Meditation is the pathway to strengthening and training this "higher" something or our connection with it. Without this as foundation, there is no possibility of freedom sufficient to begin to "know thyself."

Studying these processes, learning what is and what is not possible requires attention. How to bring the correct quality of attention, for sufficient duration, to focus in the correct direction with an understanding of what to look for is a process that can only be discovered by the individual through solitary effort, albeit with the guidance of someone already practiced in the method. Direction for the study of one's interior experiential world requires the training of a special type of attention. It is this special type of attention that Gurdjieff's method offers as a solution.

Qualities of Attention

Observation can confirm that attention comes in three basic varieties or qualities. The most prevalent is a "mechanical" attention with no real "will" of its own. It is free-floating, undirected and flows like heat. It will be automatically pulled towards the nearest, strongest attractor at the moment, then "fall," over and over, again toward the next thing that "captures" the attention. It is mechanical because there is no plan or intent behind it. Buddhism calls this "monkey mind." Everyone knows and has wrestled with this level of "distractibility." We say, "The lights are on, but nobody is home." Often, we cannot recall afterwards what it was we were listening to, looking at, thinking, during this period of random association, nor what happened to trigger it. This is our normal state of attention the vast majority of time. This can be called Mechanical Attention as there is no intention behind it and it flows according to mechanically conditioned associational chains.

Occasionally, an attractor of sufficient interest engages us emotionally and we are "caught," "riveted," held by our interest for long periods of time, sometimes even "against our will." This is a focused attention out of the ordinary. We can experience this with a book, a movie, a morbid situation, a car crash, sexual images, something fascinating to such a degree we become oblivious to our surroundings, even to the point of not hearing our name called. This type of attention can be called "Emotional" Attention because it is magnetized and held by a feeling of attraction. It has an aim, but the aim comes from the fascination with the attractor. It is not necessarily predetermined ahead of time or held in place by one's own will.

The third, and most rare, type of attention is that which is directed by one's own decision prior to the contact with the object of attention. A continual effort must be made to maintain the focus of attention against the pull of the mechanical and emotional levels. Attention must be sustained by the force of one's own choice and effort. It is usually brief in duration and must be continually renewed. This can be called "Directed" Attention. What seems to lie behind the effort to focus directed attention is a mysterious "something" that can occasionally "see" into the mind and feelings from beyond the usual conditioned habits.

Training Attention

In traditional meditation, it is this "something" that is engaged to initiate and direct its focus on a mantra, using the mantra as "home base," which serves as a point of stability. By intentionally choosing this focal point with a specific aim in mind, the directed attention is engaged. The frequent mechanical drift away from the mantra is sooner noticed and a directed return of attention to the focal point easier to reinitiate. The mantra is typically a sound, image or sensation (such as the breath or the sensation of the physical body in part or whole) or prayer of a neutral to positive emotional quality. Making this quality the object of attention decreases, or even eliminates for a while, negative thinking and feelings that trigger physiological stress responses in the first and second (body or feeling) "brains." With this hiatus in the usual flow of conditioned experiences, negativity, worry, complaining, planning, reviewing conversations past or rehearsal, all three "brains" begin to quiet, and the experience of relaxation begins. This respite in psychosomatic tension is beneficial for health and trains a person to learn to use directed attention for relief from conditioned thinking and reactions to life, real and imagined. Practiced for a long time, the resultant tranquility may lead to deeper understanding of one's hidden nature, and in some traditions, to degrees of liberation from illusions of life and ordinary self.

Restructuring the Brain

Psycho-neurological research has confirmed that the underlying mechanism for learning rests on the plasticity of the brain. When presented with new information or experiences, the brain literally begins to rewire neuronal connections to accommodate the new task. If that rewiring does not take place, there is no learning. Our brains are continually altering their physical structure in response to experience. The brains of meditators reflect changes from that activity and are different from the brains of non-meditators. We not only change our minds, but we literally change our brains to do so. Because of this fact, the great meditative traditions have found a way to transform their practitioners into types of people different from the ordinary.

Through meditation, the attention can become steadier, more capable of sustained focus, less susceptible to being continually drawn into conditioned pathways organized around worry, resentment, living in the past or future. One is better able to focus on what is actually happening in the moment with less mental/emotional overlay from memories of the past or speculation about the future, which distort the accuracy of interpreting the actual moment at hand.

Divided Attention

To bring a practice that offered the possibility of more rapid psycho-transformation and could be practiced in the flow of daily life, Gurdjieff suggested using directed attention, as is done in other practices, but rather than a single focal point, dividing attention into two or more points simultaneously. Using the interior of the body as a starting point, attention can be grounded in one or more locations by engaging sensation as the link. Holding open a space between the director/observer of attention and one or more sensitized points inside the body allows an experience of the observer as distinct from the body. Attention can then be directed onto thoughts, feelings, attitudes simultaneously while holding open this space. The experiential distance between observer and what is observed allows the possibility of noticing qualities of subjectivity within the thoughts, feelings, attitudes, interpretations that make up the stream of activity typically understood as "oneself." As the limitation and subjectivity of the content of these psychic processes are recognized, deeper levels of sincerity and objectivity can arise. "Know Thyself" means first learning what is not thyself, but rather a mechanical pattern of psychological/emotional/muscular reactions and responses to the conditioning mechanism of life. A separation of the gold from the lead requires an instrument of separation.

Gurdjieff also suggests using the potential of divided attention to look "inside" and "outside" at the same time, what his pupil Peter Ouspensky called a "double-headed arrow." How else could one discover a more accurate understanding of why one's life is the way it seems to be than by learning to watch oneself in life, in the moment, as if one were watching another person? By developing directed attention to watch what we believe constitutes "oneself" and the interior psychological/emotional responses described above — while at the same time watching the world immediately outside, including the outer movements of the body, interacting with this interior oneself, the interactions between life and one's responses become visible. The pattern of one's life becomes understandable as dependent on the pattern of one's thoughts, assumptions, attitudes, interpretations of meaning. The subjectiveness, arbitrariness, unnecessariness of many of these reactions becomes apparent. With the seeing of these links from this different perspective, something may begin to change. A different relationship, a different understanding begins to form.

The experience of working with divided attention focused on our outside movements and vocalizations, simultaneously with our interior psychological states, brings into view the question of what is directing the directed attention? What is making the decisions regarding the objects of focus? What is absorbing and learning from the new impressions flowing in from this new observational system?

There may then arise a wish to direct attention deeper to discover its source. This becomes the foundation of a rationally-based search for the mystery of Self.

On Consciousness

Dear Courtney,

Why am I writing you this unusual letter?

I am offering it as a gift, as a sharing of my current understanding, because I wish, more than anything, that you find your way to a sense of peace with yourself and others and a living experience of personal connection with the mystery of our existence. Then, everything has the possibility of becoming meaningful, and life is more vivid, and death holds no fear.

So, relax as you read, and watch the words and ideas stimulate images as they flow through your mind and heart.

Enjoy.

We can see everywhere in the natural world and the social world constructed by man that there are levels of hierarchy. Everything below is an elaboration of what is above. The lower anything is in a hierarchy, the greater its level of density, the fewer degrees of freedom it has, the more controlling influences lie above it. Take, for example, an army or corporation. It is shaped like a pyramid. The leader gives a direction to the under-leaders who send the direction lower and lower into the organization until it reaches the level designated for action. Those below follow orders assuming those above know what they are doing. The private, thus, has much less influence and flexibility than the general. Yet, it is the private who must carry out the action.

If an inspiration appears in my mind, in order to be implemented, it must be translated from image to thought to muscular movement in my voice box and/or body to have an impact on the environmental material around me, which I may then try to shape to approximate the image or idea that first appeared in my mind. Which is of a higher order or potency, the image or the object? The object only exists because it was preceded by the image. But the image must arouse sufficient emotional desire to will an attempt to bring its representation into material manifestation. So, before anything can appear in my exterior world as a result of my efforts, it must be preceded in the invisible, non-material psychological world by an impulse sufficient to give it birth outside in the "world" that we can experience through our external sense organs. Thus, the immaterial plan or wish must precede the materialized manifestation.

In nature, we see that objects of greater density are composed of something else of lesser density and those less dense components are ultimately composed of fluctuating forms of energy, sub-atomic particles. These are described as tendencies-to-exist as they seem to blink in and out of existence even as the form in which they appear continues to maintain its shape and functionality. As all living things generate complex series of interpenetrating and overlapping electromagnetic fields, it may be the fields that maintain our form as long as the field is maintained …. perhaps by Life itself.

Science studies the nature of materialized densities (objects like planets, galaxies, trees, oceans) and the invisible rules that seem to govern their interactions. Science can tell us what and, to a certain extent, how, about the material world. It cannot tell us why. Science tries to explain what we can see and measure with our external senses and instruments. It cannot address meaning. Its realm is limited to what can be observed and measured. It cannot tell us what lies behind what is observed, why it exists or where "exists" the plan behind it or the planner behind the plan.

Plato talked about the Ideal World of Forms. Take the chair you sit on while reading this letter. Where did it come from? How did the idea of "chair" come into manifestation? Most likely, a primitive ancestor, sitting on a comfortable stone, suddenly "saw" the possibility of taking it with him to another location rather than searching for one like it someplace else. Later, he saw that he might make it more comfortable by shaping it with a tool. Thus the "chair" first appeared. But where was the "idea" for "chair" prior to its appearance in our ancestor's mind? The form or concept of "chair" must have been waiting, "somewhere," outside of space and time, for a mind flexible enough to "see" it. Everything that man has discovered or created originated in someone's mind. It appeared. From where?

To think like this suggests that the "World of Possibilities" or the "World of Forms" lies outside of space/time and bits of it materialize in the minds of living creatures, dependent on the state of receptivity of that mind. Realize that everything that has been "discovered" about life and the universe has always been waiting to be discovered. The Truth precedes discovery. So, which is "higher" in the hierarchy: the potential for discovery of something previously unknown or the specific new idea which has finally has been discovered?

The sense of "higher" and "lower" implies pre-existence, less materiality and more potential vs. a resultant materialization with less potential than that from which it is derived. Where is there more potential? ... in that from which the form of the manifestation flows or in the resultant manifestation?

Today, biologists have "discovered" that biological forms and functions are "directed" by genes and are busy identifying genes that seem to correlate with manifestations. It is now commonly accepted that our genes carry the design and direct the manifestation that is "us." Clearly, there is more power and potentiality in the genes than in their product, the living animal. Reductionists ask us to believe that atoms and molecules just accidentally, through trial and error, floated together in the atomic/molecular world and began producing "living" condensations in a world of "non-living" condensations (rocks, planets, etc.). They accept that genes (invisible until the recent invention of more powerful microscopes) are the "god" of the body. They do not see that the genes did not invent themselves. They do not ask, what is the "god" behind the genes? If the genes are more "intelligent" and less "material" than the body, what is the greater intelligence behind the genes?

Let us come back to our discussion of "consciousness," starting with oxygen as a metaphor. You would agree that oxygen, a gas of much less "density," much less "materiality" than our bodies, is essential for most forms of "life" on our planet. It would seem nonsensical to talk about "my" oxygen as separate from "your" oxygen. Clearly, nobody possesses their own oxygen. We all share the oxygen that surrounds and permeates us.

Now, can there be oxygen without "life"? Our scientists tell us that oxygen molecules exist everywhere in the universe, on other planets, on comets, floating in interstellar space. There was oxygen on the earth before life appeared. But, can there be life without oxygen? Not our type of life.

Scientists report discovering life forms in the ocean depths and up to a half-mile deep in the crust that are not oxygen-based but still "alive." So, where did "life" come from? Did it emerge from clouds of oxygen? Is oxygen "intelligent" enough to design and create life?

It would seem silly to say that life, at least our form of life, evolved from oxygen. Science today believes that the process of life itself substantially raised the oxygen content of the atmosphere to its current levels. "Life" obviously is something originating from a source far above the molecular world of gases.

How could something less "intelligent" with less potentiality and power, like oxygen, create something with more intelligence, potentiality and power? "Life" obviously is something far above oxygen, something that came from beyond the world of oxygen, the molecular world of gases, and made its "appearance" in this world, at this level of density and materiality.

So, would we say that each of us possesses our own energy of life separate from the energy of life all around us? We can acknowledge that a person, dependent on their health, may manifest more or less "vitality." We see that our "vitality" ebbs when we do not eat, do not rest, are mentally distressed and is restored to higher levels when we do eat, rest and have peace of mind. This obvious ebbing and flowing suggests fluctuations in the energy of life. Do we assume that Life itself ebbs and flows or that the receptivity of the organism ebbs and flows in the quantity and quality of Life that manifests in? We don't assume that oxygen is diminishing around us if our lungs are congested and we have trouble breathing. So, it would seem that Life surrounds and permeates us in a manner similar to oxygen. Objects that do not have structures that can contain and process Life energy we call "non-living." Objects that do have these structures to manifest the effects of this Life energy we call "living." When those structures no longer function in a manner that can process the Life energy, we say the life form has "died" and is now a non-living object, a corpse. The body remains, but the invisible energy that animated it no longer manifests within it. We do not assume that the energy of Life has disappeared from the world, only the body's receptivity to its animating power.

Now, did the body invent Life? Did oxygen invent Life? Did genes invent Life? It would seem the reverse, that the energy of Life organized molecular structures to form genes which then further organized molecules which coalesced within an energy field (Life itself?) to form a body. Our bodies are at one level of materiality, which our sense organs "perceive" as "solid." Genes exist at a much less dense, less material level of existence compared to bodies. They interpenetrate bodies, but their constituent molecules can exist outside of bodies.

Is Life energy denser than bodies? Is Life energy denser than genes? Which created which? If we agree that Life created genes to help create bodies, then we must accept that Life energy existed prior to either genes or bodies. If Life created genes and bodies, then Life must come from a level less material, and of higher potency, than genes or bodies.

We have already established that bodies and molecules do not "exist" at the same level of materiality. So, in a sense, they "exist" in different, but interpenetrating "worlds" or levels of the larger universe. If we accept that Life represents a higher order than genes, which are conglomerates of molecules, then we must accept that Life comes from beyond the molecular world. We are told by quantum physicists that atoms and sub-atomic particles do not "exist" in a typical "material" sense, although most do have some small amount of mass. Rather they are now described as "tendencies to exist" of some unknown energy field that appears to under-lay the knowable universe. These tendencies-to-exist appear and disappear in a world far beyond the perceptible space/time we live in.

Now, we can probably all agree that Life is an intelligent something and marvel at its diversity, creativity, flexibility, durability. On our planet, it seems to interpenetrate and vitalize certain types of forms, but not all. Following our line of reasoning, would we assume that Life invented itself? Is Life God? Did Life create the non-organic molecules, the rocks, the planets, the stars? If it did, then the planets and stars themselves must, in some sense, be "living." If Life did not invent the non-material universe, then there must be something beyond Life. If Life did invent the non-material, what is behind Life? What does It serve? Did "something" else create Life and non-Life?

Let us look at Intelligence. Does Life seem well organized, adaptive, creative? Does the organization of Life seem "intelligent"? Does the known Universe seem well organized, adaptive, creative? Does the organization of the universe seem "intelligent" or random and chaotic?

The reductionist argument is that the universe accidentally appeared from "nowhere" a long time ago and, through random collisions over time, accidentally congealed into stars and planets, which then accidentally, through trial and error, produced organic molecules which accidentally formed bodies which somehow vitalized themselves into animation and began to become aware of the "accidental" world about them. All these higher functions and possibilities were created by forces of less possibility and potency. Finally, some of these animated "some-things" began to "think" and "feel" and "aspire" and "hope" and "long for," again as a resultant of non-thinking, non-feeling molecules.

Reductionism does assume that given enough time, monkeys and keyboards, some simian would eventually produce Shakespeare.

If this doesn't make sense, then we can return to our hierarchy model and must say that Intelligence precedes both the material and non-material forms and forces in the visible universe, including Life. There is no place left to place this Intelligence except beyond the created universe. I can speak of my level of intelligence, the level at which my central nervous system seems to operate in comparison with some other person's level. But, can I say that the energy of Intelligence is a different energy in me than that operating in you?

Let us finally return to "consciousness." As with oxygen, Life and Intelligence, would we say that the energy that we recognize as consciousness is a separate something within each of us? Is the energy that produces the experience of consciousness in me different or separate from the energy which produces consciousness in you? If not, then it would seem that, like oxygen and Life, consciousness is a "something" that permeates and interpenetrates the world around us, not just something produced by the biological functioning of life forms. We can call it an "energy" if you wish, although no one knows what "energy" is. We can only talk about "energy" as the potential to produce an effect without understanding what that potential is, where it comes from or why it exists.

Now, as we can sense different degrees of vitality from Life, we can also agree that there are different levels or degrees of "intelligence." As the intelligence of a normal man is greater than that of a dog, so we can sense that the intelligence of one man may vary greatly from another. What can we intuit about the intelligence it would take to create and run a living body or the intelligence it would take to create and organize a universe? This would seem to represent a level of "intelligence" far above our own.

Does "intelligence" require "consciousness"? We can agree that our body has an "intelligence" of its own. Medical science is still attempting to understand the complexity of the billions of interacting functions that keep us operating. Man has existed on earth without knowing, until recently, how his body works. The body, thank goodness, does not require either our attention or understanding to perform its necessary tasks. We can see that a person in a coma is typically not conscious, but intelligence continues to operate the body. Awareness of one's surroundings, awareness of being present in one's body in one's surroundings, is not necessary for the continuing operation of complex levels of "intelligent functioning." We could probably agree that the "intelligence" of my actions is increased to the degree to which I am aware of my thoughts, feelings and bodily movements in the moment. Indeed, I can see that I am often not "conscious" of myself in this way and that my life goes on. I speak and act and react and do things without needing to be aware of myself behind my thoughts, feelings and actions. Clearly, intelligence and consciousness are not the same.

So, again we can ask the question. Which is higher, intelligence or consciousness? If oxygen, Life and Intelligence are not contained individually but rather shared by all dependent on level of functioning and receptivity, so it must also be with Consciousness. If oxygen is everywhere in the universe (with higher concentrations on planets), then Life and Intelligence and Consciousness must be everywhere, perhaps with higher or lower areas of density. The difference is that oxygen, despite its rarified degree of molecular concentration, can be sensed, weighed and measured. Thus it "exists" in space/time, although at a level not directly perceivable by our sense organs. However, there seems to be no explanation for, or evidence that, Life, Intelligence and Consciousness are created from the universe of forms. Life, Intelligence and Consciousness do not appear to arise from materiality but rather originate from dimensions beyond.

What does this say about us as living forms capable of experiencing degrees of the vitality of Life, Intelligence and Consciousness? We can agree that these "somethings" or "energies" appear to interpenetrate our "world." We experience them inside our bodies, brains, and minds because they interpenetrate us along with everything else. Therefore, to access the "universe," to sense, feel and perhaps develop more understanding of the mystery underneath everything, we must go inside.

Can we agree that our body is something that surrounds us which "we" interpenetrate? Where are "we" when asleep or in a coma? Where are "we" when the body dies? We can lose many parts of the body and we are still "our Self." The outer movements of our body, speech, motion, action are (except for reflex) directed from within our psychological world at that moment. What am "I", the person I think of as myself, if not my thoughts …if not my thoughts, feelings, hopes, fears, desires, dreams? My "personality" is invisible and non-material. My "character" is invisible and non-material. I am an invisible something housed in a body that can do "my" bidding so that my "invisible self" can manifest outside in the material world in which it lives and must feed and defend itself in order to survive. On most essential survival issues, the body does not require my help, understanding or participation. It has pre-programmed functions to take care of the basics without me. My part is limited to the equivalent of looking both ways when crossing the street. My body and I must have a good working relationship, but we are not the same. But, "I" can direct its behaviors and manifestations with other people and objects in the world outside me.

So, What AM I? I am my "psychology," a combination of my current level of intelligence and consciousness. If I can increase my capacity inside my psychological world in a certain way, perhaps I can access even higher levels of intelligence and consciousness. Socrates told us, "Know Thyself." In coming to know thyself, perhaps one can come to know much more.

Love,

Dad

Meditation on Dimensions Outer and Inner

Preface

There are no new ideas in this essay. The following theme and its conclusion have been experienced, written about, spoken about, painted, composed in music countless times from the beginning of humankind. What is the purpose of recreating them here? Ideas are one thing. The actual experience behind an idea is a totally different level akin to a new dimension. To *know* is not the same as to *understand*. To make an idea real, and not just theory, we need to go beyond the hearing or reading of it to try to find a way to make it our own through some aspect of our individual experience. Exploring my own psychological functions and levels for many years has provided that quality of experience. The following represents my attempt to explore these ancient ideas through my own way of reasoning combined with my own observations inside my heart and mind. It is a reconstruction of a conversation I have been having with myself most of my life.

Dimensions: Outer

There are three dictionary definitions for the term "dimension": 1) a measure of spatial extent, especially width, height, or length, 2) extent or magnitude; scope and 3) aspect; element. In addition to these three, I would add a fourth: a realm of vastly different qualities of perception and understanding, which cannot be perceived with the senses, and yet can be known.

Our physical senses and their extension through our scientific instruments have brought us a view of the Universe and our place in it, unparalleled in history. On the one hand, we can now see the Universe as a Whole, composed of relationships between different "levels" of interlocking, networks of systems. On the other hand, we can also see that this Whole is composed of different "levels" which are discontinuous with each other in magnitude and perhaps with different roles to play in the organic Whole. The "level" of galactic superclusters is of an order of size immeasurably greater than a single galaxy while the size of a galaxy compared to a single star is, in turn, of a different order of magnitude. Stars are something of a totally different capacity and potential than planets. The life forms on a planet are infinitesimal compared with the planet of their existence yet have a life of their own and a role to play on the planet. Inside the life forms, the "level" of material we call cells exists in a "world" of its own as then does the "world" of the molecules within, which are the building blocks of cells ... as is the "level" of atoms within the molecules and then the realm of quantum particles inside the "world" of the atoms. All, together, comprise the Whole which, as they are observable, (or mathematically confirmable), seem to be the constituents of the Whole, around and inside of us. This is what is currently viewed as the Universe.

This Universe appears governed by principles, or Laws of Nature, which guide and determine their parameters. Without these "laws", the energies in the Universe could not have coalesced into the level of density we call "matter", which became stars, galaxies, planets, lifeforms, people ... you and me.

Where did these laws of Nature come from? Why are they as they are and not something else? Were they born simultaneously with the Universe, or did they pre-exist in a realm of their own, and facilitate the "birth" of what we know as the Universe?

Through our instruments we are limited to observing what happened in the Universe after its appearance, but not before. Was "what happened" to bring the Universe into existence a random fluctuation (of what?) from the Before Time? Is the precision of its structure and operation suggestive of intelligence or intention ... as religion surmises? Or ... as many (but not all) contemporary scientists suggest ... that since there is no way to confirm or investigate what happened prior to the beginning, then it is meaningless to speak of a "Before". Thoughts about "Before" thus lie in the realm of philosophy and mysticism.

It is through the lens of our subjective psychology that we experience and explore the external world. Our theories about it, the design of our investigative instruments, and our experience of the information they reveal, all occur in the realm of our minds.

For example, thinking into this question of a priori Laws from our human level in this Cosmos of interpenetrating, multiple layers, we can ask: can a rules-based game appear out of nowhere ... or must it emerge from a pre-existing concept and subsequent agreement about the rules among participants? Or can a machine build itself from a pile of material, without a blueprint originating in the mind of an inventor?

So, perhaps it is also through our psychological experience that we can explore this greatest of mysteries ... the mystery that our instruments cannot penetrate. Is there more to the Universe than we can see ... and what could have come before?

The ancient precept: "As Above, So Below", underlies Gurdjieff's observation that *"Man is, in the full sense of the term, 'a miniature universe'; in him are all the matters of which the universe consists; the same forces, the same laws that govern the life of the universe, operate in him; therefore, in studying man we can study the whole world, just as in studying the world we can study man."* (P. D. Ouspensky, *In Search of the Miraculous; Fragments of an Unknown Teaching,* p.88)

When we look around us, we experience through our senses a world of forms in a framework of height, width and depth, our familiar world of three dimensions. All this appears in a realm we call space. Within this space of three dimensions, we experience the perception of a fourth element, which we call Time. Whether this element has objective existence or not, is a question for philosophers and physicists to resolve. Our concrete experience is, for example, that if we want to meet someone for lunch, we need, not only the physical coordinates of the restaurant in Space, but also when, in Time, we are to meet. Our senses show us movement of objects in relation to other objects, such as the apparent changing location of the sun across the sky. But, unlike the other three dimensions in which movement takes place, we do not perceive Time through our senses, but rather infer it, as we observe movement in the world around us.

Based on Einstein's theories, scientists today talk about our existing in the four-dimensional realm of Space-Time. However, if one adopts the view that Time is actually a subjective experience that arises in the human mind, from that perspective it would actually belong in the realm of the Psyche. Yet, as Time is obviously a coordinate if one is to move in Space, the question is a paradox.

The existence of what we call the Laws of Nature, appears undeniable. Since we are being "philosophical", let us say for this exploration, that the Laws of Nature were somehow, a priori, to the formation of the Universe so that the Universe had a guiding framework in which to take form. We could poetically think of this as a higher "dimension" in relation to what most scientists call "Space-Time", perhaps the dimension of Universal Principles under which Space-Time operates. Since we are being philosophical, we could also wonder from "where" the Universal Principles originated. Is the search for the Initiating Impulse an endless regression?

Can our own subjective experience suggest anything about this incomprehensible question?

Look around you, dear Reader. Look at all the artificial forms in your world, your desk, this book, the chair you sit in. Think about the last meal you prepared or the last correspondence you wrote. Where did the idea, the plan for the chair or the desk come from? Where, in relation to the food, did the recipe for the meal originate? Where were the words you used in your communication prior to their expression? Human-made manifestations take form in the world outside from an idea, a plan, a wish, an impulse that originates in our psychological "world" a priori to their representation in the outer world. Since we can confirm this through our own experience, what can we make of the natural living forms around us, trees, animals, flowers … ourselves? Were there a priori factors which initiated and guided the shapes and qualities that these forms of "matter" take? Certainly, the existence of DNA prior to our conception laid the foundation for our physical and potential psychological structure and capacities. Are we not an expression of the pattern in the DNA inherited from our ancestors? We emerged from the "world" of the molecule which contained the "worlds" or the atoms and their subatomic particles.

In this sense, thinking about what came "before" in the world at our level, it is clear that man-made manifestations originate in the invisible world of our psyche. In this sense we might also speculate that the natural world originates from the pre-existing invisible Laws of Nature. This brings us back to the question, "Where did the Laws of Nature come from"?

Science has been able to explain neither the mystery of life seeming to appear out of inorganic matter, nor the invisible world of our mind, as inherent parts of the Whole we call the Universe. The fact of our sub-jective consciousness has seemed as unreachable for objective study as the question of what came before the appearance of the Universe. Yet, it has provided an arena for exploration since the beginning of recorded history, when the question of what is, and how did it appear, did not di-vide the externally perceptible world from the interior world of thoughts, dreams, epiphanies, feelings. It is through this psychological direction that our exploration will lead.

Dimensions: Inner

One factor has not been addressed so far in this exploration. The different dimensions hypothesized are the encompassing domain that results in the materialized universe and what governs its functions. What is the domain of our intellect and emotional life? *What is the realm of* our *guiding principles,* our *creative initiation?*

Every movement made by living creatures has its impetus from inside the life form, whether instinctive reactions to environmental factors or emotional or intellectual motives. Life is sensitive to and programmed to react to the worlds both outside and inside its material bodies.

In what dimension resides the home of *sensitivity, consciousness, self-awareness* and the fountain of intuitive and creative speculation that allows science to explore the physical universe … or this writer to experience the thoughts he is expressing through the use of these symbols we call "letters"?

As we live in the realm of subjective experience and we are part of the Universe, where are these subjective psychological experiences located in this hierarchy of levels? Do each of these interpenetrating dimensions have their own subjective experience with their own sense of time? In which dimension does our psyche reside? How many of these dimensions does it straddle? Is there a Dimension of Subjective Experiences?

Where do thoughts come from? Without an experience to notice or react to, what would there be to think about? How could we think? The capacity for thinking would have no content with which to exercise its potential. The library for thought-material requires a source for its experiential content. Without an author, there is no book. Without a reader, there is no reason for an author.

Without sensory organs, what would we experience of the world outside our body? Without experience, there would be no raw data needing the organizing principle of thinking. Initial experiences would be pure sensation within the womb, sounds of the mother's body and proprioception of movement, pressure, comfort and pain. At birth, vibrations impinging on newborn eardrums from the pressure waves of vibrating air molecules at first would all be meaningless noise. Visual images appear when the eyes first meet light, but without knowing the objects being seen, there would just be meaningless impressions. Shapes, colors and their movement add to the beginning library of experienced data that will later transform into meaning. Slowly, the developing capacity of the infant to organize, coordinate and explore the world of its impressions begins to take shape.

As repetitive sounds become associated with sensory impressions, the potential for imitating these sounds to reference these impressions becomes language. The sounds are symbolic short-hand for the infinitely more complex impressions of image and sensation. A child can now begin to express what it is experiencing inside its body and brain, to itself and others, in the shorthand of words. The Speaker is born. But what can be spoken about … and thought about … depends on the extent and quality of the words learned. Of course, there is intuitive perception and understanding without words, but in general, what we can think or talk about is subject to the extent of our vocabulary.

All experience occurs inside the body, whether sensations of touch from the extremities and skin, the movement of bowels and blood in the interior, the feeling states from changing hormonal mixtures in the blood, altering states of clarity and mood from changing combinations of neurotransmitters in the brain, the heart and nervous system. Cascading transformations of photons focused through the lens of the eye, striking the retina and becoming electrical impulses, re-create images of the world "outside" in the visual area of the brain. Sound, touch, taste, smell and the feel of gravity are all translated from energy vibrations of differing magnitude outside the body into different frequencies of vibrating energy inside the body to re-create an approximation of what the sensory organs initially received at their interface with the world outside. Thus, we begin to collect experiences … but all are *experienced in the brain*, even those that appear to be outside our body.

Realm of Sensitivity

All life has experience. All life is *sensitive* to the world outside and inside itself, dependent on what type of receptive apparatus the organism is endowed with. This is a fundamental definition separating what seems to be alive from what appears to be inanimate. Life is animate. Life reacts. Life responds to the interaction of energies outside and inside its bodily form. What appears to differentiate levels of life is the complexity of this reactive interaction and the degree of sensitivity the life form has of its own subjective experience.

This interior world of subjective re-activity forms an interactive system with the world of nature outside the body. The organism is made of and is part of the outside world of forms and forces called the "world," the "planet," the "universe." The vibratory resonance of this seemingly "outer" world permeates and penetrates the organism and is "re-created," and responded to, from within the body and nervous system. The subjective life of the being is inside, whether this is self-recognized or not. The subjective interior world is constantly being shaped and conditioned by the flood of energy coming into it from the outside. Organisms that don't become appropriately conditioned to respond in ways that are congruent with the external conditions cannot survive in those conditions.

If the internal mechanisms have properly formed during gestation and have not been damaged by the world they were designed to interact with, the organism lives long enough to re-produce a copy of itself before its functionality stops and it "dies." Living long enough to accomplish this requires the building of a library of conditioned patterns that are co-ordinated with the predictable demands of its environment.

We can call this memory whether or not there is subjective awareness of that memory. Memory can be seen as a fixed pattern of response to repeated stimulation. It doesn't need to be re-established with each event. It is fixed into the body's physical, chemical and neurological pattern to be available whenever conditions require its response. The organism does not need to "think" about it. We would call it "instinct" if it formed in utero and "conditioned" if built-in later by interaction with the outside after birth.

With higher mammalian life, cephalopods and birds, a degree of awareness of the interaction between this inner conditioned world of experiences and the outside world begins to manifest. Recent studies suggest a degree of intelligence, and perhaps self-awareness, for some mollusks, particularly octopuses, and manta rays. With this new quality of awareness appears problem solving, play, and unpredictability. Something other than the original survival-oriented conditioning has arisen. The world inside seems to have added another dimension ... *something* that is capable of evaluating and making choices and discoveries. And this *something* is not totally mechanical. There now seems to be a new ability to see into the library of collected impressions, into the past experiences and to anticipate the repetition of those experiences in what we call the *"Future"* ... itself a hypothesized intellectual construct.

This still operates under the influence of conditioning but with more flexibility. What is re-membered from the fragments of experiences past is still dependent on what was conditioned in the past. This determines the limits on what can be anticipated in the future. There may seem to be some choice, but that choice is both limited and, itself, may be predetermined by the conditioning of circumstance.

For example, if the time of day, the lighting and the weather is similar to a time in the past when the animal had a particular experience, the recollection of that experience from the library will be re-called due to the similarity in the conditions of the moment. The posture the animal takes in anticipation of a re-enactment of that past event is conditioned by these factors.

The build-up of hard-wired patterns in the organism as a result of repeated interaction with its surroundings, is what we call learning. The term can be applied to all conditioning whether subjectively experienced or not. Something is learning, being patterned, regardless of a subjective awareness of the process.

Again, in higher animals, the ability to mimic the behavior of others begins to lead to a transfer of information from one to another. No longer does each individual creature solely depend on its own conditioning to survive. Now the accumulated learning by others of its type can be copied through observation and practice. The accumulated learning of the interior world of one creature can now be implanted into another, shortening the time for acquisition and starting the beginning of a build-up of generational learning.

Psychosphere

The library of one animal is now shared with the library of another. The libraries are no longer stored in isolation. The *experiential* world, or what I will call here the *Psychosphere* of different animals, is now overlapping. Each, although individual in body, now begins to live in the enlarging psychic library of its species. The mind of each now begins to blend with and expand into a larger non-individualized mind of the group. The experiences accumulating in the Psychosphere expand to all animals of the type that are in experiential contact with each other. I am referring here to what has been repeatedly confirmed through observation and experience and not the hypothesized but unconfirmed "Hundredth Monkey" theory.

With animals, this requires direct, hands-on initiation of the accumulating knowledge. With the addition of symbolic language, the initiation expands exponentially. Signs are visual marks, and words are verbal sounds that symbolically convey meaning from the interior world of one person into the interior world of other people.

The information shared is limited only by the complexity of the marks and sounds and the shared understanding of their meaning. In this way, the content of the interior world of people never met or long-dead can continue to be conveyed into the inner world of the living as re-creations of experiences experienced by the never-met or the deceased. Thus, the Psychosphere expands again to include the re-presentations of lives and thoughts of all humanity.

This symbolically transferred information has limitations. The clarity of transmission is dependent on the symbolic skill of the transmitter and the shared "decoding" understanding of symbols used by the receiver. If the information transmitted is new to the receiver, the lack of equivalent background between the two may lead to unrecognized misunderstanding on the part of the receiver. The transferred information may be distorted due to coding and decoding errors.

What is the nature of what is transmitted? How is it received? Utilizing the broad definition offered by David Bohm, all aspects of the inner world are involved (*Wholeness and the Implicate Order*, Routledge & Kegan Paul, NY, 1980). The inner world is composed of all functions and activities within the body. The human being is composed of three fundamental arenas of functioning. The first and primary of these is the conjunction of physio-chemical-electrical-muscular activities that regulate, monitor and maintain all functions of the physical body. Many of these remain below the level of conscious awareness, but all are sensitive to each other and interact to maintain balance. This entire system will register every impression from without as well as collecting continual impressions about its own interactive functioning within. This level is almost entirely mechanical but learns from interactional experience. All life has this level of programmed operation regardless of degree of self-awareness.

World of Emotional Life and Interactive Relationships

The second functional capacity manifests as an *emotional life* capable of forming relationships. Mammals, cephalopods and birds experience an emotional life, with the same general range of emotions that we experience as humans. They also have relationships with others, both their own and sometimes other species. This second functional capacity manifests as sensitivity to the actions and cues from other animals, and this produces effects within their own mechanical bio-chemical physical world. The behaviors of others evoke reactions in oneself that are experienced on a continuum of comfort to discomfort, danger or safety, leading to behavioral-emotional responses in kind. For some higher animals, there are anecdotal research observations indicating an awareness of an inner world of feeling and intentions inside other animals ... what is called a "theory of mind" ... just as we know from experience inside ourselves.

The Conceptual World

In the human being is the highest reflection of a third functional capacity, encoding of experience through symbolism. We can collect, organize, reassemble and transmit experiences from our subjective interior out into the world through voice, hand and body movement so that it may be received by the sense organs of others and downloaded into their interior subjective world for processing and reconfiguration. Without the musculature of our body, we would be locked inside ourselves, unable to communicate. It is through the muscles of our face, mouth, tongue, vocal cords, hands, chest, diaphragm, and body posture that we are able to transmit. It is said up to seventy-five percent of what we are actually "broadcasting" is through this "non-verbal communication."

What and how do we transmit? We transmit through vibration and movement, thoughts, feelings, impressions collected from the entirety of our inner world. What we tend not to see clearly, if at all, is the near-total degree to which the content of our inner experiences is dependent on the transmission into us from the outside, from others. Were we to live in total isolation from others, what would there be to transmit ... and to whom? Without exposure to language, both auditory and bodily, how would we know how to transmit? Without others sharing their subjective learning, opinions and feelings with us, what content would there be for us to react to? How can we act, or even think, in a vacuum?

The majority content of our library comes from interaction with the world outside. What fills our library are our experiences. Because we are human, the librarian is not entirely programmed at birth as it is with much of animal life. Animal libraries are stored in neurological-chemical associational links that are called up automatically when required by the situation. New ones can be learned and old ones modified, but this is done without the symbolic interpretational capacity of the human brain.

We humans add a new component. Our "librarian" interprets the *meaning of experience* according to the system of interpretation downloaded into it from the outside world of human communication. Each nation, group, family has its own flavor of symbolic encoding. What we learn to pay attention to, how to make meaning of it, how to link it with previous similar experiences and how to re-interpret it back through communication is dependent on the "school" of experiential storage and retrieval learned from our human community.

Thus, the subjective world of our inner life is obviously dependent on interaction with Nature and objects but particularly dependent on the way others interact with us from their own inner standpoint. Nor are our symbolic representations, made to ourselves, independent of the physiology of our bodies. Our bodies react to the content of our minds and, in turn, bathe our nervous system in hormonal-chemical responses that influence the functioning of our brain and nervous system. In a literal way, our subjective interior "dimension" sits between the world of the body immersed in the outer life of nature and the vibrations of the invisible interior realm of communication with others and our own self-talk.

While the *Biosphere, the level of organic life,* has two components: the external biological world outside our bodies and the internal biological world inside our bodies, the *psychological world of awareness*, called here the *Psychosphere, can be aware of both its external surroundings and internal sensations, emotions and thoughts in the body's interior.*

It is obvious that all life shares in the biosphere of Nature. Our human biological forms are composed of its materials, gases, energies. We all share the same sunlight, same air, the same foods. If our senses are intact, we all see the same landscape forms and all languages have words for these forms that are translatable from one language to another. We can talk with each other about the forms and their usage.

Until contemporary times, people saw and felt themselves part of, and interactive with Nature, and experienced themselves in communication with It. They spoke to It, worshipped It, prayed to It and listened and watched for "signs" that they interpreted as Nature responding to them. Whether their sense of the meaning of all this was valid or an incomplete paradigm based on non-scientific methods, their *belief that it was valid* shaped and determined their understanding of, and what happened, in their "world."

How much do we all share in the Psychosphere? Our culture teaches us what to value and how to think about things. Our language teaches us how to symbolize what we think and value. Our institutions offer rewards and punishments for adherence or disobedience to those values, rules and validated behaviors. Our experiences with others range along the comfort-discomfort continuum and are translated into feelings and sensations. Whether we are attracted or repelled depends substantially on biological reaction, which itself is substantially influenced by how we are taught to think and feel. In our books, our schools, through conversation, through mass media and the internet, the cumulative library of all symbolic representations of all the people who have ever lived, and shared anything of their inner world with others, is available for transfer from the collective Psychosphere into our individualized Psychosphere. We have our own idiosyncratic organization of our experiences, but the content of those experiences has come or been influenced, almost entirely from the minds of others.

Noosphere: The Objective Witness

And yet ... *we can be aware of the content of our Psychosphere!* We can study it, categorize its manifestations, question its interpretations. What is this element that observes and evaluates what it sees inside its Psychosphere in the way that it also observes and evaluates the meaning of what it sees and hears in the outside world? Is this "Observer" part of the Psychosphere, or is it something representing a higher quality above that level?

Sometimes this 'something' becomes aware of itself *simultaneously* with its awareness of the interaction between its inner Psychosphere and the outer Biosphere. In that moment, it may realize it is neither the thoughts in the mind nor the body in Nature. It may then become aware of questions of its own. "Who am I? What am I? What is this all about?" Teilhard de Chardin called the world of this Observer, the *Noosphere*.*

---

* Nous, Noos; in philosophy, the mind or intellect, a postulated sphere or stage of evolutionary development dominated by consciousness, the mind, and interpersonal relationships; "creatures evolve: a new biosphere emerges, and with it a new noosphere" Teilhard de Chardin. In this essay, I am dividing the subjective dimension into two levels, the Psychosphere of ordinary psychological states and functions and the Noosphere level of the Impartial Witness.

Theosphere

It also recognizes that it, Itself, is not the "highest" level of the multi-dimensional psychological world that it now finds itself existing within. There is something else beyond it that it wishes to know about and to be in relationship with.

The world beyond itself, which the Observer senses "behind," or "above," the place of its awareness, the world from which it seeks answers to its questions, I would call the *Theosphere*.* This is the realm of mystery from which everything we can be aware of, including our awareness of ourselves, seems to originate.

Thus, we are embedded within, *and* composed of, multiple worlds. We all share these worlds, but not all of us are aware of this fact, much less have experience with all these worlds. Theory is one thing. Direct experience is something else.

Information Transfer

All life shares the Biosphere. As animal brains develop, the more sophisticated the brain, the more of the Psychosphere, can be shared through non-verbal communication between members of the same or similar species, but only the material accumulated in the group's collective Psychosphere that pertains to the world of *their* senses ... to Nature as they experience it. A group mind of accumulated and shared experiences passed on from one generation to the next begins to develop.

With the appearance of the highly developed human brain, symbolic language appears.

Just as we can share information about our location in Space and Time, we humans can share the invisible aspects of our 'location' in the Psychosphere with other humans. We can talk about and manifest our thought, feelings, moods, hopes and concerns. "How are you feeling?" and "What are you feeling?", are requests for psychological/emotional coordinates. Common questions in relationships these days are variations on: "You are not paying attention. Where are you? You keep drifting away ... where do you go in your mind when I want to talk with you?"

In a way, sometimes more and sometimes less, we literally share the Psychosphere of humanity. Our ordinary experience tells us that to access the viewpoint in the Psychosphere occupied by another human, we have

---

* Theo: from Greek "*theos*," "god."

to get them to "open up", to communicate in some symbolic manner with us, in a language we share well enough, that we can accurately decode each-others' transmissions. If what they are sharing resonates a sympathetic response within us, stimulates a resonant memory or impression from our own experience, then we can say that to some extent, we understand, we both stand under the same experience.

Intuition

But what of the information transfer that comes in dreams or intuitions or unexplainable "knowings" that we call intuition, epiphany, telepathy or clairvoyance? This seems to suggest that some information from the Psychosphere is available from channels not limited to human symbolic transmission. The fact of this, for those who have experienced it, or are willing to consider its possibility, suggests that the Psychosphere itself can be viewed as the collective mind of all of humanity and can be accessible to a sufficiently sensitive individual human mind. By implication, that level of sensitivity, that awareness of being aware of oneself watching the activity in one's psyche, would lie "deeper" or "higher" relative to the ordinary level of outside the Psychosphere. In this paradigm, that is the level called Noosphere.

What is the relationship between the materialized realm, the psychological realm and the deeper, causal realm? In physics and cosmology, at this time, the conundrum is how to reconcile the mass-based world of Newtonian physics with the wave world of quantum mechanics. It is currently accepted that light appears to be made both of particles, but also waves, depending on how the experiment is designed.

The material Universe is governed by Newtonian mathematics, while its underlying foundation appears to follow the different laws of the Quantum world. Researchers studying the mystery of consciousness inside the material brain are beginning to speculate that the interior world of our subjective experiencing appears to exist under laws of the Quantum dimension, the dimension of atoms and sub-atomic particles. Reconciliation of these immeasurably different realms has not yet been discovered.

Towards a Sense of the Whole

The current scientific search for a theory of everything is still focused on trying to reconcile the observable, measurable physical universe avail-

OUTER DIMENSIONS	INNER DIMENSIONS
Sixth Dimension Initiation	**Sixth Dimension** Will
Fifth Dimension All possible laws	**Noosphere** Objective Observing Witness
Fourth Dimension Space-Time	**Psychosphere** Experience, Thought: Individual and Collective
Three-Dimensional World Height, Width, Depth	**Biosphere** World of Material Bodies World of Cells World of Molecules World of Atoms

able to standard scientific method and instrumentation, with the baffling world of quantum mechanics. The question of *subjective experience and consciousness* is not included ... is not even considered relevant to the question by most researchers as if the scientists were looking through their consciousness and not seeing that it, itself, is the biggest mystery of all.

Looking into our brains, research instruments can "see" and measure the current of electrical impulses flowing through an infinite lattice of impossibly dense neuronal pathways. The foundation of awareness begins with a flow, a wave of electricity. This suggests that our minds lie, at the least, in the quantum realm ... if not a dimension beyond.

What could lie beyond the quantum world? One may as well ask, where did the Big Bang come from or where does awareness come from? In this exploration, that dimension is called *Theosphere*. In the old language its name was the Realm of the Gods. In contemporary scientific language we might call it the "Whatever-Lies-Underneath-the-Quantum-Level" or "Whatever-Lies-Beyond-the-Edge-of-the-Universe" or "Wherever-The-Big-Bang-Came-From" if in fact there was a Big Bang.

I have the impression that my consciousness belongs to me, that it is what makes me an "individual." Clearly, the contents of my psychological world are predominantly memories of my individual experiences. But the quality or energy of consciousness itself poses another question.

A different viewpoint is that, just as I share the atmosphere of the planet and its water and its food with all life, "consciousness" is something I share with humanity, perhaps even all of life, although in a higher degree than the lower animals because of the structure of my brain.

Conclusion

Awareness, or the state we call "consciousness," is not individualized but is a collective phenomenon shared by all humans. The implication of this proposition is that the Psychosphere is not the limit of human awareness. We are also designed to access the Noosphere, where we can not only experience a degree of freedom within and from the conditioned world of the Psychosphere but from which we touch the edge of the world above, i.e. the Theosphere.

The materialized forms of the Universe take their form and place in the Whole guided by *invisible*, prior existing principles or laws of Nature. When we recreate what we see and feel in our psychological world out into our outside world as objects or personal manifestations, is that not the same process as the Universe taking shape according to the *invisible* laws that guide the process? Our thoughts, feelings, insights, and ideas are a priori to their expression through my body into the world outside.

When we use our minds to direct our bodies to make material things, we make these things out of the substance called "matter." Matter is energy congealed into different densities and forms with different functions through an initiating impulse. In a way, Space-Time is like a uterus for the gestation of different forms under the direction of the laws which were derived from the World of All Possibilities.

As we are to the world of matter, so is the dimension of Initiation to us. Just as our creations come from our initiative into the world of matter, we too are creations, the result of an initiation inserted into matter. We retain a connection with that world of the Creative Impulse which set the laws in motion.

As ancient philosophy from the *Emerald Tablets of Hermes Trismegistus* phrases this relationship, "As Above, So Below".

Starlight

I magine standing by a still lake in early morning. The surface is smooth and reflective of sky and surrounding trees. A single drop falls onto the glass surface. A dot appears, followed by concentric waves that expand in a circle outward from the location of the original impact. Now a second drop falls and a different set of circular rings of rising and falling wavelets move out from their center. They encounter the first set of rings and begin to blend. A third and fourth drop appear. The lake surface is now rippling with the continuous fall of drops, each creating its own signature on the surface. All the ripples are now interacting and the lake as a whole is in motion, touched and energized by the combination of countless drops and their expanding, interacting patterns. We no longer speak of drops but of Rain.

Now imagine being in Space, beyond the Earth's atmosphere. What your eyes will see is the pitch-black backdrop pierced by dots of light, some brighter, some dimmer, all tiny … really only pinprick-size specks with no features other than luminosity and tint of color. In between the lights are vast swaths of black. Yet, like the drops of water in the lake, each star is radiating light out from its center, but this time in all directions, like an expanding balloon, the light of each star inflates, of course, at the speed of light. The radiations of each star expand forever towards the edge of the universe, along the way overlapping and blending with the inflating light waves of all the other stars. In this way, all suns are connected with all other suns through their expanding circles … as far as its current limits have taken it on its trip to infinity. In this way also, the collective light of all stars is subsumed in the shared light of their home galaxy. This is what we see when we look at dense areas of any galaxy. The light of individual stars melts into a bright haze denoting the shape of the galaxy when seen in different spectrums. Each individual galaxy then creates its own expanding collective radiations to overlap and blend with all other galaxies.

Astronomers tell us that space looks black because the only light we can see is that light that is both bright enough to register on our retina and directly in line with our eyes. We associate the color black with the absence of light, but in this case, space is saturated with the light of all stars and galaxies, which is invisible to our eyes unless we are looking directly at a light source. Some areas of space are also filled with dust which can intersect the flowing ocean of photons , creating a diffuse glow of reflected starlight.

Let's imagine for a moment that stars are individual intelligences, as each of us is an individual intelligence, an infinitesimal part of something larger, but still an individual within the Whole. As their continually rippling spheres of light expand and overlap, whatever information is contained in the light of one becomes blended with all the other emanating radiations; all is pooled and shared. If all the stars in a galaxy were in communication with each other, whether directly or through associated networks, this would constitute the "galactic mind."

As the light of one galaxy creates its own expanding field of illumination, it joins with all others within the range of its enlarging field of influence. As its light reaches far away galaxies on the very periphery of its own range, those most distant galaxies also have their own sphere of light, reaching outward from their center and touching galaxies beyond the direct range of the first. In this way, if all galaxies were collective intelligences, sharing data from all their individual stars, their pooled radiations would constitute a "universal mind."

This appears to be the way in which our brains work. Current estimates range between 86 and 100 billion neurons and 10 to 50 times that number of glial cells, which also receive and transmit information as well as regulate metabolism, fluid and ion homeostasis. Electricity continuously flows through this inconceivably dense pattern to energize relationships between them based on associated experiences and functions. Each cell is an individual, although an infinitesimal part of the larger whole, just as our mind is individual even though also inconceivably infinitesimal compared to the collective knowledge of all human minds combined, which could be thought of as the "collective mind-of-humankind" … or the subjective experiences of sensitivity shared with all lifeforms … a "collective mind-of-Life."

The electrical activity in one brain cell influences the electrical activity in surrounding cells and throughout the dense and expansive network in which each individual cell is located. For example, current estimates are that a given individual neuron, through its dendritic connections, may be in communication with up to 7,000 additional neurons … multiplied by each of the other 100 billion neurons. The connectivity of the glial cells amongst each other and all their associated neurons seems incalculable.

Every cell creates its own individual magnetic field, which overlaps with all the other billions of magnetic fields to form a collective field for the brain as a whole. Each neuron is an individual ... but also part of the collective, which produces a Whole greater than the sum of its parts.

When I become aware of activity in my brain ... thoughts, feelings, images, assumptions ... how am I "seeing" these phenomena of electrical activity in my neural wiring? I am seeing by the light of my attention. Attention lights up whatever I point it at ... and it continues to light whatever comes into the circumference of its awareness, even when it is drifting on auto-pilot without my direction.

Our language recognizes this apparent, or perhaps intuitive, connection. Someone who is very intelligent is called bright. Their opposite is dim. We exclaim, "Now I see it. The light just went on. I had an insight. I wish to be enlightened. What a brilliant idea. I'm in the dark ... I just don't see what you are talking about." The Bible requests, "May the Lord make His countenance shine upon you." And then, there is that strange and troubling observation that sometimes "the lights are on, but nobody is at home." Who ... or what ... is not there?

Until the harnessing of electricity, the only known source of photons, and thus light, in the Universe were stars ... and perhaps their ambassador on Earth, fire. It has recently been discovered that bio-photons, fragments of light, are spontaneously generated by living cells and may be created in the mitochondrial DNA of each cell. Along with the stars, we are the second source of light in the Universe. As every cell produces photons, so, probably, do neurons. Our minds are "lit up" with the light of electricity, allowing us to become aware of our mind's activity.

Let us imagine the drop of light that each individual awareness adds to the Whole, each mind creating vibrations in the minds around them, and each of those in the minds around them, just like the stars.

A last analogy remains to be pondered. What is observing what can be discerned in the sphere of Attention? What can be both the receiving subjective awareness of the light and, at times, its director as well? Can I cause my attention to try to shine light on this deepest of mysteries ... myself?

Are We the Universe?

The technology of our new century excites the possibility of probing ever more deeply into the mystery of existence. As cosmologists search for a theory to unify the energies underlying the material universe, neuroscientists peer into the patterns of energies flowing through the human brain, looking for clues to the enigma of consciousness.

The two directions of search appear opposite, one outward and the other interior, but is that so? Is that possible? Can a unified theory of everything exclude anything existing? Can we unify our understanding of the universe without the inclusion of ourselves? Where within a unifying understanding will we place life and consciousness? The "isness" of both commands inclusion in the search for the ultimate source of All. Without the fact of both, there would be no one to pose the question.

Consider. If life is not an inherent property of the Universe, where did the life energy come from? If life is not an inherent property of the Universe, universal throughout, then our "life energy" comes from a dimension outside the universe. Either the Universe itself is "alive," or the Universe is "livened" by something beyond the Universe itself.

If the capacity for the subjective experience of "sensation" is not inherent in the fabric of the Universe, then where did the reactivity to surroundings, displayed by all life forms and experientially confirmed by all humans, come from?

If intelligence, consciousness, awareness, wish, or capacity for will, is not inherent in the fabric of the Universe, then where does our intelligence, consciousness, awareness, wish and capacity for will come from? Either our subjective experience is part of the energies constructing and maintaining the Universe, or, whatever we are, lies outside the Universe and manifests through penetration. If so, where then is that "place"? Either the Universe is conscious, aware, and has capacity for will; or, consciousness enters the Universe from "somewhere" beyond what we know and call "the Universe."

Either "we" are the Universe, or we are something beyond the Universe, embedded within it, interpenetrated by it, and imbued with its inherent properties.

Or, perhaps, there is no "or." Perhaps both are true.

We make our world by ascribing to it "meaning." It is for us to decide ourselves what it means.

The origin of "meaning" lies beyond what we ordinarily call "the world." It arises within the invisible, psychological realm of our hearts and minds. Since man exists in the Universe and Consciousness exists in man, we cannot unify our understanding of the Universe without simultaneously accounting for Consciousness. The search out, and the search in, must be two sides of the same journey.

PART TWO

The Breadcrumb Trail

The Breadcrumb Trail
Preface

Without any outside impulse, from an early age, I felt that there must be more to life than what was happening around me. I felt there was something I was to do, that I had a responsibility to fulfill, that there was a purpose to my life that I had to discover. I felt that there was more to "reality" than met the eye, that there was another reality behind the one I was living. Starting when I was no more than three years old, there were experiences, hints of this other reality. Over the years, these began to accumulate, event by isolated event, forming what I can now discern as a trail of breadcrumbs. As if from an old fairytale, something seems to have left markers, placed from my future, along the path of my life for me to find, here and there, as I traveled my way through from my past towards that, presumably, unknown future.

In preparation for this summation of many years of reflection, I initially collected, in chronological order, all the events of my life that were imprinted in my memory with either the taste of "strange" or a sense of portent, either in the moment or on retrospection.

This list of events, spread out in time and of different forms, showed me the periodic intrusion into my awareness of experiences suggesting a current underlining the direction my life was to take. I could see ... and feel ... that this "trail of breadcrumbs" has been leading me deeper into this question of Meaning. As I now recognize, the unfolding experience with Mystery has been my teacher.

Initially, I had intended to present them all in chronological order as an illustration of how such a "mystery" timeline could weave its way through a life without its full significance being noticed until viewed in totality. As I wrote, many of them seemed appropriate for inclusion in previous essays. It lessens the drama to break them up, but the timeline has served its purpose for me. I will include a few more here, near the end of this exploration, as preparation for the summary essay of this book which explores the process my reasoning followed over many years to deal with the implications of these experiences.

As I wrote out these memories, I began to see a linkage between them. The link was the feeling of strangeness. They were experiences for which

I had no logical explanation. They were mysterious. When I looked at these events all together, I could feel them pointing me in the direction of my childhood feeling about an alternate reality. I recognized that the answer was all around me ... and, ultimately, inside me. I, you, dear Reader, all of us, are saturated in mystery ... but we are so habituated to ordinary life that we are oblivious to it, as blind as a fish is to water. To honor that mysterious quest and to offer an example for you, dear Reader, to make a map of your own journey, I offer mine as a potential model. You would not have picked up this book, much less read to this part of it, if the content were not resonating for you also.

As I have grown older, I have become increasingly interested in seeing the pattern of my life, inside and outside, to understand who I am, how I got this way and why my life has the shape it does. Recognizing the centrality of the quality of mystery in that life, I allowed my mind to free associate to the meaning and feel of the experience of mystery. Soon, memories were flowing into my awareness. I made a list as they accumulated and later put them into chronological order. As the list grew, I realized that I had compartmentalized these events in memory, not allowing them to find each other and thus not permitting me to finally see the underlying pattern of my subjective life. There, clearly, was a trail of breadcrumbs, just like in an old fairy tale, leading from the beginning of my awareness to the present moment. It is a project which I encourage you, dear Reader, to engage in for yourself ... if you share similar questions.

Hopefully, providing a taste of my subjective world may encourage your exploration of your own.

. . . .

Dream ... of Conception?

The first dream of my life I can recall occurred between 3 and 4 years of age. I was viewing a field of crisscrossing lines retreating into infinity. The experience of depth was palpable. When I was old enough to be able to talk with myself about the experience, I would think about it as lines interlaced like a spider web.

There were two diametrically opposite sensations in me. On the one hand, I had the feeling of being crushed to oblivion ... perhaps the source of my claustrophobia to this day ... while simultaneously experiencing infinite expansion and freedom!

At that young age, I did not possess such vocabulary, but I somehow understood the feelings and the paradox, nevertheless. These sophisticated words appeared when I revisited the memory in later years. Then, soon thereafter, the exact same dream occurred again! Only twice in my life have I experienced an identical repeating dream.

A therapist once suggested it was a memory of birth. I prefer to wonder whether it is a memory of the moment of conception. To this day, the feeling and impression of that dream is with me. How do I fit that experience into a view that assumes reality as limited to the material world outside?

When, a few years ago, I came across images like the one below, I felt a resonance through my whole self, body, heart and mind and the remembrance of the dream came back to me in that moment from my distant past.

Figure 6. A Resonating Image

I recently had this same feeling of confronting the ineffable when rereading Carl Jung's autobiography, Memories, Dreams, and Reflections*. At one point I experienced myself vibrating with his words:

The feeling for the infinite ... can be attained only if we are bounded to the utmost. The greatest limitation for man is the "self"; it is manifested in the experience: "I am only that!" Only consciousness of our narrow confinement, in the self, forms the link to the limitlessness of the uncon-

---

* Memories, Dreams and Reflections, C. J. Jung, Vintage Books, N.Y. 1965, pp. 325-6

*scious. In such awareness we experience ourselves concurrently as lim-
ited and eternal, as both the one and the other. In knowing ourselves to
be unique in our personal combination ... that is ultimately limited ... we
possess also the capacity for becoming conscious of the infinite. But only
then!*

*As far as we can discern, the sole purpose of human existence is to kin-
dle a light in the darkness of mere being. It may even be assumed that just
as the unconscious affects us, so the increase in our consciousness affects
the unconscious. "*

How interesting. Seventy-seven years after seeing and feeling this image in my toddler's mind, I find confirmation for my experience and intuition of the meaning of this visitation marking the beginning of my
conscious life on Earth ... like an opening and closing Do ... the chord
of a lifespan.

. . . .

My Grandfather

I recall only one real conversation of a spiritual or mystical nature in
my childhood. The memory captured an event that may not have exceeded five or ten seconds in duration. There is no trace of what led up to
this or what followed after. I am no more than ten years old, as I recall.
My maternal grandfather is holding out his hand, palm up and open to the
sky. He is telling me that each of us feel ourselves like individual fingers
and are not aware that we are all attached to the same hand, which
connects us all and, in a way, makes us all one. This quiet, gentle, and
very brief moment has been with me ever since.

In my mid-adulthood, as I entered into my second education, my spiritual training through Jung and Gurdjieff, I realized that my Grandfather
was a Mason and what that meant. I had tried occasionally as a child to
raise questions about God with my parents, but neither one could share
further than that they believed in God and there was nothing else to say
about it.

I recalled my Mother telling me that my grandfather kept asking my
father to join the Masons even though my father was not interested.
Maybe those few seconds, when I was a child, was the only time he found
a receptive audience for his own spiritual expression. Maybe, long before
my birth, he was drawn to become a Mason so that, years later, when a

child who was interested in mystery and God came into his life, he could then transfer, into me, that image and those words in that magical moment. It was a clear signpost, a finger pointing to the direction my life would eventually take.

. . . .

I Want to Talk With God

I was twelve years old. I was at Synagogue studying for my upcoming Bar Mitzva. I recall the rabbi saying that God stopped talking directly with humanity after the last prophet died. I raised my hand and said that this did not make sense to me. I wanted to talk directly with God. He replied that this was no longer possible as God had ceased direct communication several thousand years ago. Inside myself, I felt the thought, "This makes no sense. I am not interested in religion. I want to talk with God."

. . . .

The Windows of my Eyes

I believe I was in my early teens. The memory is fixed and the same whenever I remember it. I can still clearly see where I was standing in my childhood bedroom. I was suddenly experiencing myself behind my eyes, looking out through them as through windows. The essence of the feeling and inner dialogue provoked by this strange experience was as follows. I felt isolated, totally alone. Was I all by myself back here, behind my eyes and thoughts, inside my body? Was anyone else "back here"… behind the World? Would I have to spend my entire life with this sense of solitude and isolation from what lay outside the windows of my eyes? It was a mixture of sadness, loneliness and fear.

. . . .

"Seeing" Shiva

I was in my mid-teens, perhaps 14-15 years of age. It was a bright sunny afternoon, and I was alone at home in my bedroom. From my open bedroom door, I could see through my parents' bedroom and into the doorway on the other side, which led to their dressing room and bathroom. As my glance moved in that direction, I "saw," sticking out into the far doorway from behind the adjacent wall, two bare-arms, sinewy and flexible like snakes. They were undulating in the way that a rope would reproduce a "wave" when a wrist is snapping it up and down. My blood froze in horror.

Then an equally strange response occurred. I did not flee the house! I closed my door, so I would not see it. Why was I not afraid that IT would come to my door? It was a truly terrifying thought, but part of me must have believed it was not real, for, despite the fear, which I would re-experience again and again for decades whenever I recalled this event, I nevertheless waited, voluntarily trapped in my room until my mother came home a short time later. I did not tell her.

Actually, it was years before I shared this experience with a therapist. It was the only eyes-open hallucination I have ever had. It wasn't until I started working with a Jungian analyst and began studying symbols that I came across a picture of Shiva with her many undulating arms. The first time I saw this image, my blood ran cold again, and I realized that this representation of the duel aspects of the Mother Goddess, both the giver of life and the destroyer, seemed to be what I "saw" that day many years before. I won't go into my psychological and emotional issues with my mother here, but I immediately understood that I had somehow "seen" a representation of that tension projected from inside me onto the screen of the outside world.

. . . .

Clairvoyance

My love of mystery, of course, led me to reading about and exploring questions concerning unusual mental phenomena, i. e. telepathy, clairvoyance, psychokinesis. During my early graduate training as a psychologist, I visited with Drs. Montague Ullman and Stanley Krippner, directors of the Dream Laboratory at Maimonides Medical Center in Brooklyn. Krippner became famous for drawing attention through his studies of "Kirlian" photography, a process that captured on film electromagnetic discharges from objects, including living organisms. Some believed the process had captured "auras," others felt it was "only a natural phenomenon." Ullman was researching dreams. Both were major names in parapsychological research.

At the conclusion of lunch, an invitation was offered to visit the Dream Laboratory, where they were currently running experiments concerning "out-of-body" experiences. The study design had the "subject" sleep in an adjacent room while their rapid eye movements (REM), associated with dream activity, were monitored. After a period of REM, the subject would be awakened and asked if they had been dreaming and, if so, what was the content. There were several other people visiting the lab.

A volunteer was asked for to demonstrate how this experiment worked. I volunteered and was led into a small room with a bed. Electrodes were attached to my head to demonstrate how both my REM and brain electrical activity could be monitored from the control room. I was asked to lie on the bed and relax. I was then left alone in the room. A short while later, a voice came over an intercom. I don't recall which one of them was speaking.

"Steve. Look at the wall at the foot of the bed and follow it up to the ceiling. You will see a small box taped to the wall. Relax, and say what you think may be in the box."

I suddenly felt irritated and started to become argumentative. How could I know what was in the box? I felt like they were trying to make a fool of me.

"That's OK. Steve. Just take a guess. This is part of the experiment."

Still, I resisted. I felt this was ridiculous. How could I know?

"Just imagine something and make a guess," I was reassured. This was just to demonstrate the methodology.

I surrendered to the process and began to think. OK. I was in New York City. I saw an image in my mind of the skyline. I saw an image of a sidewalk café. What was light enough and small enough to fit into that box taped near the ceiling? "A postcard picture of New York," I said, relieved I had come up with an answer. A minute or so went by. Then the intercom spoke again. "How about a second guess?" it asked. I now had images of a gardening shed with tools followed by an image of a paisley pattern. After a short while, I was asked for a third guess. Now I saw a maroon background followed by an image of a woman in 1890 dress, a cream-colored outfit with long gloves going up her arms. I reported these impressions. Again, after a short pause, one of them came into the room, unhooked me and brought me back to the control room where the other visitors had been waiting.

I thought I was done volunteering, but now I was asked to look at six "target" pictures and see which one felt to be the picture that had been in the box. Again, I felt embarrassed and angry and allowed a bit of irritation to escape in my tone of voice, but I was encouraged just to look at the pictures. Three had nothing to do with my guesses. I recall clearly that one of them was a picture of an elk that was used in advertising for the Hartford Insurance Company. Of the remaining three, all were evocative of my guesses. There was a paisley pattern. There was a gardening shed. There were the vivid colors. I was surprised and confused and said all three felt related. "Pick one" was the encouraging reply. I chose one. I do not recall today which.

"Yes. That's the target card", was the reply.

Then Ullman and Krippner began to explain the experimental paradigm in more detail. The subjects in the experiment were chosen from a group of people who claimed that they "left their bodies" during sleep and could travel beyond their sleeping self. In this study, they were to prove this assertion. If they did find themselves outside their body, they were to "float" up to the ceiling and see what was in the box. Whenever their REM activity suggested dreaming, they were awakened and asked about their dreams and what was in the box. In the morning, they were shown target cards, as I had been, and asked to make their best guess selection. We were told that the study results were encouraging.

All these people were quietly listening and talking as if nothing unusual had just happened, but I was still baffled. As my perplexity continued to fuel an embarrassed anger in me, I realized that this was not a joke. These people were serious. They were saying that my demonstration was typical of results they were getting from their subjects. The anger began to subside, and I was left with bafflement that remained for decades but walled off as an "anomaly" that I had no place to situate in my quest for understanding "myself."

. . . .

Feeling the Reality of Death

Early one morning, now living for some time in our old mountain farm home, I awoke in the darkness. I was in my mid-thirties. As I rose from the bed to stand, I suddenly realized I was going to actually ... really ... truly ... someday ... die! This was not the intellectualized knowing that death eventually comes to us all. This was a full-bodied experiencing of the taste of the truth. It was a full-bodied acknowledgment of the fact. I did not experience fear, or sadness or anxiety. What I experienced was astounded amazement! I felt the reality! At no time before or since has the quality of this experiential understanding and acceptance occurred.

The fact remains in my mind, but the not experience of it.

Looking at these words on the page does not in the slightest way convey the depth of this astounding recognition. It momentarily took my breath away. Imagine being informed that you had won a multi-million-dollar lottery for which you did not recall buying a ticket or that a recent DNA test disclosed that you had actually been born to different parents in a foreign land and were the heir to a vast fortune. Really? Truly? This is a joke, right? This can't really be true. It is too improbable to accept. Yet, this was the direct experience of a fathomless, mysterious reality that I would inevitably encounter. Writing these analogies to try to describe the feeling of the experience, I now notice that they are both positive. There was no negativity to this phenomenon. It was simply … stunningly … stupefying!

Yes, people occasionally talk about the end and acknowledge that it is inescapable. Yet, we don't feel the reality of it. We only accept the idea. That night, for a long minute or two, I was standing in the awesome reality of the mystery.

. . . .

Epiphany at Baptism, Pre and Post

I had been studying Esoteric Christianity through the perspective of Jungian psychology, but it remained an understanding based primarily in my head. Now I began having experiences that revealed to me that symbols were a language from a higher dimension and that there really was a "collective unconscious" to which every person who ever lived was connected and contributing.

Now I had unexpectedly met the "Gurdjieff Work" and read a footnote in an unknown book I had just opened which said something to the effect that the Gospels were true in that they represented peoples attempt to share an un-share-able experience. Fear immediately arose throughout me because I was born a Jew. But … if the Gospels were "True" in some way … then I felt I would have to convert! I felt a responsibility to pursue the "Truth" wherever it led. There followed a two, or three, year period of intense Jungian therapy and retreats, all overlapping with my deepening experiences through the Gurdjieff Work.

During this time, I would spend hours walking around our neighborhood at night, struggling with this question. Nevertheless, I had to pursue the truth wherever it led. Then, in a moment in the middle of one of the intense retreats, I had the following recognition. The question that had been haunting me for the past couple of years was should I or should I not, convert? I saw, to the great surprise of part of me, but not another part, that this was no longer the question, should I or should I not? The conversion had already happened! Now the question was, will I or will I not accept that decision already made and follow through?

As the particular Jungian analyst I had been working with those past few years, was also an Episcopalian Priest; it had been his understanding of esoteric Christianity I was drawn to. I now saw the esoteric "hidden" inside the rituals, so I was quite comfortable with more traditional forms of Christianity, which did not seem aware of the deeper core I now felt inside of them. When I realized I had already "converted" to this way of seeing as a deeper truth, I felt that holding this perspective must therefore make me a "Christian," or at least the type of Christians I had been meeting in my analyst's circle. As he was intimately familiar with my struggle, we arranged that he would Baptize me at the Episcopal Cathedral. I wanted to perform a vigil and asked to be locked in overnight. The Baptism would be soon after sunrise. This was arranged.

So, I was locked into the Cathedral. I placed myself near the small, ornate chapel in the back by the Rose window. I had brought with me a tape recording I made of my grandfather telling me about his life. I wanted to think about my roots before "giving them up." There was a painting of the Madonna with a toddler in the chapel. I spent a long time looking at it. Then I felt something. My chest was filled with an expansive warmth. I realized I was feeling Love. I realized that Christianity, as Jesus meant it to be, was about Love. Jesus was not preaching Christianity. Jesus had come to bring the Spirit of the Law to blend with the Old Testament's emphasis on the Letter of the Law. I understood this now, not because I had read or heard it, but because I was experiencing it, right in the very moment. I felt its reality.

As dawn approached, I sat at the front of the Cathedral and looked at the Rose window. There was an image of a shepherd at the top of the complex multi-colored image. As I watched, I had the impression of movement. I started staring at the shepherd. He seemed to be swaying or slowly dancing. I rubbed my eyes. Of course, I was imagining this. I looked away and then looked back. It was still now …but … then it seemed to move again. I watched this over the next ten to fifteen minutes until someone came into the church to set up for the early service. I decided that, of course, I was imagining this movement but wondered at the meaning of my experiencing this illusion at this time. It clearly carried a celebratory sense.

In a short while my priest-therapist and a colleague came in and robed themselves for the ceremony. They dressed me as a priest like themselves. I was to offer communion next to them at the conclusion of the service. The guests arrived and stood in a semi-circle in front of the altar of the small chapel. I was placed face down with arms spread wide in the position of an acolyte prostrating himself. The ceremony was performed over me. I was not listening closely as I was experiencing a very strange and unexpected emotion. At the moment in the ceremony where there were words to the effect that I was being torn from Judaism to be absorbed by Christianity, I was, instead, experiencing myself at a wedding. I was being married, except I was the bride, not the groom. I was being "penetrated" by the groom, not physically, of course, but in some way, I still can't articulate. It was like an embrace filling me from the inside. At the moment of being pronounced "Christian," I simultaneously felt myself Jewish, equally Jewish and Christian. Rather than my being sundered from Judaism, it had become blended with Christianity. I was both and both were one.

. . . .

Premonition

When I was growing up, there had never been a divorce on either side of my extended family. My hope for the future was to find my "soulmate," raise a family of four children and remain married until death did us part in old age. I had been married a number of years and had two children when the thought entered my head that I would have three wives. I was very surprised. Where had this thought come from? In addition, the intuition revealed that my third wife would be substantially younger than me, dark-haired, and somehow connected with the archetype of Vivian relative to my archetype of Merlin, a spiritual companion in my elder years.

Years passed. Much to my disappointment and pain, my first marriage ended after nearly 24 years. She had been a partner in my Jungian interests, but we had been incompatible in ways we avoided confronting for a very long time. In time I married again, this time for twenty years before cancer took my second wife. She was a spiritual companion who could join me in a mutual love for Gurdjieff's method. I am now married for the third time in the most fulfilling relationship of my life with a younger, dark-haired woman who shares my love of spiritual work.

What does this all mean? Have I lived this life before and remember fragments? Is there an aspect of a Higher Mind that sees the entire "Time-Body" of my life at one glance? Am I psychic? Does it matter? I love the mystery and the living of it.

. . . .

The Call:

Section One: The Retreat

In my late 30's, I attended a Jungian weekend retreat run by the Episcopal Priest I recently mentioned. Two primary experiences occurred to me during this weekend. Either one alone would have changed my life, but they were both just precursors of the tidal wave that was to come. As a result of experiences at this mind-bending retreat, I "saw" the reality of both the individual and the "collective unconscious," the reality of Symbol as a living design of what lay behind it ... a metaphor for the reality of a world hidden behind the visible one in which we live.

I also felt another brush with the question of telepathy and clairvoyance from a young woman participant. For a number of years, seeking "proof" of another reality through parapsychological research, I had, from time to time, come across people who claimed to be "psychic" in some way. I would visit them, take them to lunch or dinner, and probe for some convincing evidence that they were capable of what they claimed. None of those encounters were satisfying.

This woman seemed to have information about me she could not have known as we had never met before. Oddly, there is no memory for the specifics of that encounter at the retreat. I do recall being intrigued enough to add her to my list of "psychics," and I made an appointment for two weeks hence.

Section Two: The Vision

I returned home Sunday evening, much energized by the retreat. I took out some books on symbolism and, looking at the images, again felt them to be representations of a deeper reality. I had a sense of the meaning of Jung's "collective unconscious."

A while later, I was sitting with my young son in my arms, rocking him to sleep. The logical thing to say about what "happened" next is that I fell asleep and had a dream. It didn't feel that way. It felt like I was "there" in another "place." The experience was intensely lucid.

I was in an oval space, egg-shaped. The inner space was divided horizontally. The "upper" half was a rural scene, distant woods, fields in the foreground, a house in the distance to the far right. The sky was blue and full of sun. The "bottom" part of the oval space was the black, starry void.

Halfway along the horizontal plane that split the oval in half was a round opening. In the center of that circle and vertical to it was a long straight line, like a pole. There was a man hanging onto the "pole" like a fireman halfway in his slide down at the fire station. The "man" was me. I could see myself on the outside from a distance. I was also inside myself having the experience. The upper half of his/my body was in the sunlight; the bottom half from waist to feet was hanging down into the star-filled void. From the void came "voices" (although I didn't seem to "hear" them with my ears) but rather in my thoughts. They said to me, "Let go. Let go." I replied, in my thoughts, that I wanted to but was afraid. The reply was understanding and patient. They assured me that it was OK. That when I was ready, there would be help.

I "awoke" with a start. I felt stunned. "What was that?" I wondered in surprise and a touch of awe. I looked down into my lap. My son had fallen asleep. How long had that experience taken? I put him into bed and immediately felt pressure to "write this down, or I might forget it"! I went into the kitchen to look for paper and pencil. On the counter was a 3 X 5 index card. I felt that would do to start as time was passing, and I feared I would begin to forget if I didn't write it out quickly. I found a pencil and put it on the 3 X 5 card to write notes. Instead, my hand, all on its own without intention from me, drew an oval with a diagonal, straight line running through it. That's it, I realized! That is a symbol! All I have to do is remember the symbol, and I won't need to remember words. Everything was contained in the symbol. I put the pencil down. I didn't write a word. No need. It was all in the symbol.

Then I became paranoid and angry. I wondered if the psychic I had just met was influencing me from a distance and was somehow responsible for this "vision." Rationally, I knew this was absurd, but the feeling remained. The two weeks I would have to wait were at times difficult.

Section Three: End to Parapsychology

The time came for our appointment. I recall clearly her meeting me at her door and inviting me into her home. She asked me what I wanted from her. I replied that I wanted two things. I wanted to be convinced she could do what she claimed, i. e. that she could "know" what was not possible for her to know through the senses. I wanted proof to my satisfaction of the reality of "psychic phenomena." I also wanted to understand how she did this.

At the end of the hour, I was satisfied on both counts. Again. I don't recall the details of the conversation, but it was convincing. She did know my wife was pregnant without any way of having access to this information. (As I write this today, nearly forty years later, I am recalling that she also told me I would someday write a "very strange" book. I believe, dear Reader, that what you are reading at this moment is what she predicted over forty years ago.)

I also recognized that she did not, herself, understand how the "knowing" happened. She just "saw" pictures and hunches in her mind and just "knew." I saw she was "reading" from the same mental activity that occurred in me, but somehow her "images" and hunches came from an ocean of psychic experiences into which we all contribute.

At that moment, I also recognized that parapsychological research, in which I had long been interested and done some exploration of, was a dead-end in terms of understanding the meaning of this phenomenon. Research could perhaps demonstrate a phenomenon at a certain time but could not replicate it, as psychic phenomena are spontaneous and singular. Investigation into these unpredictable experiences could not, by their very nature, be amenable to the standard scientific research model. In addition, their cause cannot be determined. However, now satisfied as to the reality and the "how" of the transmission, I walked away from parapsychology. It had been an intermediate step and was now no longer needed. The paranoia lifted, and I lost all interest in investigating "Psychics."

Section Four: Revelation

A short time later, perhaps a week, I was sitting with a friend, a physician, in his old farmhouse in a rural mountain valley to the west of my home. I had known this man a number of years. For a period of time, on Thursday evenings, we would gather with a few others to play guitar, banjo, fiddle...smoke some homemade grass grown behind his barn. It

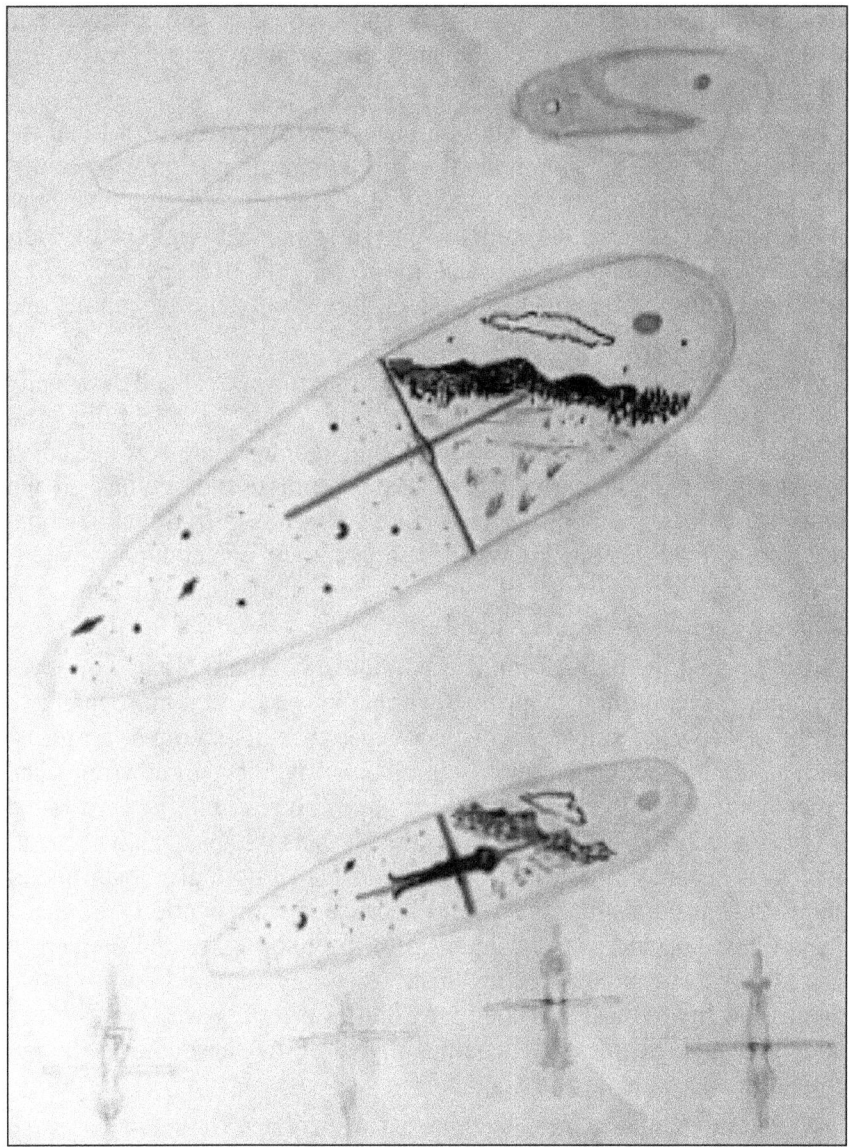

Image 5. Contemporary sketches at the time of the experience

was a wonderful period for me; the camaraderie and the magic of hearing something resembling music come through my fingers and mouth. The tuning of a guitar provided an epiphany regarding resonance, the blending of vibrations, and the magic moment when one string "fell" into tune with another. This feeling for resonance quickly generalized to an understanding of life and relationships and became central in the next step of my spiritual search about to come.

In conversation, I began to tell him about the Jungian retreat I had experienced. I began by saying that I had been in a strange group recently. He interrupted me to reply that he had also been in some strange groups in the past. He said he had something to show me that might be of interest. Leading me into an adjacent room where I had spent evenings watching him tie homemade fly-fishing lures, he opened a cabinet and selected a book to hand to me.

As I opened the book, out fell a 3 x 5 card with an oval and diagonally slashing line through it. It was the *exact* image my hand had drawn to symbolize the "vision." I was stunned, and an immediate wave of anger washed over me. The paranoia that he was trying to fool me flashed and disappeared in a fraction of a second, as I also recognized that he could not have known. No one knew. I had spoken to no one about my experience. "What is this?" I asked him. "Just something I drew when I was thinking about infinity," he replied.

As I opened the book at random and looked at the first page my eyes fell upon, several things happened within the space of no more than two or three seconds. Each was a distinct experience but so rapid in procession as to be experienced nearly simultaneously. First, I knew/felt I had come home! I had to know everything in this book. Next, my eyes found words on the page to the effect that the Gospels were somehow true attempts to record extraordinary events outside of normal human understanding. I instantly became afraid because the implication was that I would have to renounce the Judaism of my upbringing and convert to Christianity. The sense of being "disloyal" to my cultural heritage pitted against loyalty to the Truth and to my Soul was terrifying. Then, I "saw" and "felt" and "heard" a homunculus rip out of my chest and screaming, shoot out into the void and die.

At that moment, my intellectual resistance collapsed. I had always put "logic" before my heart. This time I realized that the moment had come to follow my feelings even though I had no idea what was happening or where it would lead. I looked upward and said inside myself, "I surrender."

I read the book and went back for more. It was electrifying. At some point, I asked my friend where I could learn more about this. He suggested I talk to another physician on the hospital staff, Keith Buzzell. "Keith?" I exclaimed. He was a quiet man I had been around for some time but never had gotten to know.

I sought out Keith and asked him if he knew about this material.* He replied he did know something. I asked if he would teach me. He said no. He wasn't a "teacher." but he did have interests, and as long as I shared those with him, we could work together. When our interests diverted, we would part company. Our relationship lasted over thirty-five years, sharing a common passion for this doorway to the hidden world until his recent passing.

It would be nearly three decades before I spoke of this event to anyone. As the years went by, I repeatedly discovered and re-discovered other symbolic versions of my vision. It is in the "Hanged Man" card 12 in the Tarot. It is in representations of the "cosmic egg." I see it in images of Adam Kadmon (the universal man). It is in the Seal of Solomon and the Christian cross. I found it in the work of William Blake and in some of the poems of Tennyson. I had not been aware of this history of images. Now I recognized the universality of my experience. What had called to me had been calling to others throughout the history of mankind.

. . . .

---

* The teachings of G. I. Gurdjieff on psychological and spiritual evolution.

Resonant images discovered long after the Vision

Resonant Image 1: The cover of Mutus Liber (the wordless book)

Resonant Image 2: The Yggdrasill Tree (The holy tree of Norse Legend)

Resonant Image 3: The Hanged Man, Tarot Card XII

Resonant Image 4: The Grand Man of Zohar

Susan's Visitation

S usan was my second wife of twenty years. She died of cancer in 2016. In the six months after her death, I experienced a series of inexplicable events in which she played the essential role. For reasons explained below, I felt that she had given me a gift that I was now under obligation to share with others.

On July 30, 2016, at 9:38 in the morning, I was having breakfast at a restaurant around the corner from my home with a friend. My cell phone rang. To my surprise and confusion, the name on the caller ID was Susan Dent Aronson.

My first thought was that someone was calling me from Susan's cell phone. The cell was at her daughter's house in Massachusetts. I had taken Susan's number and name off my phone account and discontinued her number. Her daughter had wanted to keep the phone. I wondered if she was calling me on Susan's phone, but that made no sense. I answered the call. The response was silence. Then I noticed a previous call at 9:11 am from Susan Dent Aronson.

When I returned home after breakfast, I entered a very emotional state, half of me hoping, of course, that Susan was contacting me, the other half searching for a logical explanation so as to avoid falling into a superstitious state. I felt again my wish for her that she had made it to the "other side" and was reassuring me that she was there (here near me) and OK. The "message" I "felt" was not in words, but distinctly was that I should "enjoy the life remaining to me and don't be afraid." The sense of her presence also reassured me that my self-recrimination for not being more emotionally present just before her death was unnecessary. She understood and there was nothing to forgive.

Not wanting to be prematurely deceived by an explainable cause for the call, I then spent several days doing research. I contacted her daughter, who told me she had not activated the phone. I used a reverse trace on the number to see if it had been reassigned to another user, but it had not.

It was then that I noticed on my caller ID that the call did not originate from Susan's iPhone but rather from our home phone! So, there was not a supernatural contact through a disconnected number. But why would her name show up on a call from the home phone? Her name had never been on that account. I checked my telephone account and saw only my name, as it should be.

Knowing now that the call came from my house while I was at breakfast, I began another line of thinking. First was the problem of her name appearing on a call from a phone registered in my name only. My son suggested that in my iPhone contacts, Susan's name might be connected to the home number. This was, in fact, the case. When I disconnected her name in my Contacts from the home number, her name disappeared retroactively from my caller ID list from that Saturday morning and was replaced by my name. This seemed very strange. Why would her name disappear retroactively when at the time of the call, it was linked to the home number? A technological explanation in terms of how the cell phone labeling operates would be a logical assumption. This seemed to explain the appearance of her name when my home phone was used to call my cell ... but, many times, I have misplaced my cell in the house, and to locate it, I would dial it from my home phone. When my cell would respond, I would follow the ring and discover where I had left it. I do not have any memory of Susan's name appearing as the caller. All I ever recall was "Stephen Aronson" on the caller ID. Had Susan's name appeared on any of these other occasions, I would have stumbled on this mislabeling earlier. I have called others from my home phone and no one ever mentioned that Susan's name appeared on their caller ID.

Now I began to ponder who could have made these two calls 27 minutes apart on that Saturday morning. I couldn't recall if I locked the door on my way out to breakfast. Typically, I did, although not always. So, assuming the door was unlocked, who would have come into the house looking for me, and not finding me would use my home landline to call my cell (they didn't have a cell of their own?). Not getting me on their first call at 9:11, they then waited in my empty house 27 more minutes and made a second call but did not respond when I answered. Then, this unknown person, who knew me well enough to know where I lived and my cell number and who wanted to reach me so badly, did not respond when I answered and then left the house without leaving a note or contacting me in the two weeks since to say they had been at my house wanting to talk with me.

Only two people would enter my house if I were not there. Susan's daughter who was in New Jersey at that time. My son David was on the other side of the city that morning. If the house had been locked, only they knew the location of the key.

I then checked my phone contacts to run one more experiment. To my surprise, Susan's contact information in my cell phone still had our home phone connected to her name. I thought I had removed it and that caused her name to disappear as the original caller and have my name replace hers. So, now seeing her name is still (or again) listed with our home number, I called my cell again to see what name would show up. This time it shows up as a combined "Stephen or Susan" with Stephen Aronson first. This continues to be inexplicable. (Later, mulling all this over, I half suspended disbelief and talked with "Susan." I apologized for being a "Doubting Thomas" but reminded her that she knew I had to "stick my finger in the wound" to be sure of my tentative interpretation so different from my rational mind.

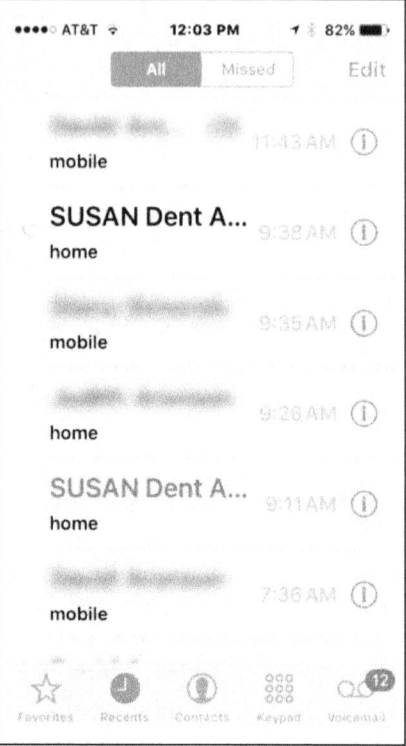

Image 6. The Call Record

With embarrassment at myself for the exercise and embarrassment for requesting "her" to make another attempt, I asked if "she" could give me one more "sign."

On Aug 22, 2016, when I went to bed, as usual, I turned on only a small baseboard night light in my bedroom, as I prefer to sleep in the dark. Across the hall from my bedroom are two guest rooms. Their lights are never on unless occupied by a guest. As I went to bed, all was dark before I turned on the night light. I awoke a couple of times during the night to go to the bathroom. All was normal darkness.

That morning when I awoke, the ceiling light in the large guest room directly opposite my bedroom door was on. It can only be turned on by the wall switch. I asked Susan if she was there as I turned off the light. I then realized I had asked for yet another "sign" to assure my rational mind of the reality of the irrational. I thanked "her."

At the memorial service, I spoke with my friend, who had been with me

342

at breakfast when the original call came in. The next to last piece of the mystery fell into place when he assured me that I had locked the door to the house when we left. He reminded me that we had a conversation about my locking the door and then I recalled that we had discussed it. He had been surprised that, as we were only going less than a mile away, I would bother to lock the door. So ... the two calls from "Susan" originated from my empty and locked house. At that moment, I remembered that I had asked for a second "sign." This conversation with him about the locked door was a shock and felt like an answer to that request.

On Aug 12, 2016, a few days before Susan's memorial, I received an email from a mutual friend in Europe, an author whose book Susan had edited shortly before her passing. He told me the following: "I have a story to share and I leave it to you if you want to read it at Susan's memorial. Susan is way further on the invisible road that we are walking. I told her so several times. She herself was not so sure. To illustrate my statement, I have the following story.

On April 10, 2016, I was training my dog in the woods. My dog had to find a wooden box, watch and bark at it until I would come. When I was at the place where the box was, the dog stopped barking and we were alone in the wood in silence. It was at that moment that I heard Susan's voice, calling my name. I said, "Are you there, Susan and she said, "Yes, I am here." Then other people from the dog school came and our communication stopped.

That night I woke up a little and Susan was in the room in beautiful light. There was a lot of warmth between us. She told me that I should enjoy my life more for the time that I have left. She also told me not to be afraid. Only someone who really has seen me can know these things about me."

Addendum

Susan died March 24, 2016. A year later, I was scrolling through my photos and discovered three consecutive, identical screenshots for a missed call(s) from Susan taken over seven months after her death. I did not take these screenshots. I was unaware of them in my phone until coming across them another six months after their reception. Strangely, the date they were received was the same date when I completed this remembrance to send to our friends, as her final wish for us all.

Extraordinary claims require extraordinary proof. So, I offer no claims.

I am left with no logical answer. The conventionally implausible explanation seems to be the only one available. I do know that this happened to me and to our friend in Europe and I have photographic evidence of the phenomenon. We are both grateful for the reminder, which I feel a responsibility to share with you, dear Reader. Enjoy the life remaining to you and don't be afraid.

November 5, 2016

PART THREE

What is Real?

What is Real?

The Place of Outside-Inside

It is difficult to know where to begin this story since it may be tainted in the eyes of many, as it was for me for a long time because the experience was facilitated by marijuana. Nevertheless, this and related experiences, both prior to and afterward, raised for me a profound question about what we call "reality." So, there are really three stories here: one about the specific experiences I will describe, another about the legitimacy of perceptions experienced under the influence of a drug and thirdly, how to know what is "real" and what is not.

Drug-Induced Alternate States of Consciousness

I was first offered marijuana at age 24 but experienced nothing from its use. A year later, I accepted another offer and "found" myself split in two. I sensed "I" was floating near the ceiling on the other side of the room and simultaneously looking back on myself on the couch. I experienced panic and pleaded with companions sitting next to me to hold my arms so I could be reassured that I still had a connection to my body and could get back into it. Bewildered, since none of them were experiencing anything disturbing, they complied, and a few moments later, the strange experience ended, and I found myself securely back in my body. This experience subsequently triggered panic reactions to any sudden, strange alteration in my sensorium. Later, as a young psychologist, I recognized the nature and source of this conditioned anxiety reaction and, using then-new psycho-therapeutic methods for treating panic attacks, I was able to cure myself of this response. As a result, I stayed away from marijuana for a number of years.

In my late thirties, a mild form of home-grown cannabis was popular among the group of young professionals, like myself, living in rural Maine. I decided to try it again, this time with pleasant results. My senses became more acute, and my intuition sharpened. It seemed to facilitate deeper understandings and perceptions, which did not disappear when the drug effects wore off but rather began to accumulate as data for a different approach to my burning question about the nature of reality and consciousness. I began to wonder about how the introduction of a few molecules could produce mind-altering effects and whether the impressions experienced in this altered state had validity. After considerable pondering on this question, a new perspective opened for me.

All my "experiences" are experienced in my mind. All the sensory input from the world around me is not really experienced at their source "out there" where they appear to be, but rather are created in my brain by the incoming electrical signals from my outer senses. These signals stimulate different molecules natural to my body, leading to changes in state and experience. I was inside my mind, experiencing these reconstructed images, sounds, smells, sensations for my viewing, like a movie. This was what I had been using, like almost everyone, for the standard of "reality." My assumption was that only experiences originating from my outer-directed senses were "real'. But then the reasoning shifted, and the following thoughts began to flow.

Dreaming

I dream at night. That is a fact. I see people and scenery. I have conversations (by telepathy!) with the people in my dreams. I have experiences, some wonderful, some terrifying, most banal. Sometimes these dreams are stories that are coherent, often very intelligently constructed, sometimes extremely funny, sometimes truly profound, and inspirational. Mostly, they seem to be bits and pieces of scenes and themes that were spliced out from their main source and thrown together randomly for a meaningless presentation to my inner eye. Another part of me seemed dedicated to producing and directing nightmares, stories of worry, terror or repeated re-viewing of humiliating or frustrating circumstances. Both themes brought with them real sensations of pleasure or fear. Sometimes the sensations were more intense than any experienced in waking life. Sometimes the intense sensation was one I never experienced in waking life, such as the experience of flying in my dreams. Yet, I believed that dreams were only dreams and, therefore, not "real."

But wait a minute. When dreaming, I am having the experience of dreaming! I can often remember parts of these experiences on awakening, and some of them I have remembered all of my life. I had heard some people say that a dream changed the course of their life. At first, I could think of no experience of mine with that effect. But on further reflection, I recalled dreams that had meaning and message for me. I recalled the feelings of awe and eternity that accompanied some "big" dreams. I remembered the strange experience of waking up inside a dream and being able to influence the direction of the dream just by thinking about it. These night-time "experiences" had a profound effect over time on how and what I thought about the mystery of myself.

So, the fact that we dream is a fact! The fact that other people report the kinds of experiences I have with dreaming ... is a fact. The fact that some dreams are vastly intelligent, organized and informative... is a fact. The fact that people have been reporting their dreams going back to the beginning of recorded culture ... is a fact. Therefore, it is a fact that there is an experience shared by all people forever and all time. The dream experience has a power to shape events in the waking world. History has recorded these stories. That is also a fact. How could I deny an aspect of what is Real to a timeless, universal event of such mystery and power? Obviously, our consciousness is not only sensitive to information coming through the sense organs from the outside, but it is also open to information coming from...? The phrase "deeper inside" comes to mind.

I then reflected on the phenomenon we call "daydreaming." I realized that my daydreaming is dreaming ... during the day! Unlike night dreams, I often created and directed my daytime dreams to entertain and amuse myself when bored. Most of the time, I myself did not intentionally set up the daydream, but rather I found myself inside it, totally absorbed as voyeur and sometimes director. Sometimes I realized I was in the daydream and other times, not until I "snapped out of it" and my attention suddenly returned to the world around me. It was like going to a movie to have my emotions manipulated but not realizing I had been dreaming until I "woke" out of the dream into the "reality" of the sense-based world.

Lucid Dreams

In one of my lucid night-dreams, there appeared a woman ... a casual acquaintance, from many years in my past. Over thirty years had gone by on the day she called me to say she was in my hometown and would like to say hello. Truthfully, she had never crossed my mind in all those years, and initially, I didn't recognize her name. We met for coffee, exchanged stories, and said goodbye, never to be in contact again. That night, she appeared in a lucid dream. Knowing I was dreaming and could change the storyline to have experiences I wished for, I realized I could turn the dream sexual for my amusement. I did so, and it was. On awakening and for almost the next 24 hours, she was in my mind accompanied by feelings that would be normal when thinking about a lover.

The power of this really caught my attention. Were dreams somehow "real worlds"? After all, the "world," which I experience outside myself, is actually experienced inside my mind. My conditioned thinking and re-acting, my assumptions and expectations filter and distort my interpretation, and sometimes even my perceptions, of parts of the "world" outside, those primarily having to do with relationships. I was actually already "creating" a "world" consisting of my beliefs and assumptions and conditioned responses ... and believing it was the actual "reality" of my life.

Was I giving life, albeit briefly, to these "people" and "places" in my dreams and daydreams? Was I responsible for what happened in this other world I was experiencing inside my brain? I vowed at that point never again to interfere in a lucid dream but rather just watch and allow to happen whatever happened. Now, many years later, I am trying to practice this non-interference in my waking life. This learning from that lucid dream both forecast and changed, over time, the direction in my inner search. Now, that is a powerful reality!

I believe many people are familiar with the phenomena of sleep paralysis. When we sleep, our large muscles become immobilized. On awakening, the ability to voluntarily move them is restored. A functional benefit is the prevention of movement during the dream state where the brain is often immersed in images of movement and, if not immobilized, when this system fails, sleepwalking and physically acting out the dream activity, acting out the dream, can occur.

Nightmares and PTSD can result in violent movement and dangerous re-enactment of the dream content. This state also becomes apparent in dreaming when movement attempted as part of the dream story is very slow or inhibited in some way. This incapacity usually becomes part of the dream storyline. The most frequent experience I have had with this phenomenon is connected with nightmares in which I am trying to escape danger and I can't move or can only move very ... very ...slowly. As the struggle to awaken from the dream takes a short while, the paralysis can continue until fully awake. Typically overlooked when this happens is the strange fact that something was awake and aware that it was asleep and dreaming, did not like the dream and intentionally struggled against the paralysis to wake the body!

On several occasions, as I was falling asleep, I could feel this state of immobility taking hold. As I have claustrophobia, this feeling was very uncomfortable, even frightening, and I would struggle against it, typically resulting in its cessation as I established re-awakening. The distinction in states was crystal clear … but I realized that I had continued to be mentally awake as my body was going to sleep. As I came to realize what was occurring, I became interested in this transition state. I periodically try to stay awake to experience the body falling asleep. During this transition period, I can watch images emerge and disappear from a background' screen'. I retain my lucidity as dreaming and body paralysis begin.

In my sixties, two other phenomena made an appearance. On a couple of occasions, as I was lying still waiting for signs of sleep to begin, I suddenly felt a sensation as if someone had grabbed my ankles and gave my whole body a strong pull towards the bottom edge of the bed. This was so startling that I reacted strongly, pulling my legs back against the sensation and looking to make certain that no one, or nothing, had actually attacked me. These experiences brought to mind the belief in incubus and succubus spirits that were believed to prey on people as they slept. I presume the sensation was caused by muscle contractions, but that was not what it felt like subjectively. I could understand how this would translate inside a non-scientifically trained mind to a supernatural explanation … or … if truly supernatural, would translate inside a scientifically trained mind as strange muscle contractions.

The second very intense phenomenon occurred on two different occasions. I was lying in bed waiting for sleep to come. I felt a moment of this pulling sensation accompanied by the usual spurt of anxiety, related to it. Then, I experienced myself beginning to "lift" out of my body and float a foot or two above the bed! I felt wide awake. I experienced fear. I hoped I was not dying. Despite rising anxiety, I was determined not to struggle against the experience but attempt to stay present for its duration and see what happened. I could sense my wife lying asleep next to me and this gave me comfort. I wondered if I was dying and literally leaving my body. I began to recite prayers that historically have helped me to be calm and stay present. I wasn't afraid to die, but I felt much too young and that I had much more to accomplish with the life on loan to me. I don't know how long the experience lasted, but the sensation of floating was intense and realistic. After a while, "I" began to float down back into my body. I had felt awake the entire time. Was it just a lucid dream? Did something actually happen?

Sometime later, perhaps a number of months, the same type of experience repeated. This time I recognized it and initially was interested in following it. As the sensation of floating out of the body began, my feet were lifting faster than the rest of me. In a moment, I was floating with feet pointing towards the ceiling and my head down near the bed. This unexpected turn of events was again disturbing. I felt wide awake but could not control the unbalanced tilt. Then, two people entered the room, one being my wife, who I knew to be sleeping next to me at the moment. These two figures did not notice me floating vertically, head down, in mid-air. In that moment, I, of course, recognized that I was indeed experiencing a lucid dream. I returned to my sleeping body but remained awake a while longer.

Experience, Interpretation, Meaning

So, years ago, when I was first pondering this question, I brought my body of reasoning back to the question of my experiences with marijuana. Although never having the more profound alterations in perception reported with powerful hallucinogens, I know that people sharing these experiences, as well as early medical research before the government shut down the academic exploration of these drugs, confirmed that these were sometimes life-altering events, just as were the visions of saints and mystics left to us in our literature and histories. I reasoned that my experiences were as valid a "reality" as all inner experiences. Whether their meaning is interpreted correctly or not is no different than the problem of correct and incorrect interpreted meaning about the outside world of other people and events. But the fact that they are real, "legitimate" experiences with enormous power makes them an aspect of a larger Reality worthy of no less attention and exploration than the world outside.

The Experience: The Place of Outside-Inside

The event which set this piece of writing in motion occurred in the mid-1980s. A tragedy had occurred. At that time, our family belonged to a Unitarian-Universalist Church and were socially friendly with two other couples. Our children played together. Then the eldest son of one of the couples was killed while on his bicycle by an automobile. While his parents grieved privately with their family, the two remaining couples went to the ocean to ponder and share our sadness, our fear, and our relief (and guilt about our relief) that this had not happened to us. The other husband offered to share a "joint" with me, and I accepted. The effect was profound and life lasting. To this day, the impression is clear, but words have not yet been found to accurately represent my experience. I will try again as best I can.

I "saw" the people with me, the sand, the ocean, the sky, as projections on a "screen." My companions were talking and moving. They had dimensionality for themselves, but as "projections" onto this screen, they seemed two-dimensional to me, certainly lacking the additional dimension I was experiencing behind the "screen." I saw that they were not aware that they were projections. I realized that their pain and fear were being expressed by their projections. Experiencing myself as behind/inside the screen, watching my own projection along with theirs, I knew that the suffering was on the level of the screen, not behind it! I also knew I could not convey this to them. I realized that I was experiencing this from a "place" simultaneously "outside" the level of the screen but also "inside" that level of ordinary reality. I still think of this "place" as the dimension of "Inside/Outside." I reasoned that if I were both outside and inside normal reality, then this must hold true for the universe. It seemed that the infinite level beyond the universe from where the material universe of stars, planets, and galaxies originated must also be connected to the tiny, invisible, infinite world where the sub-atomic particles inside of everything come from, in the deepest sub-structure of this material universe. Somehow, they felt like the same' place.' And that felt like the place of my true home, not the projected world on the screen.

Then something even stranger occurred. It is so strange and inexplicable that I hesitate to include it here in an already very strange story I am trying to reconcile with a larger understanding of what we can think of as Reality. But there is no sense in starting without finishing the whole event.

I looked toward the horizon. Hanging just above where the sky and ocean met, maybe at 10-20 degrees elevation, was a gigantic object (assuming it was at the horizon). To this day, I try to see it in my mind's eye, but I cannot accurately describe it. It gleamed like metallic polished bronze. It brought to mind an ancient weapon or sculpted religious object. There was a slight enough sense of familiarity to bring those two associations to mind, but neither was accurate or particularly useful. I had no reference for what I was looking at either then or now so many years later.

A few years ago, I was watching a documentary that presented images found on ancient pictographs around the planet. The presenter in the film was comparing those stone age images both to other symbols from the pantheistic age of the old gods and also to shapes formed when plasma is compressed by electromagnetic fields. My body reacted with a surge of "electrifying" energy in response to these images. Immediately the remembrance of what I "saw" at the ocean's edge came back into memory. Were they the same? Was there just similarity enough to evoke the emotional memory of the event? The presenter described this image as what the ancients called the "Cosmic Thunderbolt." This archetypal symbol of the power of the ancient gods immediately resonated in me, bringing back the image of what I "saw" at the ocean's horizon many years before. Recently, I have seen some images of ancient Egyptian religious objects which had the same taste of familiarity. I do not know what to make of this, and I don't try to intellectually force an explanation. I leave the experience alone in memory to remain whatever it was, without speculating about it from my ordinary mind.

Adding to the significance of this experience for me is the fact that as time has gone by, this experience has turned out to be a preview of "coming attractions." The "taste" of this "outside/inside" place has occurred again and again, most unrelated to the assistance of marijuana, bringing with it a sense that the door occasionally opens into a Reality beyond the world of my senses and the ordinary experience of what I used to call "myself."

It was one of these experiences a few years later that led me directly to the Gurdjieff "Fourth Way Work" and changed my life in ways I could have never imagined. A few years after this mind-bending experience, I stopped using marijuana for over thirty years. I was now convinced that the doorway that occasionally opened with the drug's assistance was a shortcut to another "reality" that lives side by side with or interpenetrates our "normal" sense of things. But I also felt that having received this confirmation that my search was not in vain, I needed to find my way to this other "world" on my own, without the help of this stimulant. Today, after nearly forty-five years as a psychotherapist and twenty years of psychotherapy as a patient, twelve of them in Jungian analysis and now, four decades of Fourth Way practice, I feel I have achieved that long-sought goal.

Interpretation

However, the mystery of how any of this happens remains. My initial question of whether the mind-altering effects of certain plants, gases, or other substances are "real" has now been joined by another. Neurological research has confirmed that all our experiences and reactions are facilitated by fluctuating molecular activity in our blood and nervous system. The basis of all our "instinctive" and conditioned "feelings" and reactions are the result of hormones and neurotransmitters regulated by our Autonomic Nervous System. If someone says something that my personality reacts to because it was interpreted as "insulting," the resulting surge in stress hormones will determine my reaction. If my interpretation is different, for example, if I am not "sensitive" to that remark due to my historical experiences, I may interpret it as a jest. Then a different hormonal reaction occurs in my nervous system, and I laugh. My sense of "reality" is always influenced by chemicals produced in my own body. Why should these experiences be considered more "real" than those experienced from other inner sources such as dreams, intuitions, "visions"?

Meaning

An experience experienced is an experience. The validation is in the word roots:

"Experience (n.)" late 14c., "observation as the source of knowledge; actual observation; an event which has affected one," from Old French "*esperience*" "experiment, proof, experience" (13c.), from .0 "*experientia*" "a trial, proof, experiment; knowledge gained by repeated trials," from "*experientem*."

Among the Webster dictionary definitions of this concept are several which imply that if the word "event" is recognized to mean anything subjectively experienced, then internal "events" must be included as part of a person's reality: "Something personally encountered, undergone, or lived through; the conscious events that make up an individual life, the events that make up the conscious past of a community, or the act or process of directly perceiving events or reality."

The *interpretation* of the meaning of an experience is a different journey. Perhaps the most helpful advice I received in this regard was given to me by a long-time practitioner of inner search through art, Zen, and Gurdjieff's teaching. I was fortunate to have dinner at his home one night when I was in my early fifties. After dinner, I asked for a private conversation and related my experience on the beach. I was aware, at the time, of two levels of motivation in doing so. I was searching for confirmation that what I had experienced was a different level of reality. At the same time, I saw an aspect of my personality that wanted recognition for its "achievement." Both were present and entangled but clearly discernible to me as of different natures. Because of the second, lower level of motivation, I did not mention the few inhalations of marijuana in my story. At that time, I did not want it delegitimized by the potentially contaminating fact.

He listened attentively and was quiet for a while after I spoke. I recall the essence of his reply in this way. "When we have been meditating and sincerely working for self-understanding for a long while, sometimes interesting and unexpected experiences may occur. It is best not to try to analyze the experience because this can only bring the question down to the level of our ordinary mind and its library of what it has previously heard and read. If the experience is truly novel, there are no pre-existing associations connected with it. If the experience has validity, that meaning will appear on its own, in its own time, when we are ready to understand".

I have followed this advice ever since and confirmed for myself that the process of "understanding" comes on its own when conditions are right. If the experience remains in memory but without understanding, then the time has not yet come for its meaning to be revealed.

The Author

S tephen Aronson is a psychotherapist with an eclectic training background ranging from cognitive behavioral therapy to the alchemical approach of Carl Jung. His spiritual life has been a search for verification of a deeper reality underlying the ordinary world of our senses. His personal aim has been to find a reconciliation between science and spirituality which would also allow reconciling the concept of Universal intelligence with rationality. The arcane language of specialized methods, although necessary for advanced training, is often a barrier for those seeking an initial understanding. After a dozen years in Jungian analysis and four decades of study and practice in the system of transformational psychology introduced to the West by G. I. Gurdjieff, he has sought to find an approach to illustrate these deep and complex ideas and methods in common language and universally shared experiences.

Dr. Aronson received a B.S. from Penn State University in 1965 and a PhD in clinical psychology from the University of Connecticut in 1970. After initially teaching at Arizona State and Alfred University, he left academia to pursue immersion in clinical practice under two assumptions. First, he wished to share from his personal, practical experience and not only repeat the words and impressions of others. Second, he realized that to help others understand themselves, he must first understand himself and that only direct experience could extract true understanding from intellectual knowledge.

Steve lives in rural Maine where he retired in 2013 from forty-three years in the private practice of psychotherapy, education and training. He has published on the work of G. I. Gurdjieff in *Proceedings* of the annual *All and Everything International Humanities Conference* and *Parabola*, a magazine dedicated to myth, tradition and search for meaning. In 1981 he co-authored *The Stress Management Workbook*, Appleton-Century-Croft, 1981, with physician Michael Mascia.

Stephen can be contacted at stephen.aronson@icloud.com.